# MUSICAL STAGES

# MUSICAL STAGES

## an autobiography

NEW INTRODUCTION BY MARY RODGERS

DA CAPO PRESS • NEW YORK

*To Dorothy*
*with thanks and love*

I am indebted to Stanley Green
and Rita M. Chambers for their
help in researching material
for this book.

Richard Rodgers

Library of Congress Cataloging in Publication Data

Rodgers, Richard, 1902–
    Musical stages: an autobiography / Richard Rodgers; new introduction
by Mary Rodgers.—1st Da Capo Press ed.
    p.    cm.
    Originally published: New York: Random House, 1975.
    Includes index.
    ISBN 0-306-80634-7
    1. Rodgers, Richard, 1902–    . 2. Composers—United States—Biog-
raphy. I. Title.
ML410.R6315A3   1995
782.1'4'092—dc20                                                    95-1557
[B]                                                                     CIP
                                                                        MN

First Da Capo Press edition 1995

This Da Capo Press paperback edition of *Musical Stages* is an unabridged
republication of the edition originally published in New York in 1975,
with the addition of a new introduction by Mary Rodgers. It is reprinted
by arrangement with the Rodgers and Hammerstein Organization.

Published by Da Capo Press, Inc.
A Subsidiary of Plenum Publishing Corporation
233 Spring Street, New York, N.Y. 10013

# Introduction

$\mathbf{M}$y father wrote in
room with the door wide open. He would request that we, n
I, not sing or whistle or otherwise distract him, but aside
was a rather public happening. A morning person, an e
study, and cheerfully businesslike about his work, he'd g(
at nine and was usually through by nine-thirty.

There's a kind of marvelous, rich, emotional qual
father wrote that didn't often manifest itself in his perso
be quite sharp-tongued with my sister and me, and
frightening when mad. He could also be very affectio1
finished giving you a squeeze, the implication was, "
your mother says and don't bug me."

When he died, I got letters from people sayir
the world to have lost this wonderful man, but how
for you to have lost your father." It seemed sing...
write back, "I didn't lose any more than you did, folks, because ...
what I loved about him was only what you loved—his music," but in
fact, it was true.

When you come right down to it, my father was an extremely
complicated man and deeply unhappy much of the time. (Chemically
depressed is what we'd call it now; then, we didn't know what to call
it, except tough to live with.) He had no hobbies. An occasional game
of croquet with my mother and friends—heavy English mallets, elaborate rules, and chess-like strategy—amused him on country weekends.
At times he enjoyed going to museums and galleries. But basically, he
only wanted to play theatre.

He wasn't interested in writing music in the abstract—the closest
he ever came to that were a couple of ballets. He was interested in
*stories*—that's what made him want to compose—a good, juicy, romantic, and yes, sentimental story enhanced by good lyrics. Theatre, and
theatre only, turned him on and cheered him up—all aspects of it, not
just the writing. He loved auditions (pretty girls), rehearsals, and out-
of-town tryouts especially.

New Haven, with its miserable Taft Hotel (lumpy beds, lousy
room service) and Kasey's (a greasy-spoon theatrical hangout across the
street from the Shubert Theatre, where the food was so terrible I got
sick once just from eating the pickles) was, to Daddy, a joyful excursion.

Boston, with its serenely elegant Ritz Carlton (perfumed elevators!) and Locke-Ober's for gourmet dining, was a different kind of excursion: four-star bliss instead of "a four-day bellyache."

Then, at last, New York. The final orchestra reading. Opening night. The deliciously agonizing wait for reviews—sometimes great, sometimes not, but hey! it was all part of that grand and glorious adventure called theatre that he loved so much.

After Oscar Hammerstein died, my father wrote one musical with his own lyric, *No Strings*, which fared well. He evidently didn't like the experience because he never tried it again. He never exactly said why, but he probably found it lonely working with only himself for a sounding board. Collaboration, after all, is the essence of musical theatre; you have to get along with your partner. You *want* to get along with your partner, and when you do, it's a sublime accomplishment. For that brief period when you are co-creating, you enjoy a unique, precious camaraderie you obviously cannot experience alone.

The camaraderie between my father and Larry Hart was unique, too, and God knows productive, but the working relationship was rather less tranquil. Oscar was disciplined, rational, and centered; Larry, that adorable, witty, wistful, sweet, generous (he never arrived on the doorstep without presents for us all), cigar-smoking, booze-consuming, troubled genius was not an easy companion. The best and sometimes the only way to get a lyric out of him was to lock him in a room and play a tune over and over until he came up with the words. Unless the music came first, no song got written; proximity was an obligatory factor.

Not so with Oscar. He and my father collaborated long-distance—from Pennsylvania to New York. Lyrics (which always came first in this partnership) arrived by phone or by mail. But before the actual lyric-writing process began, they met together often and intensively. They would locate the dramatic crest of each scene; that's where the song would go. They established its emotional content, its rhythm, its mood, its intention. They discussed everything you could possibly discuss about that song, short of actually writing it. Then Oscar would go off to his farmhouse in Bucks County, where he had a standing desk in the study, and struggle all morning. Time out for lunch. More struggling in the afternoon. Sometimes for as long as three weeks, until the damn thing was finally finished. Once having received it, my father would sit down at the piano and set it in no time flat; then Oscar would come into town to hear him demonstrate what he'd written. Daddy never sang—he hated singing. He much preferred whistling the tune and playing accompaniment.

Collaboration is also very like a marriage. The way you don't say to your husband, "What's that terrible thing you're wearing!"—you don't say to your partner, "Look, that's a terrible tune/lyric." Oscar, at one point, figured out something brilliant: In "Love, Look Away" from *Flower Drum Song*, the original verse was quite long (and good—I've seen it). Evidently, Oscar didn't think the music was good, or appropriate or whatever, but rather than say, "Hey, Dick, that tune's all wrong," he simply went home and rewrote the verse. It's now only two lines long. As hard as it must have been for him to rethink the whole thing (words being more difficult to write than music), it was easier for Oscar, at least *psychologically*, than to admit he didn't like what he heard—which might have led to a confrontation or awkwardness.

As for how my father handled the situation when he didn't like something of Oscar's, the world will never know. Gently and tactfully, I suppose, because this rich, rare collaboration endured until Oscar's death in 1960. My father never again found a compatible partner although he doggedly continued to grind out musicals (flawed and lacklustre work, for the most part) until his own death in 1979.

If my father were alive today, I know he'd be pleased and perhaps a little astonished at how popular his music still is. I also know, even at the ripe old age of 91, he would somehow have managed to get himself over to the rehearsals of *Carousel* at Lincoln Center Theater last spring. He would have eased himself into a seat in the tenth row or so, watched the stage with an inscrutable look on his face, delivered a few tersely-worded pronouncements about this tempo and that rhythm—and generally intimidated everyone around him.

But then on opening night, after observing with pride a whole new generation of people laughing and crying at his most favorite musical of all, he would have beamed from ear to ear.

I said earlier, he had no hobbies. I retract that: Theatre was his hobby. And his life.

I also said that what I'd loved about him was no more than what the public had loved—his music. Well, that was fifteen years ago. I retract that now, too. Granted, he was hardly your run-of-the-mill father, but *of course* I loved him. A lot. So there!

MARY RODGERS
New York City
September 1994


*An accomplished author, screenwriter, and composer, Mary Rodgers' theatre credits include the music for* Once Upon a Mattress, Hot Spot, The Mad Show, *and* Working; *her musicals have also been celebrated in a revue,* Hey, Love. *A popular author of fiction for young people, her books include* Freaky Friday *(1972; screenplay for Disney's movie version, 1977; stage musical for Theatreworks/USA, 1993),* A Billion for Boris, *and* Summer Switch.

# MUSICAL STAGES

They carried my great-grandmother's coffin down in one of those elevators that started and stopped when the elevator man tugged at a steel cable running through the car. The coffin was a plain pine box and had lain on a bed of ice on the floor for only a few hours before it was taken away. The ice took the place of embalming, strictly forbidden, and the body had to be removed almost immediately. This hurried ritual was the end of orthodox Judaism in our family. The next step was known as Reform, and even this faded after the bar mitzvah of my brother and me as a gesture to my grandfather on my mother's side. From that time on, my parents, my brother and I were Jewish for socioethnic reasons rather than because of any deep religious conviction.

If you walked south from my great-grandmother's house on Fifth Avenue down to 124th Street and turned west to Mt. Morris Park West, then walked south again to 120th Street, you would find yourself at the southwest corner of Mt. Morris Park, one of the prettiest little parks in New York. One house to the west, 3 West 120th Street, was home. Down a few steps was what was known and pronounced as an "airy-way." An iron-grill door led into the service entrance, and past two servants' rooms to the kitchen. Back of this was a pantry with a dumbwaiter serving the dining room, two floors above.

3 West 120th Street was a brownstone-stoop house. In wintertime, rubber steps and a wooden balustrade had to be put down because the stone was murderously slippery and my father's medical practice was not so small that he needed accidents at the front door. Inside was what everyone called the vestibule. A second door led into my father's province. Here we had to be very quiet because there might be a patient waiting in the reception room. Farther down the hall was the office, and beyond that a mysterious place known as the examining room, where occasionally I was allowed to watch my father pour an amber fluid into a glass tube, light a small flame under it, dip a piece of thin paper in the fluid and make a pronouncement concerning the patient. In those days the family doctor did the urinalysis himself without the luxury of an expensive laboratory.

One flight up began the living quarters for the family, which consisted of my mother's parents, my grandmother's bachelor brother, my parents, my brother and me. There was a dining room and a pantry, the terminus for the dumbwaiter. Then, facing 120th Street, came the living room. And what a room it was to me! There was a carved oak table in the center of the floor, a huge sofa and comfortable chairs covered with some kind of green material. But the main object in the room—indeed in the house, indeed in my life—was the Steinway upright near the window. It had green cloth on either side of the music rack and there was a green piano stool with green tassels. When I was little more than a baby I used to love to make the seat spin and watch the tassels fly out. It was then that I learned that exciting sounds came from the piano itself when my mother played it. This was the beginning of my lifelong love affair with music.

My passion for music was not accidental. The piano was the one means through which I could escape from the generally unpleasant atmosphere of my family life. There was hostility between my father and his mother-in-law, between my grandmother and grandfather, and between my brother and me. To find some of the reasons that produced these strained relationships, it's important to know something about the backgrounds of the people who made up our family.

My mother's father, Jacob Levy, who had come to this country with very little money, went into the silk business and ended up a rich man. He married Rachel Lewine in 1869, and Mamie, my mother, was the second of their three children. My father's parents had come from Russia by way of France and had settled briefly in a small town in Missouri named Holden. (Why Holden, I haven't the slightest idea.) William, my father, was born there but within a year his family had moved to New York. Originally the family name was rather long, but somewhere in it was a sound that approximated "Rodgers." I think that for a time the name Abrams was used, and I've been told that at least one member of my father's family used a variation of Abrams which came out Brahms. All I'm sure of is that when my father graduated from college his name was Rodgers.

William Rodgers—he was never called anything but Will—was the oldest of eight children. His father had died before I was born and his mother soon after, but I do remember my father's grandmother quite vividly—particularly her funeral and that plain pine coffin. There was little money in the Rodgers family, and as a young man Pop had to earn a living as a customs officer on the docks while simultaneously studying to be a doctor. He had been practicing medicine for about three years when he met, fell in love with and married my mother.

It was at this point that my folks made a serious mistake. My mother's parents did not want their only daughter to leave them even after her marriage. And she, being a shy, insecure woman, had neither the desire nor the strength to break the ties. So, grudgingly, my father and mother moved in with Mom's parents. This, of course, turned out to be no solution at all, and was the chief cause for the hostile atmosphere that pervaded our home.

The antagonism between my father and his mother-in-law was understandable. Both were stubborn and opinionated, but their clashes stemmed primarily from my father's financial dependence—at least initially—on the Levys, and also from his unhappiness at his mother-in-law's domination of his wife. The disaffection between the two was shown not alone with words, but most often with silence. Frequently weeks went by without either speaking to the other, a situation that left me with a deep feeling of tension and insecurity.

Almost everything in our ménage at 3 West 120th Street contradicted almost everything else. My grandfather yelled a lot, but he had a great reservoir of love for the whole family. I remember occasionally entering his room and asking for the evening paper. His answer was always prefaced by the run-together word "Goddamittohell!" Then: "Get out of here!" I would go to my room and wait. Within minutes he would appear at my door, hand me the evening paper and pat me on the cheek. I loved him dearly. He was a very short man of normal weight but extremely impressive because of his habits of dress and deportment. From his carefully trimmed Vandyke beard to his highly polished shoes he looked exactly what he was: the patriarch of the family.

I lived under the same roof with this diminutive, domineering, untutored man until I was in my twenties. To this day my wife, who never met him, cannot understand why we all loved him, with his rough voice and his demanding nature and his unwillingness to compromise. Still, there was something irresistible about a little man who wore a square bowler, dressed impeccably, and would not wait for traffic to stop when he crossed the street. My mother would say, "Poppa, you'll get hurt if you don't watch the cars." His answer was always the same: "Let them watch me!" There was also something endearing to me about a man who did not speak very much to a small boy but who would never pass the chair he was sitting in without patting him gently on the cheek.

Another contradiction in the Levy-Rodgers household was that my father and his father-in-law got along so well. Logically, it should have been otherwise. It was Grandpa who had the money while Pop was struggling to build his practice. But these two strong-willed, strong-voiced men, both disciplinarians with fiery tempers, had a beautiful relationship until the day my grandfather died. That was in 1928, and it was Pop who stayed with him at his bedside to the very end, holding his hand.

Grandma was also full of contradictions. Though born in Europe, she had few ties to the Old Country. She had obvious disdain for her husband because, among other things, he had never lost his Russian accent, whereas her English was perfect. She was an avowed atheist and even made fun of Grandpa's religious beliefs. She was such an omniverous reader that whenever anyone in the family wanted to know the meaning of a word, he never had to consult the dictionary. "Don't bother looking it up, ask Grandma," was an expression heard frequently in our house. She was a know-it-all, and I suppose this rankled my father as much as anything else about her.

My grandmother's bachelor brother, Uncle Sam, also lived with us, though most of the time we were told that he was away at his "club," whatever that was. He was a strapping, handsome man, good-natured, affectionate and full of jokes. As far as my brother and I were concerned, he added a touch of glamour to our quarrelsome household.

I suppose it's only natural, but when I was a kid I thought my father was a tall man. Actually, he was of medium height, though his military bearing did give him the appearance of being a good deal taller. He had strong, even features, and I particularly remember his bright-red hair. Like Grandpa, he too had a Vandyke beard, though he later shaved it off.

Pop played a greater part in my life than anyone else. I must have been only an infant at the time, but I can recall clearly the way he used to toss me in the air and the feeling of warm security in being caught by his strong, gentle arms. But he did have a temper. Though his anger was rarely turned on me, the strength of his voice frightened me so that even today a loud voice makes me uncomfortable.

My mother liked to recall that when I was a child I once said to her, "You're the smallest mother in the world." Perhaps she wasn't *that* small, but tiny she was, and round. Not fat, really, just round. Her voice, too, was round and deep, and her round hands were comforting on those rare occasions when she would take one of mine in hers at the dining-room table and squeeze it gently. This sort of display of affection did not come easily to her, which made it all the dearer to me. I also remember the times when I went to bed with a bad cold and awoke in the middle of the night to the sound of slippered feet padding across my bedroom floor, feel the back of that round hand on my forehead and hear a whispered "Normal. Go back to sleep." Then a light kiss and the retreating sound of slippered feet.

My brother, Mortimer (Morty, Mort), and I had a relationship that I'm sure confirms all of today's fancy psychological words and phrases. As siblings, we were ambivalent toward each other, with strong love-hate feelings for which neither of us could be blamed. I feared him because he was four and a half years older than I, much stronger, and didn't hesitate to use his strength on me. I do recall, however, one time when a bigger boy attacked me in the street and Morty miraculously appeared and sent the fellow flying. But there was reason enough for him to feel that so far as the family was concerned, I was his enemy. In those early days he was known around the house as "the big one" and I was "the little feller." Since it was "the little feller" who followed Mom onto the piano stool and got a lot of attention, "the big one" was left frustrated and belligerent.

I am sure our career decisions were greatly influenced by this. If I could do what Mom did, it was only natural for Morty to want to do what Pop did. If I got recognition in the family with music, he'd get it with medicine. And eventually he did—not only within the family, but from his colleagues and patients as well.

Taken individually, the people who made up the Rodgers-Levy household—even Grandma—were not hard for me to get along with. But mealtime, when the antagonists were all together, was sheer hell. Bickering, yelling or unnatural silence were the norm, often with one family member storming upstairs before dinner was over.

Nor was the atmosphere around the dinner table helped by any culinary imagination. Each day in the week had its own main course that was served only on that day. Monday was pot roast, Tuesday was chicken, Wednesday was fish, and so on. This never varied. The only bright spot of the week was Sunday-night supper, when we would be treated to cold cuts from Pomerantz's Delicatessen.

In a house so full of friction and tensions it was important to me to find one place where I could enjoy some measure of peace and happiness, and this was the corner of the living room with the lovely piano, which my mother played so beautifully while she and my father sang. And what did they play and sing? Songs from the current musical shows on Broadway. Both my parents were avid theatregoers, with a special passion for musicals, and since the complete vocal-piano score was always sold in the theatre lobby, Pop never failed to buy a copy. So home would come *Mme. Modiste, The Merry Widow, The Chocolate Soldier* and all the rest to go up on the piano rack. They would be played so often, both before and after dinner, that I soon knew all the songs by heart.

These were the happy moments in not very happy days. There were no loud-voiced arguments then; voices were raised only in song. And in the middle of the fun stood little Richard, who received nothing but praise and love because his ear was so quick and he sang so well. Then when company came I was called on to perform, using the hearth near the piano as a stage. More praise and more love! Is it any wonder that I turned to music as a career, and that I made theatre music my particular field? Or that sixty-odd years later I am still enchanted by it?

I don't know exactly how old I was when I first tried to play the piano, but I gather that I had to be lifted onto the piano stool. I had heard all those beautiful sounds my mother could make simply by pressing her fingers down on the keys, and I wanted more than anything else to be able to make the same beautiful sounds. I wasn't much more than a toddler when I discovered that I was able to reproduce the melodies with accuracy.

When I was about six, a girl named Constance Hyman, the daughter of a college friend of my father's, taught me to play "Chopsticks." From then on I could manipulate the bass of "Chopsticks" with my left hand so that it would fit the melody of any song I was trying to reproduce with my right hand. Formal piano lessons, however, were not successful, chiefly because being able to play by ear made me lazy and I never bothered to practice. Why waste time reading notes when I could play just about anything I heard simply by listening?

Time after time I am asked if this gift for music was inherited or if it came as the result of being surrounded by musical sounds at an early age under the happiest possible circumstances. It's the old question: Are these drives genetic or environmental? The psychologists I have talked to cannot give a clear answer, and neither can I. In my case, both motivations are possible: a mother who was an accomplished musician and parents who provided me with the joys of music at a time when I desperately needed something in my life that would give me pleasure. I quickly discovered, too, that my parents' response to my love of music was their love of me, and family friends thought I was darling. Why wouldn't I rise to all this delicious bait? Although my brother was several years older and physically many times stronger, I could beat hell out of him merely by stepping to the piano. If theatre music could win me such affection and praise, as well as making me feel like the strongest kid on the block, then that was the kind of music for me.

Naturally, no two composers for the musical theatre have the identical background and environment, nor does there seem to be any consistency in the factors that shaped their interest and talent. In the case of George Gershwin, there was no musical leaning shown by either his mother or father; of the previous generation, one of his grandfathers was an Army engineer, the other a furrier.

Jerome Kern is a little easier. His father planned a business career for him, but his mother encouraged his musical interest and was accomplished enough to give him piano lessons when he was five years old.

Cole Porter's grandfather, a tough timber-and-mining baron, wanted Cole to be a lawyer. His mother, however, was more concerned about his being accepted in society. Thinking that music would help in that direction, she made sure that he was given piano lessons when he was a child. Cole wrote his first song at the age of ten, and from then on he never stopped satisfying his mother's ambition.

Another composer-lyricist, Harold Rome, was influenced by a mother who loved to sing and an uncle who played the violin. Like Cole Porter, he first studied law; unlike Porter, he also studied architecture and art before eventually succumbing to music.

A study of Frank Loesser's life reveals little that solves the environment-genetics puzzle. Both his parents were intellectual and his father taught music, but Frank refused to take piano lessons. Even though he began improvising tunes at the age of six, most of his early career was spent as a lyricist. On the other hand, both Frederick Loewe and Jule Styne were piano prodigies who were performing with symphony orchestras even before their teens.

Vincent Youmans, Sr., a wealthy hatter, had a Wall Street career planned for his son. Although Vincent, Jr., received musical encouragement from his mother, he did not begin to compose until he entered the Navy in World War I. No one seems to know where the impulse came from, but there can be no doubt about the strength of the drive and the extent of the talent.

Arthur Schwartz lived with a father who was strongly against music and a mother who loved it. She even had him take piano lessons in secret, for which he was punished. Did Arthur lean toward music because he resented his father or because he loved his mother?

Little is known about Irving Berlin beyond the fact that his father was born in Russia and was a cantor, hardly enough to account for one of the greatest songwriting talents the world has ever known. Both Harold Arlen's and Kurt Weill's fathers were also cantors. Noël Coward's father was not, but that did not seem to hurt his career.

It is obvious from these brief observations that no definite conclusions regarding the importance of background or surroundings can be drawn, other than that the influence of either or both cannot be denied. However, it is fair to say that mothers showed greater sympathy than fathers when their sons voiced ambitions to pursue musical careers. In this respect I was especially lucky, perhaps even unique; both my parents never expressed anything but total support and encouragement.

Besides the piano in the living room, the one place I loved in my neighborhood was Mt. Morris Park. Since it was just across the street, I would often go there to coast down the hill on a sled in winter and climb the hill to the bell tower in spring and fall. This tower had been put up originally as a lookout for fires, but I don't recall its ever having been used. The view from the top is still a fine one. I also recall that every spring the Parks Department would plant masses of tulips in the center of a little island at the intersection of 120th Street and Mt. Morris Park West.

The family schedule then was to move to Long Island in May (first Arverne, later Long Beach), where my father had his "summer practice," and back to 120th Street in September for his "winter practice." The summer patients paid better because there were lots of cuts to sew up and broken bones to set on a one-time basis, whereas the winter patients, who were mostly regular, enjoyed a somewhat lower rate.

The Benjamin Feiners and my parents were old friends. They spent the summer of 1909 near us at Arverne while their son, Benjy, aged five, was recuperating from typhoid under the care of my father. When Ben was well enough to sit on the porch I was taken one afternoon to play with him. Although I was only seven I remember the occasion well for two reasons: first, Ben's head had been shaved bald; secondly, he had a brand-new baby sister, two months old. Her nurse wheeled her out on the porch, and for the first time I looked upon my future and present wife.

Returning to New York was always exciting. There were usually enough kids on the block for a game of stickball, or if no other boys were around, there was always stoop ball, in which we would throw a golf ball from the edge of the gutter against a stoop and try to catch it for a score of one. It counted ten if we caught it after it hit the leading edge of the step. Invariably, late in the afternoon a window would go up and we would hear an elderly mother—usually someone in her early thirties—cry out, "Jimmy, come in and get washed for supper!" Getting washed for supper was mandatory, since the other untidy users of the street were the horses that drew the carriages and wagons which were still the major means of transportation.

We had a subway at 116th Street and the trolleys on Lenox Avenue, but the first automobile on our street was a major event. It belonged to a Dr. Hyman, who lived just across the street from us. This imposing machine was a green Maxwell and made the doctor's son, Arthur, the envy of the neighborhood. Arthur and I were good friends, but I never got a ride in the glorious Maxwell. Not long afterward my father got his own auto, a blue two-seater Mitchell, in which he used to pay calls in Arverne. I was often allowed to ride with him; it meant company for him and excitement for me. Naturally, I was never permitted in the patient's house, but it was fun to watch my father find a ledge on which to leave his cigar while he went indoors, and I enjoyed looking at the street from the vantage point of the high, ungainly Mitchell. Occasionally there would be an emergency call and I never could understand why Pop drove so slowly. One day he explained to me, "No doctor ever saved a life by getting there half a minute sooner." Many years later, when I had a severe heart attack, I realized how wrong he could be.

The Model School, between Seventh Avenue and St. Nicholas Avenue on 119th Street, was a training institution for public-school teachers, and there I learned the rudiments of English grammar and arithmetic. Intellectually, there is nothing to remember; socially, there was one fistfight with a tough kid who beat me up. I went home with a black eye and a bloody nose, but instead of the scolding I had expected, my father cleaned me up and said, "The important thing is—what did you do to the other guy?" My mother laughed, and once again I found my family in my corner.

Because my grandfather used to be away all day at some mysterious place called "the office" in some mysterious location called "downtown," our house was left in my father's charge. His domain was the second floor, the center of which was his consulting room. It was there that my parents may have made their first mistake with me. As I was leaving for school one morning, my mother told me I was to come home at lunchtime and not loiter on the way; she was going to have a surprise for me.

All morning at school I kept thinking about that surprise. Could it be the circus? Or a baseball game? Maybe I was even going to be taken to one of those musical shows my parents loved so much. But no matter what the treat would be, I knew I would enjoy it twice as much because it meant having a half-day off from school.

As soon as the midday bell rang, I dashed home as quickly as possible. Ma was waiting for me at the door, a tense smile on her rather pale face. The surprise turned out to be the news that my adenoids were to be operated on. Right then. Before lunch? No lunch. But I wasn't to worry. It wouldn't hurt because I'd be asleep and there was a pretty trained nurse to take care of me. I was led into Pop's big consulting room. My fear and disappointment were compounded when I saw the nurse. She wasn't pretty at all; she was unattractive and I resented it.

In those days, hospitals were used only for vital illnesses and really serious surgery, so Pop's familiar office had been transformed into a complete operating room. An operating table had been moved in, along with a row of gleaming instruments, and there was a strange man (the surgeon, I supposed) as well as the nurse. After I was undressed and on the table, a mask was put over my face. I heard a terrible roaring in my ears, and the next thing I knew I was lying on my mother's bed, my throat aching. I wanted desperately to have a drink of water, but I was too busy vomiting. The whole family was sweet and kind to me, but I couldn't get over the feeling that I had been tricked.

As the Model School taught children only through the second year, I was soon shipped off to P.S. 10 at 117th Street and St. Nicholas Avenue. This was big-time stuff; it was my brother's school! It was also Bennett Cerf's and Ben Grauer's, but we didn't get to know one another until years later.

Going to school was of little significance to me. I was never a good student; I got passing grades because I was moderately bright, and in general the teachers liked me. Much more important to me was my first brush with the theatre. Only five blocks away, on 125th Street, DeWolf Hopper was appearing in *The Pied Piper*. I was taken to a Saturday matinée, by whom I don't recall, nor do I remember being interested in the plot, the rats or the children; what stirred me deeply was hearing *real* singers and a *real* orchestra. The scenery and lighting were stunning. It was 1909, when I was seven, and I couldn't eat my dinner or sleep that night. I had taken my first deep drink of the heady wine known as theatre.

A musical show called *Little Nemo* did nothing to lessen my thirst. It was based on a comic strip running in one of the newspapers and had a delightful score by Victor Herbert, which I heard my parents play and sing for weeks until I knew every note and word. Finally the great day arrived, and I was taken to a Saturday matinée at the New Amsterdam Theatre, my first visit to a real Broadway house. I was so impressed that I still know exactly where we sat: the second box from the stage on the left side. That magnificent theatre is now a grind house on shabby Forty-second Street, but then—a sister theatre to the lovely Colonial Theatre in Boston—it provided an elegant setting for Victor Herbert's exciting and tender score, with lyrics by Harry B. Smith. I can still remember a seagoing march called "Give Us a Fleet" and a children's love song, "Won't You Be My Playmate?"

Early in 1910, without any warning, disaster struck. One night I awoke screaming with pain; the maid came running in and I showed her my right index finger. She took one look at it and said, "Oh, my God!" It was flame-red and swollen almost to the thickness of my wrist. There was nothing she could do, since my parents were at the theatre. I had to lie there, writhing with pain, and wait for my father and mother to come home. Neither of them panicked. Pop simply got a scalpel from his office and had Mom hold me while he made one terrifying slash in the finger to allow the pus to escape. (This was the first episode in a horror story that lasted for many months.) The next day my father took me to a surgeon friend of his whose office was nearby. Local anesthetic was seldom used in those days, and so what followed were eight months of torture to a small boy by well-meaning men whose scientific knowledge was still limited.

As bad as the pain was the fact that my whole world—playing the piano—stopped. My right arm was in a sling all those months, and there was no way for me to play the piano or even run with the boys in the street. All I could do was wait in terror for the next visit to the doctor. The wound had to be kept open, I was told, and one time I heard the word "blood poisoning," and another, in a whisper, "amputation." I was spared both of these because my father finally arranged for me to be seen by Dr. A. A. Berg, a famous surgeon at Mt. Sinai Hospital. Dr. Berg easily attracted notice because he always wore a bright-red tie, but his fame rested on the firmer foundation of being something of a surgical genius. I was taken to the operating room and placed on a table while Dr. Berg started to inject cocaine (this was before the Novocaine era) into my finger. Even here my luck ran out. The needle broke and Dr. Berg, cursing, threw the syringe on the floor. A new one was brought and the pain stopped. Minutes later he withdrew something from the inside of the finger. The prize he found was a piece of bone about a quarter of an inch square, very thin, with a pitted surface. No one ever discovered what caused the disease, which, I was later told, went by the romantic name of osteomyelitis. Two weeks later the wound had healed and my arm was out of a sling. The finger was a mess, however, and awful to look at, to say nothing of the fact that playing the piano was still almost impossible.

A year later my father took me back to Mt. Sinai, where Dr. Berg performed what may well have been one of the earliest plastic operations: he fashioned a new fingertip for me. It is not a thing of beauty, but the important thing was that I could play the piano again. Any lack of brilliance in my playing today is not due to that illness but to the fact that technically I am just not very proficient, though good enough to communicate musically anything I have to say. The only difficulty I have, however, is due to that operation; the tip of my index finger is a little bit thicker than it should be and the space between the black keys on a Knabe is too narrow. This creates a problem that Knabe and I have managed to live with for many years.

I have always had a tendency toward hypochondria, which I try to control, but I have often wondered if this is the result of that operation for adenoids, or of a loving father suddenly appearing in the middle of the night to cut me savagely with a knife.

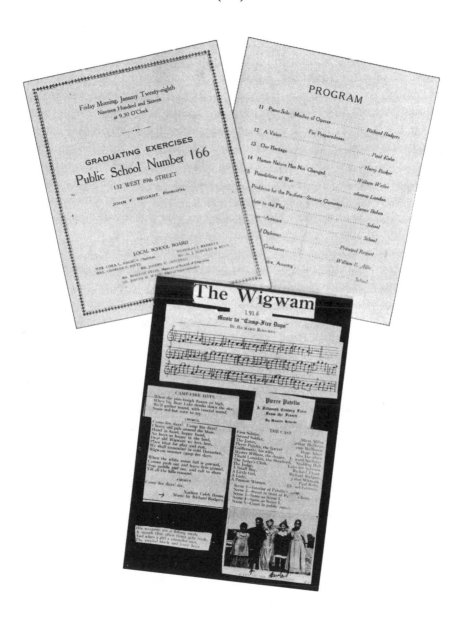

With the healing of my finger, a new phase in my life began. I was nine years old when I discovered that I could devise my own bits of melody. The appropriate harmonies were no trouble, since I already played quite well by ear. Soon I was writing complete tunes of my own. I don't remember that the family expressed any particular surprise; I suppose they just took my music for granted, something I certainly did not. I knew I gained deep satisfaction, both emotional and mental, from making up my own pieces. Of course, this was nothing more than improvising, but what is composition but formal improvisation? Certainly I was on my way, and from then on I never wanted to do anything else with my life.

About that time I recall many lengthy family discussions concerning the changes taking place in the neighborhood. Suddenly there was talk about a new apartment building about to be erected on Eighty-sixth Street between Amsterdam and Columbus avenues. The new building would have space on the street floor where my father could have his office, and a large apartment on the fifth floor where we all could live. There was one more maid's room than we needed, and this would be mine. I would also share a bathroom with the cook. It was further decided that my grandfather's room would be adjacent to mine so that I could go in and wake him up whenever he had one of his frequent nightmares and yelled in his sleep.

The move to Eighty-sixth Street meant another change of schools. This one was P.S. 166, between Amsterdam and Columbus avenues on Eighty-ninth Street. It was a good school, with what my mother considered a "better class" of boys. This meant that there were fewer tough kids and less chance that I would get into fights. At the end of each half-term there was always the big crisis of who would be "left back"—a huge disgrace—and who would be "skipped," a great honor. Being skipped meant saving a half year's work, a dispensation conferred only on very bright boys whose deportment was as good as their scholarship. One year, to my amazement, my teacher, Mr. Supnick, skipped me! Since I was never much of a student, the triumph was unbelievable, and the family seemed more impressed with this achievement than they had ever been with my music.

Nevertheless, it was my music that gave me status in the school and one more push in the direction of a career. The head of the music department was Elsa Katz. She was young, slim and attractive, but best of all, she liked me and was sympathetic to my musical efforts. She even gave me the task of playing all the music for the daily assemblies, an assignment usually carried out by middle-aged teachers who knew the technical rudiments of the piano but were uninterested, bored and wooden in performance. My job was to play the entrance and exit marches (my own improvisations), the traditional hymns and "The Star-Spangled Banner." Occasionally I made a musical joke. Whenever the principal said, "Students, sit," I would play the familiar musical doggerel "Shave and a haircut." Then, as the students sat, I'd play "Two bits." The kids never reacted, but lovely Miss Katz would always giggle.

Late in 1911 my grandfather took me to the Park Theatre, on the site in Columbus Circle now occupied by the Coliseum, to see a musical called *The Quaker Girl.* Ina Claire was the star, and I found out what it was like to fall in love with a real live actress. But beautiful and beautifully equipped though she was, I was too young and too innocent even to daydream about her. I never dared to tell this story to Ina, even when we became friendly in later years; I simply could not bring myself to say the most crushing sentence an actress can hear: "I was taken to see you when I was a child."

The Little Theatre is located on West Forty-fourth Street and is the smallest theatre in the Broadway district. My grandfather took me there the following year on another matinée excursion, this time to see Marguerite Clark in *Snow White and the Seven Dwarfs.* This time I was not intimidated by the age or the glamour of the leading lady. Miss Clark, who later became a star in silent pictures, was very young, extremely pretty and—what pleased me most—just about my size. All this made me fall so deeply in love that I spent many sleepless nights thinking about her. My prepubescent fantasies were restricted by my innocence, but as I look back on them I realize I was doing very well mentally for a ten-year-old and was clearly heading in the right direction.

With the usual logic of parents, mine decided a couple of years later that it was time for me to go away for the summer. With the usual lack of logic of parents, instead of choosing a conventional boys' camp, they decided on a place called the Weingart Institute. My guess is that they picked this particular place because the boys didn't sleep in tents, exposed to the ravages of the mild Catskill Mountains air. We were all housed in one large building that looked like a typical Catskill boarding house. I had a roommate named Bob Fisher. We didn't get along well and, frankly, I can't say that I was the most popular boy in the establishment. It may have been my personality, or it could have been that in a large group of average kids, my piano playing made me the pet of visiting parents and sisters.

I was at Weingart's in the summer of 1914, but the war in Europe was far too remote to mean anything to me or the other campers. We were involved in sports like tennis and swimming, and I was caught up in my own wonderful world of music. But there was something else; I was impatient to find out more about that grand but terrifying feeling which came over me whenever I was near a girl.

I graduated from P.S. 166 late in January 1916, and at the commencement exercises I did something only a thirteen-year-old would have the nerve to do. Without ever having seen a printed note of the music, I played a medley of operatic tunes by ear. The applause was satisfactory, and no one hissed. I didn't know enough to be grateful.

Before graduation, the family had held lengthy discussions at the dining table concerning the right high school for me. The public school with the highest standing was Townsend Harris Hall, known as T.H.H. It was a recognized fact that largely because it was a three-year school instead of the customary four, T.H.H. was the most difficult school in the city. I should have realized that it wasn't for me, but since my brother, Morty, had gone there, I figured if he could make it, I could too. To my surprise, I was admitted.

There was not much difficulty at first. I was too busy running for office —first for secretary of the athletic association, later for treasurer of the student government, better known as the G.O. By custom, boys running for office in the G.O. put up hand-lettered posters all over the school, but with the financial help of my father and brother I had *printed* posters all over the place. On the day of the election, Morty and his two best friends, Harry Phillips and Ralph Engelsman, went up to school, which was on the City College campus, and electioneered vigorously for me. How much persuasion and how much coercion they used I'll never know, but I was elected.

This victory was responsible in part for my downfall at Townsend Harris, and started a pattern I was to follow for the rest of my scholastic life: I always devoted too much time to nonacademic matters.

My grandmother and grandfather were great opera lovers and had Wednesday-night seats in the third row of the orchestra at the Metropolitan. One night my grandmother decided to stay home and let me go in her place. The opera was *Carmen* and the stars were Caruso and Geraldine Farrar. Giorgio Polacco conducted. Not being able to see the musicians in the pit, and never having heard a large orchestra before, I had no idea what to expect, but when Polacco brought his baton down on those first crashing figurations of the introduction, it was so overpowering that I thought I was going to faint. I recall that the Michaela was sung by Edith Mason, a young, lovely-looking girl who later married Polacco. Years later their daughter played one of the nuns in *The Sound of Music.*

Thanks to my grandparents I also saw the Diaghilev ballet with Pavlova and Nijinski. A few years later I stood in the back of the orchestra at Carnegie Hall to hear the great Josef Hofmann play the Tchaikovsky Piano

Concerto No. 1 in B-flat Minor. As soon as I heard the electrifying orchestral opening and the surging melody carried by the piano, I was as overcome as I had been on my first evening at the opera. My knees buckled and I had to hold on to the brass rail to keep from falling.

Because of this early love for classical music my career might easily have developed in that direction, but the musical theatre always remained my first love, perhaps because my mother and father had reached me before anyone else.

In the summer of 1916, two years after my sojourn in the sheltered atmosphere of Weingart's Institute, I was sent to a real boys' camp, tents and all, in Harrison, Maine. Camp Wigwam was owned by Arnold Lehman and Abraham Mandelstam, nicknamed Pop and Mandy. Pop was easygoing, but Mandy and I were troubled by a generation gap; I think I was too old for him. But we did have one thing in common: he loved music and used to invite first-rate musicians to perform at the camp. The one I recall most fondly was a pianist named Arthur Loesser; he never condescended to us, but played, tirelessly and sensationally, hour after hour. Years later I found out from Frank Loesser that Arthur was his uncle. Talent obviously ran in that family.

One of the counselors at Wigwam was a six-footer named Robert Lippmann, then an undergraduate at Columbia. He was a great piano player who played my kind of music, and he was also a gifted composer. But most important, he was sympathetic and encouraging despite what seemed to me a vast difference in our ages. Actually, it couldn't have been more than four years.

It was at Camp Wigwam that I wrote my first real song. I have no idea where the lyric came from, but the piece was called "Camp Fire Days" and obviously extolled the joys of spending the summer at Dear Old Wigwam. There was another song which I did not write. It was strongly discouraged by the two camp owners but sung joyously in secret to the tune of "My Bonnie Lies Over the Ocean." Since Pop and Mandy are no longer in a position to disapprove, I reproduce here the elegant lyrics:

> To Wigwam we go in the summer,
> The lousiest place on this earth.
> For this we pay three hundred dollars,
> Which is fifty times more than it's worth.
> Bring back, bring back,
> Oh, bring back my money to me, to me.
> Bring back, bring back,
> Oh, bring back my money to me.

The Standard Theatre at Ninetieth Street and Broadway was part of the "Subway Circuit," a group of theatres that booked shows in Manhattan, Brooklyn and The Bronx after their Broadway runs. It was at the Standard that I saw my first Jerome Kern musical, *Very Good Eddie*. In the cast were Georgie Mack (who had succeeded Ernest Truex), Earl Benham (who later became a successful tailor), Ada Lewis and Helen Raymond. They were all good, but it was the Kern score that captivated me and made me a Kern worshiper. The sound of a Jerome Kern tune was not ragtime; nor did it have any of the Middle European inflections of Victor Herbert. It was all his own—the first truly American theatre music—and it pointed the way I wanted to be led. On Saturday afternoons I would take my allowance and get a seat in the balcony or gallery of a Subway Circuit or Broadway theatre to see and hear whatever musicals were being shown. If it was a Kern musical, I'd see it over and over again. I must have seen *Very Good Eddie* at least a half dozen times, and even lesser-known Kern, such as *Have a Heart* and *Love o' Mike,* enticed me back more than once.

Most of the successful early Kern shows, such as *Very Good Eddie, Oh, Boy!, Leave It to Jane,* and *Oh, Lady! Lady!!,* were known as Princess Theatre musicals, in honor of the tiny theatre where all but *Leave It to Jane* first opened. Most of them were written in collaboration with Guy Bolton (co-librettist) and P. G. Wodehouse (co-librettist and lyricist). They were intimate and uncluttered and tried to deal in a humorous way with modern, everyday characters. They were certainly different—and far more appealing to me—from the overblown operettas, mostly imported, that dominated the Broadway scene in the wake of *The Merry Widow* and *The Chocolate Soldier.*

Jerome Kern's orchestral arranger for most of these early shows was Frank Sadler. Here again was something new. Sadler used comparatively few musicians, and his work was contrapuntal and delicate, so that the sound emanating from the orchestra pit was very much in the nature of chamber music. The lyrics floated out with clarity, and there was good humor as well as sentiment in the use of instruments. Actually, I was watching and listening to the beginning of a new form of musical theatre in this country. Somehow I knew it and wanted desperately to be a part of it.

While I was struggling along at Townsend Harris, my brother was applying himself diligently to his studies at Columbia University. Columbia interested me too, but not from an academic point of view. All I knew was that the big nonathletic event of the year was the annual Varsity Show. *Home, James* was the name of the 1917 production, and one Saturday afternoon Morty took me to see it at the Astor Hotel Grand Ballroom.

*Home, James* was a lot of fun and had a number of attractive melodies written by my friend Bob Lippmann. The neatly turned lyrics, I noted, were the work of a prelaw student with the impressive name of Oscar Hammerstein II, who also had a part in the show. Even I knew that anyone named Oscar Hammerstein II had to be a member of one of New York's most illustrious theatre families.

When I told Morty how much I admired what Hammerstein had contributed, my brother, who was in the same fraternity as Oscar, offered to take me backstage to meet him. Going backstage at a Varsity Show was heady stuff for a fourteen-year-old stagestruck kid, and I was overawed when I was introduced to the worldly upperclassman who had not only acted in a Varsity Show but had also written its lyrics. Hammerstein was a very tall, skinny fellow with a sweet smile, clear blue eyes and an unfortunately mottled complexion. He accepted my awkward praise with unaffected graciousness and made me feel that my approval was the greatest compliment he could receive. No deathless words were exchanged at that first meeting, but it was an occasion that years later prompted an extended disagreement between us. Oscar insisted that I wore short pants that day while I, with equal certainty, stoutly maintained that I had already graduated to "longies."

That afternoon I went home with one irrevocable decision: I would also go to Columbia and I would also write the Varsity Show. I also decided that I couldn't waste much more time before starting out in my chosen profession. I was introduced to a young would-be lyricist named David Dyrenforth, and together we created something called "Auto Show Girl." We fully expected that that topical title would guarantee the song's popular appeal; needless to say, it didn't. It was, however, my very first copyrighted song. The date was June 30, 1917.

By the end of the term it became abundantly clear that T.H.H. and I were not meant for each other. My grades were getting worse and worse, so I decided to quit before I flunked out. Because DeWitt Clinton High School was known to be comparatively easy, I got a transfer, and in the fall of 1917 I entered that cathedral of learning. The building was at Fifty-ninth Street and Tenth Avenue, on the edge of a rough neighborhood then known as Hell's Kitchen.

Clinton's charm started at the front door and pervaded the entire building; it was the faint but unmistakable scent of men's room. Schoolwork was duller than ever, and I couldn't even find other kids to raise a little hell with. The musical and dramatic activities were minimal. I was saved from total boredom, however, by my English teacher, who told me that I could buy a single Saturday-night subscription in the balcony of the Metropolitan

Opera House for only $17. That Croesus of medicine, my father, came up with the money without a question, so my Saturday nights were happy ones filled with magnificent music. Still, much as I enjoyed opera, neither my attention nor my ambition was ever diverted from the field of musical comedy.

My grandparents, Rachel and Jacob Levy in the early 1900's

My mother (1892)

My father (1896)

My first picture (1902)

With my brother, Morty (1905)

Mother and child (circa 1908)

Oscar Hammerstein and Larry Hart at Columbia (circa 1916)

Going over the script of *Poor Little Ritz Girl* (1920)

With Morty at Camp Paradox in the summer of 1920

The team of Fields, Rodgers and Hart (1927)

FLORENCE VANDAMM

A publicity shot at the ornate piano used in the film *Love Me Tonight* (1932)

PARAMOUNT

With Maurice Chevalier on the *Love Me Tonight* set

PARAMOUNT

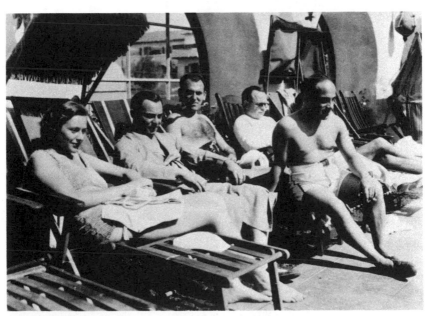

**Vacationing in Palm Springs with Dorothy, Moss Hart, Harry Brandt and Larry (1932)**

PACH

Dorothy's wedding
portrait

Mom and Pop with our daughter,
Mary, in California

A duet with Mary, California
(1933)

Mary and Linda (1937)

HARLAN THOMPSON

I wrote my first complete musical-comedy score in the fall of 1917. My brother was then a member of a local social-athletic group called the Akron Club. By that time the American Expeditionary Forces were fighting alongside the Allies against the Germans, and the boys of the Akron Club were anxious to do their bit to help the war effort. This, they decided, would be the production of an original musical comedy whose proceeds would go to a tobacco fund set up by the New York *Sun* to purchase cigarettes for our troops overseas.

The next problem was who would write the show. It was agreed that Ralph Engelsman, Morty's good friend, would be responsible for the book, but when it came to choosing a composer, the Akron boys discovered that they didn't have any members with the necessary talent. Since Ralph had been to our house frequently enough to hear me banging away at the piano, he suggested that I provide the songs. Apparently this produced some argument because of my tender age, but Ralph's enthusiasm carried the day and the club voted to accept me. This acceptance, I might add, was limited to writing the music for the show; at fifteen, I was still too young to become a member of the club.

The lyrics were another matter. I had no lyric-writer, so my father helped, my brother helped, Ralph Engelsman helped, and I contributed at least as much as they. Rehearsals lasted for months in small hired halls in the West Eighties and Nineties, or in the living rooms of cast members' parents. It was exciting to hear my melodies sung by talented young people, even though they were amateurs. Since hiring a pianist would have been expensive, I played at all the rehearsals and learned a great deal about vocal ranges and the proper keys to use.

The big night of the opening came on December 29, 1917, in the middle of a roaring blizzard. The single performance of *One Minute, Please* took place in the Grand Ballroom of the Plaza Hotel before a packed house of friends, relatives and other victims. I conducted an orchestra of five professional musicians and played the white-and-gold grand piano at the same time. I have no idea whether it was really a good show or not, but I thought it glorious. It was my first chance to examine the relationship between writing and audience reaction, to learn that what appears to be one thing on paper often undergoes a mysterious change in performance. This, I later realized, is really the answer to the question we are continually asked in the theatre: "How could such a smart man produce anything as bad as that?" The answer is that he simply does not know what he has until a live audience tells him. It is not a question of guessing; the producer, writers and composer all try to know in advance what the end result will be when the written word or note comes to life in front of human beings with their all too imponderable reactions.

Learning something about this metamorphosis began for me with the Akron Club show and I still wish I had solutions for some of these inherent problems.

A second amateur show, *Up Stage and Down,* gave me a little more experience. Sponsored by an organization called the Infants Relief Society, it played one night, in March 1919, in the Grand Ballroom of the old Waldorf-Astoria Hotel at Thirty-fourth Street and Fifth Avenue. Because I was still without a steady partner, I was again obliged to write most of the lyrics myself. My brother not only helped but also secured two new recruits to set words to my music: Benjamin Kaye, a theatrical lawyer who was my father's patient and a family friend, and Oscar Hammerstein, whom I had seen occasionally since our first meeting three years before. Hammerstein, now actually in the professional theatre as a stage manager for his uncle, producer Arthur Hammerstein, contributed the lyrics to three songs. For the record, they were called "Can It," "Weaknesses" and "There's Always Room for One More."

The show marked the first publication of my songs, an event hardly as impressive as it may sound, since my father paid the printing costs and I published them myself. We even managed to sell a few copies in the lobby.

As with the Akron Club show, I acted as both rehearsal pianist and conductor. One morning during a rehearsal Morty burst in and beckoned me away from the podium. When we were alone, he whispered, "The guys in charge don't think you're good enough to conduct. If they pull anything, pick up the music and walk out. If anyone tries to stop you, I'll murder him." Fortified by this homicidal insurance, I simply refused when the officers of the club later came to me and asked me to step down. This somehow ended the crisis, but I doubt that I would have had enough courage to take a stand without Morty's brave words.

About two months after its single performance, *Up Stage and Down* was revised and reopened for one night at the 44th Street Theatre. Now it was called *Twinkling Eyes,* for God's sake, and the beneficiary of our warmed-over efforts was the Soldiers and Sailors Welfare Fund.

Having written two complete musical scores, I saw no reason why the world should experience any further delay in appreciating my talents. Dorith Bamberger was a very pretty little girl whom I used to see fairly regularly and fairly innocently. Her mother, a widow, liked theatre music and even liked me. Trying to be of help, she took me to see an old friend of hers, Louis Dreyfus, who with his brother, Max, owned T. B. Harms, Inc., the Tiffany of the music-publishing business. Every Broadway composer of any consequence was under contract to Harms, including my hero, Jerome Kern. Mr. Dreyfus received us cordially, listened attentively to my tunes and gave me the exact advice I didn't want to hear: "Keep going to high school and come back some other time." Since I had no other choice, I kept going to high school. Later I did go back to Harms, though under somewhat different circumstances.

Fortunately, I received a bit more sympathy in other quarters. Though he was pleased that I had chosen a musical career, my father, a cautious man, still wanting to make sure that I wasn't making a mistake, took me to play for patients and friends whom he considered more knowledgeable than he was. One of them, Leonard Liebling, who had recently become the editor of *Musical Courier* magazine, was most kind and understanding. Another and even more important influence was Nola Arndt, the widow of composer Felix Arndt and the inspiration for her husband's famous piano piece, "Nola." Not only did Mrs. Arndt encourage me to go on with my music, she also gave me invaluable advice. "Don't be a so-called serious composer," she told me. "That's no life for you. And don't try to be a Tin Pan Alley songwriter, either, because you don't think that way. The place for you is the Broadway theatre. I think you'll find it more rewarding in every way than the concert hall or the popular-song field." I was also happy to learn that Mrs. Arndt was a great admirer of Jerome Kern and that she urged me to follow in the direction he was leading. Everything she said rang a loud, clear bell for both me and my parents.

I knew what I wanted to do and I knew where I was heading, but I also knew something else: every song needs words. I did not feel I was sufficiently adept at lyric-writing and I had not met anyone who I thought was. In my search for a partner I buttonholed almost everyone I knew for suggestions. Surprisingly, it didn't take long before someone did come up with the right name.

Phillip Leavitt, a classmate of my brother's at Columbia, was another one of the older boys who didn't patronize me but took my music seriously. One day he told me that there was a very good lyric-writer named Lorenz Hart, a Columbia graduate, who was looking for a composer. He explained that while Hart had had some peripheral experience in the professional theatre, he realized, as I did, that a writing partnership was of major importance in succeeding in the musical-comedy field.

Hart lived at 59 West 119th Street, just around the corner from where

I had spent my childhood, but we had never met. Early one Sunday afternoon Phil Leavitt and I rode the subway uptown, climbed the brownstone steps of the house where the Harts lived, and rang the bell. We were greeted by Lorenz Hart himself—Larry from then on. His appearance was so incredible that I remember every single detail.

The total man was hardly more than five feet tall. He wore frayed carpet slippers, a pair of tuxedo trousers, an undershirt and a nondescript jacket. His hair was unbrushed, and he obviously hadn't had a shave for a couple of days. All he needed was a tin cup and some pencils. But that first look was misleading, for it missed the soft brown eyes, the straight nose, the good mouth, the even teeth and the strong chin. Feature for feature he had a handsome face, but it was set in a head that was a bit too large for his body and gave him a slightly gnomelike appearance.

Larry was immensely jovial and led us into the back parlor, where there was a large round table, a good console phonograph, and near the window, an old upright piano. A cat ambled into the room and Larry introduced us. "This is Bridget," he said. "She's an old fence-walker." He chuckled at his joke and rubbed his hands furiously together, a nervous habit he repeated frequently. Suddenly I heard a crashing *BONG!* that lifted me out of my chair. Larry told me not to be frightened; it was only his mother's clock sounding the hour.

To calm my nerves, Phil suggested I play some of my tunes. The piano turned out to be in excellent shape, and Larry responded to my music with extravagant enthusiasm. Then we talked. And talked. And talked. Actually, Larry did most of the talking while I listened with all the reverence due a man of twenty-three from a boy of sixteen. Larry's previous writing had consisted almost solely of translating the lyrics of German operettas for the Broadway producing firm of Lee and J. J. Shubert. Only they weren't mere translations; they were actually adaptations, and excellent ones, for which he was paid almost nothing. In place of cash he got a small lifetime of experience, and as I listened I realized that here was a man who knew the musical theatre and how to write for it. His theories, and they were countless, began with his disdain for the childishness of the lyrics then being written for the stage. He felt that writers were afraid to approach adult subject matter and that the rhyming in general was elementary and often illiterate. His point was that the public was being cheated by writers who mistrusted the audience because their own level of intelligence wasn't very high to begin with.

Larry talked about a lot of things that afternoon, including arcane matters of his trade, such as interior rhymes and feminine endings, that I had never heard of before. But what really brought us together was our mutual conviction that the musical theatre, as demonstrated by the pioneering efforts of Bolton, Wodehouse and Kern, was capable of achieving a far greater degree of artistic merit in every area than was apparent at the time. We had no idea exactly how it could be done, but we both knew that we had to try. As I wrote in a magazine article many years ago: "I left Hart's house having acquired in one afternoon a career, a partner, a best friend, and a source of permanent irritation."

It wasn't long before I became acquainted with the entire Hart ménage. Larry's parents, Frieda and Max, had come from Hamburg, Germany, and both spoke with thick accents. Teddy, Larry's kid brother, looked something like Larry and had an unforgettable high squeaky voice. Later he would become a fairly successful actor. There was also Rosie, the cook, who had one bad eye but a great talent for German food, and of course Bridget, the fence-walker.

Mrs. Hart was a darling woman, tiny and sweet-faced, who talked very quietly. She used to call us for lunch by saying, "Boys, der shops iss retty." And mighty fine "shops" they were, too. I don't know if she really had any idea what Larry and I were trying to do; her role in life seems to have been nothing more than to be kind and helpful at all times to all people.

The real character was Mr. Hart. He was no taller than Larry but must have weighed in at close to three hundred pounds. He seemed to have no neck, only a chin that descended in a gentle curve to his stomach. Just to hear him talk was an experience in itself. Besides a pronounced lisp, his language—not just his English, but his language—was incredible; he was vulgar beyond belief. One night when I was still a newcomer *chez* Hart, we were served lentil soup. Mr. Hart lifted a spoonful of the thick liquid about eight inches above the plate and poured it back in. "Frieda," he roared, "it lookth like—" "Mox!" Mrs. Hart screamed while Larry and his father yelled with laughter.

Mrs. Hart had some lovely old-fashioned jewelry and the family owned three automobiles. Periodically, however, Mrs. Hart had no jewelry and there were no automobiles to be seen. I learned later that everything was always being put up as collateral in some new business of Mr. Hart's. Before I knew him, Mr. Hart had been involved in any number of companies that mysteriously went bankrupt. Larry collected the letterheads of all of these companies. I don't suppose any other lyricist can claim the distinction of writing his first songs on the back of stationery of the Pittsburgh and Allegheny Coal Company.

Larry loved to tell the story of his father warning him and Teddy that they must fast until sundown on Yom Kippur. Around noon the boys passed Pomerantz's Delicatessen on Lenox Avenue. Through the window they saw Mr. Hart not only wolfing an enormous sandwich but enjoying it in the company of a large blonde. It was some years later that I found out that beneath all this nonsense was a kind, good-hearted man who loved his family but had never learned to behave himself.

This was equally true of Larry. The difference, of course, lay in the fact that Larry had a talent so great that it overcame the lack of discipline in his work and the lack of control in his life. I soon discovered that he could never work in the morning because he never felt well enough to concentrate. This was because he loved carousing to all hours of the night. The first drink, before lunch, helped, but by early afternoon he needed more help, and by late afternoon the working day was over.

Incredibly, my parents never expressed any objections about Larry. If he was the partner I wanted to work with, it was all right with them. The only comment I can recall my mother ever making occurred one day soon after we had met. Larry had come over to our apartment, and though ostensibly there to work, was more interested in helping himself to whatever liquor he could find. After he left, my mother said sadly, "That boy will never see twenty-five." He was twenty-three then, and while Ma's estimate was off by twenty-two years, it was apparent that the seeds of self-destruction had already been planted.

Often when I arrived at Larry's house he was upstairs trying to get himself together so that we could begin work. This meant a long wait alone in the parlor, and to pass the time I would play the phonograph. There were two recordings that I particularly loved and would play over and over. One was the first movement of Tchaikovsky's Fourth Symphony (the remaining three movements were missing), and the other was Rimsky-Korsakov's *Scheherazade*. War horses though they may be, they were vigorous and highly romantic, and they further stimulated a musical appetite in me that was already pretty healthy.

Throughout the spring and summer of 1919 Larry and I wrote a number of songs we weren't ashamed of, and by August we felt we were ready to audition some of our better efforts. Phil Leavitt, who had brought us together, now took it upon himself to bring us together with a producer. That summer the Leavitt family had rented a house in Far Rockaway next door to Lew Fields and his family. Fields had first won renown as one half of the great comedy team of Weber and Fields, which had convulsed audiences during the late nineteenth century. Though he had long since split with Joe Weber, he was now well established as both a solo comedy star and a producer.

With Phil's enthusiasm paving the way, one sweltering Sunday afternoon I journeyed to the Fields' summer home to unveil the first Rodgers and Hart songs before their first audience.

Though the audition was a major opportunity to break through into the ranks of Broadway songwriters, Larry, claiming a splitting headache, begged off. I would soon discover that whenever it came to "selling" or negotiating, he would always find some reason not to be available.

Lew Fields, a man of medium build, with a deeply lined face, sad eyes and a flat nose, greeted me at the door. Expecting to play my songs before an audience of one, I was surprised to find the entire Fields clan assembled to appraise my maiden efforts. In addition to Mr. and Mrs. Fields, the family consisted of their four children: Joseph, the eldest, who bore a close physical resemblance to his father; Herbert, wavy-haired and clean-cut looking; fourteen-year-old Dorothy with the most dazzling eyes I had ever seen; and Frances, the only Fields sibling who would not pursue a career in the theatre. All six of them did what they could to make me feel comfortable, though I must admit that most of the time I found myself trying harder to impress young Dorothy than her father. When I had finished, I felt a genuine sense of accomplishment in hearing so many favorable comments from so knowledgeable a group, and I would have considered my trip worthwhile even if I had nothing more concrete than admiration and encouragement to take home with me. It turned out to be a little more than that.

Lew Fields was then starring at the Casino Theatre in a musical called *A Lonely Romeo,* which he also produced. I was stunned and slightly hysterical when he said that he would not only buy one of our songs, "Any Old Place with You," but also find a spot for it in *A Lonely Romeo.* I fumbled my thanks and appreciation, danced out of the house and rushed to the nearest public telephone to break the news to my father. "Pop," I began, trying to be funny, "I have some terrible news . . ." And then I told him what had happened. Pop was almost as excited as I was—but not until after he had first given me hell for frightening the daylights out of him.

So it was that on August 26, 1919, at a Wednesday matinée, the career of Rodgers and Hart was professionally launched. It wasn't much of a splash, but to Larry and me Niagara Falls never made such a roar as the sound of those nice matinée ladies patting their gloved hands together as the song ended. The girl who sang it was Eve Lynn; the boy was a curly-haired towhead named Alan Hale who later became famous as a hard-hitting tough guy in Hollywood pictures.

For "Any Old Place with You," Larry took as his theme all the gay things a honeymooning couple might do, hopping from Syria to Siberia and from Virginia to Abyssinia, ending with the sure-fire laugh getter, "I'd go to hell for ya,/ Or Philadelphia!" Since the lyric prescribed that this world-wide jaunt be accomplished via rail, I came up with a bouncy melody that was intended to simulate the carefree chug-chugging of a honeymoon express. It was all pretty naïve, I suppose, but we were sure that we had begun our career in the most worldly and sophisticated manner possible.

I don't believe "Any Old Place with You" had the stuff of which hits are made, but what mattered to us was that a song we had written was being performed in a Broadway show and that audiences were enjoying it. Now we were sure nothing would stand in our way. Our path was blocked many times and in a variety of ways, but we never knew enough to quit.

I have found time and again that not knowing enough to quit is one of the most important factors in theatrical success. A lot of improbable people have made it to the top, not by talent alone but simply because they were there. Young people often come to me for advice about ways of breaking into the theatre. My answer is always the same: "Take a job, any job, that will get you inside a theatre. Be an usher, be a 'gofer' [someone who goes for sandwiches and cigarettes], be anything. Sooner or later the chances are that the impossible will happen: you'll get a job as an assistant stage manager, or they'll give you a walk-on with one line, or you'll be tapped to replace someone in the chorus. A good agent—if you can get one to take you on—can be of help, but the most important thing is to be where the action is."

$B$y the fall of 1919 I was too miserable at DeWitt Clinton to continue there any longer. Columbia University was offering certain courses in "extension," which made it possible to attend freshman classes even though I had not finished high school. But what appealed to me most was that I would be accepted as a freshman socially and could write the Varsity Show—provided, of course, that I won the competition. Since eligibility requirements were obviously lax, Larry Hart also qualified to write the Varsity Show, although he had been out of Columbia for three years.

So I became a member of the class of '23 in September 1919. The very first day I arrived on campus I found out about a singing contest to be held among the four classes, with each class expected to sing a traditional Columbia song. No sooner had I heard this than I decided that *my* class had to have an original song. I rushed home, wrote the words and music, rushed back, got the class together and taught the boys the song just in time for the contest. For the edification of all, here are the imperishable words:

> C boys,
>    it's '23 boys,
>    and
> O we'll give 'em
> L.
> U boys,
>    be true boys,
>    and
> M we'll make 'em yell!
> B boys,
>    forever steadfast,
> I will for
> A.
>
> (shouted)
> C-O-L-U-M-B-I-A!
>
> '23 Hurray!

We won the contest hands down and I became the class hero. From then on, the only other freshman who approached me in fame was a chubby little fellow named Edward Roche Hardy who got his picture in all the papers because, at thirteen, he was the youngest student ever to have been accepted at Columbia.

Early in 1920 I was an extremely busy lad. First there was another commission from the Akron Club—this time, naturally, with Larry Hart as collaborator. *You'd Be Surprised* was the title of the show, which the program proudly proclaimed "An 'atrocious' musical comedy." It probably was, despite our corralling the services of three members of the Fields family. Lew Fields was credited for "Professional Assistance," Dorothy played one of the leads, and Herbert contributed the lyric to a show-stopping number about "poor bisected, disconnected Mary, Queen of Scots." The musical played the Plaza Hotel Grand Ballroom the night of March 6.

Exactly eighteen days later Larry and I had our second musical of the year, *Fly with Me,* which opened at the Astor Hotel Grand Ballroom. But *Fly with Me* wasn't just another amateur show; it was the Columbia Varsity Show of 1920.

Beyond doubt, the Triangle Show at Princeton and the Hasty Pudding Show at Harvard were classier ventures, because Princeton and Harvard were classier schools. But the Varsity Show at Columbia offered a boy like me something no other school in the country could supply: an almost professional production. There were experienced directors, a beautifully equipped stage with good lighting situated in the heart of the Broadway theatre district, and best of all, professional musicians in the pit. Here, certainly, were near-ideal working conditions; here, possibly, was an opportunity that could be of incalculable help in furthering my career.

Since writing the Varsity Show had been the sole reason I entered Columbia, one of my first priorities when I got there was to look for a suitable musical-comedy idea. Somehow Larry and I got hold of a libretto by another student, named Milton Kroopf, who promptly disappeared out of my life, and we turned the script over for revisions to our matchmaking friend, Phil Leavitt. The book was a gag-filled fantasy set fifty years in the future (in 1970!), and our locale was an island—Manhattan, of course—that was then ruled by the Soviets. Once the writing had been completed, we submitted the show to three Varsity Show judges, Richard Conried, Ray Perkins (later a comedy writer and radio personality) and Oscar Hammerstein II, whose first musical, *Always You,* was then playing on Broadway. After due deliberation the judges chose *Fly with Me* as the Varsity Show over the four other entries submitted.

Rehearsals began in January in the basement of one of the Columbia buildings, with Herb Fields staging the dances and a professional actor, Ralph Bunker, directing the book. As rehearsal pianist, I had to spend endless hours banging out the tunes on a tinny upright, but since the tunes were mine, I loved doing it. The lyrics were all Larry's except for Oscar Hammerstein's "There's Always Room for One More" and "Weaknesses," which we lifted from the *Up Stage and Down–Twinkling Eyes* score.

About a year before *Fly with Me,* Roy Webb, a Columbia alumnus, had taught me the rudiments of musical notation and conducting. Roy had also written Varsity Shows as a Columbia undergraduate, and I found him to be not only experienced but exceedingly patient and kind. It was largely his training that gave me the confidence I needed when, on the morning of the first orchestra rehearsal, I went up to the Roof Garden of the Astor and bravely faced the seasoned Broadway musicians of "my" orchestra. It must be highly rewarding for a painter to see his paintings exhibited, or for a writer to come up with a best seller, or for a business executive to complete a successful deal, but I cannot imagine anything more thrilling than standing on a podium leading—*leading*—a group of professional musicians playing your own music. I've always understood why the boy who is elected president of his class makes up his mind that eventually he will run for the Presidency of the United States. Early achievement creates a thirst hard to satisfy. In my own field, that thirst began with my early experience of writing theatre scores and then conducting them before large and enthusiastic audiences.

*Fly with Me,* which gave the first of its four performances at the Astor on March 24, was somewhat better than an amateur show, as the term is generally used. It had a large chorus of burly college men—in drag, of course—many of whom sang beautifully, some genuinely comic performers, and an entire company of passionately hard workers. In addition, the professional contributions of our director and our musicians helped give the show a near-professional look and sound. I must also say that Larry Hart, Herb Fields and I brought a good share of expertise to the construction, rehearsing and eventual performance. (Incidentally, despite a cast of talented players, we three were the only ones to seek careers in the professional theatre.)

Since Lew Fields considered Larry and me something of a personal discovery, and since his own son was involved in the production, it was only natural that he would attend a performance of *Fly with Me.* What certainly was not natural was that he was so impressed with the music and lyrics that, almost on the spot, he decided to hire Rodgers and Hart to write the score for his next production.

This was unbelievable. There I was, a seventeen-year-old college freshman, and one of the theatre's most respected producers wanted *my* songs for a major Broadway show. Even Hollywood wouldn't have dared invent that one. But it happened, though the occasion turned out to be somewhat less auspicious than I had expected.

What Larry and I didn't know at first, but would soon find out, was that Lew Fields, thoroughly dissatisfied with the score created by a team he had already hired, was desperately searching for a replacement. A number of valid reasons led to his choosing us. First, having seen *You'd Be Surprised* and *Fly with Me,* he was impressed with our ability to come up with the kind of score he wanted. Secondly, since his forthcoming production—and I can no longer withhold the fact that it was called *Poor Little Ritz Girl*—was already booked to open its Boston tryout in May, he thought he could save time by using some of the songs from our two most recent efforts. Lastly, since he had to pay off the original writers, he figured, correctly, that we would be so thrilled at the opportunity that we would willingly accept a lower fee than a team with professional experience.

But none of this detracted from our excitement, apprehension and pride in actually writing a complete Broadway score. We worked in a Broadway theatre, the Central (now the Forum), at Forty-seventh Street and Broadway. There were real live chorus girls, seductive-looking but too intimidating to touch, and experienced theatre people were all over the place. Going through the stage door each day, I became familiar with the smell peculiar to stage doors. It isn't a pleasant or unpleasant odor; it simply means Theatre. Even today I still get that stirring of excitement, that feeling of venturing into the unknown whenever I go through a stage door and smell that combination of canvas, paint and wood.

The story these experienced theatre people had come up with was a simple-minded affair dealing with a chorus girl—of the *Poor Little Ritz Girl* company—who innocently rents the apartment of a wealthy young bachelor while he is out of town. He returns unexpectedly, and . . . well, you can take it from there.

Rehearsals went uneventfully for Larry and me simply because no one paid much attention to us. Once we had submitted our songs they were out of our hands. Eventually the big moment came when, trying hard to act like seasoned professionals, we boarded the night train to Boston with the rest of the company for the world premiere of *Poor Little Ritz Girl.* The next morning when we got off, my aplomb was thoroughly shattered when I discovered that we had lost Larry. It seems that he was so small that the porter couldn't find him in his upper berth to wake him in time, so he slept his way out to the train yards. He didn't make it to the theatre until the afternoon.

*Poor Little Ritz Girl* was the first attraction to play the new Wilbur Theatre. It opened to encouraging reviews, both for the show and for the score. Though most of the songs were written specifically for the production, we did, as originally planned, use some of the numbers from our last two amateur musicals. "The Boomerang," "Mary, Queen of Scots" (which got the biggest hand) and "Will You Forgive Me?" (previously known as "Princess of the Willow Tree") had been in *You'd Be Surprised.* We also borrowed three numbers from *Fly with Me,* though all were outfitted with new lyrics: "Peek in Pekin" became "Love's Intense in Tents," "Dreaming True" became "Love Will Call," and "Don't Love Me Like Othello" became "You Can't Fool Your Dreams." This last was considered particularly original in that its theme—"You tell me what you're dreaming, I'll tell you whom you love"—may well have been the first song with a somewhat Freudian philosophy.

With such capable actors as Victor Morley, Lulu McConnell and Roy Atwell in the leads, we were all reasonably optimistic about the show's chances on Broadway. The opening, however, was not scheduled to take place until the end of July. Since there was nothing else to do for the moment, I accepted a job as a counselor at a boys' camp called Camp Paradox. It was run by a likable fellow named Ed Goldwater, who hired me primarily to compose songs for a series of Sunday-night shows put on for the entertainment of campers, parents and friends. Herb Fields was also a counselor there, and putting these shows together was great experience as well as fun.

Still, it was murderous not to be with my show during its tryout tour. What was worse was the lack of communication. I had no idea what, if any, changes were being made, and I relied on the supposition that someone would let me know if anything radical was being done.

Getting Ed Goldwater's permission to go to New York for the opening was easy. Actually, I was given the send-off of a conquering hero-to-be, and I thought of nothing but my impending triumph as I lay sleepless in my berth on the midnight train heading for New York. In the morning I rushed straight to the theatre—and received the bitterest blow of my life. Half of our songs had been cut and replaced by numbers written by the more experienced team of Sigmund Romberg and Alex Gerber. Not only that; the story had been changed (Lew Fields was now crediting himself as co-author), Charles Purcell and Andrew Tombes had replaced Victor Morley and Roy Atwell, and a new girl was playing the title role. They had even hired a new musical director, Charles Previn.

What had happened, of course, was that despite some critical indications of success, the show had not really been in good shape in Boston and had not attracted customers. So Fields simply obeyed the ancient show-business dictum that is still all too often followed today: If something is wrong, change *everything*!

Naturally, Larry and I were in no mood to be philosophical or to see any reason for a situation that ironically was something of a reversal of the one we had experienced in *A Lonely Romeo.* When our one song had been added to that show, we were thrilled at our luck and had no qualms that it might be improper to interpolate it into someone else's score. But with *Poor Little Ritz Girl* we were the original writers, and it seemed at best inconsiderate and at worst deceitful to add a total of eight numbers without even giving us an inkling of what was going on. And these weren't merely additions, they were actual substitutions. This is what hurt most of all.

The Broadway opening of *Poor Little Ritz Girl* was July 28, 1920, and even now, more than fifty years later, I can still feel the grinding pain of bitter disappointment and depression. I didn't want my parents at the opening, but since there was no way to keep them out, we sat and suffered together until they took me to the train to go back to camp—one badly bruised unconquering hero.

In fairness, I must admit that most of the changes were improvements. The Romberg tunes, though not especially original, were energetic and helpful to this sort of piece, and the cast replacements were wisely made. My father even became fond of an innocent phallic joke: "You never can tell the depth of the well by the length of the pump handle."

I was particularly surprised at the reviews, which Pop sent to me at camp. While Rodgers and Hart weren't exactly being hailed as the new white knights of Broadway, the show itself received generally favorable comments. In the New York *Tribune,* Heywood Broun wrote: "The average musical comedy is copied after the one which was produced the month before. *Poor Little Ritz Girl* may serve to break the endless chain. It shows an effort to put an ear to the ground rather than at the crack of the stage door across the street." Much to Larry's chagrin, however, the song most singled out for praise, "Mary, Queen of Scots," had words by Herb Fields. Alan Dale, the critic of the *American,* claimed it was worth the price of admission, though he loftily admonished that "some of the profanity could be advantageously deleted. H—l is no longer funny. It's merely silly."

The show ran for nearly three months, which was pretty good in those days. Today, of course, a three-month run would be disastrous, but in 1920 a Broadway production needed no more than six months to make it one of the major hits of the season. In fact, the competition *Poor Little Ritz Girl* faced made its run all the more remarkable. Theatregoers could take their pick of such fare as *The Night Boat,* with a delectable Jerome Kern score, the latest *Ziegfeld Follies* with Fanny Brice and W. C. Fields, a Hippodrome spectacle featuring girls disappearing into a tank of water, the second edition of the *George White's Scandals* (and the first to boast a Gershwin score), and Oscar Hammerstein's latest effort, *Tickle Me,* starring comedian

Frank Tinney. Best of all was *Irene,* a holdover from the previous season, with a charming score by Joe McCarthy and Harry Tierney, including "Alice Blue Gown."

Even though I now considered myself a full-fledged Broadway composer, in the fall of 1920, I did what any teen-ager is expected to do: return to school. Again all I wanted to do was to write the next Columbia Varsity Show, and again I was chosen to do it. It was called *You'll Never Know,* and I haven't the foggiest recollection of what it was about. I do know, because I still have the program, that it was co-authored by Herman Axelrod (whose son, George, became a successful playwright), that it was co-directed by Oscar Hammerstein, and that its dances were staged by Herb Fields.

Herewith I submit a list of titles of musical comedies:

*You'd Be Surprised*

*Fly with Me*

*Say Mama!*

*You'll Never Know*

*Say It with Jazz*

*The Chinese Lantern*

*Jazz à la Carte*

*If I Were King*

*A Danish Yankee at King Tut's Court*

*Temple Belles*

*The Prisoner of Zenda*

These frequently ridiculous names represent the musicals for which I wrote scores between 1920 and 1924. I cite them because since all eleven were amateur shows, they provide the best answer I can give to a question I have been asked repeatedly: "How does anyone get started in show business?" My point is that there is a great deal more to writing for the musical theatre than learning notation, the meaning of a diminished seventh, or banging away at a typewriter in some lonely room. My advice is to reject at the start the idea that "amateur" is a dirty word, and to remember that while the qualitative differences between amateur and professional productions may be vast, the resemblances are equally great. Both require singers, actors, lighting, scenery, costumes, musical accompaniment and eventually an audience. On the way to that audience, writers, whether amateur or professional, are constantly polishing and making changes; through trial and error they learn what makes dialogue funny or touching and what makes a song not only suitable but remembered.

As a showcase, the amateur production can even have immediately practical results. In the audience may be someone's uncle who knows an agent or a producer—or who may even *be* an agent or a producer—and the amateur may have taken the first giant step toward becoming a professional.

This isn't just wishful thinking; it happened to me. Because Lew Fields saw a couple of amateur musicals by Rodgers and Hart, we had been signed to write the score for *Poor Little Ritz Girl.* Even though that was a professional effort, Larry and I quickly discovered that every step was the same as in the amateur shows we had been doing. The transition was smooth simply because we had already been through the required mental and physical discipline necessary for any stage production.

$I$n 1920, most of my social life was spent with two girls. I have already mentioned Dorith Bamberger, whose mother had tried to be helpful by introducing me to Louis Dreyfus. The other girl was named Helen, and no matter how innocent we managed to keep our relationship, it was pretty daring for those days, since she was already married. Because her husband was continually away on lengthy business trips, it was possible for us to spend many hours together, mostly walking in Central Park discussing our two favorite topics, ourselves and music. Helen, who wasn't much older than I was, had no technical knowledge of music, but she had a passion for it equal to mine and an understanding far greater. She was many things to me—teacher, mother, confidante and companion. To listen to Brahms with her was a deeply emotional experience that added an extra dimension to my already all-consuming love for music.

Both Dorith and Helen had unbounded faith in my ability and were forever dreaming up ideas about the best ways I could prepare myself for that inevitable day when all Broadway would be singing my songs. Since neither girl knew the other, it seemed a significant coincidence that each of them suggested at about the same time that I should quit Columbia as soon as possible and transfer to the Institute of Musical Art, the most prestigious music school in the city (it still is today, but now it is known as Juilliard).

I was well aware that academically Columbia had little to offer me in the area in which I was concentrating all my interest. I had already achieved my scholastic goal of writing two Varsity Shows, and therefore considered myself eligible for graduation right then. My idea of heaven was a place where I would be surrounded by nothing but music, so the girls didn't have a hard job selling me on the idea.

But I dreaded the next step: telling my father. Pop was not only a college man but a strong believer in the importance of a well-rounded education. While I was grateful for his encouragement of my musical career, I had my doubts that he was ready to give his blessing to my chucking the higher academic life in favor of a specialized school. I should have known better. Pop's reaction was typical of the way he treated me as long as he lived. He listened quietly while I got the whole thing off my chest, and when I was all through my carefully rehearsed speech, he simply said, "If that's what you feel you should do, do it."

I don't suppose anybody ever went into music with less opposition or more encouragement than I. We've all heard stories of the young songwriters who have succeeded in spite of strong parental disapproval, but I cannot recall a single instance when there was even the slightest hint from my parents that I was wasting my time. The only opposition I was ever aware of came from my grandfather, even though he was a great music lover and inveterate opera goer. I have no idea where he developed the fixation, but he repeated it as if it were gospel: "Even if you are successful, they'll never pay you."

With Pop's and Mom's approval, and despite Grandpa's warning, I happily abandoned my losing struggle with geometry and French and enrolled in the Institute to learn all I could about the vastly more appealing world of music. This turned out to include just about everything except mastering an instrument, since I soon discovered that my piano playing would never be any better than adequate. (I did, however, study what was known as "secondary piano," a course usually taken by students of singing or those who majored in other instruments.) What really excited me and made me certain that I had chosen the right educational path were the lectures and the courses I took in music theory, harmony and ear-training.

Franklin W. Robinson conducted special classes in music theory, but a more appropriate name for them would be musical aesthetics. The topic may sound dull, but Mr. Robinson, who was a well-known church organist as well as teacher, had a way of making it fascinating. For instance: "The next time you go to the Philharmonic, listen to a fellow named Bruno Labate who plays the oboe. Then you will really understand what the word 'concert' means. Here is a man who plays like a soloist but always plays *with* the orchestra. Besides that, he's an exquisite musician." Thereafter, whenever I went to the Philharmonic I paid particular attention to Mr. Labate and his oboe. He was a little guy and very fat, not pretty to look at but mighty pretty to listen to. He alone taught me a great deal about music in performance.

I was fortunate to be a member of a class in harmony taught by Percy Goetschius, who was to harmony what Gray was to anatomy. He had a wonderful sense of humor and was very easygoing, his only unbreakable rule being that he would not teach more than five students at a time. Whenever Goetschius talked about ending a phrase with a straight-out tonic chord (the first, third and fifth step of any scale), he would call it a "pig," his term for anything that was too easy or obvious. Once I heard the scorn in Goetschius' voice I knew that I'd avoid that "pig" as if my life depended on it.

Ear-training was another course that sharpened my understanding of music. My teacher, George Wedge, who later became dean of the Institute, conducted these classes more like fun and games than serious academic work. By this time I had already learned how to make my own piano transcriptions (which I still do), but it was a revelation to learn that by some curious kind of musical magnetics, the fourth step of the scale was pulled down to the third, and that the seventh was pulled up to the eighth. Nobody has ever explained it scientifically, but if you take the simple phrase of the music that goes with "Shave and a haircut, two bits," you'll find that the note that goes with "two" is carried, whether it wants to or not, to the note that goes with "bits." It's almost impossible for it to go anywhere else.

In addition to regular classes, the Institute offered stimulating lectures by the leading musical authorities of the day. One of my favorites was Henry Krehbiel, the music critic of the New York *Tribune* and probably the foremost critic in the country. Whenever he was scheduled to talk, I would leave home a half-hour earlier in order to make sure of getting a front-row seat. By just listening to him expound on Beethoven, you actually heard Beethoven. As he spoke he would become so emotional that tears rolled down his long red beard. After a lecture by Krehbiel, a Beethoven symphony or sonata was a brand-new experience, as if I were listening to it with a new pair of ears.

I never got to know him well, but Frank Damrosch, the founder and director of the Institute, was always sympathetic about my ambitions, and had a surprising knowledge and appreciation of the commercial musical theatre. Dr. Damrosch *was* the Institute: he set the tone, created the atmosphere and established the traditions. One of these was the ritual of the final exams; they always took place in the evening, with the entire faculty attending in formal dinner jacket and black tie.

Another was the year-end musical revue that kidded both the school and the music world in general. Here at last was a chance for the Institute's only Broadway-bound composer to shine! In fact, my first show, *Say It with Jazz*, was such a hit that I'm convinced I won scholarships for my second and third years just to make sure that I'd be on hand to write the shows. *Say It with Jazz* was based, more or less, on Rimsky-Korsakov's *Coq d'Or*. I contributed new songs written with Larry Hart and, for insurance, a few of the better applause getters which I had written for previous amateur efforts.

For the Institute's 1922 show, *Jazz à la Carte*, we had the services of Herb Fields to stage the dances and help direct the scenes, and William Kroll, a masterly violinist who later founded the Kroll String Quartet, as musical director. Gerald Warburg, my closest friend at the Institute, also contributed a few songs. Gerry was the son of Felix Warburg, the banker and art patron. His greatest love was the cello, which he played beautifully, and like all the members of his family, he managed to combine a vocation in finance with an avocation in music. In addition to new songs, for this show I also included such tested numbers as "There's Always Room for One More" and the hit of the evening, "Mary, Queen of Scots" (done as a takeoff on Maria Jeritza in *Tosca*). The following year, under the influence of Mark Twain and the recently discovered tomb of the Egyptian king Tutankhamen, we offered something called *A Danish Yankee in King Tut's Court*. Again it was mostly a Fields, Hart and Rodgers production.

I loved my years at the Institute. I could devote myself completely to something I cared for deeply, and for the first time in my life I was surrounded by students and teachers whose addiction to music was as great as mine, even though their interests were primarily confined to the concert hall or the classroom. A good many of the students who were there went on to become famous soloists, but the majority went to the Institute to study pedagogy before returning home to teach. Because I was the only pupil there whose goal was to write for the musical stage, I felt a bit self-conscious at first in being among people whose aims in life were, at least by tradition, considered loftier. But it didn't take long before I realized that my fellow students didn't look down their noses at someone whose aim was the tinseled world of Broadway. From teachers and classmates alike I can recall nothing but an attitude of mutual help and respect, and I'm sure that's why, for the first time in my life, I was actually learning something in a school. It may be true that some men thrive on opposition and are inspired by antagonism, but I've never been one of them. I cannot conceive of being in any kind of a personal relationship based on conflict, whether teacher–pupil, husband–wife, friend–friend, or partner–partner. In school, I learned well only from teachers who were lax in discipline but firm in sympathy and understanding, and for the most part, this is what I found at the Institute.

My whole experience there was more like an adventure than going to a school. My feeling of excitement and anticipation began in the morning when I got on the subway at Eighty-sixth and Broadway for the ride up to 116th Street. By the time I reached Claremont Avenue and 122nd Street, where the building was located, I could scarcely keep from running. When I returned home late in the afternoon I was fairly bursting with stories of the wonders I had discovered during the day. There isn't the slightest doubt that my years at the Institute were far more beneficial to me than four years at college could possibly have been.

Much as I was devoted to the Institute, I never let anything keep me from seizing opportunities to get ahead in my chosen field. Perhaps to make up for my disappointing experience with *Poor Little Ritz Girl,* Lew Fields again offered me a chance to work in the professional theatre—though not as a composer and not on Broadway. During the summer of 1921, he had appeared in a Broadway revue called *Snapshots of 1921*. It wasn't much of a hit, but it fitted into the plans of Lee and J. J. Shubert, then New York's leading theatre owners and producers. Anxious to set up their own vaudeville circuit to compete with the one operated by B. F. Keith, the Shubert brothers decided on a slightly different format. Instead of following the customary practice of booking individual acts that went from city to city, the Shuberts' plan was to send entire entertainments on tour. The first half of each unit would be the customary vaudeville acts, and the second would be a truncated, or "tab," version of a recent Broadway revue. Counting primarily on the box-office attraction of the Fields name, the Shuberts chose *Snapshots of 1921* as one of the attractions to be cut down and sent out that fall, and Lew Fields chose me as the musical director of the show.

Actually, I wasn't with the show from the beginning. *Snapshots* had already started on tour when Fields sent for me to replace the original conductor, who had signed on for only two months. I arrived in Pittsburgh in December 1921 to study the show, which would require my services both for *Snapshots* and for the various vaudeville acts that preceded it. In each city the unit played, there was an orchestra rehearsal on Monday morning, followed by the show's opening that afternoon. My debut as a professional conductor took place at the Shubert-Detroit Opera House. Once I had recovered from my initial nervousness, I found that the musicians were as cooperative and as helpful as those I had worked with on my amateur shows. I learned a lot about keys, tempos and the various ways an orchestra could help a singer project a song. I also learned a lot about life beyond the confines of an orchestra pit. Working in cities like New Haven, Toronto, Buffalo, and Chicago was exciting for a nineteen-year-old kid whose only other experience living away from home had been limited to summer camps.

Among the vaudeville acts traveling with us I recall only two. The first was Belle Story, who had been a leading singer at the New York Hippodrome. She had a lovely coloratura voice and made a big hit wherever we played, particularly with her singing of "The Marriage of the Lily and the Rose." The other performer I remember was a thin young man with an odd nasal voice and a sad face with prominent pouches under his eyes. He played the banjo and sat on the edge of the stage with his legs dangling into the orchestra pit. He was a superb deadpan comic, a fact that would become even more widely appreciated when Fred Allen became a coast-to-coast radio favorite.

*Snapshots* closed on the road in the spring of 1922 and I returned to my studies at the Institute of Musical Art. I also went back to writing amateur shows. One of these was a musical version of Justin Huntly McCarthy's celebrated swashbuckler, *If I Were King,* which had to do with the way the poet François Villon saved Paris by becoming king for a day. Herb Fields, Larry Hart and I collaborated on this effort, which was written for a benefit sponsored by the Benjamin School for Girls. All the characters in the production were played by the school's students including, in the role of Villon, Dorothy Fields sporting a beard.

Somehow, possibly through Lew Fields, a Broadway producer named Russell Janney heard about our production. He sent for me, I auditioned the numbers, and he was enthusiastic enough to say that he thought they would be just right for a Broadway adaptation. Shades of Lew Fields and my first Columbia Varsity Show! Janney never went so far as to offer a contract or discuss terms, but his sincerity was obvious and I was convinced that Rodgers and Hart would soon again have their names associated with a professional show.

So I went home and waited for Janney's call. And waited. And waited. With a what-have-I-got-to-lose feeling, I eventually called him. He mumbled an apology about not getting back to me, and then explained the facts of Broadway life: his associates—that is, financial backers—were unwilling to risk money on any project, no matter how worthy, that had been created by writers so young and inexperienced.

"But don't *you* think it can be a success on Broadway?" I pleaded.

"Yes."

"And don't *they* think it has merit?"

"Yes."

"Then why can't we go ahead?"

"They won't take a chance."

It was the same routine I had experienced with *Poor Little Ritz Girl,* except that at least there I ended up with half a score. Now, almost three years later, I was being treated as an even ranker amateur. I had already shared songwriting credit with Sigmund Romberg for a moderately successful Broadway musical; I had studied at the leading music school in the city; I had toured as musical director of a vaudeville unit for the Shubert brothers; I was constantly composing songs for whatever school, synagogue or club wanted to sponsor a musical comedy or revue. Yet I was still being told that I lacked experience. And how was I to gain more experience without being given the chance to work in the professional theatre?

Surely, I felt, Janney should have more faith in his own taste. He wouldn't be the first one who did. What about that young producer Alex Aarons? In 1919 he had given a twenty-year-old piano-pounder named George Gershwin a chance to write the music for a show called *La, La, Lucille.* Now Gershwin had the assignment to write all the songs for the annual *George White's Scandals.* A couple of years before, Aarons had discovered another composer, Vincent Youmans, and hired him for *Two Little Girls in Blue.* Now Youmans, at twenty-four, had one of the biggest successes in town with *Wildflower.* And not only did both composers have show hits, they also had song hits—Gershwin with "Swanee" and "I'll Build a Stairway to Paradise," and Youmans with "Bambalina."

I tried to console myself with the knowledge that Gershwin and Youmans were both about four years older than I. But the fact was that they didn't have any reputation when they were given their first break on Broadway—nor did they have to suffer, as I had, the indignity of a well-known composer being rushed in at the last minute to decimate their scores. What's more, they were able to capitalize on their maiden efforts and to go on almost immediately to establish themselves among the foremost writers in the musical theatre.

Two and a half years after Janney had shown enthusiasm for the Rodgers and Hart *If I Were King,* he did get to produce the story as a musical, and true to the convictions of his financial supporters, he engaged an experienced and successful composer, Rudolf Friml, to write the score. Since the show, now retitled *The Vagabond King,* became one of the triumphs of the decade, I don't suppose Janney ever had any cause for regret.

So *If I Were King* ended in frustration. But I couldn't waste time brooding, particularly when Herb Fields and Larry Hart had come up with a really novel idea for a musical, which might even be timely today. In the story, our hero invents a kind of "electronic" system that obviates the use of electric wires for communication and electric power. The locale is a small city called Winkle Town (which was also the name of the play), and the plot deals with the hero's attempt—ultimately successful, of course—to convince the town fathers that the idea is both practical and beneficial.

Somewhere in the course of writing the book, we felt that the story line wasn't working out as well as we had hoped. We needed help and, almost on a dare, we went to Oscar Hammerstein. He had already established himself on Broadway with six productions—including the current hit, *Wildflower*—so we weren't counting on more than a word or two of advice. But Oscar not only read the script, he liked the concept and the songs so much that he agreed to join us as collaborator.

As it turned out, he was unable to spend much time with us, nor was he able to lick the book problems that were still plaguing us. Nevertheless, I took the completed script and all the songs I had written to a young producer named Laurence Schwab whose first show, *The Gingham Girl,* had been a big hit the previous year. I don't recall how I got the introduction to Schwab, though I do recall that he liked the songs but hated the book. By this time we had all more or less given up on *Winkle Town,* so there were no objections from Herb, Larry or Oscar when I came up with a new proposal. Knowing that Schwab was about to go into production on a musical he was writing with Frank Mandel, and also knowing that he still hadn't chosen a composer and lyricist, I offered him the use of our *Winkle Town* songs as the basis of the score for his new show.

Schwab, however, said that while he thought he might be able to work the songs into his libretto, he didn't consider his judgment regarding their merit expert enough, so he asked me if I would mind playing them for a good friend of his, Max Dreyfus of T. B. Harms. Of course I didn't mind, though I was still a bit rankled by my previous visit to that company when Max Dreyfus' brother, Louis, had told me to go back to school.

I soon discovered that Max Dreyfus was no more of a diplomat than his brother. After ushering Schwab and me into his office, this aesthetic-looking titan of the music business sat with eyes half closed as I played my songs. When I had finished, Dreyfus slowly turned to Schwab and said, "There is nothing of value here. I don't hear any music and I think you'd be making a great mistake."

I was so stunned that I couldn't say a word. My heart began to pound violently and I felt the blood rush to my face. Nothing of value? He didn't hear any music? Oscar Hammerstein had thought so much of the score that he had joined us in writing the show. Before we met Dreyfus, Schwab himself had been impressed. Now, suddenly, with two sentences, the verdict was being handed down that I had no talent. I could understand Dreyfus liking some songs better than others; I could even understand his *hating* some songs. But he didn't like anything—not even the one song that had never failed to get a positive reaction, no matter on whom we had tried it out. This was a swinging, light-hearted ode to all the joys of living in New York which we called "Manhattan."

It didn't take long for me to appreciate the reason for Dreyfus' harsh judgment. The next thing he said to Schwab was, "You know, we have a young man here under contract to us who would be perfect for the job. His name is Vincent Youmans."

The end of this little story was, of course, that Larry Schwab did not hire Rodgers and Hart for his new musical. But he didn't hire Vincent Youmans, either. By the time the show, *Sweet Little Devil,* opened in New York early in 1924, the score was the product of Ira and George Gershwin. Needless to say, they too were under contract to Harms.

Obviously, plays with music cost a great deal more to produce than plays without music. Since we seemed to be having no luck in finding a sponsor with enough confidence in his own judgment and taste to take a chance on a musical written by a couple of still-struggling songwriters, Larry and I reasoned that we should next try something more modest, a comedy perhaps, which might have an easier time getting on the boards. At the very least it would get our names known in the profession, and we could always sneak in a song or two just to let everyone know the direction in which we were still heading.

So we hashed over a few ideas with Herb Fields and finally settled on a rather simple-minded sentimental tale which, I must confess, had about it the aroma of *The Music Master,* one of David Belasco's turn-of-the-century hits. Our plot had to do with an elderly Austrian immigrant composer who is forced to earn his living as an arranger for a Tin Pan Alley music publisher. When the publisher has one of the composer's serious pieces jazzed up as "Moonlight Mama," the old man is disconsolate. Thanks to the composer's daughter and a young violinist, there is a happy ending, and poor old Franz Henkel is at last free to devote himself to the kind of music he loves.

Because of the play's theme, we made sure to include a couple of songs: the jazzy "Moonlight Mama," naturally, and as something of a burlesque on the comic songs of the day, "I'd Like to Poison Ivy."

Herb, Larry and I all contributed to the story, taking turns at the typewriter and throwing ideas around. When we finished the manuscript, the three names looked rather unwieldy on the title page, so we decided to combine our first names and give all the credit to one "Herbert Richard Lorenz." This may have been the cleverest idea we had.

In creating the main character, we consciously thought of the role as a part that would be perfect for Lew Fields, but I must say that we were all a bit surprised when he not only agreed with us but decided to put the play into production. It was, I believe, the first time that he had ever appeared in a work that was neither a musical comedy nor a revue.

We opened the show in Bethlehem, Pennsylvania, in March 1924 and kept it out of New York for two and a half months. Originally it was called *The Jazz King,* then *Henky,* and finally *The Melody Man* (if anyone wanted to confuse that title with *The Music Master,* it was all right with us).

During the Chicago tryout, Fields made the shattering discovery that he didn't have enough money to bring the show into New York. We held a hurried meeting and decided that Max Hart, Larry's father, was the only person who knew where and how to find the missing $1,000, and that I was the only person who could talk him into doing the finding. So back to New York I went, saw Mr. Hart in his office and explained the problem. As soon as I finished, Hart picked up his telephone and called Billy Rose. Rose, only about a year older than I, had already made a sizable amount of money as a lyricist, and his connection with Hart was that on more than one occasion he had paid Larry to ghostwrite lyrics for which he took the credit. I sat and listened while Mr. Hart fed Billy a line in his lisping German accent about what a tremendous success the play was in Chicago and that he might just be able to use his influence to let Billy buy into the show for $1,000. I don't know whether Rose was really taken in by Hart's fairy tale or whether he did it as a favor to Larry, but the check was in the mail the next day.

With Billy Rose's $1,000, we managed to get *The Melody Man* to open in New York on schedule, but no amount of money could have kept it running very long. The reviewers applauded Lew Fields but used the backs of their hands for the efforts of Herbert Richard Lorenz. Perhaps George Jean Nathan put it best when he wrote: "The plot is not only enough to ruin the play; it is enough—and I feel that I may say it without fear of contradiction—to ruin even *Hamlet.*"

One good thing did come out of the unfortunate experience. The part of the play's hero, the violinist, was played by a handsome young man who had had a few years of acting experience under his real name, Frederick Bickel. For *The Melody Man,* however, he was persuaded to change it to the softer-sounding Fredric March. I got to know Freddie pretty well during our only professional experience together. Whatever he did on the stage was never less than highly professional, and usually a good deal more. But offstage we would talk for hours, not about ourselves or the silly play, but chiefly about conditions in the world and the state of the arts in general. He was extremely well read and had a deep social conscience which affected his philosophical outlook. Through the years, and especially after his marriage to the lovely Florence Eldridge, Freddie and I maintained a warm affection for each other that was always deeply satisfying. Nowadays we hear the term "Beautiful People" bestowed upon members of the fast-paced, fast-buck international set. They aren't beautiful at all. To me, the Beautiful People are those like Fredric and Florence March.

Larry and I were sure of one thing after *The Melody Man:* we were never going to make it in the musical theatre by backing into Broadway with a nondescript play and a couple of satirical songs. Succeed or fail, we would have to stick with what we knew and what we did best. All this comes under the heading of Experience. We were learning—painfully—our trade with all its inherent pitfalls and misjudgments. But enough was enough. Couldn't Experience include something successful for a change?

We also knew that we couldn't afford to lose much more time. No sooner had *The Melody Man* opened than Larry came up with an idea for a story, and promptly turned it over to Herb Fields to develop into the book for a musical. An omniverous reader, Larry had long been intrigued by the theatrical possibilities of an incident in the American Revolution, when Mrs. Robert Murray, after whose family Murray Hill was named, managed by her feminine charms to detain the British general, Sir William Howe, long enough for the American forces under General Putnam to flee lower Manhattan to join General Washington's army on Harlem Heights. It was a good story, which Herb embellished with the inevitable romance, this one between an English captain and an American girl, and it gave us ample opportunity for a variety of musical expressions. We called the show *Dear Enemy.*

Confident that we had at last come up with a potential winner, during the fall and winter of 1924–25 we made the rounds of producers and publishers—and heard the same old story. We were unknowns and no one wanted to take a chance on unknowns, especially when they'd written something calling for elaborate settings and costumes. Once again we were treated to the demoralizing sound of doors being slammed in our faces.

Surprisingly, though, along the way we did pick up two important allies. One was Helen Ford, a petite, attractive actress with a lovely voice, who had scored impressively in two hits in a row, *The Gingham Girl,* Larry Schwab's first production, and *Helen of Troy, New York.* We heard that Helen was looking for a suitable new musical, and somehow I managed to persuade her to let us audition our show. This was a slightly roundabout way of doing things, but I reasoned that once Helen Ford indicated her willingness to star in our musical, she could at best find us a producer or at least make it easier for us to find one.

Helen came to my parents' apartment one evening, met Larry and Herb, and listened to us sing the songs and read the scenes. She was a wonderful audience and praised almost everything she heard. When we were finished, we looked anxiously in her direction and were treated to the exact words we wanted to hear: "I'd love to play the leading part." The words that followed, however, were *not* what we wanted to hear: "Who's going to produce it and who's putting up the money?" We had to admit that we still had no idea, and she had to admit that she had no idea either, but she assured us that she would do everything possible to help. Nothing that night could dissuade us from our euphoric belief that with Helen Ford as our intended star every producer in town would be begging us for the chance to sponsor our show.

Helen had just closed in a short-lived musical produced by A. L. Jones and Morris Green, and she was quick to set up an appointment with them. They liked what they heard, but having just lost money on their last show, they were leery of—here we go again!—taking a chance on unknown writers. Fortunately they didn't stop there.

Ever since 1919, Jones and Green had presented an annual revue, *The Greenwich Village Follies.* Even though they did not feel they could handle our show at that moment, they were impressed enough to arrange a meeting for us with the director, John Murray Anderson, who turned out to be our second ally.

Anderson, a saturnine, elegant Englishman with sad eyes and a prominent jaw, was extremely encouraging after listening to the songs and an outline of the plot. He would very much like to direct the show, he told us, and would certainly help us find a sponsor. The only trouble was that at the time he was completely occupied with directing Irving Berlin's latest *Music Box Revue,* which, since it represented his first major Broadway assignment, required his total concentration. So that, for the time being, was that.

With nothing else to do, we continued our frustrating quest. One day Anderson called me to say that he had just hung up on a young scion of wealth who was anxious to take a fling in the theatre. Anderson had talked the man into agreeing to listen to our score, but the catch was that I had to audition for him that very evening. Did he want to read the script? No, not just now. Did he want Helen Ford there or any other singers? No, not just now.

As soon as the butler ushered me into the gentleman's fashionable Park Avenue apartment I discovered that our would-be backer was not alone; he was having a party. He drunkenly introduced himself and told me to go over to the piano and start playing. So I went over to the piano and started playing. It didn't take long for me to realize that the young man couldn't care less about my songs; all he wanted was someone to provide free entertainment for his guests. There must have been eight couples there, and while I played everyone was drinking, laughing and snuggling. Despite my irritation, I found myself fascinated by the scene, so I just kept on playing and looking. Eventually, after I had performed the score straight through, my host told me I could go home. Apparently by that time everyone was all set to provide his and her own entertainment.

The winter of 1924–25 was the most miserable period of my life. No matter what I did or where I turned, I was getting nowhere. I would get up each morning, take my songs to a producer or publisher I thought might be interested, audition them—or, more likely, be told to come back some other time—and go home. This happened day after day after day. After the drubbing he had taken with *The Melody Man,* Lew Fields turned us down.

Larry Schwab never returned my call. Russell Janney was busy with his production of *The Vagabond King*. I couldn't get past the reception desks at the Shubert and Dillingham offices. And I certainly wasn't about to approach Max Dreyfus again.

None of this really dampened my confidence in *Dear Enemy*. I still felt sure that the songs were original and attractive and had good commercial possibilities, and that the story was at least as strong as anything being done on Broadway. But it seemed that no one who agreed with me was able to do anything about it.

What made things even harder to bear was that Broadway was bursting with activity. That season Rudolf Friml had *Rose-Marie,* and Sigmund Romberg *The Student Prince.* There was also Irving Berlin's fourth *Music Box Revue,* and another spectacular *Ziegfeld Follies.* But I suppose what bothered me most was that my most celebrated contemporaries, George Gershwin and Vincent Youmans, had gone on to even greater achievements. One of the biggest hits was Gershwin's *Lady, Be Good!,* starring the stage's greatest dance team, Fred and Adele Astaire. In Chicago, Youmans' *No, No, Nanette* was being acclaimed even before its scheduled New York opening. It wasn't that I didn't like their music; next to Kern, there were no two composers I admired more, both for their rhythmic vitality and the freshness of their melodic ideas. But I also had confidence in my own ability, and I just couldn't understand why, in a season that could offer over forty musical productions, everyone else managed to get a show on the boards except Fields, Rodgers and Hart.

Because of this, I was troubled at the time by severe insomnia. At night I'd lie awake in bed, tortured by the feeling that I might actually be at the end of my career. For over seven years I had been composing scores for every possible type of musical show. I had been a boy wonder. I had even made it to Broadway at an earlier age than Gershwin. Once everything had seemed to be falling into place easily; now I was twenty-two and it all seemed to be falling apart.

Since I had dropped out of college to devote myself to composing for the theatre, and since it was apparent that the theatre was able to get along very nicely without me, the next question was, What to do now? The idea of becoming a music director had a certain appeal since I enjoyed conducting, but the thought of spending my life with other people's music turned me off. I knew I could never play well enough to become a professional pianist. What about teaching? Most of the students I had known at the Institute of Musical Art were now music teachers, and from what I heard it was a satisfying life. But what category of music would I teach? Did I know enough about *any* category of music to teach it? Was I qualified to do anything besides sit at a piano and make up melodies?

Adding to my worries was the fact that I was not alone. I had a partner who was dependent on me. Larry, however, never seemed to be much concerned about our string of misfortunes. He managed to take everything in his stride, and while he may not have been of any help in auditioning or negotiating, he was a great morale booster because of his unfailingly optimistic spirit. Throughout this entire time we never had one disagreement about what course we should follow, nor were there ever any words between us about who was to blame for our lack of progress.

Then there were my parents to consider. Seeing their daily look of concern and listening to their attempts to bolster my sagging morale only succeeded in adding to my feelings of frustration, bitterness and guilt—with guilt probably the strongest emotion. At an age when most fellows I knew were already settled in their careers, at a time when my own brother was poring over medical books and laying the groundwork for a lifetime in medicine, I wasn't earning a penny. It was this aching feeling of guilt that for a while actually turned me away from music; for weeks I wouldn't even go near the piano.

Life in the Rodgers household when I was a kid had been hell chiefly because of the friction between my father and my grandmother. Even though Grandma had been dead for four years, life was still hell. There was no bickering, no yelling, no tight-faced silence. Now it was hell because I hated myself for sponging off my parents, and I hated myself for the lies I would rattle off about this producer or that publisher being so impressed with my work that it wouldn't be long before everything would be just dandy. Not once did I ever hear Mom or Pop say a single word that was not sympathetic, or show in any way that they were not behind me in whatever I wanted to do. I couldn't even get rid of my raging frustration by accusing them of not understanding me!

With desperation and despondency churning within me, I felt that the time had come for me to restore some measure of self-respect by going out and getting a job. One night I happened to unburden myself to a friend of mine named Earl. He told me about a Mr. Marvin (I don't think I ever knew his first name), a wholesaler in the babies'-underwear business with an office directly across the hall from his own. Marvin, it seems, though unmarried and fairly young, was anxious to retire and was looking around for someone he could train to take over the business when he quit. It was a one-man operation, with Marvin doing all the buying, selling and traveling on the road.

Though I had no business experience in any field, nor any particular affinity for the babies'-underwear business, I found myself intrigued by the idea of applying for the position. Why not? It mightn't be bad at all. I'd be my own boss, travel around, see the country, build the business, make enough money to enjoy life. Then, who knows, maybe someday I'd give it up and go back to composing. Larry would still be around . . . Anyway, it would be a challenge; more important, I wouldn't have to duck around the corner every time I saw someone I knew coming down the street.

So, without telling Larry or my parents, I met Mr. Marvin. We hit it off immediately; even allowing for my lack of business experience, he seemed to feel I could handle the job. Before I left his office, Marvin had made me a firm offer, with a starting salary of $50 a week. There I was, on the brink of earning what was, to me, a fantastic amount of money—and yet something held me back from accepting. Though puzzled at my sudden indecision, Marvin agreed to give me until the following morning to make up my mind.

That night at dinner I received a telephone call from Benjamin Kaye, the theatrical lawyer who, besides having written a few plays, had collaborated with me on a song for *Up Stage and Down.* Since I hadn't spoken to him for some time, I was surprised at the call. I was even more surprised at the reason. Over the phone I heard Ben's gentle, unemotional voice say, "Dick, some of the kids from the Theatre Guild are putting on a benefit show. I told them you'd be just the right fellow to write the songs."

$O$ne important element of success in any field is knowing when to say yes and when to say no. Perhaps I should have realized that Ben's offer was finally going to lead to the break I needed, but that's hindsight. What actually happened was that with my head reeling from months of frustration and my current indecision about the business world, the only words I heard were "benefit show."

"Thanks, Ben," I said, and I felt my voice tightening, "but I've been through all that before. I'm not going to do any more amateur shows. I'm sick of wasting my time. I've been doing them for over seven years, and all they've ever led me to is a dead end." Then, trying to sound casual, I added, "Anyway, I've decided to quit the music field. As a matter of fact, I've just been offered an important position with a business firm."

"Well, all right, Dick, if that's the way you feel," Ben said, "but Terry Helburn and Lawrence Langner are going to be awfully disappointed. I really gave you a hell of a build-up."

"Terry Helburn and Lawrence Langner?" My voice must have gone up at least an octave.

"Yes, Terry Helburn and Lawrence Langner. I did say the Theatre Guild."

"Then this isn't going to be an amateur show?"

"Well, not exactly. The kids who are putting on the show are mostly bit players in Guild productions. About a year ago they got together and organized something called the Theatre Guild Junior Players, mostly to do experimental plays and put them on for the benefit of the Guild management. Terry and Lawrence have been very encouraging, and now the group wants to do something to show its appreciation. After kicking some ideas around, someone came up with the notion of putting on a musical revue to raise money to buy tapestries for the new Guild Theatre on Fifty-second Street. It'll be a great opportunity for a lot of talented kids to be noticed by the public. You won't be earning any money, but since Terry and Lawrence have given their blessing, the Guild itself is planning to sponsor it."

Ben didn't have to say another word. Under the leadership of Theresa Helburn and Lawrence Langner, the Theatre Guild had become the most prestigious producing organization in the country, offering its subscribers a rich, if slightly heavy, diet of plays by the likes of Strindberg, Shaw and Ibsen. The mere fact that this was going to be the Guild's first musical—even though it would be a semiamateur benefit show—was bound to stir up considerable interest. It would mean not only a sold-out house but an audience that would certainly include important theatre people as well as critics from the daily papers. In a way it would be my final test. If I couldn't make it with this kind of showcase, I'd know I couldn't make it, *period*. But I knew that I could—I *had* to. There would never be another chance like this. Obviously, the more I thought about the project the more I found it losing its amateur status and assuming the dimension of *A Theatre Guild Production*. By the time I got to sleep that night I was sure of one thing: the world was going to have to get along with one less tycoon in the babies'-underwear business.

Ben Kaye arranged a meeting for me with Helburn and Langner in their office. They were a charming but oddly contrasting couple. Terry was a tiny, birdlike little lady who always wore a hat and looked as if she'd be more at home sponsoring tea parties than some of the major dramatic works of the century. Lawrence was an erect, courtly chairman-of-the-board type who spoke with an attractively musical accent that revealed his Welsh origin. As I played my songs for them I had to keep reminding myself that these two warm, enthusiastic people were really the Theatre Guild and not doting relatives encouraging their favorite nephew.

It was as simple as that. I played, they liked what I played, and the job was mine. Literally overnight I was lifted from despair to being the first musical-comedy composer ever accepted by the Theatre Guild.

I soon found out, however, that there was one problem, and a major one. Prominent among the Junior Players was a bright, talented actress named Edith Meiser. Even before Ben called me, it had been understood that Edith would not only appear in the revue but would also write the lyrics for the songs. Although I was scarcely in a position to dictate terms, I was adamant on one point: I would compose the songs with no other lyricist than Larry Hart. Fortunately, after some discussion, it was agreed to accept Hart along with Rodgers.

But I hadn't taken into consideration Larry's unpredictability. He didn't want to do it. He, too, was tired of the old amateur grind, with nothing in the bank to show for it. The prestige of the Theatre Guild meant little to him, and he was unhappy about the lack of time we had to put the whole thing together. But what bothered him most was that the show, being a revue, required nothing more from us than a collection of songs. He was convinced that the only way we could win recognition was to create a unified score for a book musical, with songs written for specific characters and situations. I finally talked him into the assignment by proposing that we try to incorporate a short, self-contained book musical into the revue as the first-act finale.

Since the theatre we were to play in was the Garrick, on West Thirty-fifth Street, it was decided to call the revue *The Garrick Gaieties,* and since the current tenants of the Garrick were Alfred Lunt and Lynn Fontanne, in their memorable production of Ferenc Molnár's *The Guardsman,* it was further decided to schedule two performances on Sunday, the theatre's "dark" day, May 17, 1925.

All the rehearsals took place at the Garrick. Because of the limited time, we worked, ate and napped there. Sets and costumes were kept simple, and our lighting consisted of anything we could use from *The Guardsman.* I don't think the whole production cost more than $3,000.

Although I had worked with professional actors before, I couldn't help feeling that there was something special about this particular group. They were all young and talented, but they also had something even rarer: a combination of love, loyalty, dedication and ambition that was enormously stimulating. Terry Helburn and Lawrence Langner seemed to sense it too; they never patronized us or made us feel in any way that our efforts were any less worthy than their more serious endeavors.

Thinking back on those days conjures up so many quick impressions: Philip Loeb, our deceptively mild-looking director, who could have tamed a cageful of lions with a word or a glance; Lee Strasberg, an acknowledged authority on acting even then, auditioning with the incongruous choice of "My Wild Irish Rose"; Sterling Holloway, a floppy-haired string bean, who always sounded as if he couldn't utter a word without first swallowing it; Herb Fields, whom Larry and I had brought in as dance director, trying to find enough room to work out his routines on the same cluttered stage as the singers; Libby Holman (then Elizabeth Holman), who always insisted I didn't play low enough when I accompanied her.

One morning a plump, pretty girl walked into the theatre and asked me if she could play the piano for rehearsals. She didn't even care whether or not she'd be paid. Since I had my hands full supervising the musical numbers, accompanying the singers and dancers, and writing whatever new material was needed, I was grateful to be relieved of at least one of these chores—provided, of course, that she could play well enough. She proved it simply by sitting down and, from memory, giving a note-perfect rendition of the song I'd just played, down to the exact harmonies and rhythmic nuances. This remarkable girl was Margot Hopkins (then Margot Milham), who not only played for all the succeeding *Gaieties* rehearsals but continued to be my rehearsal pianist for almost every Broadway show I did.

The Sunday of our two scheduled performances finally came. When the houselights dimmed, I crawled up from under the stage and took my place facing the eleven musicians in the orchestra. The packed audience babbled and rustled programs during the overture and applauded perfunctorily when it was over.

The curtain rose on the first number, "Soliciting Subscriptions." Since ours was a satirical revue aimed primarily at puncturing the arty pretensions of the theatre—especially the Theatre Guild—we opened with representatives of three little theatre groups, the Neighborhood Playhouse, the Provincetown Playhouse and the Actors' Theatre, explaining what each one stood for and why it merited support. At the end the trio introduced the rest of the cast with *The Garrick Gaieties* is coming down the street! Here's where we meet our meat!" And out came the kids, all holding banners with the names of Theatre Guild successes, to explain—in "Gilding the Guild" —that they were there to raise cash to help beautify the Guild's new theatre. Happily, the number achieved the primary function of any opening routine: it gave the members of the audience an idea of what the rest of the show would be like and put them in a properly receptive mood.

The first sketch, written by Ben Kaye, satirized the Garrick Theatre's current tenant, *The Guardsman,* with Romney Brent as Alfred Lunt and Edith Meiser as Lynn Fontanne. It won laughs in all the right places from the theatre-wise audience, which showed that it was at least willing to meet us halfway. Ben had also written the lyric to the next song, "The Butcher, the Baker, the Candlestick-Maker," with music by his friend Mme. Mana-Zucca. It was a jaunty piece about a girl's dalliance with the three gentlemen of the title, and received an appreciative hand.

Edith Meiser's sketch, "The Theatre Guild Enters Heaven," again ribbed our indulgent sponsors with a scene depicting St. Peter (Romney Brent) and a heavenly jury passing on the moral acceptability of recent Guild heroines. Following a dance by Eleanor Shaler, Edith Meiser came out to sing "An Old Fashioned Girl," the lone effort of the team of Rodgers and Meiser. Edith had shown me the lyric during rehearsals, and since I liked it and Larry offered no objection, I wrote an appropriately waltzing melody for it. The song was a lament for the good old days when men were men, and according to Edith's inspired line, "thought Freud was just German for 'joy.' "

Not counting the opening number, the first Rodgers and Hart song in the show was "April Fool," sung by Betty Starbuck and Romney Brent. By now there was every indication that the audience was with us, and it wasn't simply because the customers were charitable toward the young or that the tickets were cheap. Though I couldn't see the people sitting in the dark behind me, I could actually feel the warmth and enthusiasm on the back of my neck. Our show was creating that rare kind of chemistry that produces sparks on both sides of the footlights. What the people were responding to was an irresistible combination of innocence and smartness, two qualities I'm sure helped make "April Fool" one of the best-received pieces so far.

There followed another Ben Kaye sketch, "They Didn't Know What They Were Getting," an adroit takeoff on Sidney Howard's play *They Knew What They Wanted.* A backstage trio, "The Stage Managers' Chorus," won only mild approval, but Hildegarde Halliday's impersonation of monologist Ruth Draper was a crowd pleaser.

Then came our first-act finale, "The Joy Spreader." Gilbert Seldes, the drama critic and playwright, had given us the idea, and the program credited him for being "primarily responsible for this outrage." Our "jazz opera," as it was billed, was set in a department store where a salesgirl (Betty Starbuck) and a clerk (Romney Brent) have been locked in for the night. The following morning they are confronted by the puritanical store owner, but eventually they prove young love to be both virtuous and victorious. Though I'm not sure the audience quite got the hang of an opera form written in popular style, everyone seemed to appreciate our attempt at something a little daring, and the curtain came down to an extremely generous hand.

Act Two opened with "Rancho Mexicana," a number off the geographical track of the rest of the show. It was a colorful, festive story-in-dance routine, and we included it because it offered us the services of both Rose Rolando, a dancer, and her husband, Miguel Covarrubias, a well-known artist, who had designed the sets and costumes. They also brought along their own authentic Mexican music. This was our one "spectacle," and it got the second act off to a rousing start.

"Ladies of the Box Office," which followed, kidded such current examples of theatrical femininity as Mary Pickford (Betty Starbuck), a Ziegfeld show girl (Libby Holman) and the Sadie Thompson character in *Rain* (June Cochrane). A sketch by Arthur Sullivan and Morrie Ryskind, "Mr. and Mrs.," was our lone excursion into political satire. The gag here was to have President Calvin Coolidge (John McGovern) chewed out by his wife (Edith Meiser) for spending a wild evening with Herb Hoover listening to the radio and coming home at the ungodly hour of ten. The audience roared at the sight of Coolidge taking off his coat to reveal both red suspenders and a thick red belt.

I had a sense of anticipation when we began the next number—the one Larry and I had written for *Winkle Town* which, except for Max Dreyfus, everyone who'd ever heard it liked immediately. "Manhattan" was staged simply "in one" (that is, before the curtain while the scenery was being changed behind) as a boy-girl duet for Sterling Holloway and June Cochrane. Its easygoing, strolling melody and ingeniously rhymed lyric related all of the everyday pleasures to be found in New York and didn't require literal or even stylized reproduction. Though the stage was bare except for two kids, the audience could see and feel everything the song conveyed, and they ate it up. June and Sterling had to give at least two encores, and they could have given more if we had written more. If one song can be said to have "made" Rodgers and Hart, it surely was "Manhattan."

"Where Credit Is Due," a sketch about product-plugging, followed, but I was still so excited at the reception for "Manhattan" that I have no idea how it went over. In fact, I almost missed my cue for "The Three Musketeers," a second holdover from *Winkle Town,* which was sung by Sterling Holloway, Romney Brent and Philip Loeb. It was a typical revue number of the time in that it took a well-known historical situation and kidded it with modern slang (e.g., "Athos, Porthos and Aramis/We are the kittens' pajamis"). Not the best or the worst of its kind, the song benefited greatly from the trio's inventive sight gags that made it much funnier than it really was.

Two more Rodgers and Hart songs followed: "Do You Love Me?," a quizzical ballad sung by Louise Richardson, and "Black and Blue," a torchy ballad moaned by Libby Holman. "Fate in the Morning," the last sketch before the finale, did a hilarious job of skewering still another arty Theatre Guild production, *Fata Morgana.*

After the finale—a full-company reprise of "Gilding the Guild," with new lyrics—the theatre was in an uproar. I turned around to look at the audience; everyone was standing. Not standing to leave, just standing. Not just standing, either. Standing and clapping, cheering, yelling, stomping, waving and whistling. I turned back to the orchestra and had the boys strike up "Manhattan." The cast sang it. The musicians sang it. Even the audience sang it. After about ten curtain calls, the houselights went on, but still no one wanted to go. At last, slowly and hesitantly, the audience filed out, as if unwilling to leave to memory an experience that was so vivid and exciting.

Tired, exultant and wringing wet, I rushed backstage, hugging and kissing everyone in sight. We were a bunch of kids who had worked like hell and were now enjoying the almost unbearable ecstasy of having everything turn out just right. Physiologically we may have been sober but emotionally we were all drunk, and there's no greater feeling than that.

All at once we were shatteringly brought back to reality. Larry was jumping up and down, rubbing his hands together and screaming, "This show's gonna run a year! It's gonna run a year!" We all looked at one another. It wasn't going to run a year; it wasn't even going to run another day. We had only one more performance, that very night, and then it would be all over.

The evening performance went just as well as the matinée. Again there was the feeling in the back of my neck that the audience, even when silent, was loving every minute of it, and again there was wild enthusiasm at the end.

The next morning's reviews confirmed everything that had happened the day before: "absolutely fresh in word, song, dance, skit, and bit of skittishness" . . . "went over like a bunch of firecrackers" . . . "brisk, refreshing and entertaining" . . . "a witty, boisterous, athletic chow-chow" . . . "bright with the brightness of something new-minted" . . . "as spontaneous and quick-moving a show as is to be found in town" . . . "full of youth, energy and fine flashes of wit" . . . "Rodgers and Hart's stuff clicked here like a colonel's heels at attention."

With such a reception, how could we possibly let *The Garrick Gaieties* die? I spoke to Terry Helburn and she was only too happy to give us the theatre for matinées the following week—except, of course, for the two afternoons that *The Guardsman* was playing. Despite the fact that this particular week was one of the hottest on record and we had no air conditioning, all our matinées played to standing room only.

Now I was really feeling cocky. Again I spoke to Terry, this time proposing that our show be allowed to play the Garrick for a regular run. Terry smiled sweetly and asked, "And what do you suggest we do with *The Guardsman?*" Giving her the benefit of my many years of success in the theatre, I said simply, "Close it." Terry laughed and agreed to discuss the matter with the Guild's board of directors. Within two days I had my answer; *The Guardsman,* which had been running since the previous October, ended its successful run on June 6, and two days later *The Garrick Gaieties* reopened on a regular-run basis.

But not without a few changes. We decided to drop five numbers, including, ironically, "The Joy Spreader," which had been responsible for Larry's doing the show in the first place. Added were "Sentimental Me," a beautiful example of Larry's genius at combining satire and sentiment, a fast-stepping item called "On with the Dance," and a funny sketch by Morrie Ryskind and Phil Loeb based on the Scopes monkey trial. I remember that Lee Strasberg and Harold Clurman played two of the monkeys that made up the jury. To help keep the show fresh, other changes were made in the fall.

Since not all the first-string reviewers had come to see us when we first opened, we were happy to read an almost continuous stream of praise right through to the end of the run, which was late in November. There was even a critical disagreement over Larry's lyrics. Alexander Woollcott wrote in the New York *World* that they were "rich in sprightly elaborate rhymes and suffer only from the not unimportant qualification that they do not sing well." The following day Frank Sullivan answered Woollcott in the same paper. "I liked the lyrics and still do, despite the criticism of a close friend of mine that they are clever but unsingable. I think there is a soupçon of tosh to that argument, although I did not say so in so many words to him. I simply told him he was crazy."

During the run of *The Garrick Gaieties,* those of us who had a hand in the writing were given a small percentage of the gross. I think Larry and I each took home $50 a week, and I also made $83 a week, the union minimum, for the brief period of about a month that I conducted. And finally I had a music publisher. Oddly enough, despite the show's success only one, Edward Marks, showed any interest, and he published seven of our songs. This made a third source of income which, since "Manhattan" managed to catch on so quickly, further contributed to my newly acquired feeling of financial stability.

During June and early July I was living the kind of life I'd always dreamed about. Not only did I have a successful show on Broadway but I was right there every night reveling in it. What's more, I was earning good money and had plenty of time to enjoy myself when I wasn't at the theatre. My parents were spending the summer in Long Beach, so I was free to run around with the kids in the show. Occasionally, on very hot nights, I'd take a late train to Long Beach, where it was always cooler, spend the night at my folks' place, swim or play tennis the next day, and return to New York in time to go to work. Work? It wasn't work. It was my daily encounter with an adoring public, who laughed, clapped, cheered and sent vibrations to the back of my neck. What could be sweeter? Or more unbelievable? Could I really be the same guy who only a couple of months before was ready to go into the babies'-underwear business? Who can tell what would have happened if some kids hadn't wanted to do a revue and if Ben Kaye hadn't thought that his doctor's son was the right man to compose the music?

A few years later Larry and I happened to attend an opening-night performance at the Guild Theatre. Larry looked at the two huge tapestries hanging from the side walls and nudged me. "See those tapestries?" he said. "We're responsible for them."

"No, Larry," I corrected him. "They're responsible for us."

## 7

In the days when military battles were conducted on foot, it was common practice for the attacking side to keep probing the enemy lines in search of a soft spot. Once the weakness was found, the attacking troops would pour in and fan out. The reception of *The Garrick Gaieties* was the soft spot Larry and I had been looking for, and we were determined to consolidate our gains and make the most of them.

At that time there was a successful comedy on Broadway called *The Butter and Egg Man,* by George S. Kaufman. It was about a prosperous businessman from a small town who comes to New York to invest in plays, and for a while the term "butter-and-egg man" became familiar in theatrical parlance as a substitute for "backer" or "angel."

One morning I got a call from Helen Ford, our once intended star of *Dear Enemy,* who had never lost faith in the show. All she had to say was "I've got the butter-and-egg man," and I knew exactly what she meant. Actually, Robert Jackson was a good deal more than the hick comic figure of the Kaufman play. He owned a chain of stores in Canada, and later became a well-known figure in Washington political circles (not to be confused, however, with the Robert H. Jackson who served as Supreme Court Justice). But the most important thing was that he was stage-struck, and with Helen Ford as our star saleslady, we encountered little difficulty in prying loose the necessary money. After all, Rodgers and Hart were no longer nobodies; we were, if you please, the Theatre Guild's distinguished composer and lyricist who had recently displaced Alfred Lunt and Lynn Fontanne at the Garrick Theatre.

Jackson turned out to be a jolly extrovert, and he had no wish—thank God!—to interfere with us. As soon as we were assured of financial backing, Herb Fields, Larry and I met with Helen and her husband, George Ford, who was her manager. George had run a stock company in Troy, New York (where he and Helen met and married), and was a descendant of the man who had built the famous Ford's Theatre where Lincoln was shot. At Helen's suggestion George became our producer. Even before we began putting together the cast, we decided on the unusual step of previewing the show far from the regular pre-Broadway tryout route. We felt it was necessary because so many people had advised us that a musical dealing with the American Revolution might be commercially risky. But there was another reason why we wanted to test the show as thoroughly as possible before bringing it to Broadway: since Larry and I had achieved our first success with a collection of unrelated songs in a revue, *Dear Enemy* would be our first chance to demonstrate what we could do with a score that had at least some relevance to the mood, characters and situations found in a story. It's tough enough to follow a hit, but we did think it was important to come up with something totally different from what we'd done before. Of course, to do something only because it's different makes about as much sense as following up a hit with something like it only because it's almost the same. Calculation shows through in both cases, and more often than not the results prove self-defeating. Fortunately, with *Dear Enemy* we were able to go back to a show that we'd loved and lived with even before we learned how to spell "Gaieties."

George Ford found a stock company in Akron, Ohio, that was willing to let us use its theatre, the Colonial, and also to provide all the necessary actors to round out the cast supporting Helen Ford. I gave up my conducting chores at the Garrick early in July, and we all journeyed out to Akron. With George's brother, Harry, directing, we rehearsed for only one week, but our opening went well enough considering the fact that there really wasn't enough time to achieve a professional level. From what we saw and from the comments we heard, we were emboldened to go ahead with our plans to mount an elaborate Broadway production. As soon as we returned to New York, we got in touch with John Murray Anderson. We found him just as enthusiastic as before, particularly since we no longer had any problems of financial support, and he agreed to take charge of the overall staging. This meant supervising every aspect of the production, including costumes, scenery and lighting, so that there would be a cohesiveness and style to the show that set it apart from most others of the time.

Rehearsals for this production are less clear in my mind than the first reading of the score at the Knickerbocker Theatre. The orchestration had been done by Emil Gerstenberger, a tough, feisty little man who yelled a lot but never seemed to mean it. During the lunch break, Emil and I left together to get something to eat at a nearby restaurant. Walking down the street, I asked him what he thought of my conducting. "Your ass is in Egypt!" he bellowed. "Stop waving your arms around like a goddamn ballet dancer. You gotta remember to always cut the corners with your beat. Every movement's gotta be so clear that the men know whether you're conducting in four-quarter time or three-quarter time. The girls may think you're cute, but you hafta learn to make every gesture mean something to the musicians." Thereafter, I never forgot to cut the corners.

After deciding to lengthen the title from *Dear Enemy* to *Dearest Enemy,* we played a week in Ford's Theatre in Baltimore, a natural choice considering the familial background of our producer. Although there was plenty of work to be done, the most dramatic incident of the week for me occurred not in the theatre but in a delicatessen across the street. I was having lunch there one day when a gallon can of peaches rolled off the top of a huge icebox just behind me, hit me on the head and knocked me unconscious. When I came to, I managed to make my unsteady way over to the theatre for the afternoon performance, the only occasion I've ever failed to derive any satisfaction from conducting my own music.

The vibrations on the back of my neck were pretty good for this show too. Although it was a bit long, the audience was suitably impressed with the general look of the production, and it was obvious that Anderson's close attention to décor and costumes had made a difference. The audience was also taken with the play's opening scene, in which Helen Ford made a fetching entrance clad in nothing but a barrel (she had been swimming nude in the river, and Charles Purcell, as the young British officer, had stolen her clothes). It was a novel way of introducing the inevitable romantic involvement, and helped establish *Dearest Enemy* as something a little more daring than the customary Broadway product. So did an ensemble number sung by the American girls when they're told that the British are coming. It was called "War Is War," and ended with the then shocking lines: "Hooray, we're going to be compromised!/ War is war!"

One of the many useful experiences I had while working on *Dearest Enemy* was that I became aware of the multiple possibilities there are to vary that most essential of all musical expressions, the love duet. The romantic leads in any musical need a theme or motif, something that's "their" song, which is a universally accepted part of the genre. But such a song must express more than romantic attachment. First of all, it should be written in a fresh, unhackneyed way, both musically and lyrically, and it should be able to fit different situations. The repetition of a song, however, should never be used merely to plug the number in the hope of sending customers dashing to their nearest sheet-music or record store. If a song catches on, fine—every writer loves to have a hit—but it must be part of what is happening onstage. Repetition should be used not merely to drum a song into an audience's collective ear, but to make the relationship between the leading characters more meaningful through music.

In *Dearest Enemy,* the big love duet was "Here in My Arms." It was introduced toward the end of the first act and was first sung by the roguish British officer to the cute little American maid as a light-hearted plea for the girl to fall into his arms. She does, of course, suiting the action to a slight change in the lyric ("Here in *your* arms it's adorable"). In the second act, however, after the officer has been trundled off to prison for the duration of the war, the same song takes on a more plaintive tone as it expresses the emptiness of the girl's life without the man she loves. At the final curtain, the girl stands beneath a fluttering American flag, her soldier returns, and the song assumes a third aspect, revealing that now, with the war over, they will always be in each other's arms.

After a week of rewriting and cutting in Baltimore, *Dearest Enemy* had its New York opening at the Knickerbocker Theatre on September 18. The date is interesting to me principally because of the three other musical productions that had their Broadway premieres within the same seven-day period. Two nights before there had been the much-heralded *No, No, Nanette,* the Vincent Youmans show that had just completed a record-breaking year in Chicago. Three nights later came *The Vagabond King,* the Rudolf Friml operetta that was once supposed to have been written by a couple of unknown kids named Rodgers and Hart. And the next night came *Sunny,* starring Marilyn Miller, with book and lyrics by Otto Harbach and my old friend, Oscar Hammerstein, and a musical score by my idol, Jerome Kern. Thus, between September 16 and 22, 1925, first-nighters could attend openings of shows with music by Youmans, Friml, Kern—and Rodgers. Not that *Dearest Enemy* was in quite the same league as the others, nor has it been revived as frequently, but it did surprisingly well in spite of such illustrious competition.

The newspaper reviewers anointed our show with combinations of approving, if hardly ecstatic, adjectives such as "polite, sentimental and prettily embroidered," "gay, gentle and gracious," "mannerly, melodious, sane and charming" and "singularly tuneful, artistic and agreeable." Larry and I had particular cause for pride in some of the comments, especially Robert Benchley's reference to us as "that God-given team." But it was the summation of Frank Vreeland in the New York *Telegram* that really made us feel that all our years of frustration had been worth it, when he wrote: "We have a glimmering notion that someday they [Fields, Hart and Rodgers] will form the American counterpart of that once-great triumvirate of Bolton, Wodehouse and Kern." Apart from the odd implication that Kern was not an American, the comparison convinced us that what we were trying to achieve was at last being recognized and appreciated.

One evening at the Knickerbocker Theatre I remember particularly well. The Benjamin Feiners, whose son, Ben, was a close friend of mine, were sitting in the first row in the left of the orchestra with their daughter, Dorothy. She was pretty but looked very young, and though I was careful to cut the corners while conducting, I couldn't help showing off for her and her parents. A couple of months later, after I had given up my job as music director, Ben and I had a date to go to the movies to see *The Big Parade,* and I went to pick him up. Andrew Goodman, the son of the founder of

Bergdorf Goodman, was at the Feiners' apartment too, calling for Dorothy to see *Sunny.* Suddenly she appeared in evening dress. Although I had seen her at the theatre only a short time before, she no longer looked like just a young kid; in fact, she looked like the prettiest girl I'd ever seen. For the first time in my life, I knew the feeling that Oscar Hammerstein and I would express many years later in the song "Some Enchanted Evening." Ben and I may have gone to see *The Big Parade* that night, but all I saw on the screen was the bright-eyed, smiling face of Dorothy Feiner.

The opening of *Dearest Enemy* gave me two shows running concurrently on Broadway, a situation that could not have escaped the attention of Max Dreyfus. Sure enough, it wasn't long before I received the royal summons: an invitation to meet with the music publisher in his office. Summons or not, it was one meeting I was looking forward to, particularly in light of my previous unhappy encounters with both Max and his brother, Louis.

As soon as I arrived at T. B. Harms, Inc., the bustling Dreyfus headquarters, I was ceremoniously escorted in to see the great man. Dreyfus rose solemnly from his desk, greeted me warmly and immediately got down to business. Not only did he want to publish the songs from *Dearest Enemy,* he also wanted Larry and me to sign with his company as staff writers. Well, if he didn't remember having once dismissed my efforts as valueless, I certainly wasn't going to bring up the matter at this point. Of course, if my neck had been a bit stiffer than it was, I could have refused the offer, confident that I'd have no trouble finding another publisher. But this was Max Dreyfus, the publisher of Victor Herbert, Jerome Kern, George Gershwin and Vincent Youmans. To have a T. B. Harms label on the songs of Rodgers and Hart was an unequaled sign of prestige. Max Dreyfus may not have been aware that he was eating crow, but that didn't make any difference. Without a moment's hesitation I told him that Larry and I would be glad to accept his offer.

Dreyfus smiled and leaned back in his chair. Peering down his aquiline nose, he said, "There's one thing that puzzles me. Why didn't you ever bring me your songs from *The Garrick Gaieties?*" Attempting to keep calm, I told him that we had tried desperately to get someone from his firm to attend one of the special matinées but that Harms hadn't even bothered to send an office boy. Then, feeling a bit more secure, I told him that "Manhattan," the biggest hit in the *Gaieties,* was one of the songs I had played when Larry Schwab brought me to see him a few years before, and I couldn't help reminding him that he had said there was nothing of value in what he'd heard.

Dreyfus looked slightly stunned, and then quickly changed the subject by explaining the conditions under which writers worked at Harms. He would, he said, be glad to give Larry and me a drawing account similar to that given other staff writers, an offer that made no impression on me, since I didn't have the faintest idea what a drawing account was. Dreyfus explained how it worked: a number of "my boys," as he called them, were permitted to draw anywhere from $50 to $200 a week, and these sums were deducted from royalties when they became due. I suppose something of my grandfather's pride took over at this point because I found myself grandly telling him that Larry and I didn't want to work that way. We wanted nothing in advance, and would be perfectly content to wait until we received all the royalties to which we were entitled.

Dreyfus stared at me with a look of disbelief. "All right," he said, "if that's the way you want it, but I'll tell you one thing. In all my years in the publishing business, this is the first time anyone has ever turned down an advance." Then he put his arm around my shoulder, and I suddenly realized what it meant to be one of Max Dreyfus' boys. "There's one thing I want you to promise me," he said. "If you ever need money, I don't want you to go to anyone else but me. From now on, don't ever forget that I'm your friend."

I never did. Max and I, in fact, remained close friends until the day he died, nearly forty years later. It was a good relationship. Max was a shrewd bargainer and a hard man to get along with, but I never had any trouble with him, nor did he with me. I always felt that I could have gone to him for any reasonable amount of money, but I also knew that when it came to deals involving copyrights he could be really tough. He used to tell me that since he had no kids of his own, his copyrights were his children, and he was going to protect them as carefully as he could.

Max had come to the United States from Germany when he was a boy, and his first job—which I always found hard to imagine—was playing cornet on a Mississippi showboat. A frustrated composer, he gradually worked his way into the music-publishing business, first as an arranger, then as a salesman, and finally as the most powerful publisher in the field. In the late twenties, after reorganizing his firm as Chappell Music, named after the prestigious English firm he had bought, he sold part of the Harms catalogue to Warner Bros. for over $8 million.

Apart from his skill as a businessman, Max had one talent that any musician would envy. He could pick up the orchestra score of a symphony or an opera, settle himself in a comfortable chair and read it the way anyone else would read a novel. He loved to live well, and for a time he and his wife had an elaborate estate in Bronxville, from which they would commute to a large cattle farm in Brewster.

As long as I knew him, Max was always what is generally described as "painfully thin." In his case, however, the adverb was not hyperbolic. Throughout his life there was hardly a time when he was not afflicted with some illness, often a serious one. In the early thirties, shortly after Dorothy and I were married, he was so sick that when we drove up to Bronxville to see him, we fully expected that it would be for the last time. But Max fooled everybody; when he died in 1964 he was in his ninetieth year.

Soon after the opening of *Dearest Enemy* I formed another valued and enduring friendship. I have already mentioned the three other major musicals that opened in the same week as *Dearest Enemy*. In addition, a drama that had its premiere on the very same night as *No, No, Nanette*—September 16, 1925—was to serve as my introduction to one of the theatre's supreme talents.

The play was *The Vortex*, and the author, in his first Broadway appearance, was Noël Coward. A daring study of upper-class decadence, *The Vortex* was a resounding hit, and I was fortunate to get tickets to a Saturday matinée. Though I was impressed with the writing and acting, the high point for me, possibly because it was so unexpected, occurred in a party scene early in the second act. Urged on by his friends, the character Noël was portraying sat down at the piano to play a dance number which turned out to be my own song, "April Fool," from *The Garrick Gaieties*. It was not then, nor has it ever been, well known, and since I was aware that Coward himself was a gifted songwriter, I took it as a tremendous compliment that he would choose "April Fool" over something better-known, or something that he himself had written.

A couple of days later I went to Rudley's, a restaurant in the theatre district, for lunch. Rudley's was below street level, and as I walked down the steps I happened to notice a couple seated at a side table. The man's trim elegance and the slightly Oriental cast to his features could belong to no one else but Noël Coward. We had never met, but I knew that I had to speak to him. Although well aware of his reputation for cutting remarks and the fact that he could devastate my naïve enthusiasm with no more than a raised eyebrow, I boldly walked over and introduced myself. "I'm Dick Rodgers, and—" I began. No sooner did I get the words out than Coward jumped up from his chair, threw his arms around me and proceeded to shower me with praise. Every time I tried to get in a word about how much I admired his play and his music, he would top me with a new expression of admiration for *my* music. When I finally left his table, I was so overcome that I simply walked back up the steps and out of the restaurant. It wasn't until I was halfway down the block that it dawned on me that I hadn't had any lunch.

This sort of enthusiasm for other people's work was typical of Noël Coward, just as his criticism was as outspoken as it was deft. Perhaps his outstanding quality was style. He wrote with style, sang with style, painted with style, and even smoked a cigarette with a style that belonged exclusively to him. Despite his ability to do so many things so superbly, he always had to endure the put-down that anyone so versatile could not possibly be a first-rate talent. What nonsense! Versatility on so high a level needs no excuse. Even one of his lesser-known operettas, *Conversation Piece,* contains more charm, skill and originality than fifty musical plays put together by men specializing in particular fields.

These were cup-runneth-over days for Larry and me. We had written songs for a successful revue, we had proved we could also write a complete score for a book musical, Max Dreyfus was our publisher, and couples were asking dance bands to play "Manhattan" and "Here in My Arms." Recording companies were beginning to record our songs, including a medley from *Dearest Enemy* performed by the Victor Light Opera Company, the nearest thing then to an original-cast album. To top off the year, we were admitted to membership in the American Society of Composers, Authors and Publishers, that impressively titled organization which makes sure that composers and lyricists are compensated whenever their works are performed publicly for profit. Today it isn't hard to join ASCAP, but in those days it was an exclusive outfit, and being accepted as members was further proof that Rodgers and Hart had not only arrived but were considered by their peers to be more than just transients.

Surprisingly, there were few changes in my personal life. I still lived at home with my parents and was still expected to let Mom know if I'd be late for dinner. I honestly felt that the achievements of my brother, who had already begun his medical practice, were far more worthy of praise than mine. My friends were the same neighborhood kids I'd gone around with all of my life. I may have been making more money than ever before, but that wasn't saying much.

Had I come from a very poor family, the change in my life style would probably have been more noticeable. Perhaps I would have lost my head and bought more clothes than I needed, or spent my late hours in those forbidding haunts known as speakeasies. But my family was middle-class, sympathetic and understanding, yet never indulgent, and it simply didn't occur to me to behave differently. My folks had seen me through some miserable times when I certainly couldn't have been a joy to have around the house, and now that things seemed to be working out, it was great fun to share my happiness with them. In fact, my father was the organizer and keeper of my scrapbook, carefully pasting in anything he found in the press about me.

Our newly attained successes also made little difference in Larry's life. Basically he was the same sweet, self-destructive kid I had always known.

A second reason that contributed to my keeping on an even emotional keel was the nature of my work. Though I write the songs and may even conduct them, the audience sees and hears someone else. To paraphrase Oscar Hammerstein, a song becomes a song only when someone sings it. It's the singer up there in the spotlight who gets the applause and who is identified with what is being sung. This is as it should be, but what it can do to a singer's ego is another matter, and it frequently takes an iron will to keep the performer from considering himself the creator.

For example, I'm sure I still recall vividly the thrill of meeting Noël Coward only because my life has not been spent bowing and blowing kisses to my dear public. I enjoy conducting, but that's a purely personal enjoyment. My ego is satisfied merely by hearing my music and knowing that others also derive pleasure from hearing it. I can think of nothing more emotionally satisfying than driving all alone in a car late at night, switching on the radio and listening to one of my songs come at me out of the dark.

Another factor that helped me stay relatively level-headed during those first success-filled months was the precarious nature of the theatre itself. No one has ever had a life in the theatre consisting solely of successes. Anyone entering the field must be conditioned to accept a certain amount of failure; he can only pray that the averages turn out in his favor. At the age of twenty-three I had already painfully learned about failure in my career before *The Garrick Gaieties,* and I knew that my life would not continue forever as blissfully as it was now. No matter how long it runs, every show must have a final curtain, and nothing is to be gained from continuing to savor a success or brood over a flop. When one show is finished, the only thing to do is go on to the next one—and hope.

By the end of 1925 I was already working on the next one—except that it wasn't on Broadway or even in a regular theatre.

As mentioned earlier, the only way we had been able to get *The Melody Man* on Broadway the previous year was when Larry Hart's father hoodwinked Billy Rose into investing $1,000 in that hopeless enterprise. But Billy and Larry had remained friends—partly, I suspect, because Billy, who was still primarily known as a songwriter, needed a handy ghost whenever he got stuck for a lyric. In addition to writing songs, Billy had been operating a speakeasy. But he longed for respectability and felt he could attain status by remodeling a mansion on Fifth Avenue and turning it into a theatre-restaurant. In those days Fifth Avenue was still the site of a number of elegant town houses, and though their owners took a dim view of this commercial invasion, it didn't faze Billy. No liquor was to be served at his Fifth Avenue Club, but customers were assured of getting two things besides food: a steep $5 cover charge and a complete Broadway-type musical revue.

When Billy approached Larry and me to write the songs for the opening show, the idea sounded interesting and we turned out nine or ten numbers. Both the club and the show opened in January 1926, but neither remained open very long. The expected carriage trade found little of attraction in a legitimate, booze-free cabaret, nor was life made any easier by constant complaints from the club's affluent neighbors. Billy sold the place after only a couple of months.

This experience gave me the opportunity to get to know the very shrewd, highly complex and oddly likable character known as Billy Rose. Billy, who was only slightly taller than Larry, was forever churning up new ideas, each more adventurous than the last. Even when one of his schemes fell through, it was never for want of boldness or imagination, nor was it ever from being excessively open-handed. Billy could be pretty tricky, as we discovered when the promised royalties for our revue score failed to arrive. As I recall it, we never collected a dime for our efforts, but Billy was the kind of promoter who somehow made you feel he had paid you double.

Working on the show for the Fifth Avenue Club gave us more time to think about what our next Broadway effort should be. Since we had already written the score for a costume musical, it seemed logical to show what we could do with an up-to-date theme and locale. Six-day bicycle races had recently become a big attraction at Madison Square Garden, and it occurred to Herb Fields that it would make an appropriately topical subject for a musical comedy. He pasted together a plot that was hardly destined to become a classic, but it was lively enough and inconsequential enough to serve the expected function of a musical-comedy book. We called it *The Girl Friend,* after one of the songs in the show.

Most of the songs Larry and I were writing during this period were in the traditional form of song construction at the time. That is, there would be a verse, or lead-in, followed by the refrain, or main body of the song. The verse could be any length, but the refrain was almost invariably limited to thirty-two bars. Construction within the thirty-two bars was also pretty standardized. First there would be a main melodic theme of eight bars, which was then repeated for another eight bars. The third eight—called the "release"—would be a different theme, with the final eight bars returning, often with some variation, to the main theme. This was called the "AABA" form. Another thirty-two-bar form—the "ABAB"—gave equal weight to two melodic themes, though here, too, there might be some variation in the final section. "Thou Swell," which came a bit later, was written in the "ABAB" form. Though occasionally I did play around with the formula —"Manhattan," for example, has no release, or "B" theme, at all—Larry and I never felt restricted but rather enjoyed the challenge of coming up with something fresh within the prescribed regulations.

"Blue Room," which we wrote for *The Girl Friend,* is an interesting example of what I mean. In form it is strictly "AABA," but in writing the main melody, I began the second, third and fourth bars on a C natural— the fifth note of the scale in the key of F—and followed it with a note rising a half tone in each successive bar. This gave Larry the idea of using a triple rhyme on the repeated C note, and then, for emphasis, repeating the word "room" on the rising half tones:

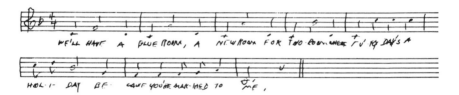

Note how effectively this combination of rhyming and repetition conveys the emotion: "blue room," "new room," "for two room," and then, in the second eight bars, "ballroom," "small room" and "hall room." For the final eight bars, Larry decided against the anticipated repetition and boldly introduced the unexpected references to "trousseau" and "Robinson Crusoe," saving the "blue room" reference until almost the very end of the song. A listener, of course, may not be aware of the technique behind a song, but he is certainly aware of the effect when it turns out right. In "Blue Room" it did.

*The Girl Friend* brought Rodgers and Hart right back to the man who had given them their start in the professional theatre. Lew Fields had lost money on *The Melody Man* and had been unimpressed with *Dearest Enemy,* but he liked our latest effort and agreed to produce it. For our leads, we had the husband-and-wife team of Sammy White and Eva Puck, two warm, gifted people who had the knack of being funny even when their material wasn't side-splitting. We'd first met Sammy and Eva when they appeared in *The Melody Man,* and they'd impressed us so much that we promised that someday we'd write a show just for them. Unlike most such promises, this one was kept.

*       *       *

When *The Girl Friend* opened in March 1926, it looked as if we were in for our third Broadway success in a row. The first-night audience laughed and applauded with enthusiasm, and most of the reviews were highly favorable. But few things are predictable in show business. Perhaps theatregoers weren't attracted to a story about a six-day bicycle racer; whatever the reason, the show barely limped along for the first week or so, and it looked as if it would have to close. Drastic steps were needed and were taken. Herb, Larry and I agreed to a plan that I think was then unprecedented in the theatre: we offered to suspend our royalties if Lew Fields would keep the show running. Within weeks, word-of-mouth comments and the popularity of the songs "The Girl Friend" and "Blue Room" helped to build our audiences, and soon we were doing great business. *The Girl Friend* played until December, ending up with an even longer run than *Dearest Enemy.* All of which proves that temporary financial sacrifice can sometimes assure eventual financial success. But there are never any guarantees.

During this period I saw a good deal of Lew Fields. Despite that early unhappy experience when he brought in another composer to share the writing of my first Broadway score, our relationship had turned into one of genuine mutual affection. Lew—Mr. Fields to me—was about twenty-five years older than I, and possibly because he had given me my first break, always seemed to have a paternal feeling toward me. He had one habit I used to love. Instead of shaking hands, he would pat me on the cheek, a gesture I found especially endearing since it was so like the kind of thing my grandfather used to do. In all, we were associated in seven Broadway productions, and there was never a single harsh word between us.

At about the time of the opening of *The Girl Friend,* I received a call from Terry Helburn. Since *The Garrick Gaieties* had turned out so profitably, she and Lawrence Langner were all for putting together a second edition, using most of the same people but with all new material. Though we agreed to do it—who could refuse the Theatre Guild?—Larry and I had qualms about the project. The first *Gaieties* had sneaked into town, first as a benefit show, then for a week of matinées, and finally, due to genuine popular demand, for a regular run. What we'd lacked in polish we'd made up for in fledgling enthusiasm, and audiences and critics appreciated the show for what it was. To attempt a similar revue just one year later, it seemed to us, would be extremely risky, for the vital elements of surprise and spontaneity would be hard to recapture. On the other hand, we had no other new project lined up, and we knew it would be fun to be working again with all those talented people. Besides, it was very much in the tradition of the time for popular revues—from the opulent *Ziegfeld Follies* to the intimate *Grand Street Follies*—to spawn successive annual editions.

In the second *Garrick Gaieties* we again kidded the theatre in general and the Theatre Guild in particular, along with other ready-made targets that were fair game for a bunch of smart-aleck city kids. Fully aware that we were sticking our necks out by inviting comparison with the previous *Gaieties,* we tried to disarm the audience by frankly admitting in the opening number:

> We can't be as good as last year,
> For the last year was great.
> How can we compare with the past year?
> It is sad but such is fate.
> We've lost all that artless spirit
> With our Broadway veneer.
> Then it was play
> But we're old hams today,
> So we can't be as good as last year.

Well, we weren't, and critics told us so, but strangely enough, it didn't hurt at the box office. Those who had either seen our show the previous year or who had heard about it couldn't have cared less; *The Garrick Gaieties* was back in town, and that was good enough for them. The second edition ended up running only about a month less than the first.

Two musical numbers from that production are worth mentioning. In the first *Gaieties,* Sterling Holloway and June Cochrane sang "Manhattan"; in the second, Sterling and Bobbie Perkins (June Cochrane was now in *The Girl Friend*) sang a song called "Mountain Greenery." Here, instead of the boy and girl finding the city "a wondrous toy," they decide to leave the city to discover a more romantic setting in the country. The whole attitude was one of urban sophistication amid a rustic atmosphere, which gave Larry a chance to play around with such tricky interior rhyming as "Beans could get no *keener re-/* Ception in a *beanery,/* Bless our mountain *greenery* home." For one of the encores, he even managed to come up with: "You can bet your *life its tone/* Beats a Jascha *Heifetz tone.* "

The other musical number was our first-act finale, "The Rose of Arizona," which, like the previous *Gaieties'* "The Joy Spreader," was a self-contained mini-musical with a book by Herb Fields. Here, for what may have been the first time, a musical revue included a burlesque on the musical theatre itself. We kidded the Kern-Bolton-Wodehouse Princess Theatre shows with a "Till the Clouds Roll By" kind of song called "It May Rain When the Sun Stops Shining" (even ending with "We'll see a sunny day/ For love will find a way/ Till the clouds go rolling by"). We also kidded the heroics of the Friml operettas ("All you Shriners and Elks and Pythian Knights/ And Babbitts of low degree,/ Just listen to me"). Then we had a chorus of flowers sing and dance to the patriotic ode to "The American Beauty Rose," which was full of purposely horrible nonrhymes such as "drizzle" and "Brazil," and "replenish" and "Spanish." "The Rose of Arizona" turned out to be one entry in *Gaieties* No. 2 that most people found superior to its predecessor in *Gaieties* No. 1.

The vigor and originality of the American musical stage during the mid-twenties were much admired, and even envied, by British producers, who began importing Broadway musicals in ever-increasing number. *No, No, Nanette,* in fact, had had a London production even before its New York production, and the Gershwins' *Lady, Be Good!,* starring Fred and Adele Astaire, and *Tip-Toes,* as well as *Sunny,* by Kern, Harbach and Hammerstein, were all reigning favorites. What's more, both Kern and Gershwin had already turned out original scores specifically created for British musicals.

During the winter of 1926, Cicely Courtneidge and Jack Hulbert, a popular English musical-comedy couple, were co-starring in New York in their London success, *By the Way*. It was Hulbert's first time out as producer as well as performer, and while in New York, he and his partner, Paul Murray, spent as much time as possible scouting Broadway musicals for possible importation. Apparently they liked Rodgers and Hart's efforts well enough to get in touch with us, even though stories about the American Revolution and six-day bicycle racing seemed hardly the stuff of which successful West End musicals were made.

Hulbert was an ebullient Englishman with a half-moon smile and an aggressively jutting chin, and Murray was a likable Irishman with a good deal of persuasive charm. Since neither one of our book musicals was deemed appropriate, they came up with the idea that Larry and I write the score for a musical, *Lido Lady,* for which they already had the libretto and in which Hulbert and his wife were planning to appear. This was especially intriguing because Larry and I had recently seen *By the Way* and were very much taken with Cicely Courtneidge's wacky but ladylike clowning. The only problem we could see was that in the musicals we had written with Herb Fields, the three of us had always worked closely together, and we weren't sure we'd feel comfortable outfitting a score to the specifications of an already written libretto. But who were we kidding? The whole enterprise sounded like an exciting adventure, and we were ready to pack our bags that night.

Presently our plans began to enlarge. The show was not expected to begin rehearsals until early fall, and since its locale was the Lido, it was of utmost importance—we kept telling ourselves—that we first repair to Venice to soak up the atmosphere. Another event contributed to our expanding itinerary: on June 8, 1926, at the Ambassador Hotel, my brother married a girl named Ethel Salant. I was best man, and since Morty and I had shared so much during the past couple of years and had become so close, I found the occasion surprisingly emotional.

Suddenly I got an idea. Not only would Larry and I go to Italy, we'd also meet up with Morty and Ethel on their honeymoon. We'd do a little sightseeing, swim in the Adriatic, and end our trip in London writing a show.

What a dull, miserable grind my life was becoming! What could possibly have made me decide against going into the babies'-underwear business?

## 8

**Vanderbilt Theatre**
48TH STREET, EAST OF BROADWAY
DIRECTOR — — LYLE D. ANDREWS

FIRE NOTICE: Look around NOW and choose the nearest
Exit to your seat. In case of fire, walk (not run) to THAT Exit.
Do not try to beat your neighbor to the street.
JOHN J. DORMAN, Fire Commissioner.

WEEK BEGINNING MONDAY EVENING, DECEMBER 2d, 1926
Matinees Wednesday and Saturday

LEW FIELDS and LYLE D. ANDREWS
present

HELEN FORD
in
A New Musical Comedy
"PEGGY-ANN"
with
LULU McCONNELL

Book by Herbert Fields
Music by Richard Rodgers
Lyrics by Lorenz Hart
Book Staged by Robert Milton
Musical Numbers and Dances arranged by Seymour Felix
Settings designed by Clark Robinson
Costumes designed under Mark Mooring
Under the Personal Supervision of Lew Fields
Entire Production

Characters as They First Speak
Mrs. Frost ............................ Lulu McConnell
Mr. Frost ............................ Grant Simpson

PROGRAM CONTINUED ON SECOND PAGE FOLLOWING

---

**New Amsterdam Theatre**
42nd Street, West of Broadway
The New Amsterdam Theatre Planned and Designed by A. L. Erlanger
and P. Richard Anderson, and Executed by Herts and Tallant, Architects
NEWAM THEATRES CORPORATION
ERLANGER, DILLINGHAM & ZIEGFELD
Directors

FIRE NOTICE: Look around NOW and choose the nearest
Exit to your seat. In case of fire, walk (not run) to THAT Exit.
Do not try to beat your neighbor to the street.
JOHN J. DORMAN, Fire Commissioner.

BEGINNING TUESDAY EVENING, DECEMBER 28, 1926
Matinees Wednesday and Saturday

FLORENZ ZIEGFELD
Presents
NEW MUSICAL COMEDY
"BETSY"
with
BELLE BAKER

Words by Irving Caesar and David Freedman
Staged and revised by Anthony Maguire
Lyrics by Lorenz Hart and Music by Richard Rodgers
STAGED by SAMMY LEE
Costumes by Charles Le Maire
under the personal direction
of Victor Baravelle
Orchestra

Characters
.......................... AL SHEAN
.......................... PAULINE HOFFMAN

END PAGE FOLLOWING

---

**GAIETY THEATRE**
STRAND · W.C.
SOLE PROPRIETORS THE GAIETY THEATRE CO., LTD.
LICENSED BY THE LORD CHAMBERLAIN TO WILLIAM C. GAUNT

WEDNESDAY, DECEMBER 1ST, AT 8.0, AND EVERY EVENING AT 8.15
MATINEES: WEDNESDAY AND SATURDAY AT 2.15

JACK HULBERT and PAUL MURRAY
present
The New Musical Comedy
"LIDO LADY"
Written by RONALD JEANS
Based on the Book by GUY BOLTON, BERT KALMAR and HARRY RUBY
Music by RICHARD RODGERS    Lyrics by LORENZ HART
Devised and arranged by PAUL MURRAY and JACK HULBERT

PRODUCED BY JACK HULBERT

Characters in order of their appearance

| | |
|---|---|
| Marjorie Wilson | PHYL ARNOLD |
| Mollie Doone | MURIEL MONTROSE |
| "Peaches" Stone | JOHNNIE CLARE |
| Benson (Mr. Blake's Butler) | LAURENCE GREEN |
| Spencer Weldon (Mr. Blake's General Manager) | HAROLD FRENCH |
| Rufus Blake (a wealthy Manufacturer of Sporting Goods) | BOBBY COMBER |
| Luis Valese | HENRY DE BRAY |
| Bill Harker (an American Friend of Harry Bassett) | BILLY ARLINGTON |
| Rita | APRIL HARMON |
| Harry Bassett | JACK HULBERT |
| Fay Blake (Mr. Blake's Daughter) | PHYLLIS DARE |
| Peggy Bassett (a Motion Picture Actress and Cousin of Harry Bassett) | CICELY COURTNEIDGE |
| Master-at-Arms | ROWLAND HILL |

The Gaiety Dancers—DORA FITZGEORGE, HARRY WHITE, FRANK TURNMAN, JOE GERALD, and BILLY SHAW
Visitors to the Lido—MARJORIE GAUGHAM, MYRA HOWARD, SYBIL FREDERICKSON, NANCY BIGG,
ANN CUTHBUT, CYNTHIA CARLTON, DAR-ETTE ANDREWS, LILIAN DU ROY, LILIAN LOGAN, VERA
RUDGE, MARY DU PONT, MARJORY DAVIDSON, ERIS BURKE, PHEOLA BAXTER, RICHARD GARRARD,
ELLA LORNE, RUBY STEWART, ARNIE THORLBY, MARJORIE BELL, MOLLY NEASHE, THELMA MORLAND,
VISTA SWART
Visitors to the Lido—DENNIS RAY, DONALD AXELL, PAUL FRENCH, CHARLES ELLO, PERCY GALE, GEORGE
GUNNERY, ARTHUR IVES.

As befitted the historic occasion of our first transatlantic crossing, Larry and I chose to make the journey on a ship with the most impressive and musical name we could find. The *Conte Biancamano* may not have been the grandest ship in the Italian fleet but it was roomy and comfortable, and Larry took endless delight in rolling the name around his tongue as if he were speaking Italian. Amid all the hoopla attending ocean trips in those days, we left New York in midsummer. Like most such journeys, ours was both restful and festive. Larry spent most of his time hanging out at the bar when he wasn't hanging over the rail, and I spent most of my time hanging around whatever attractive and unattached girls I could find.

The weather turned balmy as we entered the Mediterranean, and on the night we docked in the Bay of Naples everyone was out on deck to listen to the Italian musicians pouring out such syrupy Neapolitan melodies as "O sole mio" and "Santa Lucia." The music, the star-filled sky and the view of Vesuvius hanging threateningly over the city made the whole scene unforgettable.

But there were even more thrilling sights to come. To get to Bertolini's Palace Hotel, our car had to go halfway up a mountain on the outskirts of the city. Then we had to get out and walk through a tunnel that took us to the center of the mountain, where we boarded a lift that went straight up through rock to the top floor of the hotel. That's where the lobby and the restaurant were located, with the bedrooms below. The view from the top was so breath-taking that even Larry was impressed—at least temporarily.

After spending a couple of days in Naples, we took the wriggling Amalfi Drive down to beautiful Sorrento. But its charms were somewhat ruined for me the morning I awoke and discovered that I had been attacked by an aggressive type of flea that had a nasty habit of burrowing under the skin. From Sorrento we went to Milan, where we had a reunion with my honeymooning brother and his bride. Morty, previously a pretty somber fellow, was practically bubbling; married life obviously suited him.

The automobile drive across the Dolomites to Venice may be one of the most beautiful in the world, but I don't advise it for anyone intimidated by mountain passes. It's a frightening sight to see a bus coming at you on one side of the road and a drop of a thousand feet on the other just as you are rounding a curve with no protective wall. I loved and hated it at the same time, but Larry just hated it. As far as he was concerned, "these mountains are just a lot of rocks."

Venice with its canals, gondolas, St. Mark's Square and Doge's Palace is stamped forever in the mind of anyone who has ever seen a travel folder, but somehow the reality was even more unreal than the image. When one visits Venice, one must of course also visit that luxurious sandbank known as the Lido which separates the city from the Adriatic Sea. One morning Larry and I boarded the public boat that makes the short run from the city to the beach. Seated across the way from us was a woman in her mid-thirties, obviously not Italian. She was blond, slim, patrician-looking without being haughty, coolly oblivious to the heat or the crowd, and I thought she was the most beautiful woman I had ever seen in my life.

As soon as we arrived at the Lido, Larry went in search of the nearest bar and I went for a stroll on the beach. Suddenly I heard a friendly English voice calling my name. To my joy it was Noël Coward, whom I had not seen since our first accidental meeting in the downstairs restaurant in New York. We quickly filled each other in on the reasons why we were there. Noël was in Venice, he told me, visiting an American friend he was sure would love to meet me. We strolled over to his friend's cabana, and I was introduced to a slight, delicate-featured man with soft saucer eyes and a wide, friendly grin. His name was Cole Porter, but at that time neither the name nor the face was in the least familiar to me. However, he was thoroughly familiar with my songs and was almost as effusive in his praise as Noël had been when we had first met. When I told the two of them that Larry Hart was staying with me at a hotel in Venice, Porter insisted that we both join him for dinner that evening at the place he had rented in the city.

Promptly at seven-thirty, Porter's private gondola pulled up outside our hotel. Larry and I got in, were wafted down the Grand Canal and deposited in front of an imposing three-story palace. This was the "place" Porter had rented, which we later found out was the celebrated Palazzo Rezzonico, where Robert Browning had died. We were assisted out of the gondola by a liveried footman wearing white gloves, and ushered up a massive stairway, at the top of which stood Noël, Cole and his wife, Linda. To my happy surprise, she turned out to be the stunning woman I had seen on the boat that morning.

During the delicious and elegantly served dinner Cole kept peppering me with questions about the Broadway musical theatre, revealing a remarkably keen knowledge of both classical and popular music. Since he impressed me as someone who led a thoroughly indolent, though obviously affluent, life, the sharpness of his observations was unexpected. Unquestionably, he was more than a social butterfly.

It wasn't until after dinner, however, that I was to appreciate his remarkable gifts. We went into the music room, where at my host's request I played some of my songs. Then Noël played. And then Cole sat down at the piano. As soon as he touched the keyboard to play "a few of my little things," I became aware that here was not merely a talented dilettante, but a genuinely gifted theatre composer and lyricist. Songs like "Let's Do It," "Let's Misbehave" and "Two Little Babes in the Wood," which I heard that night for the first time, fairly cried out to be heard from a stage. Why, I asked Cole, was he wasting his time? Why wasn't he writing for Broadway? To my embarrassment, he told me that he had already written four musical-comedy scores, three of which had even made it to Broadway. But little had come of them, and he simply preferred living in Europe and performing his songs for the entertainment of his friends. Later he did admit that he hoped someday to be able to have the best of both worlds: working on Broadway and living in Europe. What's more, he said, he had discovered the secret of writing hits. As I breathlessly awaited the magic formula, he leaned over and confided, "I'll write Jewish tunes." I laughed at what I took to be a joke, but not only was Cole dead serious, he eventually did exactly that. Just hum the melody that goes with "Only you beneath the moon and under the sun" from "Night and Day," or any of "Begin the Beguine," or "Love for Sale," or "My Heart Belongs to Daddy," or "I Love Paris." These minor-key melodies are unmistakably eastern Mediterranean. It is surely one of the ironies of the musical theatre that despite the abundance of Jewish composers, the one who has written the most enduring "Jewish" music should be an Episcopalian millionaire who was born on a farm in Peru, Indiana.

That night is still as clear in my mind today as it was then. Though I was unaccustomed to such glittering grandeur, Noël and the Porters turned the occasion into one of the warmest, most relaxed and happiest evenings of my life. Everything else in Venice seemed a letdown after that.

Next stop: Paris. Larry and I took a neck-craning train ride from Venice in high anticipation of the pleasures of life in that fabled city. But Paris was a disappointment. We had no friends there and had to be content with the usual Eiffel Tower–Arc de Triomphe–Louvre–Sacré Coeur sightseeing round. Perhaps it was the weather or perhaps it was just us, but everything seemed drab, and I don't think we saw one smiling face the entire two weeks we were there. Somehow I had the feeling that every Parisian, from taxi driver to head waiter, was trying to take advantage of a couple of innocents abroad. We were reconciled, however, by the prospect that after Paris came England, where we'd be getting back to work and meet all sorts of interesting people who spoke our language.

Our stay in England began promisingly enough. We took the ferry from Calais to Dover and got on the London train in time for tea. Sharing our compartment was a middle-aged, properly tweeded Englishwoman who watched quietly as she saw us struggle over the frustrations of the English monetary system. Apologizing for intruding, she asked if she might be of help. She helped in two ways: first, by spending the rest of the trip to London patiently explaining the British system of pounds, shillings and pence; and secondly, by revealing that, contrary to legend, the English people are not cold and unapproachable. This initial impression has been reinforced almost every time I've had occasion to visit the country.

Of course there are always exceptions found in any such generalization, and it was just our bad luck that the two exceptions we found on our first trip to London happened to be our producers, Messrs. Jack Hulbert and Paul Murray. They had booked us into the Savoy Hotel, but instead of the large rooms with a sweeping view of the Thames that we had been promised, we had to be content with two small dark rooms with no view at all. The Hulberts and the Murrays were well aware that this was our first visit to London and that we didn't know a soul there, but apparently they couldn't have cared less. I recall our having dinner one night at the Murrays' home, but that was the extent of our producers' concern for the composer and lyricist they had specially imported from New York. Since rehearsals were still some weeks off, we had little more to do than write our songs and take in the tourist attractions. There was one difference: unlike Paris, where we were thrown by the language barrier, among other things, we could enjoy the theatre. Not only did we see such transplanted Broadway hits as Gershwin's *Lady, Be Good!,* still starring the Astaires, and *Tip-Toes,* we also had fun at such home-grown entertainments as *Cochran's Revue of 1926* and the long-running *Co-Optimists,* with Stanley Holloway.

Making songs fit into an already written script (some fluff about a flapper tennis champ on the Lido who is pursued by an unathletic suitor) was certainly less stimulating than the give-and-take sessions we were accustomed to having with our old librettist buddy Herb Fields. To make matters even less appealing, we soon found out that the role of the young heroine would be played by an actress who, though unquestionably popular and talented, was pushing forty and looked it. Without much effort we managed to come up with the required number of songs which, "inspired" by our recent sojourn on the Adriatic, included a tune called "Lido Lady" and another called "You're on the Lido Now." Paying due respect to the city in which we were toiling, we also contributed a duet called "A Little

Flat in Soho." And since "Here in My Arms" was unknown in England and could easily be fitted into the story, we dusted off the hit song of *Dearest Enemy* and added it to the new score.

But we were becoming so bored with the project that once we finished the songs, we told Hulbert that if there were no further need of our services we'd be just as happy to pack up and go home. Not surprisingly, no one objected. The London assignment that we had looked forward to with such anticipation had turned so sour that we didn't give a damn whether or not we ever saw *Lido Lady.* What really bothered us was that we never did discover the reason why, after being so friendly and enthusiastic when we first met in New York, Hulbert and Murray had turned so cold and distant in London.

We booked passage on the *Majestic,* the next available ship for New York, and a day or two later we took the boat train for Southampton. The *Majestic* was to make one stop, at Cherbourg, to pick up passengers from France, and printed lists were handed out of the passengers who would soon be coming aboard. I quickly flipped through the list to see if I could find a familiar name. Could I indeed! There, in bold letters, I read:

MR. AND MRS. BENJAMIN FEINER
MISS DOROTHY FEINER

Miss Dorothy Feiner was, of course, that lovely-looking girl I had seen a year before when I called for her brother, Ben. By now she would be old enough to take a long look at, so when we pulled into Cherbourg harbor and the tug with the new passengers came alongside, I was at the rail waiting for her. Even a short look convinced me that I was not going to have a lonely voyage.

Dorothy seemed to be as pleased to see me as I was at the sight of her. The seas were calm and the weather warm, and the two of us spent all our waking hours together, from the morning walks around the promenade deck to the late-at-night sessions on the sun deck. By the time we reached New York we had managed to get to know each other well enough to know that we wanted to know each other better.

As the *Majestic* steamed into New York harbor, the sound of singing and band music sent everyone scurrying to the starboard side of the ship. There, alongside the *Majestic,* was a tugboat with a large banner reading "WELCOME HOME, DICK AND LARRY." Dick and Larry? That's us! Aboard the tug were all the kids from *The Garrick Gaieties* singing the songs from the show and waving to us. It may have been a press agent's gimmick, but it was one hell of a homecoming.

Now that I had got to know Dorothy, I had a special reason to be glad to be home. But having graduated from Horace Mann the previous June, she would soon be leaving for Wellesley, and I would be able to see her only on weekends. With just a week before her departure, we took advantage of the brief time by spending every evening together. She was so bright, so quick-witted and so lovely to look at that I knew then that I would never look anywhere else.

Fortunately, I had plenty to do to keep me from mooning while Dorothy was away at college. Just before Larry and I left for Europe, Herb Fields had discussed with us the possibility of joining him in a highly original concept. Many years before, Lew Fields had produced a musical called *Tillie's Nightmare,* starring a hefty comedienne named Marie Dressler who later became popular in the movies. Herb thought the show could be rewritten and modernized with a new score and a younger, more attractive leading lady. Larry and I liked the idea immediately and began working on it early in the fall. It wasn't hard to sell the show to Lew Fields, and he agreed to produce it with Lyle Andrews, the owner of the Vanderbilt Theatre. Originally we called the show *Peggy,* but by the time it reached Broadway it was renamed *Peggy-Ann.*

Back in 1920 Larry and I had written a song called "You Can't Fool Your Dreams" for *Poor Little Ritz Girl,* which may well have been the first Broadway show tune to have indicated that its lyricist had at least a passing knowledge of the teachings of Dr. Sigmund Freud. By 1926 Freud's theories, though much discussed, had not yet found expression in the theatre, and the time seemed ripe for a musical comedy to make the breakthrough by dealing with subconscious fears and fantasies. That's exactly what we did in *Peggy-Ann.*

To begin with, the entire show, except for a prologue and epilogue, was all a dream. In one scene Peggy-Ann finds herself on board a yacht, where she is to marry the leading man. Her mother, acting as minister, performs the ceremony using a telephone book as a Bible. Peggy-Ann shows up for the occasion in her underwear. After the yacht is wrecked, the wedding party is towed ashore by an enormous fish. They land in Cuba, where Peggy-Ann and her husband go to the races and win the entire island. It was all absurd but meaningful in an avant-garde sort of way. Luckily, the daily critics appreciated what we were doing, and praised us in such terms as "far from the familiar mold," "sprightly and imaginative," "futuristic," "a really bright piece of nonsense" and "far different from the usual pattern."

Working on *Peggy-Ann* was a joy because the whole production was a family affair. In addition to being reunited with Herb and Lew Fields, we were happy, after much delay, to have the leading role played by Helen Ford. Others in the cast were Lulu McConnell, a lovable comic we'd known ever since *Poor Little Ritz Girl,* and Edith Meiser and Betty Starbuck, both of whom had been in *The Garrick Gaieties.* Even the music director, Roy Webb, was the man who had taught me the rudiments of musical notation and conducting during my amateur-show days. The genuine fondness and admiration we all had for one another made it doubly gratifying when *Peggy-Ann* became one of the successes of a season crowded with no fewer than forty-seven new musical comedies and revues. It remained at the Vanderbilt for ten months, and then toured for four.

It is in the nature of things that we live in a balanced world. We expect a certain amount of happiness and a certain amount of unhappiness; we are conditioned to a life in which failure can easily follow success, just as success can easily follow failure. After the coldness of our association with *Lido Lady,* the warmth of our association with *Peggy-Ann* seemed a natural and inevitable antidote. Perhaps it is this element of apparent inevitability that makes us philosophical about the vagaries of life; we can even see a certain justice in them, particularly if the wins exceed the losses. Yet it's hard to think there was anything balanced or inevitable about the mess Larry and I deliberately got ourselves into while we were working on *Peggy-Ann.*

One day Florenz Ziegfeld called. Though Larry and I were now well established on Broadway, as soon as I heard the name Ziegfeld it was like Moses hearing the voice of God on Mount Sinai. Ever since 1907, with his first *Follies,* Ziegfeld had been the acknowledged master producer on Broadway. He was the Great Glorifier, whose shows were the most dazzling and whose stars were the most celestial. The Ziegfeld name on a *Playbill* was an acknowledged guarantee of quality, glamour and success, and so when Florenz Ziegfeld called, Dick Rodgers went running.

In an excessively ornate office I came face to face with a heavyset, gravel-voiced man of authority with a face dominated by a large crooked nose. Ziegfeld lost no time in outlining his idea. He and his millionaire friend and backer Replogle (he was never called anything but Replogle) had just returned from Europe on the same ship with Belle Baker, a tiny woman with a huge voice whose stage appearances until then had been confined to vaudeville houses. Both he and Replogle, Ziegfeld told me, had been "bowled over" by the singer when she performed at a ship's concert, and they were both convinced that she had the makings of a major Broadway attraction. The producer had already commissioned a couple of writers, David Freedman and Irving Caesar, to create an appropriate vehicle, and had even begun lining up a supporting cast. Now, if Larry and I would agree to do the score, the show, which was to be called *Betsy,* would be all set to go into rehearsals in a few weeks.

"A f-few weeks?" I stammered. "We couldn't possibly have it finished in a few weeks. We're already working on a show for Lew Fields."

"I know all about that," Ziegfeld said. "But you two are the whiz kids of Broadway. I'm sure you can do it. Besides"—and here his voice became ever so buddy-buddy—"I wouldn't think of doing it with anyone else but you."

Well, I was only twenty-four and it was the Great Florenz Ziegfeld speaking, and if he felt that way about us, how could I possibly refuse? What a way to end the year—a score for a Ziegfeld production!

I quickly got in touch with Larry, who grumbled a bit but said okay. Apparently even he was impressed by the magic of the Ziegfeld name. When I got home that evening, my parents were surprisingly unenthusiastic. No specific reason, just a feeling. My hunch is that Mom and Pop somehow had the same instinct that makes a lioness apprehensive for its cub. Because *Betsy* turned out to be the worst experience of my career—the worst, that is, until I did another show for Ziegfeld.

During the short period allowed us to create the score, Larry and I seldom saw Freedman or Caesar, and there was hardly any effort at genuine collaboration. I don't think we had more than one meeting with La Belle Baker. Ziegfeld, whose function should have been that of a coordinator, rarely paid any attention to us. There was nothing else for us to do but go our not very merry way trying to write songs that might fit a story for which we had been given little more than a rough outline.

At first I felt rather proud of myself for being able to juggle two scores at the same time. After Dorothy had been at Wellesley for about a month, I wrote her about it:

> I have been doing a terrific amount of manuscript work in the past few days, and I'm delighted with the way my eyes have been behaving. However, it leaves me awfully groggy. There's something like two hours' work on each manuscript and though I have worked hard at it, there are at least twenty-five numbers still to be done. Of course, there are more things to write, and when both shows are seriously in rehearsal I expect to give up eating and sleeping entirely.

By mid-November, with both musicals now scheduled to open on Broadway almost simultaneously the following month, a serious problem had developed with *Peggy-Ann:* we still didn't have a leading lady. Our first choice had been Helen Ford, but she was on the road in *Dearest Enemy*. Then we tried to get Ona Munson, a bright ingénue who had played the title role in *No, No, Nanette* both on tour and in New York, but we let her get away. We held audition after audition, but still couldn't find anyone to play the part.

Within a few days, however, I was able to write Dorothy:

At this particular moment I feel much as though I'd been passed very slowly through a wringer and hadn't been hung out to dry. It's been one of those tough days, with nothing happening badly but everything happening with difficulty.

But as the saying has it, after the R. comes the S. Following two disheartening hours trying to squeeze a glimmer of intelligence from the latest applicant for the part of Peggy, Herb decided to give Helen Ford one more try. We got her on the phone in Cincinnati—and Herb leaves tomorrow night with a contract and a manuscript! It seems *Dearest Enemy* is to close next week and Helen will be Peggy after all! It's been a strain, you see, because we're sure we have a good play to begin with, and we have the best directors there are, and to be forced into such a disagreeable position was rotten. Now I hope everything'll be all right.

In Mr. Ziegfeld's office yesterday morning was assembled all the cast and all the authors and all the directors. The purpose of the meeting was to read the book and play the score. It was a most unpleasant session for me, as I hate to play for friends, much less a bunch of actors whose only thought is exactly what and how much each is to do. However, the book is funny, at any rate, and you realize how important that is. Rehearsals begin definitely today, so we're off! God be with us; it's going to be a terrible siege!

Which, as it turned out, was hardly an overstatement. A week later I wrote:

There was a terrible blowup Friday evening when Z. and his general manager bawled me out for not appearing at enough rehearsals. Z. said some rotten things, and I told him I was through with his lousy show. The general manager also made some cracks and I raised hell.

Yesterday morning Dreyfus sent for said g.m. who came over to Harms to apologize to me. Last night Z. and I were walking around rehearsals with our arms about each other's waists. That's that . . .

My earlier prediction of giving up eating and sleeping while the two shows were in rehearsal was pretty accurate. But I still found time to dash off a letter to Dorothy:

> *Peggy* is such a daring idea and is being done to the limit, while *Betsy* is so much applesauce. I started work early this morning and quit at 12:30 to go out for a sandwich. After 3 o'clock in the afternoon I feel like an old man and act it. I haven't shaved since Wednesday night, and Thanksgiving Day was spent at three different rehearsals . . .

One day early in December, Ziegfeld telephoned to ask Larry and me to join him for dinner that evening at his home in Hastings. Great, I thought; now at last we can really thrash over many of our problems. (Despite his concern for my attendance at rehearsals, Ziegfeld was always too busy to have any time for serious discussions.) He sent his chauffeur-driven Rolls Royce to pick us up—a sure sign of our favored position—and we were greeted at his home by his wife, Billie Burke, who couldn't have been more gracious. We enjoyed a sumptuous meal and the conversation flowed, but every time either Larry or I broached the subject of *Betsy*, our host would always find something else to talk about. After dinner we repaired to the drawing room, where at last Larry and I discovered the reason why we had been so grandly entertained. It seemed that now *we* were obliged to do the entertaining: Ziegfeld simply instructed us to go to the piano and perform all the songs from *Betsy* for the amusement of his nine-year-old daughter.

*Betsy* was an enormous show with dozens of elaborate scenes, a large cast and hundreds of little chorus girls milling around like mice in an endless stream of "production numbers." It should have been kept on the road for months before being allowed to open in New York; instead, it had just one week at the National Theatre in Washington. During that week panic took over. Freedman and Caesar fought with each other, Larry and I fought with Freedman and Caesar, and Ziegfeld went charging around the theatre, screaming like a wounded water buffalo. After the Washington opening I wrote Dorothy: "I don't like it at all. The book, if you can call it that, is terrible, and the score has been such a source of extreme annoyance that I am anxious only to have it done with."

A fitting climax to this whole sorry episode came opening night in New York. Almost at the last minute, without saying a word to anyone, Ziegfeld bought a song from Irving Berlin and gave it to Belle Baker to sing in the show. Not only did the interpolated number get the biggest hand of the evening at the premiere, but Ziegfeld also had arranged to have a spotlight pick out Berlin, seated in the front row, who rose and took a bow.

My mother, whom I took to the opening with me, was too unsophisticated to understand what Ziegfeld's slippery piece of showmanship meant to me, but Dorothy, who was there with a friend, was outraged.

It really didn't take a trained ear to appreciate that the Berlin contribution, "Blue Skies," was a great piece of songwriting, easily superior to anything Larry and I had written for the production, but at the time I was crushed by having someone else's work interpolated in our score—particularly since Ziegfeld had insisted he wouldn't think of doing the show with anyone else. A few words in advance might have eased our wounded pride, but Ziegfeld could never be accused of having the human touch—at least not where men were concerned. He did show consideration for girls, but even there his overriding ego, or insecurity, would occasionally take over. I recall one night at a *Betsy* rehearsal when, for some minor infraction, he turned on Madeleine Cameron, a featured member of the cast, and blasted her to bits in front of the entire company. Even her hysterical tears failed to stop him. No, Ziegfeld was not a nice man.

Anyway, I got my wish: a Ziegfeld production to end the year. There was some solace in the fact that *Peggy-Ann,* which had opened the night before *Betsy,* was on its way to success, but there was scant balm to the ego in the fact that Rodgers and Hart and Florenz Ziegfeld had ended 1926 with the biggest flop of their respective careers.

Naturally, such a disastrous experience made me take stock of what I was doing and where I was heading. From May 1925 through December 1926, Larry and I had written the scores for six Broadway musicals, one night-club revue, and one musical in London. By today's standards, this was an almost unbelievable body of work within so short a time; yet somehow I had managed to find time to conduct, travel to Europe, and fall in love.

In trying to reassess what we had done, Larry and I discovered, without surprise, that we were most stimulated and did our best work for those assignments that were the most challenging, such as the first *Garrick Gaieties, Dearest Enemy* and *Peggy-Ann.* Of equal importance, we found that we needed to work with people who were not merely professionally competent but also easy to work with. Productions such as *Lido Lady* and *Betsy,* which brought us into contact with indifferent or antagonistic people, resulted in what we both felt were inferior scores. It was obviously foolhardy for us to succumb to the temptations of working in a foreign locale, like London, or for a legendary impresario, like Ziegfeld, if we did not believe in the show we were writing.

By the beginning of 1927, the Rodgers and Hart track record was as solid as anyone else's on Broadway, but to keep it solid we knew that we would have to be particularly careful of our future commitments. Being careful, however, did not mean playing it safe; if anything, it meant being careful not to.

There was no question that *Betsy* had been an emotion-draining experience. What Larry and I needed was to get away and try to relax a bit before deciding on any new projects.

To our amazement, we had been getting word that *Lido Lady,* after receiving moderate notices, had become a sellout in London. This seemed as good a time as any to discover what wonders had been wrought on the show that we had walked out on before the opening. Late in January, we sailed for London to take a look.

*Lido Lady* was a hit, all right. The packed audience roared with laughter at the antics of Cicely Courtneidge and Jack Hulbert, and there was enthusiastic applause after every number. It was gratifying, of course, but also mystifying. We still didn't think it was much of a show. The book was infantile, the jokes stale, the aging ingénue hadn't gotten any younger, and even the songs didn't strike either Larry or me as anything to boast about. Two days later I tried to explain it in a letter to my girl at Wellesley:

> The show has broken all records for the Gaiety Theatre and is playing to constant capacity. No one can tell us whether it or *Sunny* is the biggest hit in London. For a personal opinion, that's another matter. Were I a stranger paying for my seat I doubt if I'd have a particularly wonderful evening, but I'm not, so what's the difference?

At the end of the letter I added a lonely cry: "Why the devil aren't you here? The fun we could have is simply awful! London is in full swing now and there is so much to do . . ."

Hulbert and Murray were no more hospitable this time than on our first visit, but since we didn't expect anything different, we weren't disappointed. After a few weeks, fully rested, Larry and I were all set to return to New York and face the what-do-we-do-next problem when, unexpectedly, we got a call from Charles B. Cochran. Getting a call from Cochran in London was akin to getting a call from Ziegfeld in New York. "C.B." was acknowledged to be the leading producer of the London stage, and his musicals were famed for their opulence, taste and superb showmanship. What could we lose?

Cochran's office was a wonderfully old-fashioned establishment in Old Bond Street. Physically, the producer was not especially distinguished-looking, but it didn't take long for us to appreciate what a unique person he was. Not only was Cochran a man of obvious great experience and keen judgment, he also knew how to deal with people and put them at their ease. We couldn't have been with him for more than ten minutes before we were chatting as if we'd been friends all our lives.

C.B.'s idea wasn't exactly world-shattering; he simply wanted Larry and me to provide the songs for a new revue he was planning for his theatre, the London Pavilion. Because we still had no plans of our own and there were no pressing reasons to return to New York, we looked at each other and said yes on the spot.

Since it was mid-February and the show wasn't to open until sometime in May, Larry and I took off for Paris, primarily to convince Russell Bennett, who was then living there, to do the orchestrations for the score. Russell, even at that time among the most creative arrangers in the theatre, probably has the most amazing powers of concentration of anyone I've ever known. When he eventually joined us in London, I remember walking into his flat one morning to discover him working diligently on the score while listening to music blaring from a radio.

Another reason why we went to Paris was to see if we might not have misjudged it the first time we were there. Somehow, this time the French seemed more friendly, or perhaps it was just that we were getting used to the Parisian way of life. What made our stay doubly enjoyable was that we ran into two girls we had known in New York. With Rita Hayden and Ruth Warner, we made a happy foursome taking in all the expected sights—and a few unexpected ones, too.

While we were escorting the girls back to their hotel one night in a taxi, another cab darted out of a side street and missed hitting us by a matter of inches. As our cab came to a halt, one of the girls cried, "Oh, my heart stood still!" No sooner were the words out than Larry casually said, "Say, that would make a great title for a song." I told him that he was a crazy fool to be thinking of song titles at such a time, but I guess I'm a crazy fool too, because I couldn't get the title out of my head. When the cab stopped at the girls' hotel, I took out a little black address book and scribbled the words "My Heart Stood Still."

After Paris, Larry and I went to the south of France for a few days, but I couldn't help thinking about my freshman in Massachusetts. I wrote Dorothy from Cannes:

> Just before we left Paris there were three letters in a bunch from you. You see, you are every bit as nice as I said you were. And how I enjoyed them! *En passant,* why don't you get yourself fired out of school for smoking! That would settle your problems so well.
>
> Anyway, one helluva good time was had in Paris. We tore the old

place wide apart in a nice way with no ill effects. There were ten days of nearly complete joy. The "nearly" means you, because we could have had fun. No? . . .

When we returned to London, Louis Dreyfus, Max's brother and the head of Harms's London office, suggested that if we were going to stay awhile in the city, we should rent a "service flat" rather than stay in a hotel. A service flat, we quickly learned, was like an apartment except that all the services, including housekeeping and the preparation and serving of meals, were taken care of by the management. The place that Louis told us about was beautifully located, at 29 St. James's Street, between Piccadilly and St. James's Palace. Actually, Larry and I had separate flats on the same floor, with mine conveniently equipped with its own piano. "Here am I back in London at work," a letter to Dorothy announced, "which consists of getting up late, going to rehearsal and making a few pithy suggestions, having dinner somewhere or other, and 'going out.' I'm full of sympathy for myself and don't see how I can stand it."

Cochran's new revue was to be called *One Dam Thing After Another.* Even without the *n* in "Dam," this struck Larry and me as a racy title for an English revue. Others apparently thought so too, since the show was usually referred to as *The London Pavilion Revue.*

While in London, Larry and I went to see another musical, *Lady Luck,* which included two of our songs from *Betsy,* "Sing" and "If I Were You." Opening the program, we read our credit line, "Additional numbers by Rogers and Hart." Even today my name is frequently misspelled, but it no longer bothers me as it once did. (Though it still bothers my wife!) In the mid-twenties, however, whenever I saw a newspaper piece about me in which the *d* was left out of "Rodgers," I was ready to shoot the editor. One day, after having seen my name misspelled in three different articles, I told my father that the only course left was to give up the struggle, admit defeat and drop the *d* myself. Pop bristled slightly, but as usual he didn't give me a flat answer. He thought for a bit, then said, "I'll tell you what: you just make the name so well known that the accepted way to spell it will be with a *d.* " I knew I couldn't win that argument.

Larry and I spent a lot of time working in our adjoining flats in St. James's Street. It was enjoyable, chiefly because Cochran was so encouraging and appreciative of everything we did. He lined up an impressive cast for his revue, including, in her first major part, a very young, bright-eyed and toothy doll of a girl named Jessie Matthews. Also in the cast was Edythe Baker, a brilliant American pianist, whose trademark was a large white piano. A second pianist, for the pit, was Leslie Hutchinson, an extremely personable black man known as "Hutch." He used to appear at all the society parties and was so popular that it was a real coup to have him play in the theatre orchestra.

One morning in my flat I was looking for a telephone number in my address book and came across the words "My Heart Stood Still." Now what the devil could that mean? Then I remembered that night in Paris. It was early and Larry was still asleep, so I simply sat down at the piano and wrote a melody that seemed to express the feeling of one so emotionally moved that his heart has stopped beating. Later, when Larry came in, I grandly announced, "Well, I've set that title to music."

"What title?" Larry asked.

" 'My Heart Stood Still.' "

"Say, that's a great title. Where did you get it?"

He had completely forgotten the taxi incident, but after I played the tune for him he finished the lyric in no time at all. In my entire career this is the only time I can recall in which a specific, totally unrelated incident triggered the creation of one of my songs.

More important than its genesis, of course, is the song itself and the way it illustrates a facet of Larry's talent that has often been overlooked. His ability to write cleverly and to come up with unexpected, polysyllabic rhymes was something of a trademark, but he also had the even rarer ability to write with utmost simplicity and deep emotion. Just look at the lyric to "My Heart Stood Still." With the exception of six two-syllable words, every word in the refrain is monosyllabic. But how direct and affecting it all is with, for example, its tender reference to "that unfelt clasp of hand" and its beautifully contrasting conclusion:

> I never lived at all
> Until the thrill
> Of that moment when
> My heart stood still.

With lovely Jessie Matthews singing it in *One Dam Thing After Another* and Edythe Baker playing it on the piano, this song easily turned out to be the hit of the show.

It will not have escaped the reader's notice that this stay in London was far more enjoyable than the first. The man most responsible for this was unquestionably Cochran, who entertained us frequently in his home and who went out of his way to introduce us to many interesting people. Cochran himself was an admirable blend of gentleness, intellect and courage. His interests were catholic. He brought Russian ballet to England, promoted championship prize fighting, sponsored concerts and produced everything from the heaviest dramas to the lightest musicals. He was a lovely man and I was deeply fond of him.

It was at Cochran's home that I first met Edythe Baker, who was popular with a fascinating segment of London society. Her steady beau, whom she eventually married, was Gerard "Pops" d'Erlanger, the son of Baron Emile and Baroness Catherine d'Erlanger. All the d'Erlangers were great lovers of the arts, including Pops's brother, Robin, and Robin's vivacious wife, Myrtle. Since Larry had discovered his own group of friends, I spent a good deal of my free time with the always exciting and stimulating d'Erlanger clan. Myrtle, in particular, threw some of the gayest parties I've ever been to. Even after her divorce from Robin—when she was given the title, definitive article and all, of "The Mrs. Farquharson of Invercauld"— our friendship continued, until her death during World War II. Today I am still close to the d'Erlanger family through Zoë, Myrtle's daughter, and Zoë's children.

I first got to know the Prince of Wales at Myrtle and Robin's home. He loved all kinds of music, but especially that of the American theatre, and Edythe and I enjoyed playing for him. Because of his friendship with Edythe, the Prince came to the opening night of *One Dam Thing After Another*. I was all agog over this, not only because I was pleased at his being at the show but because I was sure that the resulting publicity would be of tremendous box-office value. Cochran, however, wise to the ways of London audiences, warned me that it could spell disaster, since, given the choice, Britons much preferred spending an evening watching royalty than what occurred onstage.

As the show progressed, it looked as if C.B. was absolutely right. No matter what was happening in the revue, everyone was staring at the royal box, as if to await a signal indicating when to laugh and when to applaud. The Prince was obviously enjoying himself, but by the time the people in the stalls and the circles got the message, they reacted in all the wrong places.

During the intermission Larry and I mingled with the crowd in the lobby, where we overheard two properly starched ladies discussing one of our songs. "That was certainly a hot tune," said one dowager. "Oh, no," corrected her friend. "Mr. Rodgers does the tunes. Mr. Hart does the lyrics." A little later a bejeweled *grande dame,* on meeting Larry, said ever so sweetly, "It's funny, Mr. Hart. It's very amusing. But I don't like funny shows. I like pretty shows."

After the final curtain fell to no more than perfunctory applause, Larry and I went backstage to see Cochran. "Well, boys," he said matter-of-factly,

"I don't know whether to try to make this thing run or close it now and book a film into the theatre." Then the three of us went to his office to have a drink and discuss the show's fate. Neither Larry nor I could offer concrete advice, since we knew next to nothing about London theatre management, but C.B. did agree to keep the show going for a while. Surprisingly, the reviews turned out to be extremely encouraging, and helped the show remain alive until an unexpected piece of luck came our way.

Larry and I had already returned to New York when, three weeks after the show's opening, we received a bundle of newspaper clippings. Though the Prince of Wales had inadvertently almost killed our show on opening night by his mere presence, he now became the one most responsible for turning it into a success. According to the newspaper accounts, he had gone to a dance in Plymouth at the Royal Western Yacht Club and had asked the orchestra leader to play "My Heart Stood Still." Teddy Brown, the leader, didn't know the tune, nor did any of his men, but that didn't stop the Prince. Since he had heard Edythe and me sing and play the number many times, he knew it well enough to hum the melody until the musicians were sufficiently familiar with it to play it. One newspaper, the London *Evening News,* had a big headline blazoning THE PRINCE "DICTATES" A FOX-TROT. Underneath was a subhead, THE SONG THE PRINCE LIKED, and underneath *that* were the printed words and music of the first sixteen bars of "My Heart Stood Still." This royal seal of approval was enough to send Londoners queuing up at the Pavilion box office and scurrying to music stores to buy the sheet music and recordings of the song. Thanks to the Prince of Wales, our revue ran for seven months and Cochran was never forced to book that film.

Our Cochran revue had given Larry and me a breather from the inevitable decision we had to make about our next Broadway show. On returning to New York, we knew we could not postpone it any longer. One thing was certain: it would have to be different from anything we'd ever done before. Apart from our own inclination to try something new, we were well aware of the number of producers and writers who, having had one hit, simply tried to duplicate the formula the next time out—or even worse, tried to copy someone else's formula. Rarely, if ever, did these imitative productions succeed in being anything more than hand-me-down products.

Indeed, there was an appalling monotony of subject matter in even the best musical shows of the twenties. The themes seemed to be built almost entirely around the boy's pursuit of the girl, their breakup in time for the first-act finale (you gotta make the customers want to come back to see how it all turns out), and the eventual reconciliation. There were plenty of variations on the Montague-Capulet theme or the Cinderella—or its variant, the Pygmalion—theme, in which the poor girl ends up beautiful, rich and the Queen of the *Follies*. And there was always the one about the poor girl chasing the rich boy or vice versa—until they both turn out to be either rich and happy or poor and happy. The important thing was that everyone had to end up happy so that the people who bought tickets would leave the theatre happy.

There was essentially nothing wrong with this except that it kept the musical theatre within a structurally uncreative bind. As a composer I should not have been too concerned about this. The simpler and more predictable the story, it might be argued, the more ready the audience is to appreciate the music. If the plot is especially fresh or daring, the theory goes, the composer risks audience resentment at the intrusion of his songs. But this seemed to me both nonsensical and self-defeating. I have always believed that the story and the music must be closely interrelated, and that each component should be strong enough to help the other and contribute to the overall effect. Why should songs rescue a juvenile, hackneyed story? Or even, though less likely, an intelligent, adult story save a weak score? Why can't they both be equally bright, original and enjoyable? I'm not claiming that I was alone in my view. All the major composers of the twenties—such as Kern, Gershwin and Youmans—were constantly seeking ways to break out of the conventional musical-comedy mold, though they often had to write for formula entertainments.

That's why it was always so much fun to work with Larry and Herb Fields. We all liked and respected one another and what each one of us was contributing. After our London sojourn, it was almost inevitable that Larry and I would do our next Broadway show with Herb, and when we got together again to toss around ideas it was also almost inevitable that we would think only of the most challenging and intriguing subjects we could find. This led directly to *A Connecticut Yankee*.

Back in 1921 Larry, Herb and I had seen a moving picture adapted from Mark Twain's *A Connecticut Yankee in King Arthur's Court*. We all thought the story wonderfully funny, with an irresistible combination of fantasy and social commentary, and were sure it had the makings of a first-rate musical comedy. At the time making a musical comedy out of an accepted literary classic may not have been frowned on by producers, but it wasn't exactly encouraged either. But we liked it and wanted to do it; it was as simple as that.

Well, not quite. Charles Tressler Lark, a flinty-eyed character, was the lawyer for the Mark Twain estate. When I first outlined to him our plans to turn the story into a stage musical, Mr. Lark agreed, to my amazement, to let us have the rights without payment. But that was in 1921, when Larry,

Herb and I were still unknown and unable to get a hearing. By 1927 our option on the book had lapsed and when we tried to pick it up again, Mr. Lark, well aware of our successes, made sure that the estate would receive both a high fee and a whopping royalty arrangement.

As the producer who had sponsored most of our past musicals, Lew Fields was our obvious choice to present *A Connecticut Yankee* (the slightly shortened title that we used), and in the summer of 1927 we gave him the Mark Twain novel to read while he was in London directing the English version of *Peggy-Ann*. Surprisingly, he cabled back that he could see nothing in the book that would make a good musical. Still confident that we would have little trouble finding a producer once the script and songs were finished, we went ahead with the project anyway. What Herb Fields did primarily was to update the modern part of the story and use the dream flashback in Camelot as a means to introduce anachronistic humor involving current slang and business technology at the court of King Arthur.

After Lew Fields returned to New York and read what we'd written, he became as enthusiastic as we were and agreed to produce the show. In order to get the Vanderbilt Theatre, where we had thrived with *The Girl Friend* and *Peggy-Ann*, Fields again went into partnership with Lyle D. Andrews, the theatre's owner, who put up a good deal of the capital.

At about the same time, early September of 1927, we were approached by Charles Dillingham, one of Broadway's most respected producers, to write the score for a musical comedy to star Beatrice Lillie. Both Dillingham and Miss Lillie knew of the hit that "My Heart Stood Still" had made in London, and as soon as we had agreed to do their show they both told us how anxious they were for Bea to introduce it to Broadway. Now, Larry and I were well aware that Bea Lillie was a great attraction and a great clown, but we also knew that she simply didn't have the voice to introduce "My Heart Stood Still" to anyone. To get her off our backs, we simply told her that she couldn't have the song because it was already slated for *A Connecticut Yankee*. Of course, once we used the excuse, we had to make sure that the song really was in the show. This meant getting permission from Cochran, since it was still being sung in his revue. He agreed, but only on the condition that Larry and I accept a cut in show royalties. Thus, we found ourselves paying for the right to use our own song, though I have to admit that it turned out to our ultimate advantage.

To play the title role in *A Connecticut Yankee*, we chose William Gaxton, a restlessly dynamic performer, well known in vaudeville but still untried in a Broadway book musical. Constance Carpenter, the love interest, was an English actress who had appeared in the Gershwin musical *Oh, Kay!* the previous season. And directing our dances was an imaginative young man with limited Broadway experience who answered to the highly unlikely name of Busby Berkeley.

Rehearsals were fun, as most rehearsals are, and everyone seemed optimistic about the show's chances. Because of the title, we decided to open out of town in Stamford, Connecticut, but the production was still so ragged that the citizens of the Nutmeg State could hardly have considered it much of an honor. The only really enjoyable part of our stay in Stamford was that Dorothy came down from Wellesley for the opening. She did her best to like the show, but I knew she was being kind. By the time we got to Philadelphia, however, we were in good shape, and we played there for four weeks to sellout business. We did have one major disagreement, which was over the song "Thou Swell"; Lew Fields wanted it cut out of the score. While it is often necessary to remove a particular number if it is inappropriate or slows down the action, in this case there seemed to be no sound reason for dropping the song, and I simply refused to allow it.

Our conductor for *A Connecticut Yankee,* as he had been for *Peggy-Ann,* was my close friend Roy Webb, and because of my confidence in the song and the show, I asked his permission to conduct the first-night performance in New York. On opening night I climbed into the pit, received a polite greeting and led the musicians through the overture. Instead of opening directly into the first act, we began with a prologue in order to separate the show's real world from its dream world. The scene, set in a hotel ballroom in modern-day Hartford, contained two songs, the second being "My Heart Stood Still." Here, I was certain, we would really grab them. To my dismay, however, the song, while greeted cordially enough, didn't produce the enthusiastic reception I had expected. Oh, well, on to Act One. It was here that we began the dream sequence in which Billy Gaxton, having been hit on the head in the prologue, dreams that he is back in the days of King Arthur. In the first scene, the road to Camelot, he meets the fair Connie Carpenter, and after a few words of who-hit-me–where-am-I banter he begins singing "Thou Swell." Billy wasn't more than eight bars into the refrain when I began to feel that something on the back of my neck. It wasn't the steady, growing sensation I'd felt during the first *Garrick Gaieties,* nor was it the more subdued, all-is-well feeling I had during *Dearest Enemy.* This time the audience reaction was so strong that it was like an actual blow. Though there were no audible sounds, I could feel the people loving Gaxton, adoring Carpenter and going wild over the song. The applause at the end of the number was deafening, and Billy and Connie returned to give several encores. That did it; from then on, the show was in. Nothing, I knew, could stop it from being a smash.

After the final curtain there was a genuine ovation, and most of the company went next door to The Tavern, a popular theatrical restaurant, to await the critical verdict in the morning papers. Though there were some reservations about the book, all the reviewers confirmed my feeling that we had a major hit. Brooks Atkinson, in the *Times,* liked everything about it, and gave my music as enthusiastic a review as it has ever received. I have enough company in my affection for Brooks to lead me to believe that this review was not the only justification for my feeling that he was the best critic the American theatre has ever had. Gilbert W. Gabriel, in the *Sun,* was also unreservedly enthusiastic, but it was not until years later, when we became good friends, that I realized that he was the only theatre critic writing for the New York press who had a musician's knowledge of music. I also got a kick out of the notice written by Frank Vreeland of the *Telegram.* Taking his cue from "The Sandwich Men" number in the show, he penned his own sign:

---

GO, THOU SLUGGARD,
AND ENJOY
"A CONNECTICUT YANKEE"
AND TELL
YE COCKE-EYED WORLDE
THOU HAST HAD
YE HELLUVA TIME

---

The success of *A Connecticut Yankee*—the biggest one Larry and I had during the twenties—further confirmed my feeling that taking chances was the only safe thing to do. Unfortunately, however, I was not always able to adhere to this conviction. Being human, I could still be persuaded to take assignments that, if looked at with more objectivity, I should have refused. *She's My Baby* was just such a project.

In 1927 Ziegfeld's only possible rival in America in fame and prestige was Charles Bancroft Dillingham, and Larry and I were eager to write the songs for his new Beatrice Lillie production. Dillingham's office was just above the entrance to the Globe Theatre, which he owned. Oddly enough, I had never met him before, nor did I have any idea of what he looked like. Expecting to meet another rough-and-tough Broadway producer, I was surprised to be greeted by a tall, courtly, neatly mustached gentleman who treated me as if I were doing him the greatest honor merely by visiting him. Briefly, he outlined his plans for *She's My Baby.* He was confident that he'd found an ideal vehicle for madcap Bea Lillie in a farce devised by Guy

Bolton and the team of Bert Kalmar and Harry Ruby, who were considerably better known as songwriters than as librettists.

Since I had long admired Bolton, I was particularly anxious to work with him, and knowing and liking both Kalmar and Ruby was another factor in persuading me to join the new venture. Though the story they had devised didn't strike me as being a world-beater, I felt that Larry and I would not only have fun working with these people but could also learn something from them. And who could resist the temptation of writing songs for Beatrice Lillie, whose irrepressible antics had made her a great favorite in New York ever since *Charlot's Revue of 1924*?

Soon after the successful launching of *A Connecticut Yankee* early in November, we began working on *She's My Baby*. We had already surmounted the first hurdle by keeping "My Heart Stood Still" away from Bea and putting it in *A Connecticut Yankee*. Our second hurdle had nothing to do with the show or the score: it was me. About halfway through the job I got a severe case of flu and had to be bedridden for a couple of weeks. With rehearsals almost ready to begin, I managed to get out of bed and totter down to see Dillingham. He took one look at me and said, "You look terrible. Pack a bag and go down to Atlantic City. Stay there for four or five days and don't do a thing. And remember, you're my guest during the entire time."

That was the kind of man Dillingham was—generous, considerate, always more concerned about people than about business. The kind of man I was? I was a nut. I told him no thanks, that I'd been holding things up long enough and felt that I had to stay home and finish my work as quickly as possible. And I did.

As a producer, Charles Dillingham was tremendously prolific, with an impressive career of over fifty shows, including such hits as *The Red Mill, Watch Your Step* and *Sunny*. Yet I found him an enigma as far as our musical production was concerned. Once we'd all signed our contracts, he immediately lost interest in the project. I remember that we had a run-through in Washington, with a dress rehearsal the following night. At the end of the first act of the dress rehearsal, I saw him calmly strolling out of the theatre. "Mr. Dillingham," I called out after him, "what about the second act?" Without breaking stride, he said, "Oh, I saw it last night. I don't have to see it again." I'm sure he must have been at the New York opening, but I can't recall seeing him there or ever hearing another word from him about the show or the score.

In addition to Bea Lillie, *She's My Baby* had an interesting cast. The ingénue was played by Irene Dunne, whose voice and beauty were then just beginning to be appreciated. Clifton Webb, who played a sort of comic romantic lead opposite Bea, was little different from his later Hollywood image—suave, soigné and unflappable. And there was Jack Whiting, whose wavy red hair and ear-to-ear smile made him the epitome of the Broadway juvenile.

*She's My Baby,* which opened early in January 1928, received only tepid notices, with most of the blame going to the book and most of the praise going to Bea Lillie. Probably because the better songs were written as specialty numbers for Bea, Larry and I didn't come up with anything that lasted beyond the show's two-month run in New York.

So it was another setback for Rodgers and Hart. Not that the experience was in a class with *Betsy*. There were no fights and no bitterness on anyone's part. No one was to blame except myself for having become involved in a show I should have avoided.

During my siege of influenza I had received especially loving care at the hands of both my parents. Pop, of course, was my doctor, but Mom never left the apartment until I was well again. Primarily to show my appreciation for their kindness, I decided to treat them to a trip to Europe. The winter of 1928 was particularly cold and miserable in New York, and with nothing pressing at the moment, I managed to persuade them to take a vacation in Paris and the warm, balmy south of France. A week after the opening of *She's My Baby,* the three of us sailed on the *Columbus,* and were welcomed in Paris by the worst snowstorm the city had had in years. After a day or two of being confined to our hotel, we decided we'd had enough and took off for the Riviera. There was no snow there, but the weather was freezing and the clouds were ominously gray. We weren't licked yet! With stubborn determination we reasoned that all we had to do was to go a bit farther south, to North Africa, where surely we would find a tropical paradise.

We sailed for Algiers on a crowded, filthy little tub with the grand name of *La Moricière*. The crossing was rough, the food almost inedible, and the sole privilege enjoyed by the family Rodgers was sharing the only private bathroom on the ship. We found Algiers fascinating, but only for a day or so. Then the weather turned cold and wet, and once more we found ourselves unable to leave our hotel. Were we depressed? Damn right. Were we defeated? Not on your life. So determined were we to have our elusive, fun-filled holiday in the sun that we hired a car, a big Renault, and a good French chauffeur-guide to drive us over the Atlas Mountains to Setif, on the edge of the Sahara. We drove through the mountains and spent the second night of the trip in a hotel at Constantine. Up early the next morning for the final leg of what had become something of a holy mission, we discovered that the car had broken down and wouldn't budge. Lesser men might have given up right then, convinced that fate had decreed that they would be forever frustrated in their quest for a little warmth and sun. But not the undaunted Rodgerses! We simply hired the only taxi in Constantine to drive us the remaining distance to Setif, and there, at last, we found what we had been searching for ever since we left New York—a bright-blue sky and a warm, sunny climate.

The only trouble was that it had taken us almost a month. Since I was now needed in New York to begin work on a new show, we could enjoy our discovery for only a single day before heading back. Still, we could say "Mission accomplished," and with pride in our fortitude, we took a train back to Algiers, the *Roma* across the Mediterranean to France, and the *Olympic* from Le Havre to New York.

It must have been about five o'clock in the morning when we reached the mouth of the Hudson. Something awakened me, probably tugboats, and I looked out the porthole. There were huge chunks of ice on the Hudson, so the weather was obviously no warmer than when we had left, but the sky was unusually clear and the stars looked as if all I had to do was reach up and touch them. I dressed quickly and ran up on deck to see the breath-taking Manhattan skyline illuminated in the brilliant early-morning glow. As we passed street after street on our way up the river to our pier, I felt the exhilaration of a prisoner about to be set free. The freezing weather bothered me not at all; all I cared about was that I'd soon be home again, seeing Dorothy again and doing the work I loved again.

## 10

Larry and I never had any kind of agreement, either written or verbal. Even a handshake would probably have seemed too formal. We simply knew that as long as we both could do the work we did, we would always remain partners.

Our relationship with Herb Fields was much looser. Although, curiously, Herb never seemed to have any great love for the theatre, he was easy to get along with and was always full of ideas, and we enjoyed working with him more than with any other librettist. But none of us ever thought of ourselves as part of an indissoluble trio, even though, up to 1927, Herb had never written with any other songwriters. Early that year, however, before we began working on *A Connecticut Yankee,* he had accepted an offer to join another team, Clifford Grey, Leo Robin and Vincent Youmans. His first effort without Rodgers and Hart turned out to be considerably more successful than any of our early book shows without him, since *Hit the Deck* was one of the decade's most memorable productions.

Having done so well with a musical comedy about the U.S. Navy, Herb began dreaming up an idea to involve another branch of the service, the United States Marines, and this time he brought it to us.

The show was called *Present Arms.* Because we were concerned about a musical dealing with Marines coming on the heels of one dealing with sailors, we did what we could to make the new show as different as possible. Instead of taking our servicemen to China, as in *Hit the Deck,* we took them to Pearl Harbor. Instead of having our heroine chase our hero, we had our hero chase our heroine, and instead of making her a New England seamstress, we made her a titled English lady. Try as we did, though, it all came out as a variation on *Hit the Deck.* This resemblance was reinforced by a particularly short-sighted bit of casting. To play our Marine hero we chose a round-faced, breezy song-and-dance man named Charles King who had just finished playing the sailor hero in *Hit the Deck.*

At the time we went into rehearsals, however, this did not bother us because we were more concerned with other members of the cast. As I wrote to Dorothy about a week before we opened out of town: "The show is quite a problem. We're rather sure, for us, of the book and the score, but the cast remains an unknown quantity. Charlie King looks great, but we don't know about the leading lady, a sweet-looking little English blonde named Flora Le Breton. She does everything well, but she seems to have for most of us the same attraction as a small canary . . ."

Our dance director for *Present Arms,* as for *A Connecticut Yankee,* was Busby Berkeley. This time, however, he wasn't satisfied with just directing the dances; he also tried out for, and got, the second male lead in the show. What may surprise some people today is that it was Busby who, with a juicy little grape of a girl named Joyce Barbour, introduced the musical's most popular song, "You Took Advantage of Me."

This brings up one of the eternal mysteries of the musical theatre. Despite good reviews, it is often next to impossible to predict whether or not a show will be a commercial success. We first learned this with *The Girl Friend,* which got rave notices and almost closed in a couple of weeks. But one might think that predicting a song hit would be easier. Anyone knows that all that is needed is to keep plugging away until the public is so saturated with a number that it is sure to love it forever. But the fact is that no amount of plugging can make people like something they don't respond to, though there are certain songs that, with a little extra help, can achieve popularity. We had hopes for "You Took Advantage of Me," but we had even greater expectations for the more romantic duet, a sweet, charming, tender and eminently appealing ballad called "Do I Hear You Saying, 'I Love You'?" Consequently, we made sure that it was generously reprised throughout *Present Arms.* It was sung in the first scene and in the third scene, it was played during intermission, it was part of the finale, and it was the last music the audience heard as it filed out of the theatre. But people forgot it as soon as they reached the sidewalk. Maybe the title was too long, maybe the music was too delicate, maybe maybe maybe . . . As it turned out, the number everyone did remember—and still does today—was the sassy, unregretful "You Took Advantage of Me."

Since *Present Arms* was about the Marines, we were in agreement that the show would be different in at least one respect from most musical comedies: there would be no effeminate young men in the chorus. We ended up with the toughest, burliest-looking group of singers and dancers ever seen onstage. This turned out to be a mixed blessing when we got to Wilmington for the out-of-town tryout. What we hadn't counted on was that our Marines not only looked like real Marines, they also tried to act like them. Most of their hours when they weren't onstage were spent going from bar to bar and getting thoroughly soused. On one occasion, after spending the night carousing through the city, they returned to their hotel, rode up to the tenth floor and hurled a heavy pot of sand through a window. Fortunately, no one was hurt. Another time they ended a similar spree early in the morning by going from door to door of people's homes and helping themselves to bagfuls of freshly delivered rolls. After satisfying their hunger, our playful chorus boys then proceeded to have a fight with the rolls in the street and in the hotel lobby. One more day in Wilmington and we all would have been thrown out.

The show's New York opening—on April 26, 1928—took place at the

Mansfield Theatre. The performance went well and the next day's reviews were mostly raves. Still, at least half a dozen critics couldn't help pointing out the resemblance between *Present Arms* and *Hit the Deck,* which had opened exactly one year before. Perhaps because of this, the show lasted only a little more than four months.

It was during the run of *Present Arms* that I had my first and only brush with a member of New York's underworld. One of the girls in the cast had actually adopted the stage name of Hotsy-Totsy, but before the opening we managed to talk her into using something a bit more conventional, and she settled on Demaris Doré. She had a solo, "Crazy Elbows," which came toward the end of the first act. One night I was standing in the back of the theatre when the drummer made a mistake during her song and Hotsy-Totsy used a one-syllable vulgarity to express her displeasure that was easily audible in the rear of the house. As the audience let out a collective gasp, I rushed backstage and told the stage manager to get rid of her. Louis Shurr, the agent, sent us a cute little kid as replacement, but because her voice was weak we had to turn her down.

The following night Dorothy and I went to see Marilyn Miller in *Rosalie,* the big Ziegfeld hit at the New Amsterdam. While we were standing on the sidewalk during the intermission, Shurr, his face chalk-white, dashed over to us and told me that we were all in great danger. It seems that the girl we had just turned down was a particularly close friend of one of Brooklyn's most notorious gangsters, and he was determined to avenge this slight to his inamorata. According to Shurr, Larry Fay, another gangster and friend of the Brooklyn hood, wanted to see me that very night and would be waiting for me at twelve-thirty at Texas Guinan's speakeasy.

Putting up a brave front, I told Shurr to go home and assured him I could smooth things over. As nonchalantly as possible, Dorothy and I returned to our seats for the second act of *Rosalie,* though neither of us had the foggiest idea of what was going on. Despite my objection, Dorothy insisted on staying with me after the show. Because we were early for the scheduled encounter, we first went to our favorite late-night port of call, Montmartre, until it was time to learn whether my lack of artistic appreciation would condemn me to be taken for a ride or dumped in the river. When we arrived at the appointed hour, Texas Guinan seated us at an isolated table in the corner. Presently she returned with a tall, black-haired, gray-faced man with a sagging jaw who looked like an undertaker—which, in a way, he was. Before saying anything to me, Larry Fay stared at our departing hostess and muttered, "She's a son of a bitch." Even in the dimly lit room I could see Dorothy blush; language like that was simply not used in what was then called mixed company, and it served to make both of us even more apprehensive. Fay then turned to me, reached across the table, squeezed my wrist, and in a voice of gravel, said, "As a special favor to me, Dick, wouldja let the girl go on for one performance?"

When Larry Fay asks for a special favor like that, how could any fearless composer possibly refuse? The next night the girl went on, and she was terrible. As I left the theatre during the intermission, Fay was waiting for me at the curb. Uh-oh, I thought, here it comes. Now he's going to tell me she's another Marilyn Miller and as a special favor to him I'll have to give her the leading part and put her name in lights. Fay looked at me coldly and said, "She stinks, and what's more, I'm gonna tell her so myself." Then he squeezed my wrist again and said pointedly, "Listen, if there's ever anything you want done, just let me know and I'll take care of it for you."

That was the end of the matter and also the end of my association with the underworld. But I must confess that there have been two or three times in my life when I was sorely tempted to avail myself of Fay's generous offer.

One afternoon in the spring of 1928 I was working at the piano at home when suddenly my grandfather appeared in the doorway and said, "Richard, I don't feel well." I got him to his bedroom and phoned down to my father's office on the first floor of the apartment house we lived in. Pop was in our apartment within minutes, and his immediate diagnosis was that surgery was imperative. Grandpa wasn't strong enough to be moved to a hospital, so we had to turn his bedroom into an operating room. But the operation wasn't successful and a week later he died. It hit me terribly hard. I adored the old man, as did my brother and my parents. I knew he had no faith in the theatre as a career, but his hope that I would go into a more conventional line of work was motivated only by his deep concern for what he felt was best for me. When I did achieve a measure of success, he never hesitated to tell me how proud he was of me and of what I'd accomplished.

After Grandpa's death I felt that I had to get away alone for a while, so I took a brief trip to Colorado Springs. While there, I began getting frantic telephone calls from Larry and Herb about a new idea they had for a musical. It was to be based on a novel called *The Son of the Grand Eunuch*, and they were both convinced that it had the makings of a sensational musical. Sensational was right. I bought the book, read it, and thought they were both crazy. The story was about a young man in ancient China who did everything he could to avoid being castrated, a prerequisite for inheriting his father's exalted title. This didn't strike me as a theatrically adaptable subject for the musical stage, but Larry and Herb had already talked Lew Fields into producing it, and I found myself in the uncomfortable position of being the lone holdout.

When I returned to New York, we continued thrashing the matter around until I finally agreed to go along. They were all so sure of themselves that I didn't want to be the one to torpedo a project they all believed in so deeply. One factor that helped influence me was that while I found the story distasteful, I had to admit that it was a daring departure from the average Broadway musical-comedy subject. Maybe we could shock people into liking it. *Present Arms* had turned out to be a fair success, but there was nothing out of the ordinary about its theme and I certainly didn't relish hearing people compare it to *Hit the Deck*. With *Chee-Chee,* which was the name of our castration musical, there surely wouldn't be any danger of its being compared to anything. Furthermore, from a strictly creative stand-point it offered the challenge of introducing an entirely new concept within the framework of musical theatre.

Larry and I had long been firm believers in the close unity of song and story, but we were not always in a position to put our theories into practice. *Chee-Chee* gave us that chance. To avoid the eternal problem of the story coming to a halt as the songs take over, we decided to use a number of short pieces of from four to sixteen bars each, with no more than six songs of traditional form and length in the entire score. In this way the music would be an essential part of the structure of the story rather than an appendage to the action. The concept was so unusual, in fact, that we even called attention to it with the following notice in the program:

NOTE: The musical numbers, some of them very short, are so inter-woven with the story that it would be confusing for the audience to peruse a complete list.

*Chee-Chee* also brought up a specific problem about the actual writing of the score. With the exception of *Dearest Enemy* and about three quarters of *A Connecticut Yankee,* all our other previous musicals had had modern settings, mostly in or around New York City. For *Chee-Chee,* my job was to compose music for a story set in ancient China. Obviously it would have been inappropriate for me to write typically "American" music, but equally obviously, even if I could have written "Chinese" music, Broadway audiences would have found it unattractive—to say nothing of the impossibility of Larry's finding the proper words to go with it. The only solution was to compose my own kind of music but with an Oriental inflection, reproducing a style rather than creating a faithful imitation. Frequently composers try to reproduce the musical sound of a specific age or locale, often with some success, but I think it's a mistake. It leaves the writer wide open to compari-son—usually unfavorable—with the real thing, and at best only reveals re-creative, rather than creative, skills.

With Mitzi Green, pianist Edgar Fairchild, George Balanchine and, at far right, producer Dwight Deere Wiman at a rehearsal of *Babes in Arms* (1937)

Playing the score of *I'd Rather Be Right*. Standing are producer Sam Harris, Larry, Moss Hart, George S. Kaufman and George M. Cohan (1937)

Taking a bow on the stage of the Met with Marc Platt and Mia Slavenska after conducting the premiere of *Ghost Town* (1939)

John O'Hara rewriting a scene for *Pal Joey* (1940)

With Larry, working on *Pal Joey*

Ray Bolger relaxing at a *By Jupiter* rehearsal (1942)

Max Dreyfus at his farm (circa 1942)

With Oscar at a rehearsal of *Oklahoma!* (1943)

Catching a bouquet after conducting the 2000th performance of *Oklahoma!* (December 4, 1947)

The oak tree and house at Black Rock Turnpike (1944)

Ethel Merman and Irving Berlin rehearsing *Annie Get Your Gun* (1946)

Governor Robert Kerr
welcoming Theresa Helburn
and me to Oklahoma City
in November, 1946

With Oscar in the Public Garden, Boston, reading the reviews of *Allegro* (1947)

With Dorothy and Oscar and Dorothy Hammerstein at the Hammersteins' farm in Doylestown (1948)

Writing "Bali Ha'i" at lunch in Josh Logan's apartment (1949)

With conductor Salvatore Dell'Isola, Barbara Luna, Mary Martin and Ezio Pinza listening to the playback of Columbia's cast recording of *South Pacific* (1949)

At my surprise birthday party at Rockmeadow (June 25, 1950)

Giving Mary a farewell present onstage after her last Broadway performance in *South Pacific,* June 1, 1951. Josh Logan and Leland Hayward are on the right.

One special pleasure I derived in composing the score for *Chee-Chee* was a musical joke that I used toward the end of the second act. As the son of the Grand Eunuch was being led off for his emasculation operation, he was accompanied by a triumphal march, in the middle of which I inserted several bars of Tchaikovsky's *Nutcracker Suite*. I found it gratifying that at almost every performance there were two or three individuals with ears musically sharp enough to appreciate the joke.

But no matter what we did to *Chee-Chee* it was still a musical about castration, and you simply can't get an audience at a musical comedy to feel comfortable with such a theme. If I learned anything from this experience, it's that if there's a basic problem with a show—and *Chee-Chee*'s was as basic as you can get—no amount of beautiful scenery, theatrical effects or musical innovations can hide it. We opened in New York late in September 1928 and were greeted by a barrage of critically ripened fruit, though there were a few posies tossed at the music and the imaginative way it melded into the story. The production remained on Broadway for exactly thirty-one performances, and achieved the distinction of having the shortest run of any musical I've ever written.

Including *Chee-Chee*, I had composed twelve theatre scores in four years—ten in New York and two in London. Since successes outweighed failures by about three to one, I was able to be somewhat philosophical about my latest disaster. I had developed enough self-confidence in a field notably lacking in this quality to realize that failures are an inevitable part of the game, and that they need not prove fatal if you learn from your mistakes. If you don't, you have no business being in the theatre—and you won't be for long.

Having achieved a certain amount of fame, I found myself at about this time meeting a number of people who did a good deal to alter my social life. I was single, I played the piano, I was presentable. Basically, I was the same person I'd always been, but now that I was a minor celebrity I found myself constantly being invited to parties given by a mixture of high and café society. I loved every minute of it. I don't suppose there's a person in the world who doesn't enjoy receiving compliments on his work, and these people were extremely appreciative of my accomplishments. Nobody ever complained about my piano playing (which had never improved), and my hosts seemed to feel some kind of special distinction just because the composer of "Manhattan" or "My Heart Stood Still" was playing his very own songs on their very own Spanish-shawled Steinways. As my friend Adlai Stevenson once said, "Flattery is all right if you don't inhale." Knowing the vagaries of a profession in which all too often you are only as good as your last success, I was delighted to enjoy—without inhaling—whatever adulation came my way.

Because of this never-ending flow of social dinners and parties, I did something none of my bachelor friends did: after a suitable period of mourning for *Chee-Chee,* I reciprocated the many invitations I had received by throwing my own party in mid-December of 1928 at the Park Lane Hotel. There were over a hundred people from the theatre, the arts, and what used to be called the Four Hundred, and it was such a social event that newspapers carried feature stories about it. Oddly, considering all the glittering, witty and talented guests, the only incident about the evening that I can still remember was the meeting between my father and Mayor Jimmy Walker. Because Walker had one of the most familiar faces there, Pop's idea of a joke was to put out his hand and say, with feigned sincerity, "I'm sorry, but I didn't get the name."

Despite rumors at the time, the failure of *Chee-Chee* was not the reason for the breakup of the Fields, Rodgers and Hart partnership. As a matter of fact, there never really was any breakup, because Larry and I later worked with Herb again on two shows and three movies. But after *Chee-Chee,* Herb was getting other offers, and so were Larry and I, and it was perfectly understandable that we take advantage of the best available opportunities.

Early in 1929 I received a call from a producer named Alex Aarons. Aarons was the perceptive chap who a decade before had given both George Gershwin and Vincent Youmans their first opportunities on Broadway. With his partner, Vinton Freedley, he had presented a string of Gershwin hits since 1924, including *Lady, Be Good!, Oh, Kay!* and *Funny Face.* Larry and I knew and liked both Alex and Vinton, and we had always hoped that someday we might get together with them professionally as well as socially.

What Aarons had in mind was making a musical of a play by Owen Davis called *Shotgun Wedding,* with Davis himself doing the adaptation. Owen, whom I knew as a man of great humor and kindness, had won a Pulitzer Prize for his drama *Icebound,* but what interested Larry and me even more was that his comedy, *The Nervous Wreck,* had recently been turned into a hugely successful musical for Eddie Cantor called *Whoopee.*

Owen's story, which was renamed *Spring Is Here,* was not particularly strong, but coming after *Chee-Chee* it seemed the epitome of wit, charm and dramatic skill. Frankly, it was just one more bit of fluff dealing with flirtations among the "Tennis, anyone?" Long Island social set, and it took the entire evening to unscramble a plot that was hard to find in the first place. The reader may well ask what had happened to those daring, innovative musicals that Larry and I were supposed to be dedicating our lives to create. The answer is that we didn't write our own stories. When Herb Fields wrote

*Dearest Enemy* or *Peggy-Ann* or *A Connecticut Yankee* we were right there with him, but by 1929 the only other trailblazing musical—and the one that towered over everything else during the decade—was Oscar Hammerstein and Jerome Kern's *Show Boat.* No other librettists besides Fields and Hammerstein seemed concerned with anything really fresh and imaginative, and Oscar certainly had no need of another lyricist for his scripts. Since Larry and I simply could not wait around for the odd chance that something novel and worthwhile would turn up, we had to accept the best offers we could get. Hence, *Spring Is Here.*

Back in January 1928, on the opening night of *She's My Baby,* I had met an imposing gentleman named Jules Glaenzer who had come backstage to congratulate Bea Lillie. Jules, who was the vice-president of Cartier's, not only loved the theatre but enjoyed even more giving parties for people in the theatre. It wasn't long before I became a member of what was known as the Glaenzer Party Set. Jules and his beautiful young wife, Kendall, had made their series of parties famous for bringing together social registrants, business tycoons and theatrical luminaries in an atmosphere of good talk and music. Though he was a wonderful host, Jules could at times be autocratic. Whenever one of his guests sang or played, he made such a point of there being absolute quiet that he became known around town as "Shush" Glaenzer. It's hard to believe that anyone would have to shush people while Gertrude Lawrence was being accompanied by George Gershwin, but the Glaenzers always made sure there was a steady flow of champagne, which had the unfortunate habit of loosening tongues at the wrong moments.

Jules and Kendall had a lovely house on the beach at Westhampton, and I was often invited there for weekends, as were other composers, including Gershwin. I'll never forget one August day when George sat down at the piano, a lean, swarthy, intense figure totally absorbed in his music, yet equally aware of his audience and the effect he was achieving. It was the first time I'd heard *An American in Paris,* and like everyone else I was captivated by the vividly evocative work. When I told George how much I admired it, he looked surprised and said, "I didn't know you were like that."

"Like what?"

"I didn't think you'd like anybody's music but your own."

Coming from anyone else, this remark would have been insulting, but George always said what was on his mind and expressed himself in such an innocent way that you knew no offense was intended. His appreciation of his own work was equally innocent. Once when we were both at a party near Westhampton, the orchestra played a new Gershwin number from a current show. When I told him that I thought it was a great tune, he simply replied, "Yes, isn't it?" Actually, it would have been impossible not to love all of Gershwin's music, and he had the added ability to perform his works at the piano in such a way that they always took on a special glow. No one could ever play a Gershwin tune like Gershwin himself, and I can still clearly recall those steely fingers racing through "Fascinating Rhythm" or lovingly caressing the notes to "The Man I Love."

One weekend when I was with a few friends at Jules's Westhampton place, Dick Hoyt, a member of the Glaenzer Party Set who lived nearby, invited us to fly back to New York on Sunday in his private seaplane so that we could all attend a party at the Glaenzers' apartment. This was early in 1929, when flying in any kind of a plane was a major adventure, and we were happy to accept.

Never having flown before, I felt tremendously stimulated by the flight. We landed in Port Washington Bay, and Dick had his car meet us and drive us to town. When I arrived at my parents' apartment, where I was still living, it was too early to dress for the party. Still keyed up by my aerial adventure, I did something I rarely do. I walked over to the piano and began improvising a melody, which to my surprise sounded good. Later I played the tune for Jules at the party. He became so enthusiastic that when Alex Aarons arrived he insisted I play it for him. When I finished, Alex leaned over, kissed me on the forehead and said, "This has got to be in our new show."

The next day Alex had me play the music for Vinton Freedley, and it almost caused the end of the Aarons and Freedley partnership. For reasons he never bothered to explain, Freedley simply didn't want the song in the show. I later was told that after I left, the two men fought furiously about it, but somehow Alex got his way and the tune was included in the score of *Spring Is Here*. Larry wrote one of his most affectingly ardent lyrics for it, and Lillian Taiz and John Hundley introduced "With a Song in My Heart."

Recalling the writing of "With a Song in My Heart" brings up a subject that is a touchy one to most people in the arts. I have always cringed at the word "inspiration." It is simply impossible to create something solely as a result of the stimulation of a single experience. I firmly believe that the single experience, whatever it is, becomes part of the totality of one's personality, and it is this personality that expresses itself through whatever medium the individual uses. My first plane ride did not inspire me to write "With a Song in My Heart," any more than a near traffic accident had inspired me to write "My Heart Stood Still." It is the excitement of the event combined with the excitement of having a job to do combined with one's background combined with one's talent that results in the song, painting or novel. I've never believed that after a man has an affair with a beautiful girl he is inspired, almost as a reflex action, to dash to the nearest piano, canvas or writing desk and pour out his emotions in a lasting work of art. The affair simply becomes part of the man's experience, which in turn helps form his personality.

In my own case, I found emotional stimulation in music when I was very young by listening to my mother play the piano. There was further excitement when my grandparents introduced me to opera, and going to the Broadway theatre was even more fascinating. But what compelled me to express myself through music was never a single stimulus; rather, it was a great number of them, combined with heredity, environment and a certain native ability. Later, increased activity and technical knowledge contributed to the proficiency I gained through the years.

One other element was also influential: the encouragement of people whose judgment and values were important to me. Because my parents loved theatre music and nurtured my love for it, I found myself going in that direction because of my desire for continued parental approval. This also gave me the impetus to work harder so that I might feel worthy of that approval.

Along with the popular misconception about "inspiration" is the concomitant one that anyone involved in the arts must be unbalanced, since creative work and logical behavior are somehow considered mutually exclusive. One evening at a dinner party a woman of apparent intelligence kept asking me questions about my working habits. As I described them I watched her expression change from skepticism to utter disbelief. It was incredible to her that I liked working in the morning because I felt fresh after a good night's sleep, or that two highballs made it impossible for me to work at all. I could see that she wasn't buying any of it, so I finally blurted out, "Look, I've been lying to you. I never get to work before two in the morning, I have to be blind drunk before I get any kind of idea, and on top of the piano I always place a small naked girl." I don't think she bought that line, either, because she suddenly stopped talking to me.

In 1927 Alex Aarons and Vinton Freedley had a theatre built for them on West Fifty-second Street which they called the Alvin, derived from the first syllable of each man's first name. Alex had a suite of offices on the top floor, and Vinton had his just below. Partly because of the argument over "With a Song in My Heart," I became much closer to Alex than to Vinton. Alex, whose father, Alfred Aarons, had been both a composer and a producer, was a bald, bespectacled man with a great fund of jokes and an enormous love for music. Almost every afternoon at five he made a ritual of meeting in his office for cocktails. Usually we were joined by Alfred Newman, the music director for all the Aarons and Freedley shows. Apart from being a fine musician, Al was a wonderfully warm and gregarious person, and for a time the three of us were almost inseparable. Actually, it was really six of us, since these five o'clock sessions were generally the prelude to dinner with Alex's wife, Ella, Alfred's wife, Beth, and my future wife, Dorothy.

Working on *Spring Is Here* was far more rewarding for the congeniality of the company than for any creative accomplishments of our run-of-the-mill show. Even the spotlighting of the brilliant duo-piano team of Vic Arden and Phil Ohman was a familiar attraction from the Aarons-and-Freedley Gershwin musicals that had gone before. Probably the only unusual aspect of the production was that we signed a Hollywood leading man for the starring role. Glenn Hunter was boyishly handsome and personable and had scored a success in a film called *Merton of the Movies*, but he did have one drawback as a musical-comedy actor that went undetected on the silent screen: he couldn't sing a note. Originally we had intended to give him the chief ballad, "With a Song in My Heart," but one rehearsal was enough to make us change our minds. After an emergency conference we decided to give the song to the vocally talented John Hundley, even though he played the role of the hero's rival. Glenn had only two numbers, one of which was "Yours Sincerely." The piece was created in the form of a letter set to music, and he recited the lyric with the orchestra carrying the melody.

When *Spring Is Here* arrived at the Alvin in March 1929, it was greeted by an enthusiastic press. To my surprise, it was pointed out that we had an amusing, if conventional, story, a youthfully energetic company, and a score that was variously described as "graceful," "tuneful," "beguiling," "lively" and "lovely." Once the notices were in, coupled with the appeal of our Hollywood star, we fully expected a lengthy run. But *Spring Is Here* ran only three months—which was all it really deserved.

Every year Jules and Kendall Glaenzer spent a number of months in Paris, where Jules attended to the affairs of Cartier's home office. Soon after *Spring Is Here* opened, they insisted that I join them in Paris for a party at which they would introduce me to their European friends. The fact that I agreed to cross the Atlantic just to go to one party gives a pretty good idea of the kind of life I was leading in those days. On arrival in Paris I rented a small apartment in the Hotel Astoria, an unassuming but charming hotel facing the Arc de Triomphe. The party itself, at Restaurant Laurent in the Champs Elysées gardens, was a posh affair, and the account in the Paris *Herald* was crowded with an eye-popping guest list, including members of both theatrical royalty and real royalty. The following day I set off for the Riviera for a few days in the April sun, and upon my return to Paris I threw a party for the Glaenzers at the Ritz with just about the same guests as the ones who had been at their party for me.

With my appetite for party going and party giving thoroughly sated, I sailed home on the *Olympic,* the same ship I had taken following the African adventure with my parents. The *Olympic* was my favorite ocean liner. I loved its paneled staterooms and its elegant Ritz restaurant, where passengers who did not wish to eat in the regular huge dining room could enjoy the finest French food, wine and service at any hour of the day. The ship made a fare reduction for those of us luxury lovers who dined at the Ritz, and we were billed separately.

In the summer of 1929 I came to a difficult decision. I was twenty-seven years old, financially independent and yet still living with my parents. They certainly weren't restrictive, nor did they interfere with my life in any way, but I felt strongly that the time had come for me to live alone. Just as Queen Victoria needed a room of her own, I needed a place of my own. Moving out was painful for all of us, but my mother and father never said a word against my leaving. Nevertheless, I knew that Mom in particular took it hard, since she had remained with her parents even after she was married; I'm sure she found it difficult to understand why anyone who was single would want to live independently. Now, for the first time in almost thirty-three years of married life, my parents would finally be alone.

The apartment I chose was on the nineteenth floor of the Hotel Lombardy on Fifty-sixth Street, between Lexington and Park avenues. It had three good-sized rooms and an enormous terrace. There was only one other apartment on the floor; it was similar to mine but facing in the opposite direction. I didn't find out who lived there until after I had moved in. One morning the hotel manager called me into his office to show me a letter he had received from the occupant, who turned out to be the novelist Edna Ferber. Miss Ferber, then spending the summer in Europe, voiced strong objection to the hotel's renting an apartment on *her* floor to a songwriter. She was sure there would be wild parties every night, to say nothing of my banging away at the piano all day. The manager confessed that he didn't know quite how to placate the lady and asked if I had any suggestions. Of course, the mere fact that he brought the matter to my attention may have been his way of warning me that now that I was living on the fashionable East Side I'd better learn to mend my debauched West Side ways. Still, I could understand his concern, and I calmly told him that all he had to do was to let me know the day before Miss Ferber was due back from her trip, and I was sure I could smooth all the lady's ruffled feathers.

When the day came, I had masses of flowers sent to Miss Ferber's apartment with a card reading "From your Nearest Neighbor." The following evening, just as I opened my door to go out, Miss Ferber opened hers and we met in the hallway. She was so overcome by my gesture that she threw her arms around me and told me how delighted she was to have me living next door. Then, to my amazement, she began berating me for not having bothered to get in touch with her when we had both been staying at the same hotel in Colorado Springs the previous year. My protestations that I did not know her at the time and that there was no one to introduce us made not the slightest impression. I suppose this was her way of telling me that she liked me, but I found it perplexing. Over the years I was to discover what a truly indecipherable woman Edna was—demanding, loving, funny, angry, generally impossible, but always a loyal and dear friend.

*Spring Is Here* may not have been good for more than one season, but Aarons and Freedley apparently liked our work well enough to sign Larry and me for their next musical. Called *Me for You,* it was also written by Owen Davis. The story was all about a wealthy roué, played by Victor Moore, whose daughter, Betty Starbuck, has no idea that her old man is a bootlegger. To keep Betty away from her boyfriend, district attorney John Hundley, Victor has his seagoing partner, Jack Whiting, become her legal guardian for a month, and everything gets straightened out when Betty and Jack fall in love.

At least this was the story we started with. The idea of dumpling-shaped, mild-mannered Victor Moore as a rumrunner seemed so incongruous, at least during rehearsals, that we all thought it a brilliant stroke of casting. When we reached Detroit for the first stop in our tryout tour, however, we quickly realized that all the clever dialogue and funny routines just weren't going over. It didn't take long for us to discover the flaw: audiences simply would not accept lovable Victor Moore in the unlovable role of a smuggler, nor did they care much for a story that ended with the heroine ditching a district attorney to marry a lawbreaker.

What to do? We had a score that the audiences seemed to like, a talented cast, and attractive scenery and costumes. Now, if this were a Hollywood backstage musical, the director would gather the cast and crew together and say, "Listen, kids. We've got lots of talent and some sure-fire numbers and some beautiful sets and costumes. All we have to do is change the story. So if we all work real hard, I know we'll have ourselves a great big smash." So everyone works real hard and they have themselves a great big smash. But real backstage life is not to be confused with the Hollywood version—except that in this case we did exactly what they would have done in the movies. The only trouble was that for reasons beyond our control, the show did not turn out to be a great big smash.

After two weeks in Detroit, Aarons and Freedley closed *Me for You* and we all returned to New York. But not before the producers had already hired two new librettists: Paul Gerard Smith, who had performed a similar salvaging operation on the Gershwin show *Funny Face,* and Jack McGowan, the co-author of *Hold Everything,* one of the previous year's biggest hits. Together, the two men worked frantically to fashion a story that would at least utilize whatever cast members, songs, sets and costumes we decided to keep. Now the story had Victor Moore playing a lovable cook who works aboard a yacht which, unbeknown to its owners, is being used for smuggling. Leading man Jack Whiting now became a more acceptable hero as a Coast Guard officer, and Betty Starbuck, while still in the show in a major comic role, was succeeded by Barbara Newberry in the romantic lead. We even found a spot for a skin-and-boneless dancer named Ray Bolger who had previously appeared only in one or two Broadway revues.

For some reason our revised musical was called *Heads Up!* when we opened in Philadelphia on October 25, 1929. Shortly thereafter we were faced with a problem that no amount of script changes could solve. On the day before the opening, Alex Aarons came charging down the aisle of the Shubert Theatre with the staggering news: "Boys, you can forget about the show. You can forget about everything. The bottom's just dropped out of the market!"

None of us was rich enough to be badly hurt by the Wall Street crash, but there was no question that until that fatal day everyone had been living through a period of unbelievable affluence. I remember a young elevator boy in my hotel telling me one afternoon, "Well, Mr. Rodgers, I did pretty well in the market today. I just made a thousand dollars." Overnight everything had changed, and like every other business, the theatre was going to be in for a long, painful period. It certainly was not the right time to open a large, expensive musical production, but after spending so much time and effort and money, there was no thought of turning back. Despite Alex's emotional outburst on the day of the crash, we were all victims of that compulsive attitude that makes the show the only thing that really matters. We simply could not allow our world to come to an end, no matter what was happening in the real world.

Despite the blanket of gloom that hung over the country, *Heads Up!* had a well-attended first night in Philadelphia, and our Broadway opening at the Alvin received a warm greeting from the audience. By and large the press was encouraging but we were all well aware that, particularly now, rave reviews were no harbingers of financial success. Surprisingly, the show didn't do badly and ended its run with 144 performances.

Two songs from *Heads Up!* still mean a good deal to me. One was "Why Do You Suppose?," an uptempo number with a lyric that had fun comparing the mating habits of animals and humans; the other was "A Ship without a Sail," which had an unusual construction, at least for 1929. I have already mentioned the fairly rigid "AABA" or "ABAB" thirty-two-bar form. For this ballad I divided the refrain into twelve-, eight- and twelve-bar sections, thereby achieving a mild breakthrough with an "ABA" form. It was still thirty-two bars, of course, and I don't suppose many people noticed it, but I enjoyed getting away even slightly from the accepted strictures of songwriting. When I first played the melody for Larry, he said it sounded like a barcarole. Since the show had a nautical setting, the idea of comparing one's lovesick emotions to a ship without a sail was a particularly felicitous notion and Larry developed it into one of his most beautifully crafted lyrics.

*Heads Up!* didn't do much for any of us, except possibly Messrs. Moore and Bolger. To give you some idea of what passed for humor in those days, I remember one line Victor had that always brought down the house. When the smugglers took over the yacht, one of them poked Victor in the ribs with his pistol and asked him if he knew what a mutiny was. "Oh, sure," piped Victor, "it's a show that they give in the afternoon."

Once the initial shock of the Wall Street crash began to wear off, most people confidently expected that conditions would soon begin to improve. President Herbert Hoover, that starched, well-meaning symbol of probity, reassured the country that business and industry would soon turn the corner, and of course we all wanted desperately to believe him. Indeed, at the close of 1929, Broadway could still offer a remarkably varied assortment of over forty plays and musicals to entertain or bore the public.

Many of us, however, were not convinced that prosperity was just around the corner. We knew that we were in a precarious business. Nobody *had* to go to the theatre. In the world of entertainment, it cost a great deal less to see a movie or a vaudeville show—and it cost nothing at all to stay home and listen to the radio. With the market continuing to slide at a rapid pace, we couldn't help but worry that our world was in danger of being destroyed.

Still, during this period of vain hopes and dire fears, Larry and I were incredibly lucky. No sooner had *Heads Up!* opened than we received two important offers in rapid succession. The first came from Charles B. Cochran, who was in New York for the opening of his imported London hit, Noël Coward's *Bitter Sweet,* which had been unveiled six nights before *Heads Up!* He told Larry and me that he had seen nothing on Broadway that he wanted to produce in London. What he did want was an original show with a score by Rodgers and Hart, but this time he thought it should be a book musical instead of a revue. Not an operetta like *Bitter Sweet* but something in a more contemporary vein, yet equally imaginative and pictorially appealing. If Larry and I could come up with an outline for a suitable story, he'd put a librettist to work on it right away.

*Bitter Sweet,* which was told in flashback by an elderly woman reliving her youth, was a great vehicle both for the American actress Peggy Wood, who originated the role in London, and for the British actress Evelyn Laye, who played it in New York. Cochran wanted our new show to provide an equally strong starring role for Jessie Matthews, that charming singer and dancer who had introduced "My Heart Stood Still" in *One Dam Thing After Another.* Since a musical requiring an actress to play both a young girl and an old woman had recently proved so successful, Larry and I hit upon a variation that we felt would be equally effective in revealing Jessie's talents. Our idea was that to gain publicity, a girl in her early twenties passes herself off as a woman in her sixties whose youth has been preserved through the science of modern cosmetics. Complications arise when the young man she loves balks at the prospect of marrying a woman more than twice his age. Because the girl is an aspiring actress as well, Cochran could also indulge in his penchant for elaborate spectacles that didn't have much to do with the story but did impress theatregoers. We called the show *Ever Green*.

Cochran had returned to London by the time we finished the outline; soon after we sent it to him, he wrote us that he thought it would work beautifully. There would, however, be a delay; because of the uncertain economic outlook and because he was already committed to produce Noël Coward's *Private Lives* early in 1930, he had decided to postpone *Ever Green* until the late spring.

If it hadn't been for this postponement, Larry and I would probably never have had anything to do with the second offer we received at about the same time. Understandably, the mere fact that the offer came from Florenz Ziegfeld would have elicited a firm "No, thanks" after our unhappy experience with *Betsy*. But in the closing days of 1929 it was not the time to refuse any reasonable proposal. I couldn't afford to wait for the stock market to recover or for Cochran to start work on the new show for one compelling reason: on December 7 I became engaged to Dorothy, and I knew that within months I would have to face many new responsibilities. Even before the crash, the theatre was a risky place in which to earn a living, and now I was planning to get married at the beginning of what could be a severe, prolonged depression.

Larry and I talked it over and agreed to do the show for Ziegfeld. Our enthusiasm for the venture, called *Simple Simon,* was stimulated almost exclusively by the fact that Ed Wynn was going to star in it, and we were both crazy about him. Ed was an original; there's never been a comic like him before, nor will there ever be again. He wore clownish costumes, made up silly puns, dreamed up zany inventions, and looked on the world with a wide-eyed, childlike innocence that made everything he did seem uproariously funny.

The first time we met Wynn was when we went to his apartment one evening to discuss ideas for the production. He lived on East End Avenue, and I remember that his son, Keenan, who was then about fourteen, was also at home. Basically a shy, retiring man, Ed overwhelmed us with his warmth and sympathetic understanding when we told him of our previous experience with Ziegfeld. We went home that night thoroughly convinced that no matter what our problems with Ziegfeld might be, Ed would be on our side.

And he was. But Ziegfeld was too much for Ed, who, as the co-author of the book with Guy Bolton, had enough problems of his own. Bolton was then the most prolific librettist on Broadway, but *Simple Simon* didn't win him any new laurels. It was little more than a tailor-made tale for the star, in which Wynn played a Coney Island newsstand owner who falls asleep and dreams about such Mother Goose characters as Cinderella, King Cole, Jack and Jill, and Snow White. The idea was as ridiculous then as it would be today, except that Ziegfeld's stage designer, Joseph Urban, turned the production into a spectacularly attractive show. And there was Ed Wynn. All he had to do was come out and say, in that comical lisp of his, "I love the woodth," and the audience would go wild.

Late in January 1930, after the Boston opening, Wynn came up with an idea for a musical scene in which he would accompany Lee Morse, one of the featured singers, but not on any ordinary piano. Ed designed it so that it could be mounted on wheels and he could ride it like a bicycle, with the girl sitting on top. This later became one of his standard routines. All that was required from Larry and me was a new song, which we wrote one afternoon at the Ritz-Carlton. Called "Ten Cents a Dance," it was rushed into rehearsal just as soon as the ink was dry.

The first evening the song was to be performed, Ziegfeld, in an unprecedented show of friendliness, invited me to sit with him in the audience. Wynn, the bicycle-piano and Lee Morse made their entrance and were greeted with applause. Everything would have been fine except that Miss Morse had had a few too many and couldn't remember either the words or the music. It was a distressing, dispiriting introduction for a new song, and Ziegfeld was so enraged that he fired Lee immediately. To replace her he hired a slim blond singer named Ruth Etting who had just closed on Broadway in Ruth Selwyn's short-lived *9:15 Revue*. Miss Etting had made a great impression in this show belting out Harold Arlen's first hit, "Get Happy," and we were sure she would be equally effective with our song. By now we had left Boston, and since there were no New York previews, the first opportunity Ruth had to sing the ballad before an audience was on opening night. She scored such a resounding hit that thereafter "Ten Cents a Dance" became her musical trademark.

Larry and I were particularly proud of this taxi-dancer's lament because it may have been the first show tune to express the emotions of a person caught up in one of the more unsavory areas of employment. Certainly it was influential in expanding the themes of torch songs beyond the "My Bill—My Man" threnodies that were concerned only with women being mistreated by their men. Later the same year, in fact, Cole Porter was emboldened to deal with the ultimate sordid profession in his bitter exhortation of a streetwalker called "Love for Sale."

Although Ziegfeld never faltered in his admiration for "Ten Cents a Dance," he was strangely hostile toward one of our other songs in *Simple Simon* and insisted that it be dropped. A few months later we added it to the score of the Cochran musical, *Ever Green,* and "Dancing on the Ceiling" easily became the most popular number in the show.

Ziegfeld scheduled *Simple Simon* to follow *Bitter Sweet* at his lavish Ziegfeld Theatre. I cannot recall the opening-night audience reaction, but in going through the press notices I find that the reviewers all loved Ed Wynn but were scathing in their appraisal of the libretto. "Dull," "cumbersome," "banal," "humorless" and "grim" were some of the terms used. The critics were also divided about the score; only one reviewer, Burns Mantle in the *News,* mentioned "Ten Cents a Dance," which he described as "particularly effective." It may come as a surprise that *Time* magazine called "I Still Believe in You" "one of the best tunes Rodgers and Hart ever wrote," and *Variety* proclaimed "Send for Me" the "hit number" of the show.

Of course this wasn't the first time that critics praised songs that were quickly forgotten, and virtually ignored the ones that later continued to be performed. Rereading reviews such as these makes it easy to scoff at the judgments of play reviewers. But critics are not seers. They simply react to what they are hearing for the first time, and their reactions vary just the way most people's do. Of all the elements they must comment on in reviewing a show, music is probably the one that most strongly resists interpretive appraisals. Music produces an emotional response, and it is little wonder that the terms used to describe it are often imprecise. Perhaps this is because most critics are not musicians—but for that matter, neither are most of the people in the audience. The difference is that the critics' views are in print and are likely to influence vast numbers of people. Because of this responsibility, in addition to the fact that there are usually over a dozen songs in a show, I have always thought that reviewers should have access to the entire score, either in the form of sheet music or records, before they cover a production. At least familiarity should give them a greater understanding of what has been written and why. I venture to say that my ear is at least as well trained as any theatre critic's; yet, unless the music is extremely simple and childlike, I wouldn't dare to pass judgment on a Broadway score on the basis of only one hearing. I don't think anyone can come away from a score after listening to it for the first time with a feeling much more specific than that the music is either good or bad. It is only after repeated listening that a person can appraise the individual songs with any degree of analytical judgment. Critics, however, are called upon not only to comment on music and lyrics after only one hearing, but also to make intelligent observations about every other area of the production. And of course they must never equivocate. Every time I read in a review that a score is weak or tuneless, I am amazed that a writer, after a single hearing, could make such a rash and damaging statement. I can never help wondering if such a judgment might not be entirely different if the critic had the opportunity to become familiar with a score before rendering his verdict, the way critics of "serious" music do.

Sometime following the opening of *Simple Simon,* and after displaying what I thought was admirable patience, I paid Ziegfeld a visit to ask him for the long-overdue royalties for the score. Upon telling the secretary that I wanted to see him, I was asked to wait in the outer office. So I waited— and waited. After an hour I began to get the idea that the Master knew very well why I was there and that he was counting on me to give up and leave. People kept going in and out of his office but I was prepared to stick it out if it took all night. I must have been there for about three hours when I suddenly recalled that Ziegfeld had a reputation for being terrified of an organization of theatre writers called the Dramatists Guild. Since Larry and I were members of the Guild, Ziegfeld had to sign what was known as a minimum basic agreement, and part of this agreement contained the clause that writers must report to the Guild if a producer failed to pay royalties on time. Once a producer was reported as being in arrears no other Guild writer—which meant virtually every writer in the theatre—could work for him until he paid up. It didn't even require any court action—simply a meeting of the Dramatists Guild Council to render its decision to act in behalf of the writer.

By now thoroughly fed up with Ziegfeld's waiting game, I told the secretary that I'd had enough and that her boss would next be hearing from the Dramatists Guild. The minute that message was relayed, the doors to Ziegfeld's office flew open and the producer came out with his arms outstretched and a broad smile pasted on his face. Without even the formality of asking me what I had come to see him about, he sent for his bookkeeper and told him to make out checks to Larry and me for whatever amount was owed us. If it hadn't been for that magic name, "Dramatists Guild," I don't think we would have collected a dime.

As mentioned earlier, my reason for taking on *Simple Simon* was chiefly motivated by the decision Dorothy and I had come to late in 1929. One evening while we were having dinner at Montmartre we found ourselves discussing our future together as if it were the most inevitable thing in the world. I don't think there was even a formal proposal. Suddenly the seriousness of what we were saying hit us, and without even finishing our dinner we went bounding out of the restaurant to Dorothy's house to break the news to her parents.

Parents always seem to have a strange way of knowing things like this even before they are told. As soon as we walked into the Feiners' apartment, and without our saying a word, Dorothy's mother dashed across the room to tell us how happy she was. Her father, never the most voluble member of the family, said little, but at least he didn't look unhappy. The following night there was a repetition of this mind-reading act when I went to see my parents, who were by now living at the Gotham Hotel. I no sooner had said, "I have some great news for you—" when Mom completed the thought, "You're engaged to Dorothy Feiner!"

With both pairs of parents apparently happy, the only problem arose over what kind of wedding to have. The Feiners wanted a large affair and I wanted a small one. So we compromised: there would be a small group at the ceremony—just the immediate families and close friends—which would take place at the Feiners' Park Avenue apartment, but there would also be a large engagement party to proclaim the coming event. It was held in the Ballroom of the Park Lane Hotel on Sunday, the twelfth of January, with Emil Coleman's orchestra providing the dance music.

The wedding itself took place on March 5. The service was performed by that impressively leonine man, Rabbi Stephen S. Wise, who had also married my mother and father, my brother and his wife, and Dorothy's brother and his wife. Morty was best man, and Larry Hart and Herb Fields were officially "ushers," though there really weren't enough people there for them to ush. While it's an old saying that all brides are beautiful, mine was the most beautiful of all, and in the past forty-five years I've never found any reason to change my mind.

Not wishing to spend our wedding night in a hotel, Dorothy and I boarded the S.S. *Roma*, bound for Italy. That night we had champagne and caviar all by ourselves in our stateroom, and then retired with the heady thought of how romantic it would be to awaken the next morning far out to sea. When we got up the next morning we found that we were still tied up at the North River dock. There had been some engine trouble and the ship didn't sail until midafternoon.

Naples was our first stop, just as it was on the first trip Larry and I had taken to Europe almost four years earlier. My return to the fabulous Bertolini's Palace Hotel was even more thrilling now that I had my bride with me. After a few days in Naples we took the night train down the Italian coast and across the Straits of Messina on the train ferry to Sicily, and proceeded to the ancient city of Taormina. The hotel we stayed in was a converted monastery and we slept in what had once been a monk's cell, but the awesome sight of the Mediterranean on one side and Mount Etna on the other was ample compensation.

From Sicily we took a ship to Cannes, where we stayed at the Carlton Hotel, all luxury, style and rich food. That's where I discovered that my wife loves to gamble. As for me, I simply have the wrong temperament. If I lose, I translate the loss into the cost of a pair of new shoes; if I win, I feel as though I were taking money that doesn't belong to me.

London, our last stop, gave me the opportunity of getting back to work. Charles Cochran was now ready to proceed with his production of *Ever Green,* and I had arranged with Larry, who was then traveling through Germany, to meet us in London. Since we would be working in the city, it seemed impractical to live in a hotel, but after looking at a number of service flats, including those in St. James's Street where Larry and I had previously stayed, I discovered that what had once seemed comfortable and attractive when I was a bachelor now looked dingy and cramped.

One of the friends I had made through Myrtle d'Erlanger on my last trip to London was Beatrice Guinness. At dinner one evening Beatrice told Dorothy that her daughter, Zita James, owned a house at 11 York Terrace, right on Regent's Park. Since Zita was then away on a prolonged trip, Beatrice was sure that she would be happy to rent us her house for as long as we liked.

Dorothy and I took one look at the place and promptly fell in love with it. It was a charming Regency-period town house, exquisitely furnished, with a lovely view of the park from the rear windows. There were even three sleep-in servants. But what really sold us was that Larry could move in with us and have the entire top floor to himself. It was a perfect arrangement: he would have his privacy and we would have ours.

Or so we thought. The first evening Larry was with us, we heard a persistent ringing of our front door bell after he had gone to his room. We opened the door to discover a strange woman frantically pointing to a stream of water flowing out of a drainpipe on the top floor. It didn't take long to discover what had happened: after turning on the water in his bathtub, Larry had promptly forgotten about it when he became absorbed in a book. Fortunately, no damage was done to Zita's lovely house.

Dorothy and I had expected to have our breakfast alone, but Larry was always in the dining room waiting for us. Then we discovered a tiny library and arranged to have breakfast served there. Still, Larry had no trouble finding us and invariably showed up in need of a shave, wearing a stained bathrobe and smoking a big, black, smelly cigar. But once I'd explained to him, as diplomatically as I could, that Dorothy and I preferred privacy at this time of day, Larry good-naturedly left us alone.

Dorothy had good reason for being especially sensitive at this time. After visiting a doctor whose name was—on my honor—Beckett Ovary, she received confirmation of what we both suspected: she was pregnant. At the beginning there were no unexpected ill effects and Dorothy's normal round of activities was completely unhindered. As for housekeeping, she had no problems once she mastered the intricacies of British currency and remembered, among other things, that a sweet was a dessert and a biscuit a cracker. Dorothy taught the cook to make coffee in the American way, and our English friends, who were used to the thin beverage that was always brewed a day before, loved to sample Dorothy Rodgers' special brand.

As I knew they would, Myrtle d'Erlanger and Dorothy took to each other immediately, and the entire d'Erlanger clan made sure that we were, quite literally, royally entertained. One evening at a large gathering at the home of Lord Louis and Lady Edwina Mountbatten, my host eased me over to the piano and asked me to play. Presently a slim young man came over and sat on the piano bench beside me. He surprised me by asking to hear such musical esoterica as opening chorus numbers and verses to obscure songs, and was even familiar with tunes I didn't know. I had no idea who he was, and expecting him to be a well-known composer whom I should have recognized, I was startled to be told later that my knowledgeable friend was the Duke of Kent. Obviously I was born to be chummy with the British royal family.

Benn Levy, who is best known today as the author of *Springtime for Henry,* was the librettist whom Charles Cochran had chosen to write *Ever Green.* As before, C.B. was a pleasure to work with, and Levy turned out to be a congenial and diligent collaborator. The only problem was that Cochran again found it necessary to postpone the show, this time until the fall. With the score almost completed and with no further reason to remain in London, Dorothy and I and Larry returned to New York.

Home for the newlywed Rodgerses was my apartment at the Lombardy, though it was not to be for long. Shortly before my marriage I had received a call from an executive at Warner Bros. offering an attractive contract for the services of Rodgers and Hart as movie songwriters. With the advent of "talkies," Hollywood had naturally discovered that the best way of showing off the marvels of film *and* sound was to specialize in stories that could not be made as silent movies. Which of course meant stories with songs. Since there were few songwriters then in Hollywood, the major studios went on the hunt for all the best-known Broadway and Tin Pan Alley writers they could find. What they offered was hard to refuse. They put people under contract for a specific number of years, gave them handsome salaries and comfortable offices, and in general provided the kind of security that could not be found in the theatre even during its most prosperous years.

Our arrangement with Warner's called for Larry and me to write the scores for three musical films. What made it especially attractive was that the agreement also included the services of Herb Fields as scriptwriter. Though we enjoyed working with other writers, up to this time Larry and I had never had the kind of theatrical successes or creative stimulation that we'd enjoyed with Herb. Now we were being offered a fresh opportunity for all three of us which, we hoped, might rekindle something of the spirit that had marked our early Broadway endeavors. Apart from *Fifty Million Frenchmen,* which Herb had written with Cole Porter, none of our recent musicals had done well. Maybe what we needed most was simply a change of scenery which might also help our work for the stage. And there surely could be no quarrel with the money. From every point of view except one, the Warner Bros. contract was highly attractive.

The exception was Dorothy. Her pregnancy was beginning to give her extreme discomfort and she did not feel well enough to travel to California. Though I had to go where my work took me, our leave-taking wasn't easy, both because of Dorothy's health and because it was the first time we'd be separated since our marriage.

After settling in at our hotel, Herb, Larry and I were driven to Burbank, where the studio was located and where we were to meet Jack Warner, the most prominent of the four brothers who owned the company. Warner, who was having lunch with his aides in the executive dining room, was a slim, dapper man who looked very much like a movie version of a gambling-casino owner. He gave us a flashing smile, and then proceeded to speak in the thickest Yiddish accent I'd ever heard. "I dun't van't none of your highbrow sunk-making," he warned us as his smile quickly vanished. "Music mit guts ve got to heff—sunks mit real sediment like the 'Stein Sunk' and 'Mit Tears in Mine Eyes I'm Dencink.' "

My God, I thought, could this really be the powerful Jack Warner? Then I noticed that the half-dozen or so men around the table all had their backs to us, and their sides and heads were shaking as if they were laughing uncontrollably. I realized that this was Warner's idea of a joke. Ever since the first self-made merchants and nickelodeon owners had gone West to organize film studios as movie-manufacturing plants, there had been a steady stream of gags about the illiterate immigrants who had created a new world of entertainment in and around Hollywood. Samuel Goldwyn and his celebrated Goldwynisms had become a universally accepted model of the breed, and Warner, apparently a bit self-conscious about the image, enjoyed assuming the caricature for the entertainment of his staff. I can't say I thought the routine exactly side-splitting, but from then on Jack and I got along fine. He furnished Larry and me with a luxurious office, and even made sure we had a secretary. No one gave us any idea what a lyricist and a composer were supposed to do with a secretary, and after a day or two we persuaded the studio to assign her to someone else.

Initially, the film that Herb, Larry and I worked on was to have starred Marilyn Miller, but for some reason the feminine lead went to Ona Munson, with Ben Lyon and Walter Pidgeon as her romantic rivals. The picture, *The Hot Heiress,* was so called because it was about a riveter (Lyon) who accidentally tosses a bolt into the boudoir of an heiress (Munson), and then falls in love with her when he arrives to put out the fire.

Though the story was puerile, we rather liked the idea that it used music not for spectacle, but naturally, as if the songs were part of the dialogue. However, *The Hot Heiress* was hardly a notable screen debut. We ended up with only three songs in the final print, and neither they nor the film created any stir.

I can't say that I learned much about moviemaking during this first visit to the West Coast, but I was fascinated by the process of putting a story, particularly a musical, on film. In those days, for example, there was no such thing as prerecording, and every time someone sang, the entire studio orchestra had to be on the set. What interested me most of all, however, was the work of the film editor, which, though unappreciated by the average moviegoer, is of enormous importance in determining the finished product.

One of the pleasantest aspects of this trip to Hollywood was not only that Dorothy eventually felt well enough to join me but that she even coaxed my parents into taking the trip with her. We all returned to New York in mid-August—and within a month I was forced to leave again. This time it was a call from C. B. Cochran. *Ever Green* was proceeding well, but Larry and I were needed in London for rehearsals. A transatlantic crossing was certainly not advisable for Dorothy, and once more I was forced to make a trip without her.

Saying good-bye to someone you love is always hard; saying good-bye to Dorothy at this time was extremely difficult. Her pregnancy was again causing her great distress, and I was leaving for a job that would keep me away for at least two months.

On shipboard Larry, as usual, kept himself occupied at the bar. I spent most of my time working on the piano manuscripts while sitting in a deck chair, since it would have been embarrassing to play the piano in a public room. This not only helped pass the time on a dull ocean trip, it also gave me more leisure once I arrived in London. But the problem was what to do with all that leisure. I was just plain miserable without Dorothy, and full of self-blame for doing the kind of work that would keep me away from home for such a long period. Under the circumstances there was little anyone could do to make me feel much better.

But many people tried. My mother and father came over for a visit, and my English friends helped enormously. The d'Erlangers and their group had all grown fond of Dorothy during our first trip, and their concern for her health was obviously so sincere that it helped ease the pain of our separation. Noël Coward again proved a loyal friend, and Cochran did everything he could to make me feel comfortable. Of course he was well aware that I was chafing to return home, but there was no way I could leave before the out-of-town opening. And that—in Glasgow—was still a month away!

In the meantime the Cochrans, who always seemed to know when I needed morale-boosting, took care of my weekends by inviting me to their summer home in Egham, an imposing mansion with heavy mid-Victorian furniture and glorious gardens and trees. The only trouble with the place was that there was just one bathtub and loo for everyone to fight over.

Cochran also showed extreme solicitude for my opinions on everything to do with the show, even including the costume designs. In fact, from the standpoint of mutual cooperation and admiration, I can't recall ever having worked under such pleasant circumstances.

One night after a rehearsal, C.B. took me to a prize fight which turned out to be one of the strangest events I've ever witnessed. The referee wore white tie and tails, and most of the audience was dressed formally. Except for an occasional muted cheer, the spectators sat in deadly silence, which made the sound of leather against flesh seem even more cruel. The whole evening had the unmistakable aura of the upper classes getting uninvolved pleasure from two members of the lower classes beating each other up, and it rather soured me on the British sporting scene.

Early in October I left for Glasgow alone to attend orchestra rehearsals, since, unlike in America, the Scottish orchestras rehearsed for days before a performance. The trip north was horrendous. It took ten bumpy, sleepless hours to get there, and once I arrived I had to endure a period of almost mind-numbing loneliness. During the day I could occupy my time with orchestra rehearsals, but at night there was nothing to do but have dinner alone, take in a movie or a show alone, return to a depressing hotel and be in bed by ten.

A week later the *Ever Green* company arrived. As the hotel was part of the railroad structure, it was necessary only to get a porter to carry the bags into the hotel through its rear lobby entrance, but for some reason Larry couldn't be convinced that the hotel was right at the station. After huffing and puffing at a cabdriver, he managed to get the confused man to load his luggage and drive him around the corner to the main entrance on the street.

The dress rehearsal of *Ever Green* went exceedingly well and proceeded to disprove one of the theatre's ancient saws that a good dress rehearsal means a poor opening-night performance. Cochran had assembled a truly sumptuous production, with colorful scenes depicting such locales as the Albert Hall in London, a *Folies-Bergère* type of revue in Paris, an elaborate street fair in Neuilly, and even a religious ceremony in Catalonia, Spain. What helped immeasurably was that our revolving stage, which was being used for the first time in Britain, worked without a hitch or even a sound.

Jessie Matthews scored exactly the kind of triumph Cochran had hoped for. Her naïve charm, gossamer dancing and liquid voice won praise, even adoration. It was *Ever Green* that led to Jessie's movie career, in which she reigned as the queen of British musicals.

Initially, however, everyone thought that Cochran was taking a chance with Jessie. The British public has always been loyal to its idols, and Jessie had recently tangled with Evelyn Laye, a long-time favorite, over the affection of Evelyn's husband, Sonnie Hale, which resulted in the breakup of the marriage. Jessie and Sonnie had subsequently married, and since he was playing the male lead in *Ever Green,* it was feared that loyalty to Evelyn might turn the public against Jessie. Fortunately, these fears proved unfounded.

Our songs were also well received. "Dancing on the Ceiling," rescued from *Simple Simon,* was performed by Jessie and Sonnie all around a huge inverted chandelier that rose from center stage like an incandescent metal tree. The song itself is worthy of some comment because its creation throws further light on the unusually close collaboration between Larry and me. I had composed the music first, and there was something about it that gave Larry the feeling of weightlessness and elevation. This in turn led to the original notion of a girl imagining that her distant lover is dancing above her on the ceiling. Note that in the first two bars—on the words "He dances overhead"—the notes ascend the scale in a straight line, then descend in the third, and then suddenly leap a seventh, from D to C on the words "(ceil)ing near," at the beginning of the fourth bar:

Because the song was written in the "AABA" form, these notes are repeated in the second and third "A" sections. This is particularly effective at the end, when the leap occurs on the words "a danc(ing floor)," and then, as a variation, rises even higher on "Just for," before unexpectedly dropping a seventh for the final words "my love."

Once *Ever Green* was successfully launched in Glasgow, there was no further need for me to remain with the show for its London opening. Knowing how desperately I wanted to be with Dorothy, Cochran told me I could leave for New York whenever I wanted to. The day after the tryout opening, I took the same bumpy train ride back to London and caught the next ship sailing for New York. By happy coincidence it was the *Majestic,* that lovable liner on which, more than four years before, Dorothy and I had first gotten to know each other.

On reaching home, I was determined to remain with Dorothy until the birth of our child. But Herb, Larry and I were still under contract to Warner Bros. for two more films. Had the contract not involved the two others, I would have tried to get out of it, or at least postpone it, but with no ties of their own, Herb and Larry were anxious to get started and I simply could not walk away from my obligation both to them and to the studio.

We had no idea of what we wanted to do, but when we discussed it with the Warner people in New York there was a certain amount of hemming and hawing, and they advised us to go to California to talk the matter over with Jack Warner. I had to go, but by this time I was thoroughly fed up with assignments that meant my constantly packing and unpacking a suitcase. Before I was married I'd had one show after another on Broadway; now that I had a wife at home there didn't seem to be any work for me nearer than three thousand miles in either direction.

As it turned out, this trip to the West Coast kept me away for a much shorter period than I had expected. Even before we had a chance to bring up the subject of the new movie, Jack Warner hit us with the news that musical films, which had been a major attraction for every studio during the past year, had suddenly become a glut on the market. No one wanted to see song-and-dance movies any more. Why there should have been such a turnabout has never really made sense to me, except that there were probably so many inferior productions that they created a negative reaction against *all* musicals. Whatever the reason, it was the condition that prevailed and there was nothing we could do about it; Warner simply wanted out. We hired a Los Angeles attorney to arrange a satisfactory financial settlement for the two canceled films, and returned to New York as quickly as we could.

During the subsequent weeks I really began to feel the effects of the Depression. For the first time in many years my telephone was not jangling with offers from producers to write new shows. As in the days when we first started, it was up to Larry and me to get together with a librettist and create a story and score that would interest a producer. Herb Fields was in the same situation, and it occurred to the three of us that a show built around the crazy world of Hollywood would make a timely and amusing musical. Based in part on our own recent experience, we slapped together a piece about two kids who go to Hollywood, where the girl becomes a silent-screen star. With the sound revolution, it's the boy who makes good while the girl, as happened so often in real life, proves unable to maintain her success when she is heard as well as seen. True love, of course, turns out to be the only remedy for the girl's bruised ego. While it was an ordinary plot, we did manage to avoid one stereotype: our studio mogul was an Irishman named Dolan. In tribute to Mary Pickford, who had nothing to do with the show, we called it *America's Sweetheart*.

Now to find a producer. By the end of 1930 some of the most highly respected men in the theatre were in serious financial difficulty and there was general retrenchment all down the line. Even though Alex Aarons and Vinton Freedley had a big success with *Girl Crazy,* they were unwilling to take a chance on another musical in the same season. Lew Fields, who had a flop with *The Vanderbilt Revue,* vowed he'd never do another Broadway show—and he never did. Dillingham had been hit hard by the crash and was in virtual retirement. Theresa Helburn and Lawrence Langner of the Theatre Guild, who had just sponsored another *Garrick Gaieties* (without Rodgers and Hart), didn't think our new musical was for them. Billy Rose was just beginning his career as a Broadway showman, but he was almost as much of a credit risk as Ziegfeld—and we sure as hell weren't going to go back to Ziegfeld.

Fortunately the Broadway reunion of Fields, Rodgers and Hart did have enough appeal to win the support of one prominent producing team, Laurence Schwab and Frank Mandel. I had known both men for a long time, though we had never before been associated in a theatrical production.

Schwab, in fact, was the man who had first taken me to see Max Dreyfus on that miserable occasion when the publisher told me that my music had no value. Since then they had had considerable success, primarily with romantic Sigmund Romberg–Oscar Hammerstein operettas *(The Desert Song, The New Moon)* and breezy, modern musical comedies *(Good News, Follow Thru)* by the Bud De Sylva, Lew Brown and Ray Henderson team. They were both thorough men of the theatre who could write as well as produce (Mandel was co-author of *No, No, Nanette*), and though shrewd, careful businessmen, were extremely likable and easy to work with.

At the recommendation of Herb Fields, the producers signed a bearded, sharp-tongued director named Monty Woolley who had previously worked with Herb on two Cole Porter musicals. For the male lead there was unanimous agreement that the part was ideal for smiling Jack Whiting, Broadway's most popular juvenile, who had been in *She's My Baby* and our last musical, *Heads Up!* For the female lead we auditioned a number of actresses and then settled on a tiny, round-faced blonde with an oddly appealing nasal voice. Her name was then Harriette Lake, but by the time she emulated the show's heroine and went to Hollywood herself she had become known as Ann Sothern.

In the midst of rehearsals—on January 11, 1931—Dorothy gave birth to our first child at Lenox Hill Hospital. The obstetrician was my brother, Mortimer. Mary was a healthy, lively, generally happy baby, and naturally the brightest and prettiest little girl two nutty parents ever clucked over.

I was spared some of the more disagreeable chores of early parenthood because eight days after Mary was born I was off to Pittsburgh for the first stop in *America's Sweetheart*'s tryout tour. The reception was encouraging, and after a week we opened at the National Theatre in Washington.

In the score of *America's Sweetheart,* Larry and I had a song that was one of the few we wrote which made a passing reference to the country's economic condition. It was called "I've Got Five Dollars," and in it, a marriage proposal takes the form of an offer of, besides five dollars, such itemized possessions as six shirts and collars and a heart that hollers. The mood was jaunty and optimistic, and the use of repetitive note patterns helped convey the desired effect of a light-hearted inventory.

*America's Sweetheart* opened in New York in February, but received little help from a divided press, with comments ranging from "sounds like discarded cues from *Once in a Lifetime* set to music" (John Anderson, *Journal*) to "New York will clasp it to its bosom until we get back our light wine and beer" (Robert Coleman, *Mirror*). I'm not sure about that bosom-clasping but we did last the season, which in 1931 was all that anyone could reasonably expect.

Larry and I were happy to be back on Broadway after a full year's absence, but it didn't take long before the exhilaration of opening night disappeared. Having a musical on Broadway and even having a creditable run were not enough. We had to start planning our next production as soon as possible. At first we hoped to continue the newly reactivated Fields, Rodgers and Hart trio, but Herb soon got an offer to write Hollywood scripts. Larry and I tried batting story ideas around, but nothing seemed to work. Even if we did come up with something that we thought promising, there was always the problem of finding a solvent producer. Still, with Hollywood closed to us, we had no other alternative but to try to keep active and hope that something would turn up.

What did turn up was totally unexpected. During these doldrum days for song-and-dance movies, one screen entertainer, the irresistibly exuberant French singer Maurice Chevalier, had managed to appear in a succession of hit musicals. Chevalier's movies were gay, bubbly confections, usually set in Europe and directed by that master of continental comedy, Ernst Lubitsch. They succeeded when others failed, I suppose, because they were concerned with glamorous people in glamorous locales far from the troubled shores of the United States, because they offered moviegoers something a bit spicier than the ordinary domestic product—and because they had Chevalier. And just how did Rodgers and Hart fit into all this? We were the songwriters Paramount wanted for the next Maurice Chevalier picture.

## 12

L/arry and I went to Hollywood with a contract for one picture and stayed for two and a half years. My second experience in the film capital started out brightly enough—*Love Me Tonight* is still considered to be among the most imaginative screen musicals ever made—and I derived a certain amount of satisfaction from one or two other assignments. But two and a half years? What on earth could have compelled me to devote so long a period of time to what was, for the most part, the most unproductive period of my professional life?

I could give many valid reasons why I did not head for home as soon as it became apparent that Hollywood and Rodgers were not made for each other. There was my fascination with film technique, coupled with my feeling that I could make a genuine contribution to the medium. There was the appeal of the sunbaked, affluent life that I found all around me. There was the attraction of parties and social affairs where Dorothy and I enjoyed meeting the idols, moguls and other fawned-over fauna of the area. There was the benefit of bringing up a child in a healthier atmosphere than a crowded, dirty city.

But I would gladly have chucked it all had it not been for the strongest of all chains that bind a man to a life he finds unrewarding: money. The Depression didn't last just a year or two, it lasted almost an entire decade, and the years from 1931 to 1935 were the hardest of all. A man with a family to support, particularly given the ephemeral nature of my profession, had to acknowledge the financial importance of a contract with a major studio. The arrival of a substantial weekly pay check can go a long way in assuaging dissatisfaction with working conditions—or the lack of working conditions.

Moreover, during this period the New York stage was hard hit by the country's economic woes, so whenever I began longing for the sweet misery of sweating over a bar of music at two in the morning during a hectic rehearsal in New Haven, I consoled myself by rationalizing that Broadway had had it and that the screen was not only the most popular but also the most challenging and exciting form of entertainment in the world.

At first I didn't have to do any such rationalizing. It really looked as if I had made the right decision in going West when I did. If a film of the quality of *Love Me Tonight,* I reasoned, could be created when screen musicals were in disfavor, surely when they regained popularity Rodgers and Hart would be in the vanguard. But it didn't turn out that way. Ironically, the resurgence of film musicals that began in 1933—sparked by the Busby Berkeley extravaganzas and later by the Astaire-Rogers pictures

—had almost the reverse effect on the career of Rodgers and Hart. When no one else was making musicals, we worked on one of the screen's most highly praised achievements. When everyone else was making musicals, we had a contract but no work.

When Larry, Dorothy, Mary and I arrived in Hollywood in November 1931, the director assigned to *Love Me Tonight* was George Cukor. He seemed an excellent choice, since he had worked with Ernst Lubitsch on the previous Chevalier-MacDonald film, *One Hour with You.* A week later Larry and I were surprised to learn that Cukor was out and that Rouben Mamoulian had been tapped to succeed him. Mamoulian did not seem as good a choice. A Chevalier picture needed a deft, delicate touch, and on the basis of such melodramatic offerings as *Applause* and *Dr. Jekyll and Mr. Hyde,* Mamoulian didn't appear to have this attribute. As soon as we met him, however, Larry and I quickly realized that there could be no better director for *Love Me Tonight.*

Owlish, with a thick crop of black hair and an exuberant manner, Mamoulian had a concept of filming that was almost exactly what we had in mind. Like us, he was convinced that a musical film should be created in musical terms—that dialogue, song and scoring should all be integrated as closely as possible so that the final product would have a unity of style and design. Fortunately, he was the producer as well as director of the film and had complete autonomy. One of the first things he insisted on was that I compose all the background music, not simply the music for the songs. This was—and still is—highly unusual, since film scoring has generally been left to composers specializing in the field. It is more or less stop-watch composing, with the writer creating musical themes to fit precisely into a prescribed number of frames. I had no background in this sort of work but I found it extremely challenging and fun to do, and it certainly helped in giving the film the desired creative unity.

One sequence I was particularly proud of was the scoring for the deer hunt. In it, I had to create two contrasting and intercutting themes, one— on the brass—for the pursuing dogs and horses, the other—on the strings —for the frightened deer. Mamoulian staged the entire sequence as if it were a zoological ballet.

Primarily, however, *Love Me Tonight* gave Larry and me the opportunity to work with one essential tool of the musical film that heretofore had not been properly utilized: the camera. In almost every musical, the camera would be set up, a boy and girl would be stuck in front of it, and it would photograph them while they sang or danced. It was all done within the limits of one prescribed locale. What we had in mind was not only moving the camera and the performers, but having the entire *scene* move.

There was no reason why a musical sequence could not be used like dialogue and be performed uninterrupted while the action took the story to whatever locations the director wanted. Mamoulian loved the idea, and fortunately the script for *Love Me Tonight* provided us with the perfect situation in which to try it out.

Early in the picture there is a scene in Paris in the tailor shop owned by Maurice Chevalier. He has just made a morning suit for a portly bridegroom-to-be, and in expressing their mutual delight at the results, the two men are no longer able to contain their emotions in ordinary dialogue but break into rhyming dialogue:

MAURICE:   The tailor's art/ For your sweetheart.
CUSTOMER:   That's like poetry in a book./ How beautiful I look.
MAURICE:   The love song of the needle/ United with the thread,
        The romance of the scissors . . .
CUSTOMER:   So Claire and I could wed.

With the musical mood established in rhyme, Maurice exclaims, "Isn't it romantic?," and suddenly the music takes over. Following the verse ("My face is glowing, I'm energetic,/ The art of sewing I find poetic"), the refrain finds Maurice anticipating marriage to an adoring and subservient wife who will scrub both the floor and his back, cook him onion soup and provide him with a huge family. (Incidentally, the lyric in the film is different from the one Larry later wrote for the commercial version.)

Once Maurice has finished the song, the music is picked up by the customer, who expresses admiration for the "very catchy strain." Still humming and singing, he bids Maurice good-bye and jauntily walks down the street. A passing taxi driver hears him and begins whistling the tune, which in turn is repeated by his fare. The fare turns out to be a composer on his way to the railroad station who starts writing down the music, singing each note as he goes along. With no break in musical continuity, the scene cuts quickly to the interior of a railroad car, where the composer is now busily putting words to the music. The song is overheard by a group of French soldiers who, in another abrupt change of scene, now sing the piece in march tempo as they hike through the countryside. Suddenly the camera pans away from the soldiers to a gypsy boy who is listening intently. He dashes back to his camp and plays the theme, now oozing with romantic passion, on his violin. By this time night has fallen, and in a long shot we see a nearby château with a single lighted room. The camera dollies in, and there is Jeanette MacDonald, as a lovesick princess, looking wistful on a balcony. Now it is her turn to be affected by the music she hears coming from the gypsy camp, and she expresses her longing for an unknown prince in armor who will kiss her hand, bend his knee and be her slave.

Thus, from a tailor shop in Paris to the sidewalk, to a taxi, to a railroad car, to a country road, to a gypsy camp, and finally to a château far from the city, one song is used to provide the romantic link between hero and heroine, even though they are miles apart and have never met.

Another effective sequence in the film was the opening, which in quick, dramatic shots establishes the sights and sounds of an awakening Paris, all orchestrated—without an orchestra—into a steadily accelerated rhythmic pattern. This was entirely Rouben's idea; in fact, he had already used it in a different setting for the 1927 play *Porgy* (later to become the Gershwin opera, *Porgy and Bess*). Just as he had previously coordinated the early-morning Catfish Row activities, now Rouben coordinated a succession and accumulation of activities in a Paris neighborhood—workmen digging up the street, a baby crying, a woman sweeping her steps, men grinding knives, shopkeepers opening their stores, auto horns honking, whistles tooting, smoke belching out of chimneys. Every shot and sound is synchronized until the orchestra, at first almost imperceptibly, takes over for Chevalier's first song, "That's the Song of Paree." Is there any wonder that Larry and I were stimulated by a man as brilliant as Mamoulian?

Actually, our story really wasn't much—merely a satirical variation on the Cinderella and Sleeping Beauty themes—but it was perfectly suited for a variety of dramatic, comic and musical innovations. In fact, many of the techniques we used—particularly moving from one location to another during one song, and the quick cutting and undercutting of scenes—are still very much a part of moviemaking today.

Though Larry and I were primarily concerned with the cinematic quality of the score, we did not forget that having Maurice Chevalier introduce our songs would help them enormously in winning popularity. Indeed, Chevalier had already done so well in immortalizing the charms of such ladies as Valentine and Louise that we decided to write a perky little piece for him about a girl named Mimi (somehow the film's dialogue made it apply to Princess Jeanette). We also wrote four other songs that we felt confident were just right for the Chevalier delivery: a romantic title song, which both Maurice and Jeanette were to sing as solos but which, thanks to a split screen, would be made to appear as a duet; a dramatic number about life as an Apache; "Isn't It Romantic?"; and "That's the Song of Paree."

One memory that will always be with me was of the day Larry and I performed our songs for Chevalier. Unlike the luxurious office we had at Warner Bros. when we were toiling over *The Hot Heiress*, Paramount had assigned us to a cell-like cubicle on the first floor of one of their buildings. It couldn't be dignified by being called an office; if we went over to the tiny window and stuck our noses right up against the glass, we could see a patch of about six inches of sky. One day we heard a knock on the door, and there, with eyes twinkling and teeth gleaming, stood Maurice Chevalier. Everything he wore was blue—blue jacket, blue sport shirt, blue scarf, blue slacks, blue shoes—which accentuated the incredible blueness of his eyes. He greeted Larry and me as if we were old friends, told us how happy he was that we were writing the songs for his picture, and asked if we would mind playing some of them. With Chevalier practically sitting on my lap in our cramped quarters, I played the music and Larry and I took turns singing the words. Chevalier sat silent throughout, his usually expressive face without a trace of either approval or disapproval, and when we'd finished he simply rose and left without saying a word. We were stunned. The only conclusion we could reach was that he didn't like what he'd heard. Now what? Should we start all over again? Would the studio replace us with another team? And what about our reputation once it got around that Chevalier, the screen's leading musical star, had turned thumbs down?

The next morning we tried to sneak into our little room without anyone seeing us; we were certain that word of Chevalier's displeasure had already spread and that it was only a matter of time before we'd be called into the front office to be dismissed. We couldn't do any work; we simply stared at each other and at the walls like prisoners in Death Row, a feeling heightened by the cell-like atmosphere of the room. After a couple of hours the door burst open and there again stood our smiling blue boy. "Boys," Chevalier said, throwing one arm around Larry and the other around me, "I just had to come back to tell you. I couldn't sleep a wink last night because I was so excited about your wonderful songs!" *He* couldn't sleep a wink last night! Why he couldn't have told us the day before I'll never know, but suddenly the weight was lifted from our shoulders, and it was a tough job for Larry and me to conceal our feeling of relief.

Maurice and I became friends and saw quite a bit of each other socially during my stay in Hollywood. His personality was very much what it was on the screen—warm, ebullient, full of vitality. Though extremely gregarious, he was not a quick man with a dollar, which was probably a result of his poverty-stricken youth; in fact, he was the only man I've ever met who would accept a cigarette and put it in his pocket.

Jeanette MacDonald, whom I had known slightly when she was a Broadway ingénue during the twenties, had already attracted notice as Chevalier's leading lady in two films. In *Love Me Tonight* she had a song, "Lover," which, though treated as a joke and never reprised, somehow managed to catch on. Jeanette sang it in an outdoors scene while riding in a horse-drawn cart. Still yearning for an unknown lover, our lonely princess sings the romantic lyric with sincerity, except that certain words and phrases are directed to her occasionally frisky horse. As, for example:

> Lover, when you find me
> Will you blind me with your glow?
> Make me cast behind me all my—WHOA!
> Kiss me, hear me saying
> Gently swaying I'll obey
> Like two lovers playing in the—HEY!

Not many people know that Jeanette was an accomplished horsewoman, and that she insisted on doing all her own riding in the film. In the finale she was called upon to ride a horse fast enough to overtake a rapidly moving train, jump off the horse and force the oncoming locomotive to come to a halt by standing defiantly on the tracks. Our cameras were set up on a train running parallel to the one being filmed, and Jeanette had to race furiously between them. It's hard to understand why the studio allowed her to take such a risk, but she managed to get her way. It was not for nothing that she was called the Iron Butterfly.

The most lasting friendship I made during *Love Me Tonight* was with Myrna Loy, one of the most charming, witty and perceptive women I have ever known. Before getting the part of the man-hungry countess in *Love Me Tonight,* Myrna had been cast almost exclusively as an Oriental vamp, and this film gave her the first opportunity to show her rare gift for comedy. She had the best line in the picture. After the frail Princess Jeanette has fainted, someone rushes up to Myrna and asks, "Can you go for a doctor?" "Certainly," she answers, batting her large almond-shaped eyes. "Bring him right in."

*Love Me Tonight* served to establish Larry and me as a motion-picture team very much in the same way that *The Garrick Gaieties* had established us on the stage. It proved that a movie musical produced at a time when everyone was certain there was no market for it could be both artistically and commercially successful. It even supplied us with a bonus: "Lover," "Isn't It Romantic?" and "Mimi" became Rodgers and Hart's first song hits to emanate from Hollywood.

Unfortunately, things began going downhill almost immediately thereafter. Paramount was impressed enough with our work not only to offer us a contract for a second film but also to provide us with an outward symbol of our new eminence—a luxuriously appointed office to work in. On paper, our next screen assignment, *The Phantom President,* seemed like a welcome change of pace. It was to be a satirical musical concerned with political skullduggery during a presidential campaign, with the leading role to be played by Broadway's legendary Yankee Doodle–Song-and-Dance man, George M. Cohan.

Larry and I had never met Cohan. Though as a composer he was hardly up there with the Kerns, Berlins or Gershwins, I did admire the infectious vitality of his songs, and I had great regard for him as an actor. No matter how simple-minded or corny his shows were, he never failed to give a highly skilled, even subtle performance.

But the times had almost passed Cohan by, and he was in semiretirement when he signed the contract with Paramount for what was to be his first screen role. I'd heard that he had been promised the opportunity of doing some of the writing on the film, but a change in the studio hierarchy ended whatever verbal agreement might have been made. At any rate, neither Larry nor I had been directly informed about this, though we were aware that we had the questionable distinction of being the first lyricist and composer other than George M. Cohan himself to write songs for him.

This, coupled with the fact that Cohan seemed to feel that the studio did not treat him with the deference that was his due, produced tension right from the start. There was never anything overt, simply a curtness and a disdain that he displayed not only to us but also, with rare equanimity, to everyone who had anything to do with the picture. One just knew that he felt he could direct better than the director, write a script better than the scriptwriters, and write music and lyrics better than Rodgers and Hart. During the shooting he never remained on the set when he wasn't required in front of the cameras, but always returned directly to the seclusion of his dressing room. I don't recall that he ever deigned to grant interviews, sign autographs or speak a civil word to anyone. It was obvious that he felt miserable about making the picture and he wanted us all to know it. (After the film was completed, he did let off steam in a newspaper interview. "If I had my choice," he said, "between Hollywood and Atlanta, I'd take Leavenworth.")

Probably because of the frigid atmosphere on the set, I don't remember much about the making of *The Phantom President.* I do recall that Claudette Colbert was in it, and so was Jimmy Durante—who never called me anything but "Roger." I also know that, like *Love Me Tonight,* the picture offered Larry and me opportunities to work out our concepts about incorporating songs within the action of the story. Our most ambitious number was the presidential convention in which the entire session—including speeches by candidate Cohan and sidekick Durante, as well as the reactions of the delegates—was all set to music. We tried getting away from the usual treatment of a love song by having a trio of twittering birds sing the ballad "Give Her a Kiss" to the timid Cohan while he is sitting next to Claudette in an open-top automobile.

*The Phantom President* was made early in 1932 and released just in time for the Roosevelt-Hoover election campaign. I think even Hoover was more popular than the film.

A month or so after finishing work on the Cohan picture, Dorothy and I were hit with a tragedy from which it took us both a long time to recover. Soon after moving into a furnished house on North Elm Drive, we were told that Dorothy was to have a second child. This was joyous news because it meant that Mary would have a companion near her age at a time when she most needed one. Suddenly, almost at full term, Dorothy began having a series of premature contractions. Late one night she was rushed to Cedars of Lebanon Hospital, where the baby, a girl, was born but lived only a few minutes. I had never before realized how traumatic such an experience is. Dorothy was physically depleted and emotionally drained.

With two movies released at about the same time and one of them a success, Larry and I could sift through a number of offers before deciding on our next project. In dealing with a presidential election, no matter how outlandish, *The Phantom President* had given us the opportunity to handle a contemporary theme. For *Hallelujah, I'm a Bum*, the picture we were asked to do next, the theme was equally contemporary but far more daring. It was the first and probably the last musical ever made in Hollywood that concerned itself almost entirely with the problems of the Depression. During those years so many people lost their jobs, money and homes that they were forced to live wherever they could find a few yards of vacant ground. In our picture we focused on bums living in Central Park, with Al Jolson playing the part of Bumper, their leader, Harry Langdon playing Egghead, a radical who calls the police "Hoover's Cossacks," and Frank Morgan as a Jimmy Walkerish mayor who is always at least two hours late for appointments and who spends most of his time at the Park Casino. We tried to keep the score relatively light, but we were defeated by the theme. The subject of homelessness at a time when it was such an urgent national problem didn't strike many people as something to laugh and sing about.

*Hallelujah, I'm a Bum* was produced by Joseph Schenck at United Artists, with Lewis Milestone directing. Milestone, who had already handled such grim epics as *All Quiet on the Western Front* and *Hell's Angels,* was a highly imaginative director who shared with Mamoulian an abiding hatred of doing the same kind of movie twice.

Most of the shooting of the Central Park sequences took place at the Riviera Country Club, in Pacific Palisades. One of the unusual aspects of the filming, since there still was no technique for dubbing of music, was that a large orchestra, conducted by my old friend Alfred Newman, was ensconced right on the golf course so that the songs could be performed in their proper exterior setting. At that time, probably as a convenience to studio orchestras and to save money, the conventional method was to shoot all exterior musical sequences indoors and try to make them look as if they were being performed outdoors.

*Hallelujah, I'm a Bum* gave us the opportunity to expand on the innovation, already tried out in *Love Me Tonight* and *The Phantom President,* of what was then called rhythmic dialogue, though a better term might be "musical dialogue." We simply used rhymed conversation, with musical accompaniment, to affect a smoother transition to actual song and to give the entire film a firmer musical structure. It was similar to recitative in opera, except that it was done in rhythm and was an authentic part of the action.

In one scene Jolson and his buddies, street cleaner Harry Langdon and hobo Edgar Connor, are walking through the park when they hear the insistent sound of a clock ticking (which is actually performed by the orchestra). They discover the clock attached to a lady's handbag in Langdon's sanitation bin and comment on it:

> CONNOR:  Tick tick tick
>     That sure am slick
> JOLSON:  Not so quick
> CONNOR:  Tick tick tick
> LANGDON:  What's that thing?
> JOLSON:  It's a lady's bag
> LANGDON:  The aristocratic rag
>     Of a plutocratic hag . . .

When they examine the contents of the bag, Jolson finds a letter addressed to the owner—which, being in rhyme, conveniently lends itself to song. Suddenly the dialogue and the tick-tick-tick music become more agitated as the three argue about what to do with a thousand-dollar bill they also find in the bag. This leads directly into the number "Bumper Found a Grand," in march tempo, in which the news is conveyed from one tramp to another as they all try to get cut in on the money. Jolson ends the scene by addressing the crowd ("Friends, rummies, countrymen") and extolling the virtues of poverty in the song "What Do You Want with Money?"

Unlike our experience with Cohan on *The Phantom President,* Larry and I found working on *Hallelujah, I'm a Bum* almost as exciting as *Love Me Tonight.* Jolson, who I had been told might prove difficult, turned out to be a sweet man who at the time was undergoing one of his frequent estrangements from his wife, Ruby Keeler. He was completely cooperative, though it often took a little patience to corner him to get down to business.

During part of the time I worked on the picture Dorothy was back in New York visiting her parents. A letter I wrote to her in October 1932 gives an account of an unusually nerve-racking day:

> Today was one of those mad ones that made me satisfied that you were away. It started with writing, manuscripts to be done, conferences about rehearsals, orchestrations, and everything else. I had half an hour for dinner, alone, at the Derby, and then back to a rehearsal. Jolson wouldn't work because he wanted to go to the fights. I agreed to go with him if he'd promise to work with me later. So to the fights we went (terrible ones) and then to his apartment where I rehearsed him for an hour. Then to meet the boys at Milestone's house to hear the final dialogue scenes, then home. It's two a.m. and I'm pooped . . .

Late in the year Larry and I got a call from Irving Thalberg, the young production head at Metro-Goldwyn-Mayer, who offered us not only a contract but a choice of assignments. He had been greatly impressed with what we had achieved in *Love Me Tonight* and was sure that either one of two stories his studio owned could be adapted with equally effective results. One was a then popular comic novel that we would work on with its author, Thorne Smith; the other was a Hungarian play about a banker whose wish comes true when he marries an angel. Larry and I thought the Hungarian fantasy had greater screen possibilities, and with everyone's blessing we went to work with a young writer named Moss Hart who had been assigned to do the screenplay. Moss, no relation to Larry, was the co-author of a successful Broadway play, *Once in a Lifetime,* in which he had ridiculed the sham, pretensions and frustrations of Hollywood. Our experiences with *I Married an Angel,* the name of our fantasy, could easily have provided him with enough material for a whole new play.

Moss was an intense, almost Mephistophelian-looking fellow, fairly bursting with ideas. The three of us worked closely, and within a month or so completed the entire story and score. Louis B. Mayer, who was Thalberg's boss, had intended the picture as a vehicle for his newest contract star, Jeanette MacDonald, and had even lured her to sign with the studio because of his enthusiasm for the project. But when we were all finished and everything was set to roll, Mayer called God into conference and issued a royal decree: fantasies were uncommercial and he was canceling the production. The fact that he had approved the studio's purchase of the story, signed Jeanette MacDonald on the basis of her doing it and had nothing but praise for our treatment made not the slightest difference. No one could budge him, and that was the end of it.

Well, not exactly. Years later we did make *I Married an Angel* as a Broadway musical, and years after *that* M-G-M decided it would be just the thing for Nelson Eddy and—yes, indeed—Jeanette MacDonald. Thus, Larry and I ended up in the curious but happy position of being paid for the same material three times: as a movie that was never filmed, as a stage musical, and as a movie that was filmed but—from what I've heard about it—never should have been.

After working on the first *I Married an Angel,* however, we had no thought of any future monetary rewards. We had wasted our time, and it was back to the bars for Larry and back to the tennis courts for me. Moss was smarter than either of us; he returned to Broadway, where he and Irving Berlin put together a show called *As Thousands Cheer* that was one of the great revues of the decade.

My disappointment was somewhat mitigated by an event that occurred in Washington at about the same time: the beginning of the Presidency of Franklin D. Roosevelt. FDR's decisive defeat of President Hoover in the 1932 election had been a stimulant for the entire Depression-weary country. With confidence exuding from his voice, his jutting jaw, the tilt of his cigarette holder, his bright, piercing eyes, he became so much the physical embodiment of the nation's longing for optimism that it was easy to ignore the fact that he was unable to walk without crutches.

From the very start of his presidency, Roosevelt churned up and turned out a dizzying succession of ideas, programs and laws. One of the first things he did after he had taken office in March was to declare a Bank Holiday in order to stop the alarming number of bank failures. During the week-long period while the government established laws to control banking, everyone had to live on whatever cash he had on hand. Ever since moving to California, a year and a half before, I had been sending my folks a weekly check because Pop was then in virtual retirement. As soon as the Bank Holiday was declared, my father telephoned me. To my amazement, he told me that he had dutifully cashed the checks I had been sending but had never spent any of the money. Instead, he simply put the bills in a safe-deposit box, and since he was sure I could use some cash he would wire me the money. Because of Pop's foresight, I was among the few people in the country with more cash than they needed during the emergency.

By 1933 the team of Rodgers and Hart had three movies in circulation, which had, we thought, helped to evolve the screen musical into a form that was indigenous to the medium. Had *The Phantom President* or *Hallelujah, I'm a Bum* succeeded, who knows? Maybe our kind of musical would have set the standard. One thing we did know: in March 1933 Warner Bros. released a backstage movie with a series of dazzling production routines which, more than any other film, was responsible for the rebirth of the screen musical. It was *42nd Street,* and all our innovations in music-and-story integration, in using one song to carry the action through a number of different locales, in bridging songs with rhythmic dialogue were quickly forgotten. Everyone wanted backstage musicals with lavish spectacles. Our old friend Busby Berkeley, who had choreographed two Rodgers and Hart shows, had revitalized an entire cinematic form with his daring overhead shots and his ingenious kaleidoscopic effects.

Buoyed by the country's renewed interest in musicals, the M-G-M hierarchs again thought of Rodgers and Hart. This time, however, Thalberg wanted us to sign a one-year term contract rather than one for a specific film. While he could not assure us that our experience with *I Married an Angel* would not be repeated, he was convinced that with musicals once again in demand, there would be plenty of work for us. Still, Larry and I remained dubious. A term contract would put us under obligation to do exactly what the studio wanted, whether we liked the assignment or not. It also meant that if it chose to, the studio could ignore us entirely. We had known too many writers who had been sold the benefits of a term contract, only to find themselves with little to do except collect a weekly pay check. We did, however, become a bit less dubious when Thalberg told us what our weekly pay check was going to be, but what really clinched the deal was opening the *New York Times* one morning to discover that there was a total of exactly five shows then running on Broadway. What was I to do? Run home for the unlikely prospect of making it six? Suddenly I realized how hollow was my long-held belief that I could chuck Hollywood any time I really wanted to and take up where I had left off in New York.

Well, what the hell. There was bound to be work; there was certain to be a fat salary; the year would go fast enough. Besides, there was no alternative. So Larry and I accepted our sentence: one year at soft labor at M-G-M.

Our period of servitude began, surprisingly, with a bang—though not the kind I ever want to hear again. We had been given a large studio in which to work, and one afternoon while playing piano for some friends, I suddenly heard a roaring sound and a deafening crash, followed by the incredible sight of the piano moving away from me. We were in the middle of an earthquake! Luckily the studio was on the first floor of the building, and we simply dashed for the nearest window and jumped out.

Since telephone lines had been damaged and road travel was temporarily halted, I had to spend anxious, frustrating hours worrying about Dorothy and Mary. At the time we were living on Angelo Drive and when I was finally able to return home, I almost collapsed with relief to find my family safe and our house only slightly affected.

The next day I discovered that the deafening crash I'd heard was caused by a brick wall falling on an empty rehearsal hall adjacent to my studio. If the wall had fallen just a foot closer, we would have been killed. The aftershock of this experience lasted for months, and to this day the passing of a heavy truck makes me acutely sensitive to the trembling of the ground beneath.

Larry and I were under contract to M-G-M for a month before anyone knew what to do with us. At the time Howard Dietz was the studio publicity chief, though he was a good deal more than a company flack. With composer Arthur Schwartz he had written some outstanding songs for Broadway revues, including "Dancing in the Dark" and "I Guess I'll Have to Change My Plan." He was a dynamic, extremely able man who easily wore more than one hat and looked great in each one he put on.

What Howard had in mind was the screwball picture to end all screwball pictures, with a cast including every available comic on the M-G-M lot, some guest-star appearances, and a score by Rodgers and Hart. After many changes along the way, the picture was eventually released as *Hollywood Party,* with Howard serving as co-author and co-producer. For the comedians, he managed to round up Jimmy Durante, Jack Pearl, Charles Butterworth, Polly Moran, Lupe Velez, Ted Healy and the Three Stooges, Laurel and Hardy, and even Mickey Mouse.

The picture turned out to be a real hodgepodge, and by the time it was released there had been so many directors assigned to it that none was credited—or blamed. (While Larry and I were working on the film, the man in charge was Edmund Goulding, but at least three other directors had a hand in it.) We submitted about a dozen songs, but only three were retained in the final print.

One of our ideas was to include a scene in which Jean Harlow is shown as an innocent young girl saying—or rather, singing—her prayers. How the sequence fitted into the movie I haven't the foggiest notion, but the purpose was to express Jean's overwhelming ambition to become a movie star ("Oh, Lord, if you're not busy up there,/ I ask for help with a prayer/ So please don't give me the air . . .").

For some reason the scene was never used. A few weeks later we were asked to write something for a Harlem night-club sequence in *Manhattan Melodrama,* a nonmusical starring Clark Gable, Myrna Loy and William Powell. Since I rather liked the melody for the discarded "Prayer," Larry came up with a new lyric and Shirley Ross sang it as "The Bad in Every Man" ("Oh, Lord, what is the matter with me?/ I'm just permitted to see/ The bad in every man . . .").

But that still wasn't the end of the song. While under contract to M-G-M, we were also under contract to its music-publishing company, then run by a man named Jack Robbins. Robbins was so enthusiastic about the song's possibilities that he assured us that if Larry would write a more commercial lyric, he'd get behind the number and plug it from one end of the country to the other. Larry came up with the third lyric, Robbins was as good as his word, and the song became the only success we ever had that was not associated with a stage or screen musical. This is the way it began: "Blue moon, you saw me standing alone,/ Without a dream in my heart,/ Without a love of my own . . ."

One final word about *Hollywood Party.* In one scene Jimmy Durante was supposed to say, "I'm the lord of the manure," but Howard Dietz was afraid he couldn't get away with it. He telephoned the studio front office for a ruling and was advised that the line could not be used. The censors wouldn't allow the word "lord."

With the completion of our work for *Hollywood Party,* Larry and I received a few offers for individual songs from various studios. Since we had no assignment at M-G-M, the studio lent us to Samuel Goldwyn to write an appropriate ballad for Anna Sten to sing in her first Hollywood film.

Remember Anna Sten? Anyone who lived through that period and was at all aware of movie stars must recall the round-faced Russian beauty with soulful eyes whom Goldwyn chose as his entry in the "another Garbo" sweepstakes. With some of the most persistent drumbeating that ever preceded the appearance of a screen personality, Goldwyn vainly tried to make Anna a star before anyone even saw her on the screen. Perhaps it was a case of oversell, for American moviegoers did not take to her, and she left after making only a few films.

Goldwyn's idea was to launch his discovery in a new version of Emile Zola's *Nana,* in which she would be obliged not only to act but also to sing. Dorothy had to return at that time to New York for a minor operation, and I wrote to her about the new assignment:

> When I got back to Larry's house, he had already written a lyric for the tune I had for the movie. We rushed down to United Artists

and played it for Al Newman, who's conducting. Al raved about it and we took it right up to Goldwyn. Well, sweet, we've had reactions in our time, but this was the top! He yelled and screamed and phoned Sten to tell her it was the best song he'd ever heard. His parting remark was, "Boys, I thank you from the bottom of my heart!" Of course, now I'm in love with Goldwyn! You know what a fool I am for anyone who's kind to me or likes my work. Well, this guy was so unaffected and naively enthusiastic that I was really touched.

Unfortunately the song, "That's Love," never did catch on with the public, but for a while Sam had us convinced that we had come up with another "Lover." One day he asked me to play it for Frances Marion, a sweet, precious little woman who was one of Goldwyn's favorite screen writers. Al Newman was also there. When I finished, I looked up from the keyboard and was startled to see the lady standing with her eyes closed as if in a trance. When Sam asked her what she thought, she slowly opened her eyes and said, in her sweet, precious little way, "Sam, this song is the essence of Paris. I've never heard anything so Parisian in my life." With that, Goldwyn wheeled around to Newman and commanded, "Newman, in the orchestra eight French horns!"

This is the kind of story that always prompts patronizing laughter, and it is a funny line. But I think I understand what Sam meant and why he said it. It was simply his way of telling Newman to go all out in supplying the proper Parisian flavor for what he had just been assured, by a woman he considered brilliant, to be a genuinely Parisian song. He was expressing both his delight and his gratitude, and I found this kind of warm, impetuous reaction disarming.

It is unfortunate that in making fun of Goldwyn and his Goldwynisms we often forget the man's brilliance. His innate good taste was responsible for what was probably a higher percentage of quality pictures than any other moving-picture producer. He never did anything just because someone had told him it was the commercial thing to do. When Sam said, "I make my pictures to please myself," he wasn't merely mouthing a line that would look good in print; he really meant it. It's also important to remember that since he used his own money and never depended on large-company backing to finance his projects, he was probably the only really independent producer in the business. My theory about Goldwyn and his language problem has always been that since he was foreign-born and didn't arrive in the United States until he was in his twenties, his mind worked so quickly that his tongue was simply never able to keep up with it. His thinking was always far ahead of his speech.

David O. Selznick was another major film executive I got to know well in Hollywood. Actually, I had known him ever since we went to the same public school in New York. In 1933 he had just been brought over to M-G-M from RKO Radio Pictures by his then father-in-law, Louis B. Mayer. One of David's first pictures was *Dancing Lady*, a rather blatant follow-up to *42nd Street*, into which he had poured an all-star line-up including Clark Gable, Joan Crawford, Franchot Tone and, making his Hollywood debut, Fred Astaire. In our contract with M-G-M, Larry and I had signed to write only complete moving-picture scores, not individual songs, but since we had already done one song for Goldwyn, we could hardly refuse when Selznick asked us to provide a number for the *Dancing Lady* finale.

The song was to be sung by Nelson Eddy and was intended to accompany a lavish production routine all about the pell-mell pace of modern living. After Larry and I put together something we thought appropriate, we were asked over to an enormous studio where we were obliged to perform the number before King David and his retinue of sound men, cameramen, wardrobe people, publicity people and anyone else they could find who wasn't doing anything. When we finished to applause and many complimentary words, David thanked us profusely.

Feeling satisfied about the song's reception, I took the next day off to play tennis at the Beverly Hills Tennis Club. I was in the middle of a game when I was told I was wanted on the telephone, so I jogged over to the clubhouse.

It was Selznick. "Dick," he said, "I want to tell you how crazy all of us are about the song you played yesterday."

"Thanks, David."

"It's really just what we need for the finale."

"Glad you feel that way. Is that all you called me about?"

"Well, no, Dick. Er . . . as a matter of fact, I do have one thing I'd like to ask you."

"Yes, David?"

"Could you make it a little better?"

Could I make it a little better? As patiently and with as much control as I could, I explained that it's impossible to make a song "a little better." It's like making an egg a little better. It's either a good egg or a bad egg. If it's a song, that's it; good or bad, there's nothing that can be done about it. Slightly flustered, David thanked me for my elementary lesson in composition and assured me there would be no problem.

But this wasn't the end of Selznick's uneasy feeling about the song. During rehearsal the dance director, Sammy Lee, needed about eight bars of the melody to help him convey the proper rhythm to the dancing chorus. A recording was made of these eight bars and Lee played it over and over until the dancers became thoroughly familiar with the beat. One day I got a memo from Selznick reading, *in toto:* "I like your tune very much, but don't you think it's a bit monotonous?"

At this point, of course, I am expected to show what a really unappreciative boob Selznick was by revealing the name of a song that is so familiar it will prompt the reader into whistling all thirty-two bars. Hardly. The song was called "That's the Rhythm of the Day," and today even I have difficulty remembering how it goes. I guess I should have made it a little better right from the start.

And that was the way Rodgers and Hart spent the year 1933: one score for a film that wasn't made; one score, mostly unused, for a film no one can recall; one song for Goldwyn; one song for Selznick.

It's bad enough to know you're wasting your time and not accomplishing anything; what really hurts is to realize that others are aware of it too. One morning, reading the Los Angeles *Examiner,* I came across the following query in O. O. McIntyre's syndicated Broadway column: "Whatever happened to Rodgers and Hart?"

The comment scared me so much that my hands began to tremble. I was only thirty-one, Larry wasn't yet forty, and McIntyre was writing as if we no longer existed. But the phrase meant more to me than that; what had happened inside us that could impel us to accept money without working for it, spend day after day on the tennis courts or in the local bars, and simply allow our talents to rot? How could we have let ourselves be caught in this trap? What *had* happened to us?

No sooner had I read the piece than I told Dorothy that we simply had to leave Hollywood and get back to the real world as soon as possible. Then I telephoned Larry. The item had hit him exactly the same way, and he was perfectly agreeable to my doing what I could to get us out of our contract. Without even tentative plans for the future, I called our agent and told him I didn't give a damn how he did it, but that Larry and I wanted out. The agent did what he could, but for reasons unknown the studio flatly refused to let us go.

Possibly motivated by our desperation at having nothing to do, Thalberg signed us up to write the score for his next movie, *The Merry Widow,* which would star Maurice Chevalier and Jeanette MacDonald. Actually, he didn't sign "us," he signed Larry, since Franz Lehár had written a pretty fine score without any help from me. But because Larry and I had one of those "whither thou goest I will go" contracts with the studio, the lyrics were officially credited to "Richard Rodgers and Lorenz Hart."

There's no question that Larry was a highly adaptable lyricist, but Viennese musical pastry was simply not his dish and he loathed every minute of the assignment. What made it even tougher was that the only thing Larry and Ernst Lubitsch, the movie's director, had in common was their fondness for big black cigars. Though he was the acknowledged master of gaiety and sophistication, Lubitsch was an autocrat on the movie set, with a decidedly Teutonic approach to film making. He insisted that Larry be punctual for all meetings, and that his lyrics be submitted on neatly typewritten sheets. He took it as a personal affront when Larry would show up late and fumble through his pockets for scraps of paper on which he had scribbled the lyrics. Still, Larry did manage to turn in his usual creditable job, and many people have sung his words to "The Merry Widow Waltz" and "Vilia" without realizing that he wrote them.

And what was I doing all the while Larry was working on *The Merry Widow?* Tennis. I was doing tennis.

Eventually our contract ended, and Dorothy, Mary, Larry and I packed up and went home. On my final day as an employee of Metro-Goldwyn-Mayer, I thought it only polite to say good-bye to Irving Thalberg, who had, after all, thought enough of us to sign us up originally. I drove over to the studio, went directly to the cottage on the lot in which Thalberg worked, gave the receptionist my name and in a few minutes was ushered into Thalberg's office. There I found the producer seated at a conference table with five men flanking him. I walked over and said, "Larry and I are leaving today and I just wanted to say good-bye." Thalberg looked up with an uncomprehending, glassy stare on his boyish face, and I suddenly realized that he hadn't the faintest idea who I was.

This incident vividly demonstrated to me the kind of dehumanized, impersonal world that existed under the factory system the studios then maintained. To Thalberg, we were all faceless, anonymous cogs. Whenever we were needed, all he had to do was press a button and we'd hop over to help turn the company's wheels. I had no definite plans when I left Hollywood that day but I was sure of one thing: I would never again tie myself down to this kind of spirit-breaking situation.

I'd like to emphasize, though, that my feelings about Hollywood had nothing to do with moviemaking *per se.* My dislike was solely for the system of binding a creative person to a particular studio for a particular length of time. What an appalling waste of money, time and talent! Brought up on the old-fashioned idea that people should only earn money because they work for it, I found it impossible to adjust to this unpressured, indolent existence. Everyone said the same thing: Don't knock yourself out, enjoy life, get some sun on your face, brush up on your tennis game. The living was so easy that it was unbearable.

I know that there were many writers in Hollywood during those years who were constantly and gainfully employed. But, perhaps for reasons of insecurity, studio moguls always seemed to have a certain antipathy toward people from the Broadway theatre. They used us when they had to, but they were never really happy about our being there. For our part, I don't suppose there were many Broadway writers who were happy about being there either. He never told me in so many words, but Jerry Kern must have been miserable in Hollywood, and I know Oscar Hammerstein was. The people who succeeded in moving pictures—and I'm talking primarily about lyricists and composers—were those who did not have an extended background in the theatre.

Part of our adjustment problem was that we were used to writing complete scores of anywhere from a dozen to twenty songs. In Hollywood they thought a score was four or five songs. Or they would only need one. They also had the sneaky habit of comparison shopping. They'd ask three or four writers for a song and then would choose the one they liked best. So far as I know, I was never involved in any of these little competitions.

In a way, I have always had a feeling of gratitude toward M-G-M. If its management had tossed Larry and me only a few more crumbs, we might have been lulled into staying longer, and that would have been the end of Larry Hart and Dick Rodgers. I'm sure I would have ended up as a neurotic, a drunkard or both.

$\mathbf{F}$or months Dorothy and I had been dreaming about going home, but when we got there we found that we didn't have a home.

Three years earlier, soon after Mary was born, we had moved to larger quarters at 50 East Seventy-seventh Street, an apartment building that was actually part of the Hotel Carlyle. When we were on our way to Hollywood, we had subleased the apartment to an elderly couple, and since they'd taken such good care of it, when they left after about a year we felt emboldened to sublease the place to an affluent, newly married couple. Naturally we had advised them when we would return, but to our astonishment they were still there when we arrived. The girl had had a baby some weeks before and they simply did not want to leave. In fact, when we walked in early in the afternoon the young mother was fast asleep. I'll never forget the look on Dorothy's face when she saw the woman in her bed.

What was even worse was what they had done to our home. Despite our request that there be no animals, they hadn't been able to resist buying a puppy, who in turn couldn't resist using the legs of our tables and chairs for teething or relieving itself all over our carpets. A tray with glasses had been dropped, and there were liquor stains and pieces of glass everywhere. Chewing gum was stuck under the chair arms, vases and china pieces were broken, the walls were covered with fingerprint marks, and some of our drapes were torn. Even our dining-room table was ruined because their butler had used it as an ironing board on which to press the master's trousers. Welcome home, Dorothy and Dick!

One remark I shall never forget. Dorothy took one look at the kitchen —filthy stove, grease marks on the walls, dozens of unwashed dishes piled in the sink—and raged into the bedroom to confront our reclining tenant. "Yes, I know," the young lady replied sweetly, "I went in there once and never went back."

The only thing to do was to move into a temporary apartment—which we luckily found right in the Hotel Carlyle—and exert whatever pressure we could to get these Kallikaks out. When we finally did, we were then faced with the huge task of cleaning up after them. Dorothy looked at the mess around her and blurted, "Oh, I wish there were one magic place that I could go to and say, 'There it is—you fix it.'" Instinctively I came up with the logical question: "Why don't you start a business like that yourself?" Eventually Dorothy did exactly that: a year and a half later she founded Repairs, Inc., whose function was to serve as a single agency that would hire skilled craftsmen to repair any kind of broken or damaged objects.

But in the spring of 1934 the main task for me was to repair my own damaged career. Mine and Larry's. We made calls and we saw people, but things were just as bleak as we had feared. A few shows were running— the Moss Hart–Irving Berlin revue *As Thousands Cheer;* Jerry Kern and Otto Harbach's *Roberta;* a Shubert-sponsored *Ziegfeld Follies;* Leonard Sillman's first *New Faces* revue—but between March and June not a single new musical opened on Broadway, and the prospects for the fall weren't encouraging. Lew Fields was no longer producing shows, Terry Helburn and Lawrence Langner of the Theatre Guild were tied up with long-range plans for a Gershwin musical based on the play *Porgy,* Schwab and Mandel had split up, as had Aarons and Freedley (though Freedley was continuing alone), and Ziegfeld was dead. But the Shubert brothers were still active and a new flock of producers had come into prominence while we were away. There really was nothing else for us to do but dig in, make the rounds— and hope.

The offer that did materialize was from a totally unexpected source, and once again from Hollywood. While working on the one song for Sam Goldwyn, I had become friendly with his production chief, Arthur Horn-blow, Jr. Possibly because Arthur's roots were in New York—he had been a playwright and an editor for *Theatre Magazine,* which his father had founded—he was particularly sensitive to the plight of theatre writers in Hollywood. He had recently left Goldwyn to become a producer at Paramount and he offered Larry and me the chance to write the score for his first musical, which was called *Mississippi.* W. C. Fields was to star in it, along with a new singing hero, Lanny Ross. Neither Larry nor I was exactly thrilled at the prospect of returning to Hollywood so soon after leaving, but it was our only firm offer and we needed desperately to get back to work. Besides, as we kept telling ourselves, it would only be for five or six weeks.

Feeling guilty about leaving Dorothy alone to supervise the renovation of our apartment, I rented a house in Rye, New York, for her and Mary for the summer, and by July I was back in the land of make-believe. No sooner had I arrived there than I received news that made me want to turn around and go home: Dorothy was pregnant again.

As for the actual writing assignment, however, things really couldn't have been better. "This is the first time since *Love Me Tonight,*" I wrote Dorothy early in August, "that I have felt satisfied with myself. This appears to me to be a complete, well balanced score with three good tries for popularity, a couple of amusing musical sequences, and plenty of musical material for the camera. I'm really excited about it. Fields will be excellent, but my one doubt is Ross. Perhaps careful direction will do something for him."

Those "three good tries for popularity" were "Down by the River" and "Soon," which made it, and "Roll, Mississippi," which didn't. Two out of three wasn't bad predicting.

Actually, there *was* a third song from *Mississippi* that became popular but it wasn't written until I returned home. As soon as Larry and I were safely back in New York, Paramount got a new studio boss. He took a hard look at the film's rushes, decided that production on the film be halted at once and that, at Arthur Hornblow's suggestion, Lanny Ross be replaced by Bing Crosby. I couldn't quarrel with his judgment so far, but then the new studio head decided that the Rodgers and Hart score would have to be scrapped and that an entirely new one was needed. Hornblow didn't simply object; he told the man that if our score was thrown out, he'd walk out, and apparently this was enough to guarantee that our songs remained. It was also enough to guarantee that Arthur Hornblow and I would remain lifelong friends.

But there was still another problem; now it was decided that Bing needed another number. Without returning to California, Larry and I wrote it in New York, made a recording of it, and mailed it to Hornblow. The song was—and turned out to be—"Easy to Remember."

Shortly after our return to New York, I bumped into Harry Kaufman on Broadway. He was an amiable but shrewd theatre man who was then the actual producer of the Shubert brothers' musicals. The brothers had hired him as something of a good-will gesture, since they were well aware of their reputation as tough men to work for, and they felt that Harry might attract people who otherwise would have nothing to do with them. Harry, who had just produced the *Ziegfeld Follies* and *Life Begins at 8:40,* two highly regarded revues, asked me if I had anything in mind that the Shuberts might be interested in.

I sure did. While Larry and I were in Hollywood during our last trip, we had read in a trade paper that RKO, having recently completed *The Gay Divorcee,* was looking for something new for its dancing stars, Fred Astaire and Ginger Rogers. Since we both had long wanted to write a score for Astaire, we naturally started talking about what kind of story might be suitable for him. Astaire had made his fame as both a ballroom and tap dancer, and it seemed to us that he might be receptive to a story that would allow him to demonstrate his skill in a different area. So we began tossing ideas around, and eventually came up with the saga of a former vaudeville song-and-dance man who composes and performs a modern ballet with a classical ballet company. There would be some kidding of the ballet form, and of course Fred would become involved with the glamorous ballerina before returning to the cute little trick he really loved. We called it *On Your Toes*.

Larry and I wrote a two-page outline and two or three songs, and then invited Fred to our rooms at the Beverly Hills Hotel to try to sell him on the idea. He was receptive to it but ultimately turned it down; he was afraid his public wouldn't accept him in a role that would not allow him to wear his trademark attire of top hat, white tie and tails.

When I told Kaufman about *On Your Toes* and our meeting with Astaire, he said he thought the story had the makings of a great musical, but he had another dancer in mind. All he had to say was "How about Ray Bolger?" and I knew it would all work out. This spidery, sparkling dancer, who was then appearing in *Life Begins at 8:40,* had made a great hit in *Heads Up!,* and there was no question that he was a perfect choice for the lead. On the strength of the story outline and Harry's enthusiasm, Lee Shubert put the show under contract and gave Larry and me an advance against royalties.

Once we had finished the dialogue and about half the songs, we auditioned the material for Lee Shubert. I had been warned that holding an audition for Shubert was an experience, and indeed it was. His leathery face, protruding nose and slicked-down black hair gave him the look of an Indian chief, and his impassive, stony stare could easily wither the bravest of the braves. But that wasn't the worst of it, I was going through the third number in the score when I heard an odd sound, and I looked up. Lee Shubert was fast asleep, snoring peacefully.

Obviously Shubert was somewhat less than fired with enthusiasm for the project and did nothing to get it going. Whenever I asked about it, he would insist that he was planning to get started very soon, and that I should just be a little patient. Since so much was riding on this project, I was extremely apprehensive. Larry and I had been away from Broadway for four years and we could not allow this chance to slip away. Besides, it wasn't just *any* show; this was all ours—lyrics, music *and* story by Rodgers and Hart.

On March 5, 1935, our fifth wedding anniversary, Dorothy and I received a beautiful gift: our daughter Linda. Mary, who was then four and in the kindergarten of the Brearley School, was excited and a bit confused about the birth and the anniversary occurring on the same day. She was acting in a play performed by her class and proudly announced to one and all that her mother had just had a baby and couldn't possibly come to see the play because she was getting married.

While Larry and I were being kept dangling by Lee Shubert, we got a call from our old friend Billy Rose, now a Broadway producer. Actually, Broadway couldn't hold Billy. He had a grandiose scheme to mount a production that would be part circus and part musical comedy, and had already taken a lease on the venerable Hippodrome, at Sixth Avenue and Forty-third Street, which had once been the home of the most dazzling stage spectacles ever presented. But he wasn't content merely to hire a hall; his idea was no less than to gut the entire interior of the theatre and have it redesigned and rebuilt like a circus tent, with the audience in banked seats looking down on a single "ring." All the action—story, song-and-dance numbers and circus acts—would take place either in the ring or, for the aerial acts, high above it.

Billy wasn't going to stint on a thing and was getting the best designers, directors and writers available. Jimmy Durante and Paul Whiteman and his Band would be in the show, and his agents were scouring Europe for the greatest jugglers, tumblers, clowns, animal acts and trapeze artists they could find. It was, he assured us, going to be the most mammoth attraction of its kind, and appropriately, he was calling it *Jumbo*.

Billy's request that Larry and I write the score came at a particularly opportune time. By now it was clear that Shubert had no intention of producing *On Your Toes*. We had taken it to another producer, but work could not begin until Shubert's option had run out. We still had qualms about Billy, since we remembered all too well that he had never paid us for our last assignment for him, but his enthusiasm was so infectious that we agreed to do the show without even seeing the script.

As befitting the super-showman that he was, Billy seldom thought along conventional lines. For his story, he went to Ben Hecht and Charles MacArthur, the co-authors of *The Front Page* and *Twentieth Century*, who had never before written a musical-comedy book. Though he was certain that they would come up with a plot that was fresh and different, what they produced was another Romeo and Juliet variation, in which the daughter of one circus owner falls in love with the son of his bitterest rival. It was, however, convenient enough for the purpose, though there was scarcely any actual collaboration between the librettists and the songwriters.

The official billing for *Jumbo* read: "Entire Production Staged by John Murray Anderson." Actually Murray, who had been so helpful ten years before in putting on *Dearest Enemy,* was primarily concerned with the physical aspects of the production—the scenery, lighting and costumes—and didn't really care much about the story or the way the songs fit it. I recall once just before the show's opening when he took me backstage to demonstrate the workings of a huge, complicated lighting switchboard. "Each one of the lights is controlled by its own special switch," he explained. "It's all pre-set. All you have to do is just touch a switch and you get exactly the lighting effect you want." Then he started to giggle. "See this little yellow one here?" he said, pointing to a tiny toggle switch at the far right of the board. "Do you know what that's for? That's for the book." A single light switch was all the plot of the musical meant to him.

For the man who *would* be concerned with the book, Billy hired a director whose experience heretofore had been solely in nonmusical plays. George Abbott was a tall, sharp-featured ramrod of a man who, more than anyone else, was responsible for tying all the disparate elements of the production together. *Jumbo* was the beginning of what would be a number of fruitful associations between Abbott and Rodgers and Hart.

Like many people in the theatre, Billy Rose had a vision that far exceeded his finances. By the time the show opened—after many delays—it had cost in the neighborhood of $340,000 (most of it supplied by Jock Whitney), which I think was a record up to then. Billy, however, never parted with a dime if he didn't have to. He even managed to get a special ruling from Equity, the actors' union, that he was not obligated to pay the performers during the lengthy rehearsal period because the show was classified as a circus, not a regular theatrical production. Billy had a curiously personal attitude about money. He hated to have anyone ask him for a delinquent payment, not so much because he didn't have the money or didn't want to pay it, but because it hurt his pride.

One of Billy's idiosyncrasies was that he would not allow any of the songs for *Jumbo* to be played over the radio, giving the reason that people wouldn't go to see his show if the airwaves were saturated with its songs. This, too, was really a matter of pride. He simply felt that his show was so great that it didn't need any further plugging from a rival form of entertainment. Pride or no pride, his decision was a serious blow to us. In our score were "The Most Beautiful Girl in the World," "My Romance" and "Little Girl Blue." We were confident that they had the potential for popularity, and eventually they did catch on, but by the time Billy had lifted his ban, the show's run was almost over and nothing could help it. The reviews were great and the production certainly gave customers their money's worth, but big, fat, colorful *Jumbo* was just too expensive to keep running and it closed after only five months.

Still, what mattered most to Larry and me was that we had returned to Broadway with a highly acclaimed show, and that despite the myriad attractions it offered, our work did not go unnoticed. No one would again have to wonder whatever had happened to Rodgers and Hart.

     *    *    *

With *Jumbo* out of the way, we could now devote all our efforts to getting on with *On Your Toes*. Once Shubert's option ended, Dwight Deere Wiman, the producer who had already expressed interest in the musical, was ready to go ahead with it any time we were.

Wiman was a curious anomaly in the frequently rough-and-tumble world of Broadway. Though he had been producing plays ever since the middle of the twenties and had already presented such hits as *The Road to Rome, The Little Show* and *She Loves Me Not,* something about him made people take him for a dilettante. He was what my mother called a "swell." He had inherited wealth, plus the manners, accent and appearance to go with it. He may have lacked that certain drive and dedication associated with producers, yet he probably had more profitable attractions than most of the more aggressive members of the breed.

Wiman liked *On Your Toes* from the start, but since neither Larry nor I had had much success in writing anything but songs, we took our script to George Abbott for advice. In addition to being a director, George had had considerable experience as a playwright, including at least two hits, *Broadway* and *Three Men on a Horse*. He told us what he liked and disliked about the script, and what he said made so much sense that we asked him not only to rewrite the book but to direct the production. He agreed, rewrote the book, and just before the show was to go into rehearsal, abruptly left to spend the winter playing golf in Palm Beach. There was no further explanation; George simply wanted to get away, and that was that. This left us in a terrible hole. We had everything and everyone ready, including Ray Bolger, so there was nothing else to do but get ourselves another director.

Our opening in Boston late in March 1936 turned out to be so bad that we knew drastic measures had to be taken. No one else could get us out of this jam but Abbott, so I sent him a telegram. He was, after all, the co-author of the show and he must have *some* concern about its success. Fortunately for all of us, he did. He arrived in Boston and saw the show, but didn't make a single note nor say a word about the performance after we left the theatre. When I suggested that Dwight, Larry and I go back to the hotel with him to talk things over, George shook his head. "Boys," he said, "there's nothing to talk over. We'll have plenty of time after we start rehearsals tomorrow. Now let's get some girls and go dancing." Which is exactly what we did.

What Abbott did the next morning was simple—and radical. Because our other director had made so many changes in his script, all George did was cut out the new material and go back to his original book. And it worked. In almost no time we were right back where we started, and from which we should never have left.

One of the great innovations of *On Your Toes,* the angle that had initially made us think of it as a vehicle for Fred Astaire, was that for the first time ballet was being incorporated into a musical-comedy book. To be sure, Albertina Rasch had made a specialty of creating Broadway ballets, but these were usually in revues and were not part of a story line. We made our main ballet an integral part of the action; without it, there was no conclusion to our story. During the dance, two gangsters enter a theatre box intent on shooting the hero at the conclusion of the ballet. Seeing their guns aimed at him, he beckons the conductor to continue the music so that he can keep on dancing to avoid being a target. Finally the police come, and the hero falls to the floor exhausted.

This ballet, called "Slaughter on Tenth Avenue," had always been part of the script, but we knew that much would depend on getting the right man to choreograph it. George Balanchine was a leading European choreographer who had worked with impresario Sergei Diaghilev and had recently settled in New York, where he founded the American Ballet Company. The previous year his company had given a highly praised recital at the Adelphi Theatre, which had led to its being signed as the resident ballet company for the Metropolitan Opera. Once Larry and I had seen his work, Balanchine was the man we wanted.

I met with Balanchine one afternoon in his studio to play the music. I didn't know a thing about choreography and told Balanchine that I was unsure how we should go about it. Did he devise his steps first and expect me to alter tempos wherever necessary, or did he fit his steps to the music as written? Balanchine smiled and with that wonderful Russian accent of his said simply, "You write. I put on." And that was the way we worked. He used the music just the way I had written it and created his dance patterns to conform. I don't think that our arranger, Hans Spialek, had to change more than thirty-two bars.

*On Your Toes,* and particularly his dance in "Slaughter on Tenth Avenue," made Ray Bolger a star. It didn't hurt Rodgers and Hart, either, especially as a showcase for a song called "There's a Small Hotel." It was the melody—romantic, unsophisticated, youthful—that suggested the theme to Larry of an idealized country inn with its wishing well, one-room bridal suite and view of a nearby church steeple. This was another example of his ability to convey the appeal of the simple life. There is no question that Larry was a big-city kid who thrived on the vigor and pace of Broadway, yet he could write longingly about quiet pleasures far from the razzle-dazzle world. "Mountain Greenery" was an early attempt, though it was obviously the work of a Manhattan sophisticate. More sincere was his tribute to the isolated "Blue Room" that was "far from worldly cares," or his description of "A Tree in the Park" as an oasis in the noisy city. Larry loved having people around him, but when, in "There's a Small Hotel," he wrote the lines "Not a sign of people—Who wants people?" he made you believe that a rural retreat was his idea of heaven.

The Broadway season of 1935–36 offered many good musicals. There was the colorful Howard Dietz–Arthur Schwartz revue, *At Home Abroad,* starring Beatrice Lillie and Ethel Waters; Gershwin's monumental opera, *Porgy and Bess;* the elegant *Jubilee,* by Moss Hart and Cole Porter; Oscar Hammerstein and Sigmund Romberg's romantic *May Wine;* a glittering *Ziegfeld Follies* with Fanny Brice and Josephine Baker; and a new *New Faces,* with Imogene Coca. But when the season ended, the two longest-running musicals turned out to be *On Your Toes* and *Jumbo.*

Larry and I had come back, finally, from the limbo of Hollywood. No longer would we ever have to take an assignment just for the money or simply to have our names attached to a Broadway show. More than anything else, the rebirth of our career had given us the security, both financial and professional, to do the kind of creative work that had long been our goal.

## 14

From the fall of 1935 through 1942 was a period of almost unbelievable productivity for Larry and me. We had ten shows in those seven years, all but one a success. It seemed as if nothing we touched could go wrong. We had the freedom to do what we wanted and the satisfaction that what we wanted to do, others wanted to see. We could experiment with form and content not only in our songs but in the shows themselves. We should have been the happiest of men in the happiest of worlds.

Most of the time, in fact, we were. Larry was never easy to work with, so nothing he did really surprised me. He'd always drunk too much. He'd always do anything to avoid getting down to work. He'd always loved staying out late and carousing until dawn. But now the years of dissipation began to show. Not in his work, of course; if anything, this was better than ever. But there were signs. Now, instead of being an hour late for a meeting, he'd be two hours late. Or he'd disappear for days. Or he'd show up and I'd take one look at him and know he couldn't begin to put pencil to paper.

At first I chose to ignore it. I was too full of the euphoria of being back on Broadway with one hit after another. We were constantly showered with offers. People who only a year or so before had been too busy to see us were now taking us out to lunch and inviting us to parties. Somehow, our renewed activity seemed to be mirrored throughout the country. Roosevelt won re-election in a landslide, and economic conditions appeared to be improving. And though some of us were deeply concerned about what was happening in Germany under Hitler, the idea of another world war still seemed remote.

Larry even went in for self-improvement at about this time—at least, his idea of self-improvement. Always somewhat concerned about his height and general appearance, he now started wearing Adler elevator shoes to make him appear taller and began taking treatments to restore his falling hair.

One of the better influences on Larry was his maid, Mary Campbell, a sharp-tongued, no-nonsense black woman who was never one to hide her displeasure at the behavior of either her employer or his friends. Among the guests at one dinner party was the glamorous black entertainer Josephine Baker. Josephine, who grew up in St. Louis but was then living in Paris, batted her eyelashes at Mary and asked grandly, *"Donnez-moi une tasse de café, s'il vous plaît."* Mary shot Josephine a look of incredulity mixed with contempt. "Honey," she said, "you is full of shit. Talk the way yo' mouth was born!"

But even Mary couldn't curb Larry's prodigal habit of inviting people to his home without a thought of how many were coming or whether he even knew them. One Sunday when Larry and his mother were at our house for lunch, Dorothy asked Mrs. Hart, "Don't Larry's parties ever disturb you?" Mrs. Hart smiled and said, "No, not ferry much. Except dot night ven Paul Viteman came mit his whole band!"

Another time, when Larry asked Lawrence Riley to dinner, the playwright asked, "About seven?" Larry's answer was "Hell, bring as many as you like."

There are many examples of Larry's generosity and his almost compulsive habit of check-grabbing. Once when I was in London, Dorothy's mother and father gave a dinner party at the Berkeley Hotel to which they invited my parents, who were visiting London at the time, and Larry. When the waiter brought Mr. Feiner the check after dinner, Larry leaped up from the table and tried to tear it out of his hand. It was slightly embarrassing, but those of us who knew Larry also knew how frustrating it was for him to let anyone else ever pay for anything.

One year, on my birthday, Larry told Dorothy and me that he was sending us "a little ashtray" as a present. The little ashtray turned out to be a bronze nude figure in the center of a large marble receptacle which must have measured nearly two feet in diameter.

Larry's generosity even resulted in a fistfight on one occasion. I hadn't seen him for about a week and had the feeling he was purposely ducking me. When we finally met for lunch, I was shocked at his appearance. He had black-and-blue marks on his face and a gash above his left eye. What had happened, he explained, was that a stranger had telephoned him with greetings from a mutual friend in California. After chatting a bit, Larry invited the fellow to his apartment for dinner. As the evening wore on, the man got drunk—which wasn't a difficult thing to do at Larry's place—and also somewhat unpleasant. Finally Larry escorted him down to the street, hailed a taxi for him and turned to go upstairs. For some reason the man suddenly started to curse and then threw a right which knocked Larry down. No one came to his rescue; a few taxi drivers in the area simply stood around watching the mayhem.

The story upset me terribly. "Oh, don't feel sorry for me," Larry said with a mischievous smile. "As soon as I got my breath I kicked the son of a bitch in the nuts and he's still in the hospital."

This was typical of Larry. First he told the story exactly as it had happened, leading me to believe that he was the one who had been seriously hurt. Only after I had expressed my concern and sympathy did he reveal the ultimate outcome of the brawl.

*　　　　*　　　　*

In the fall of 1936, Larry and I thought it might be challenging to try something away from either the stage or the screen. At the request of Paul Whiteman, we wrote a narrative concert piece for soloist and symphony orchestra called *All Points West.*

Though the work had only a few performances and is barely remembered today, it was a further attempt on our part to expand the scope of our writing. I had already composed extended musical sequences for the film *Love Me Tonight,* and also the ballet "Slaughter on Tenth Avenue" for *On Your Toes,* but this was something entirely different: a self-contained work, billed as a "symphonic narrative," which was created specifically for the concert hall. Whiteman conducted it at the Academy of Music, in Philadelphia, at the end of November with the Philadelphia Orchestra and with baritone Ray Middleton as soloist. After the concert was over I caught a glimpse of Paul Whiteman's score. To my astonishment it was complete with arrows and exclamation points, and in red pencil little remarks such as "LOOK OUT!" and "WARNING!"

In answer to the inevitable question about why we had written *All Points West,* I told a newspaper interviewer, "We wanted to do something with more freedom. We wanted to escape the conventions that hedge in the musical-comedy song. For one thing, you're supposed to work in your title in the first eight bars and then to repeat it at the end. If you're bursting with independence, you might add a few bars here or take away a few bars there, but the form is almost inflexible. Also we got pretty tired of writing about nothing but love."

The form of *All Points West*—and I can't recall whether it was Larry's idea or mine—was a soliloquy sung by a train announcer at Grand Central Station. In it he reveals the frustrations of a life that keeps him tied down while others are on their way to exciting, distant places. Suddenly a prisoner on his way to Sing-Sing escapes from the police and the announcer, caught in the ensuing gunfire, is killed. At last he gets his wish to go on a journey to a faraway land. Pretty sentimental and melodramatic, I admit, but it was a faltering step in a basically right direction. Later I would be able to take firmer steps, even within the confines of the musical theatre.

Sometime during the summer of 1936, while Larry and I were strolling through Central Park, we noticed a bunch of children in a playground who were making up their own games and rules. We began talking about kids and what might happen if they were suddenly given adult responsibilities, such as finding ways to earn a living. One way might be to put on a big benefit show that would turn out to be a hit. And that's the way *Babes in Arms* was born.

The idea appealed to us for a particular reason. Every musical production on Broadway seemed to be dependent on at least one big star, and we thought audiences might welcome something youthful and unassuming for a change. By casting our show with talented but largely unknown performers, we hoped theatregoers would welcome the opportunity to discover future stars themselves.

We put together a serviceable book and took the idea to Dwight Deere Wiman. Though Wiman was inclined to be lavish in his taste, he turned out to be easy to sell. I don't think the whole production cost him more than $55,000, and even with a top ticket price of $3.85, it turned a nice profit.

Actually, *Babes in Arms* was one of those shows that worked right from the start. About a week before our Boston opening in March 1937, I wrote Dorothy: "Yesterday afternoon we had a run-through of the whole piece. It still looks encouraging. Naturally, we can't be sure of our values, but as far as material is concerned, we're in excellent shape to open. The cast is holding up well and there have been definite improvements. The numbers looked very good and are nearly all set now. Dwight and everyone else, especially Larry, were very happy about the whole thing."

Most of the kids in the show were really kids. I think Mitzi Green was sixteen; Ray Heatherton, in his mid-twenties, was the oldest; and for those looking for future stars, there were Alfred Drake, who sang the title song, and Dan Dailey.

Since there was a good spot for a ballet, we again hired George Balanchine for the choreography. We had particular fun with the scene in the kids' show in which Wynn Murray sang "Johnny One Note." For some reason that I can't recall, it was performed in an Egyptian setting, but instead of going in for exotic scenery and costumes, we emphasized the do-it-yourself nature of the show by having the cast come out wearing such household appliances as towels, bath mats, coat hooks and scrub mops.

In creating a story which contained a show within a show, we had a certain leeway, since "Johnny One Note" was just a specialty number. "My Funny Valentine," however, was very much about a specific character in the book; in fact, before the show opened we even changed the character's name to Val.

"Where or When" was probably the most popular song in this score, at least during the run of the show, and it had an interesting theme that was hardly typical of a musical-comedy song. We have all experienced the psychic phenomenon of "déjà vu" at one time or another—that is, doing something for the first time and being certain that we have done it before —but Larry was the first to use it in a lyric. He and I even received letters from college psychology professors telling us they were using the song to help illustrate their lectures.

Hollywood was making noises again. This time the call came from Warner Bros., the studio for which Larry and I had written our first movie score. The picture was to star Fernand Gravet, the latest French import, and Carole Lombard, and one of the attractions was that we would again be working with Herb Fields, who, with his brother Joseph, was writing the screenplay. Larry and I had already agreed to do a Broadway show in the fall, so with no assignment to keep us in New York, we went to California in June. The picture? *Fools for Scandal.* If you remember this choice little exhibition, raise your right hand.

Larry and I wrote a complete score for the film, and since everyone was pleased and predicted great things, we returned to New York and thought no more about it. Then one day sometime in March of the following year, I received a telephone call from the head of the Warner Bros. office in New York. He said, *"Fools for Scandal* is opening at the Music Hall next week."

"Great! We'll all go and make a party of it."

"Not exactly, Dick. In fact, I'm calling you to ask you to promise that you won't go to see it."

"Why shouldn't I?"

"Well," said the gentleman from Warner's, "because if you do, there'll be a certain number of deaths. Either you'll shoot yourself or you'll shoot everybody at Warner's, and I'm not looking forward to dying so soon."

So I never saw *Fools for Scandal.* It turned out that they had cut almost every song out of the picture and had simply used the score for background music. Our only recourse was to stay away.

I recall little about this particular stay in Hollywood except for one tragic event that happened while I was there: the death of George Gershwin. The best way I can indicate how his illness and death affected me is to quote my letters to Dorothy. On July 10, 1937, I wrote:

> I don't like what I hear about George. He's had a complete mental collapse and they don't know what to do with him. They'd like to send him East to a sanitarium as they don't trust the ones out here, but he's too ill to be moved. Moss [Hart] tells me that he can't eat or even talk and is in a house which they've taken for him and turned into a hospital.

The next day I wrote:

> I'm so upset at the moment I can hardly think enough to write. I phoned Cedars [of Lebanon Hospital] a little after ten-thirty and was told that George had just died.
>
> It shouldn't have been such a shock to me as I've been in close touch with the situation for days through Moss, but I just can't believe he's gone. I've been interrupted at least five times since I started this by people calling up. Moss just phoned, crying so he could hardly talk. It's pretty tough on him as he's been very close to the family and has stood the brunt of all the hospital arrangements . . .

Again, in a letter the following day:

> The town is in a daze and nobody talks about anything but George's death. There seems to be a certain amount of mystery as to the reason why no diagnosis was made until the night before the operation, but since we don't know the details it isn't possible to have an opinion. It's just awful . . .

George's death left such a pall over my stay in Hollywood that I was especially eager to return home and get started on a new project.

Engendered by the widespread cynicism that developed during the Depression, one of the distinctive forms of musicals in the thirties was the topical revue or topical musical comedy. The best of these never went in for preaching or propaganda but managed to make their comments on the conditions of the world without forgetting that the basic function of entertainment was to entertain. The Gershwin brothers had supplied the scores for the antiwar musical *Strike Up the Band,* the presidential lampoon *Of Thee I Sing,* which won the Pulitzer Prize as the best drama of the season, and its less successful sequel, *Let 'Em Eat Cake.* Irving Berlin wrote the songs for a musical about New York City police corruption called *Face the Music,* as well as for the revue *As Thousands Cheer,* which was created entirely in the form of a newspaper.

George S. Kaufman, the co-author of the three Gershwin shows, and Moss Hart, the author of the two with scores by Berlin, now thought the time was ripe for them to collaborate on the most daring political satire of them all, and they wanted Larry and me to write the songs. Their idea was nothing less than a musical-comedy lampoon about President Roosevelt himself. Though Presidents had been depicted before in musicals—Calvin Coolidge in our first *Garrick Gaieties* and recently Herbert Hoover in *As Thousands Cheer*—this would mark the first time that the leader of our country would be seen as the protagonist of a book musical.

When Hart and Kaufman outlined the idea to us, we fell in love with it right away. All four of us were ardently pro-FDR, but we were sure we could have a lot of fun sticking pins into such current phenomena as the New Deal and its alphabetical agencies, the packing of the Supreme Court, and the outlandish idea that Roosevelt would dare break tradition and run for a third term. Though we might make a few people squirm a bit, we felt that the show could be done with taste and without giving real offense. Besides, creating such a musical comedy at this time was in itself an affirmation of the freedom we had always enjoyed and had long taken for granted. Hitler, who had come to power in Germany the same year Roosevelt first took office, had already instituted repressive measures against non-Aryans and "enemies of the state." Abolition of all forms of dissent was also part of Mussolini's Fascist regime in Italy and of the aggressive military leaders in Japan. Spain was in the midst of a civil war led by Franco, with the blessing and backing of Hitler and Mussolini. In one country after another, one saw the extinction of human life and liberty. Suddenly all those who had been moaning about what had happened to us during the Depression were beginning to realize that ours was one of the few nations on earth where people weren't afraid of their leaders. We could talk against them, we could vote them out of office—and we could even put them up on a Broadway stage as the butt of ridicule in a song-and-dance show.

The idea of working with two such imaginative craftsmen as Kaufman and Hart was exciting, and the idea of doing this kind of show—which, at Dorothy's suggestion, was eventually called *I'd Rather Be Right*—was even more so. But then Kaufman and Hart told us the name of the actor they were getting for the leading role: George M. Cohan. When I heard the name I must have turned at least a dozen shades paler. Dammit, Larry and I had already had our fill of Cohan in *The Phantom President*. Didn't they know that he was a disgruntled man with no respect for anyone's work but his own? Didn't they realize what they were getting themselves into?

Moss tried to reason with me. Cohan, he confided, had nothing but the highest regard for Larry and me. It was simply that he was unaccustomed to working in Hollywood, and the studio had really treated him shabbily. This was going to be different. This would be Cohan returning to Broadway in a musical comedy after an absence of almost ten years, and he was anxious and grateful to be getting back to work. Besides, the show was to be presented by Cohan's closest friend and former partner, Sam H. Harris. Everyone knew that Sam was one of the sweetest men on Broadway and that he was just about the only person in the world who could keep Cohan in line. What's more, Cohan had only recently appeared in Eugene O'Neill's play *Ah, Wilderness!* for the Theatre Guild and from all reports had been a model of cooperation.

Well, I hated to see this opportunity going to someone else, and maybe Moss was right; maybe it *was* just Hollywood. Surely this was a great way for Cohan to cap his career, and he'd be crazy to blow it. Larry and I were also aware that we couldn't get just anybody for the part. It needed an outstanding star, and whatever we might feel about him personally, Cohan was exactly that, possibly the only one in the musical theatre who could play Roosevelt. So, heeding the famous Lee Shubert dictum, said about another actor, "Never have anything to do with that son of a bitch unless you need him," we agreed to do the show. And of course everything turned out to be even worse than we had feared.

Our first encounter took place on a lovely day early in September 1937 on the occasion of the first playing of the score for our star. Because I was apprehensive about the way Cohan would receive it, I thought it would be helpful to get away from the customary rehearsal hall or office where auditions usually take place. For the occasion my friend Jules Glaenzer kindly let us use his elegant East Side apartment, which had a living room so spacious that it contained two pianos.

All of us showed up at Glaenzer's that day—Harris, Kaufman, Hart, Larry and me—and when Cohan arrived, we seated him midway between the two pianos. I played one piano and Margot Hopkins, my rehearsal pianist, was at the other. Moss Hart did the singing. He didn't have a trained voice, of course, but he had excellent enunciation and an oddly charming way of putting over a song. All during the performance Cohan sat with his arms folded, his eyes half closed, his mouth drooping. No matter what the number, neither his expression nor his position changed. He never moved his head, smiled, frowned or said a word during the hour it took. This didn't bother me much, since I'm a quiet listener myself, but once we were finished, Cohan rose from his chair, walked over to me, patted me on the shoulder, mumbled, "Don't take any wooden nickels," and then walked out the door.

That was that. We all looked stunned. I tried to reassure the others by saying, "Maybe it will be like Chevalier," recalling the time when Maurice was equally noncommittal after hearing our songs for *Love Me Tonight*, only to return the next day full of praise. But we knew it wouldn't be, and it never was. Throughout our entire association with Cohan, Larry and I were treated with only thinly veiled patronizing contempt, and when we weren't around, we were told, he never referred to us by anything other than the sarcastic nicknames of "Gilbert and Sullivan."

One of the problems, which none of us was fully aware of before production began, was that Cohan hated Roosevelt. On our opening night in Boston he even added his own lyrics to an encore of "Off the Record" which were particularly cruel to the President. The pretext for this addition, according to Cohan, was that he objected to lyrics that Larry had written about Al Smith which *he* thought were too cruel. Actually, those particular lyrics had been discarded weeks before. The only reason Cohan put in his own lines was simply for his own ego—to show everyone that he could still beat us at our own game. Trying to make a joke of it after he sang the lines, Cohan confided to the audience—though of course for our benefit—"I'll probably get my two weeks' notice for doing that."

As soon as the performance was over, Larry and I raised hell with Sam Harris, and Cohan promised that he'd never do it again. Then, to our amazement, the next morning's New York *Herald Tribune* carried the entire story of the blowup with the following headlines:

COHAN REFUSES
TO SING LYRIC
ABOUT AL SMITH

IN BOSTON TRYOUT HE CUT
LINES, PUT IN HIS OWN
AND WRITERS OBJECT TO IT
BUT ALL'S HAPPY NOW

"GILBERT AND SULLIVAN OF
U.S." REWRITING THE PART

All hell broke loose again. Cohan was furious because he thought I had planted the story, and I was fuming over the "Gilbert and Sullivan" crack. Sam Harris prevailed upon me to try to placate our high-handed star, but there was little I could do. Luckily, there were no further incidents of this sort.

I can't say that my relationship with George S. Kaufman was much better. I'd known and liked Moss ever since our frustrating days in Hollywood writing *I Married an Angel,* but Kaufman's acerbic sense of humor never appealed to me. I was also amazed by his attitude toward musicals. Though he had been associated with some outstanding productions, both as writer and director, he had no love of music. He even told me that with *I'd Rather Be Right* he was deliberately setting out to prove that the book was more important that the songs. I'm quite willing to admit that our score for *I'd Rather Be Right* may not have been one for the ages, but it did seem a curious attitude for someone to express, especially to a composer. Anyway, Kaufman managed to convince Sam Harris that he was right, with the result that Kaufman and Hart got a higher royalty percentage than Rodgers and Hart.

*I'd Rather Be Right* may well have been the most eagerly awaited musical of all times. Our out-of-town tryouts were covered as if they were Broadway opening nights. Newspapers ran editorials about what a wonderful country we lived in where shows like this could be presented. Gags from the show were repeated all over town even before the official New York premiere. Perhaps expectations were too high because for the most part the reviews were not the out-and-out raves we had hoped for. Cohan, however, got ecstatic notices, and I'll be the first to admit that he fully deserved them.

Although our production was billed as "a musical revue," it did have a thin story line. A young couple in Central Park talk about getting married but the boy's boss won't give him a raise until Roosevelt balances the budget. In a dream, the boy and girl meet Roosevelt, who tries to do what he can to help. This somehow strengthens their resolve because once the dream is over they decide to get married anyway. Most of the time the show was merely a series of scenes that lent themselves to topical wisecracks and songs—a cabinet meeting, a fireside chat, a birthday party (with a dour Alf Landon as the butler) and a press conference. Dorothy's favorite lines were in Treasury Secretary Morgenthau's song:

> I'm quite a busy man right now—
> I'm Secretary Morgenthau.
> I have achieved, you must admit,
> The biggest goddam deficit!

This was part of a number called "A Homogeneous Cabinet" sung by leading members of Roosevelt's cabinet. Not exactly a catchy commercial title; nor was it meant to be. In fact, almost every song was written to express some viewpoint on major topics of the day, as revealed in such titles as "A Little Bit of Constitutional Fun," "Sweet Sixty-Five" (about Social Security), "We're Going to Balance the Budget," "Labor Is the Thing," "Off the Record" (for the press conference), and "A Baby Bond." Out of town, we had a romantic piece as the title song but this was changed before New York to an uptempo number with a political slant. Even our one remaining ballad, "Have You Met Miss Jones?," was introduced simply as one way of getting the President's cabinet to become sympathetic to the young lovers' plight.

*     *     *

After our experience with George M. and George S., Larry and I were anxious to return to people with whom we enjoyed working and with whom we shared a mutual respect. Our two experiences with Dwight Deere Wiman—*On Your Toes* and *Babes in Arms*—had proved so pleasant, as well as profitable, that we had made plans to do our next show together even before we began working on *I'd Rather Be Right.*

As I've already mentioned, back in 1933 Moss, Larry and I had collaborated on a screen treatment of *I Married an Angel.* One night at dinner I began telling Dwight all about the project—including, of course, the fact that M-G-M had never done anything about it. Without hearing a note or reading a word, Dwight gave us his assurance that if he could buy the property from the studio, he would present it on Broadway.

After protracted discussion, Wiman and M-G-M finally came to terms —and remarkable terms they were. The company gave Larry and me the right to make a stage musical out of all the material written for the unproduced film, provided that they would retain the right to pick up an option on the stage production for possible filming in the future. Within a week after the show opened, M-G-M did pick up the option and eventually made the picture.

For the musical stage version of *I Married an Angel,* Larry and I decided to return to the original Hungarian play rather than to Moss's scenario. Since we had recently written our own libretto for *Babes in Arms,* we felt confident that we could do at least as well with the new story.

Just as *Jumbo* had brought George Abbott into the musical-comedy field, so *I Married an Angel* was instrumental in adding another brilliant director to the ranks. Although Joshua Logan had been associated with Wiman in the past and had recently directed Dwight's highly acclaimed production of *On Borrowed Time,* he had never before directed a musical. One meeting, however, convinced us that he could handle the job with ease.

Josh Logan is a big hulk of a man with a flamboyant personality; he is also a diligent worker and a great worrier. After *I Married an Angel* had been in rehearsal for a week, he came to Larry and me and told us he was upset with the way things were going. That very night the three of us met in Larry's apartment to thrash things out. Almost every idea Josh offered made sense, and we decided to start immediately on a thorough rewrite. With his prodding, we threw out about a third of what we had written, adding new dialogue and situations, even entire scenes. All three of us took turns dictating to a secretary, and by the time we were finished, at six in the morning, we finally had a script that worked. I don't think there were more than half a dozen changes thereafter.

This show had some wonderful people in the cast. Dennis King had already had a solid career both in the classics and in operetta; Vivienne

Segal had been playing leading roles in musicals for some twenty years; Walter Slezak, like Dennis, was a highly versatile actor, with experience both in Europe and New York. But the one who stole the notices and the applause was Vera Zorina, here making her Broadway debut as the Angel. Dwight Wiman had been extremely impressed with her when he saw her in the London production of *On Your Toes*. Not wanting to oversell her, however, he cautiously mentioned that he thought she might be good in a small part in *I Married an Angel*. A little while later, when I was in Hollywood for the *Fools for Scandal* assignment, I was at a party when in walked a breath-takingly lovely young girl with a charming European accent who quickly had everyone crowding around her. The next day I sent Dwight a telegram: SMALL PART NOTHING HAVE JUST MET VERA ZORINA THATS OUR ANGEL.

In our play, we made no effort to condescend to our audience's imagination by putting the story in the form of a dream. Dennis didn't fall asleep or get bopped on the head to make it easier for people to accept the preposterous idea of a man marrying an angel. In effect, our attitude was take it or leave it; this fellow actually marries a real angel. And as so often is the case when you respect your audience, everyone was happy to go along with us.

The theme of the play was that it's possible for someone to be too good. Our angel nearly ruins her husband's life by her truthful but undiplomatic remarks. It is only when, under the expert tutelage of Vivienne Segal, she becomes devilish instead of angelic that the marriage is saved.

One of the scenes we added to the show during that all-night session was a takeoff on the Radio City Music Hall stage show which we called "At the Roxy Music Hall." It was a satirical fantasy, choreographed by George Balanchine, with a line of well-drilled Rockettes consisting solely of Vivienne Segal and Audrey Christie, and an arty underwater ballet with Zorina as a sea nymph. I haven't the faintest recollection of how the Radio City Music Hall got involved in a show set in Budapest, but in those days motivation was not among the most important factors in a musical comedy. If it worked, it worked, and this one did.

On opening night, however, it seemed to me that nothing was working. As Dorothy and I sat in the last row of the Shubert Theatre, I was certain that the show was dying before our eyes. There were only sporadic laughs and hardly any applause. During the intermission we both ran out for a drink at the nearby Astor Hotel bar—three drinks, as a matter of fact. Possibly because I was so well fortified, the second act seemed to go slightly better. Still, after the curtain I was sure we were going to have a hard time keeping it open for any kind of a run.

The next morning I picked up the *Times* fully expecting Brooks Atkinson to confirm my worst fears, and read: "*I Married an Angel* perches on the top shelf of the Rodgers and Hart musical cabinet. For this is no grinding of the Broadway hurdy-gurdy, but an imaginative improvisation with a fully orchestrated score and an extraordinarily beautiful production . . . Musical comedy has met its masters, and they have reared back and passed a Forty-fourth Street miracle." Wow! Could we have been at the same opening? Still slightly dazed, I read Richard Watts, Jr., in the *Herald Tribune:* "Thanks to a characteristically delightful score, imaginative settings, and the enchanting performance of Vera Zorina, it is a thoroughly charming musical comedy."

The afternoon papers were almost all on a par. "It has the most delightful score Mr. Rodgers has written in several seasons and some of Mr. Hart's drollest lyrics," wrote the *Post*'s John Mason Brown, who ended with: "Altogether a very pleasant and most unusual evening." Richard Lockridge in the *Sun* called it "a gay and capricious delight, full of jauntiness and grace and happy songs." To Sidney Whipple in the *World-Telegram,* it was "lavish entertainment," and John Anderson, the *Journal-American*'s critic, hailed it as "a winged wonderwork from the musical heavens of Rodgers and Hart."

In hindsight it is easy to say that I should have had more confidence, and that I should have known from experience that first-night audiences are notoriously inaccurate barometers. Those who give opinions are invariably the victims of wish-fulfilment, hoping the production will be good or bad, depending on their attitudes toward the people involved. But though I am very much aware of the many ultimate failures that are cheered passionately on opening night and the great successes that are received with coldness, I still cannot be oblivious to what I see and hear around me. Because of the first-night reception, I was certain that *I Married an Angel* was going to fail; it turned out to be our biggest hit in about ten years.

Chronology does not always give an indication of the time span during which shows are written. *On Your Toes* was ready before *Jumbo,* but was produced five months later; *I Married an Angel* was in the works well before *I'd Rather Be Right.* Hence, it shouldn't surprise anyone that the idea for *The Boys from Syracuse* came to Larry and me when we were busily involved with writing *I Married an Angel.*

That was early in 1938. We were on a train heading for Atlantic City, where we thought the fresh sea air might help to stimulate some new ideas. For some reason we began discussing Shakespeare, which led to our discovery that no one had ever thought of using one of his plays as the basis of a musical comedy.

The mere fact that it had never been done before was reason enough for us to start thinking that it should be our next project. The problems of *I Married an Angel* were pushed aside for the rest of the trip as we began tossing around titles of plays. Even eliminating the tragedies and histories, we had a pretty large field to choose from.

But one play attracted us from the start, and for a very personal reason. Larry's younger brother, Teddy, was a clever comedian best known for such George Abbott farces as *Three Men on a Horse* and *Room Service*. He was short and dark, and though he looked a good deal like Larry, he was always being mistaken for another gifted comic, Jimmy Savo.

"Why don't we do *The Comedy of Errors?*" Larry said, rubbing his hands together as he always did when a good idea hit him. "Teddy and Jimmy would be a natural for the twin Dromios." Nepotism notwithstanding, we both realized that it was an inspired casting idea, and once *I Married an Angel* was behind us, we got down to serious work on the show that eventually became known as *The Boys from Syracuse*.

When we started talking about a director for this kind of musical farce, we could come up with only one name: George Abbott. Moreover, George was so enthusiastic that he decided to produce the show himself. At first Larry and I were supposed to collaborate on the script with him, but he had it all finished before we could get started. The book was so sharp, witty, fast-moving and, in an odd way, so very much in keeping with the bawdy Shakespearean tradition that neither Larry nor I wanted to change a line.

There was one line, though, that George appropriated directly from the original play. This was the Seeress's "The venom clamours of a jealous woman poisons more deadly than a mad dog's tooth." Lest anyone unfamiliar with the classics accept this as a sentence he had thought up all by himself, George had Jimmy Savo follow it by sticking his head out from the wings and proudly announcing to the audience: "Shakespeare!"

The cast for *The Boys from Syracuse* was full of talented young people. Besides Teddy and Jimmy, we had Eddie Albert and Ronald Graham as the Antipholus of Syracuse and the Antipholus of Ephesus. There were also three notable charmers for our leading ladies: Marcy Westcott, Muriel Angelus and an energetic cream puff named Wynn Murray.

Abbott whipped the show into beautiful shape, and George Balanchine was again with us to stage the dances. It was fortunate that everything went so smoothly because Larry's disappearances had become more frequent than ever. When he was there, he worked rapidly; all we had to say was that we wanted a new line or two or a complete new verse and it wouldn't take him long to come up with exactly what was needed. Once Abbott and I were deep in conversation at a table and Larry was sitting with us. Our animated talk didn't bother him in the least; he just kept scribbling away and when he was finished he'd written the verse to "Falling in Love with Love."

Last-minute changes are fully expected in the creation of a musical, and Larry was certainly aware of how important it was to be with the show during its tryout. But when *The Boys from Syracuse* company took off for New Haven, he was nowhere to be found. Luckily, the show was so well set that no further work was needed, but how much longer could our luck hold out?

We found out soon enough, and the answer, as I had feared, was not reassuring. A few weeks after *The Boys from Syracuse* opened successfully on Broadway in November 1938, George Abbott came to Larry and me with the idea of doing a rah-rah college-football musical called *Too Many Girls*. The script was by a writer named George Marion, Jr., who had done some of the writing for *Love Me Tonight*, and though the story had originally been conceived for the movies, it was easily adjusted to the requirements of the stage. Larry and I were drawn to the idea, I suppose, because it gave us the chance to work again with talented young people who were not yet anointed as "stars." We signed Marcy Westcott, who had been in *The Boys from Syracuse*, and Mary Jane Walsh, who had been in *I'd Rather Be Right*. Our All-American backfield consisted of Richard Kollmar, Desi Arnaz, Eddie Bracken and Hal LeRoy, and our cheerleaders were led by Diosa Costello and Leila Ernst. We were back in *Babes in Arms* country again, and it was fun.

Larry, however, was no fun at all. It was almost impossible to find him when we needed him, and this time we needed him desperately. The show had many rough spots and we were constantly cutting and rearranging the songs. I vaguely remember that I came up with the idea for the opening number in the show, "Heroes in the Fall," in which the football players of Pottawatomie College lament the brevity of their tenure as campus luminaries. Since Larry was nowhere to be found, I had to supply the necessary lyric myself. This happened on a few other occasions as well.

All the major songs, however, did have lyrics written by Larry. Because our story dealt, more or less, with an institution of learning, in "I Didn't Know What Time It Was" he came up with the idea of discovering both love and wisdom, and in "Love Never Went to College" he personified love as an ignorant but all-powerful ruler. Two songs in the score even allowed us the chance to express our feelings in a light-hearted way about situations of current concern. We had already serenaded our romantically idealized city in "Manhattan," and now, in "Give It Back to the Indians," we turned things around and pointed out its blemishes. Some of the problems we touched on are still very much with us today:

Broadway's turning into Coney,
Champagne Charlie's drinking gin,
Old New York is new and phoney—
Give it back to the Indians.
Two cents more to smoke a Lucky,
Dodging buses keeps you thin,
New New York is simply ducky—
Give it back to the Indians.
Take all the reds on the boxes made for soap,
Whites on Fifth Avenue,
Blues down in Wall Street losing hope—
Big bargain today,
Chief, take it away!
Come, you busted city slickers,
Better take it on the chin,
Father Knick has lost his knickers,
Give it back to the Indians!

Larry even wrote the lines "We've tried to run the City/But the City ran away," probably the earliest admission in song that New York is ungovernable.

Our other beef was registered in "I Like to Recognize the Tune," in which we voiced objection to the musical distortions then so much a part of pop music because of the swing-band influence. We really had nothing against swing bands *per se,* but as songwriters we felt it was tough enough for new numbers to catch on as written without being subjected to all kinds of interpretive manhandling that obscured their melodies and lyrics. To me, this was the musical equivalent of bad grammar. On the other hand, once a song has become established I see nothing wrong with taking certain liberties. A singer or an orchestra can add a distinctive, personal touch that actually contributes to a song's longevity. I can't say I'm exactly grief-stricken when something I've written years before suddenly catches on again because of a new interpretation.

*Too Many Girls* was not one of Broadway's immortals, but it received enthusiastic notices and had a respectable run. To tell the truth, I scarcely cared; overshadowing everything was Larry, and he worried me greatly.

At about this time I was commissioned by the Ballet Russe de Monte Carlo, then the foremost ballet company in the world, to compose the score for a new work. I was particularly appreciative of the chance, since *Too Many Girls* had provided little that was creatively challenging, and I was also glad to get away, however briefly, from the Larry Hart problem.

It was Gerald Murphy, the wealthy ballet patron and artist, who first interested me in doing this score. At the time, the Ballet Russe specialized in the classics or in new works by European choreographers and composers, and Gerald was anxious to see the Paris-based company expand its repertory by adding ballets that would be completely American in theme and choreography. A young dancer named Marc Platt had an idea for a ballet based on the gold rush, and Gerald brought us together to work on the libretto. Our tale, which we called *Ghost Town,* concerned an old miner in a ghost town who tells a story to a couple of tourists about a gold prospector and his fortunes and misfortunes. As the story unfolds, the scene changes to the days of the gold rush, and at the end, the old miner turns out to be the protagonist of his story. We brought in a lot of characters, including Jenny Lind and Algernon Swinburne, and I'm afraid it was too cluttered and involved for its own good. But it was given a sumptuous production with some of the company's most gifted dancers and it did serve its purpose of introducing a native American work into the repertory. Years later the Ballet Russe would do far better with other Western ballets, most notably Agnes de Mille's *Rodeo,* but at least *Ghost Town* was the one that started the trend.

I conducted all the New York performances. What made the first evening truly memorable was that my family—Dorothy, Mary, Linda, Mom and Pop—was in the audience, beaming down on me from a box. Little Richard, who used to show off for company in front of his parents' living-room fireplace, was now showing off in the pit of the Metropolitan Opera House.

One rehearsal incident I'll never forget. I was naturally nervous about conducting the famed orchestra of the Ballet Russe, and one day, following a run-through, the first trumpeter jumped up from his chair and yelled "Rodgers!" Now I knew I was in trouble. No one yells "Rodgers!" to the conductor—and composer!—unless there's something wrong. Then, breaking into a wide grin, the man said, "Rodgers, Broadway composer, from you I expected hot licks!"

*Higher and Higher,* the next musical on the Rodgers and Hart agenda, was a classic example of my theory that it's impossible to redesign a show once the basic concept proves unworkable. With Vera Zorina such a tremendous success in *I Married an Angel,* it was only natural for Larry and me to attempt a musical tailored to her specific and considerable gifts. Josh Logan brought us an amusing story about a maid who is passed off as a debutante, and we thought it would work just fine.

Zorina was then in Hollywood making, among other films, *On Your Toes,* and was unable to return to New York because of her screen commitments. Perhaps we should have waited for her, but at the time it seemed best to have the play rewritten to fit someone else. Which decision led straight to disaster. The Hungarian actress Marta Eggert was chosen to play the lead, but she was an entirely different type from Zorina—for one thing, she was a singer, not a dancer—and the show suffered. It wasn't that Marta wasn't good, but the part wasn't good for her. It had taken me years to learn that a show can be altered, songs can be added or dropped, and actors can be replaced, but once the basic structure of the production is set, it is suicide to try to change it.

If *Higher and Higher* is remembered at all today it is probably not because of its cast or songs but because of a trained seal. This leads to another of Rodgers' Irrefutable Rules: If a trained seal steals your show, you don't have a show.

In the summer of 1940, two events had a profound effect upon me.

The war in Europe had begun the previous September, but apart from my hope that it would somehow end quickly with the destruction of Hitler, it did not concern me directly. For a while, in fact, there was so little military action that it was dubbed the "phoney" war, and it appeared that some kind of settlement would be agreed to. Then, suddenly, Germany began its lightning invasion of Norway and Denmark, followed by the conquest of Holland, Belgium and France. Obviously England was the next target, and news from our friends in London was not reassuring. Myrtle d'Erlanger, our closest friend over there, was so concerned for the safety of her daughter that she cabled us to ask if Zoë and her nurse could live with us for the duration of the war. Zoë was a charming, bright child, about a year older than Mary, and for the three and a half years she was with us, she was almost as close to Dorothy and me as our own daughters. It was fortunate that she came at the time she did because only a few weeks after she arrived, England was subjected to the devastating Battle of Britain.

The other event, which occurred early in September, was the death of my mother. For the past few years my parents had made a custom of taking extended vacations at the Traymore Hotel in Atlantic City. This time they had been away for about a month when I got a telephone call from my father. With a voice that was ominously unsteady, he said, "Richard, your mother's very sick." When I told him that Dorothy and I would catch the next train down, he said, "Don't rush, don't rush. It's too late."

Dorothy and I and Morty and his wife went down to Atlantic City together to bring Pop home and to be of whatever help we could. What had happened was simply that Mom had awakened in the morning, complained of a pain and suddenly died of a stroke.

At the time of Mom's death, my folks were living at the Hotel Croydon, at Eighty-sixth Street and Madison Avenue. When Pop walked into the apartment he did the kind of inexplicable thing all of us are likely to do in times of crisis. He went straight to his desk and said he had to write some letters. When I asked what letters could be so important that they had to be written at a time like this, he said he was writing to the magazines to which he subscribed advising them to change his subscription address from the Traymore Hotel back to the Croydon.

During the first few months after my mother's death, my father continued to be remarkably composed until one evening when Dorothy and I were taking him back to the Croydon in a taxi. Without any provocation he suddenly burst into tears. Neither Dorothy nor I said anything, but we knew what he was going through.

Ours was a close family and Mom's death affected us all deeply. Her understanding and sympathy, particularly at the time when I was floundering around at the beginning of my career, were something I shall always hold dear, and for which I shall always be grateful.

## 15

Thursday

Dear Dick:

I don't know whether you happened to see any of a series of pieces I've been doing for *The New Yorker* in the past year or so. They're about a guy who is master of ceremonies in cheap night clubs, and the pieces are in the form of letters from him to a successful band leader. Anyway, I got the idea that the pieces, or at least the character and the life in general, could be made into a book show, and I wonder if you and Larry would be interested in working on it with me. I read that you two have a commitment with Dwight Wiman for a show this spring, but if and when you get through with that I do hope you like my idea.

All the best to you always. Please remember me to the beautiful Dorothy and say hello to Larry for me. Say more than hello, too.

Faithfully,

John O'Hara

I was in Boston with *Too Many Girls* in October 1939 when the letter reached me. John and I had known each other for a few years, but it had never occurred to me that there would be a point at which our professional careers might meet. The letter was a total surprise, and a welcome one.

Since *Jumbo,* Larry and I had had phenomenal luck with most of our shows, but the problem of what to do next was constantly with us. I knew that *Too Many Girls* was not in the same league as our previous musicals, and I had certain misgivings about *Higher and Higher,* the Wiman commitment O'Hara referred to in his letter. But a musical based on O'Hara's Pal Joey stories in *The New Yorker* could be something really special. The "hero" was a conniver and braggart who would do anything and sleep anywhere to get ahead. The idea of doing a musical without a conventional clean-cut juvenile in the romantic lead opened up enormous possibilities for a more realistic view of life than theatregoers were accustomed to.

As I expected, Larry was equally enthusiastic about the project. He had spent thousands of hours in exactly the kind of atmosphere depicted in the stories and was thoroughly familiar with the Pal Joeys of this world.

Not only would the show be totally different from anything we had ever done before, it would be different from anything anyone else had ever tried. This alone was reason enough for us to want to do it.

I didn't make O'Hara wait long before sending him a telegram expressing our interest. He was then in California writing film scripts, and we had a long correspondence discussing various aspects of the project.

Almost as soon as I began writing to John, I had decided on the actor I wanted for the leading role. A week after *Too Many Girls* opened, Dorothy and I went to the opening-night performance of William Saroyan's play *The Time of Your Life*. In the small role of an aspiring entertainer was an especially engaging young man named Gene Kelly. The stage was aglow with life whenever he appeared, and his dancing was superb. The next day I wrote O'Hara that we had our Joey.

What John had in mind was not a musical based on any single story, but something that would borrow scenes and characters from a number of stories. As the plot developed, it turned out to be about Joey's affair with a wealthy woman, what she does to help him get ahead, and her ultimate disillusionment with him. Next to Joey, the show's most important role would be that of the benefactress, and since Vivienne Segal had been so right as the worldly cynic in *I Married an Angel*, she seemed like a natural for the part in *Pal Joey*. She was.

Work on *Pal Joey* began in earnest soon after the opening of *Higher and Higher*. There were problems right from the start. The Larry Hart problem I knew about, and with luck I could cope with it. But I was unprepared for the problems with O'Hara and with George Abbott, who had agreed to be both producer and director.

Strangely, though it was O'Hara who first broached the idea of a musical-comedy *Pal Joey*, he turned out to be rather indifferent, after he came East, to the creative aspects of the show. Like Larry, he proved difficult to nail down to do any work. There were periods during which I didn't hear from him for several weeks, and I couldn't even get him on the telephone. Finally, in desperation, I sent him a wire: SPEAK TO ME JOHN SPEAK TO ME. But nothing could change him, so a lot of the rewriting fell to Abbott himself—though occasionally John would drop by to make revisions of the revisions.

The problem with Abbott was of an entirely different nature. This was the third Rodgers and Hart musical produced by Abbott, and the first one that presented any differences about money. One day he informed me that he felt Larry and I were getting too much of a royalty and that we should agree to take a cut. He was never specific about why he thought so, and I told him that I couldn't understand his attitude. We parted without either of us giving in. A day or so later I saw him again, and this time he told me that he had been talking to his general manager, who had convinced him to pay us our regular royalty. I was pleased to hear this, of course, but I couldn't help wondering why George needed—or heeded—someone else's advice on such a matter.

The whole issue was curious, until two incidents gave me some inkling of the way George's mind was working. The first came at a meeting I had with Jo Mielziner, who was designing the show. When I made certain suggestions about the sets, he said, "You know, George told me to spend as little money as possible on production costs." Why? "Well," said Jo, "George hasn't got much faith in this show."

This disturbing attitude was confirmed soon afterward by Bob Alton, our choreographer, who told me that he needed two more girls for the chorus. I suggested that he call Abbott and say so. Bob did, and then relayed the startling message that George had told him that if he wanted two more girls in the chorus, he should get me to pay their salaries.

The next morning in George's office I told him about my meetings with Mielziner and Alton, and then said calmly, "George, I think you ought to give this show up. I don't think you're the right one to produce it. It's obvious that you have no faith in it, and the best thing all around would be for us to find someone else who does."

Apparently this was enough to straighten things out. Abbott may not have been wild about doing *Pal Joey,* but, by God, he wasn't about to let anyone else get his hands on it. Mielziner got the money for the settings, Alton got his two extra girls, and Larry and I never heard another word about a royalty cut.

Why George put us through all this I really don't know. Perhaps because of the daring nature of our show he thought he was sticking his neck out a bit too far. Apparently people must have told him that it wasn't commercial to do a show with such a disreputable character for a hero, and he was apprehensive about losing money on so risky a venture.

But whatever his personal attitude, the production George staged was a beauty. Nothing was softened for the sake of making the characters more appealing. Joey was a heel at the beginning and he never reformed. At the end the young lovers did not embrace as the orchestra swelled with the strains of the main romantic duet; in fact, they walked off in opposite directions. There wasn't one decent character in the entire play except for the girl who briefly fell for Joey—her trouble was simply that she was stupid.

Throughout our score for *Pal Joey*, Larry and I were scrupulous in making every song adhere to the hard-edged nature of the story. Taken by itself, "I Could Write a Book" is perfectly straightforward and sincere; in the context of the plot, however, Joey, who had probably never read a book in his life, sang it for no other reason than to impress a naïve girl he had just picked up on the street.

Because of the night-club setting of most of the musical's action, Larry and I were able to have fun writing numbers burlesquing typically tacky floor shows. We had all our chorus girls parade around with little on except headdresses representing flowers (in "The Flower Garden of My Heart") and colors ("That Terrific Rainbow"). But of all the songs, the one that has endured the longest is unquestionably "Bewitched, Bothered and Bewildered." Here we tried something that is particularly effective in comedy numbers—the contrast of a flowing, sentimental melody with words that are unsentimental and self-mocking: "Lost my heart, but what of it?/ My mistake, I agree./ He's a laugh but I love it/ Because the laugh's on me." At the end of the show, we used the melody again, but now the lyric expressed the reverse:

> Romance—finis
> Your chance—finis
> Those ants that invaded my pants—finis—
> Bewitched, bothered and bewildered no more!

There was no question that *Pal Joey* was radically different. Brooks Atkinson, of the *Times*, the most influential of all the critics and usually among the most discerning, referred to the story as "odious," and ended his review by asking, "Although it is expertly done, can you draw sweet water from a foul well?" Fortunately, other appraisers were more appreciative, including Wolcott Gibbs, of *The New Yorker*, who wrote: "I am not optimistic by nature but it seems to me just possible that the idea of equipping a song-and-dance production with a few living, three-dimensional figures, talking and behaving like human beings, may no longer strike the boys in the business as merely fantastic."

We had reason to be proud of *Pal Joey*, and despite legend that the show lacked popular appeal, it did have a successful eleven-month run, followed by a three-month tour.

But legends die hard. In 1952, when Jule Styne, who was then a producer as well as a composer, secured the rights for a revival of *Pal Joey*, he met with tremendous difficulties in raising the necessary money. At one point things looked so bleak that I pleaded with him to drop the project. But Jule had a stubborn faith for which I shall be eternally grateful, and eventually he managed to get the show on. With Vivienne Segal, looking not a day older and again playing the feminine lead, and Harold Lang now in the title role, *Pal Joey* was greeted as the freshest, most exciting musical of the season. This time the slightly gloating Wolcott Gibbs wrote: "Standards apparently have changed because up to now I have met nobody who found anything embarrassing in the goings on." Brooks Atkinson admitted that though he had been less than enchanted by the show when he first saw it, a second viewing convinced him that the musical "was a pioneer in the moving back of musical frontiers, for it tells an integrated story with a knowing point of view . . . Brimming over with good music and fast on its toes, it renews confidence in the professionalism of the theatre."

In a personal appraisal, which appeared in the *Times* on the occasion of this new production, I wrote: "Larry Hart knew what John O'Hara knew —that Joey was not disreputable because he was mean, but because he had too much imagination to behave himself and because he was a little weak. While Joey himself may have been fairly adolescent in his thinking and his morality, the show bearing his name certainly wore long pants and in many respects forced the entire musical-comedy theatre to wear long pants for the first time."

*Pal Joey* was the most satisfying and mature work that I was associated with during all my years with Larry Hart. And how did I follow it up? By taking piano lessons. My sight-reading had never been good, and I felt that if I didn't do anything about it now, I'd never get around to it. I also had a particular reason: I wanted to play well enough to be able to join a few other musicians from time to time to perform some of the standard chamber-music works.

My teacher was an old friend, Herman Wasserman, who was extremely helpful. I had a marvelous time practicing four or five hours a day, and it did a great deal of good not only for my playing but for my composing too. I'm afraid, however, that I never really progressed far enough to perform chamber music. Besides, after the United States became directly involved in the war, there simply wasn't anyone around to play with.

One morning early in May 1941, after Mary, Linda and Zoë d'Erlanger had gone off to school, Dorothy and I received a cablegram informing us of the death of Zoë's mother, Myrtle, in a German air raid. The news was shattering. That morning Zoë was appearing in a school production of *The Mikado,* and Dorothy and I had promised to attend. All we could think about as we saw her singing and acting on the stage was that we would soon have to tell her the dreadful news.

Later in the day, after we had returned home, we sat Zoë down and told her as gently as we could what had happened. During the entire time she just sat looking at us, betraying not the slightest sign of what was going on inside her. When we finished, all she said was, "Don't tell Linda." At such a time, this remarkable child could think only of protecting the feelings of another child five years younger.

There is little that anyone can do to console a person in such a tragic situation. By coincidence, however, Dorothy and I had recently made a decision that helped slightly to mitigate the pain: we had decided to move out of the city. Though we had always considered ourselves city people, we found that living in a New York apartment with three growing girls did make life a bit cramped, particularly since my work required me to do much of my writing at home. We had friends who had bought homes in and around Fairfield, Connecticut, and we always enjoyed the feeling of spaciousness and serenity whenever we visited them. It was close enough to the city and far enough away to give us what we thought would be the best of two worlds.

We found a place on Black Rock Turnpike in Fairfield that seemed suitably large enough for the kids to romp around in. It was a Colonial house, built on a high knoll, with fifteen rooms and five baths and situated on about six and a half acres. The house was more functional than attractive, but we decided to buy it because Dorothy and I fell in love with a tree standing in the front yard. It was a massive oak with a ninety-foot spread and we thought it the most magnificent tree we had ever seen. So in June, after the children's school year, the Rodgers family—including Zoë d'Erlanger—packed up and moved to Black Rock Turnpike. We were not to have a permanent New York address for the next four years.

During August the Duke of Kent, who was Zoë's godfather, visited President and Mrs. Roosevelt at Hyde Park. Because he was anxious to see Zoë, the Roosevelts invited the Rodgerses and their young English charge to visit them. (The invitation failed to include the Rodgers children, an omission that Mary found especially hard to endure.)

The Duke and the Roosevelts were all at Val-Kill Cottage, Mrs. Roosevelt's private house, when we arrived. I could not help but notice that the President's granite-like head and muscular shoulders and arms looked incongruous in contrast to his painfully feeble legs. When we shook hands, mine actually seemed to disappear into his. Later Mrs. Roosevelt took Zoë for a swim in her pool so that the Duke could tell us the horrible circumstances of Myrtle d'Erlanger's death. She had been killed during one of the most devastating air raids over London and her body was not discovered until four days later.

My memory of this visit will always be dominated by that remarkable woman, Eleanor Roosevelt. One incident was especially revealing. After making a graceful dive into the pool, she quickly swam to the shallow end and then bounded out of the water to join us. We were all impressed with her skill, and Dorothy commented that it was obvious she had been swimming and diving all her life. Mrs. Roosevelt beamed. "Oh dear, no," she said. "I learned to dive only recently. It was my grandchildren. They were making fun of me because I didn't know how, and I was determined to show them I could do anything they could do!"

Zoë d'Erlanger remained with us for almost three and a half years. Dorothy and I often talked about how much we would love to adopt her, but we were sure that her family would never allow it. The war was still going on when she was told that she would have to return home because her great-uncle was very ill and wanted to see her before he died. Seeing her leave under any circumstance would have been painful, but at this time it was almost unbearable. With her English nanny, Zoë had to make the perilous trip by freighter to Lisbon, then by plane to England. Dorothy and I spent many a restless night worrying about her, but fortunately she was unharmed during the journey and the remaining years of the war. Now married, with a family of her own, she is still very close to the Rodgers family and her annual visits are always happy ones.

Nineteen forty-one was the first time in six years that Rodgers and Hart did not have a new show on Broadway, and the reason, I'm afraid, was Larry.

The drinking, the staying out all night and the disappearances were increasing to an alarming degree. It was now almost impossible to rely on him to keep an appointment, and if he did, he was seldom in condition to do any work. He no longer seemed to give a damn about anything. He still wore elevator shoes to make him appear taller, but he'd given up his hair-restoring treatments and looked as if he slept in his clothes.

Larry Hart was not my responsibility except insofar as our professional collaboration was concerned. Still, because of my deep affection for him, it would have been inhuman if I didn't do what I could to help. Not that he felt that he needed help. From the start he had made it clear that he led the life he wanted and was not about to change it for anyone, though I knew it bothered him that, as he once told me, his mother was constantly nagging him to "settle down like Dick and marry a nice girl." But the fact remained that I had known him for over twenty years. We had worked together, struggled together and succeeded together, and I simply could not look the other way while this man destroyed himself.

One way I could help was with money. Larry was never in need of money, but he had no concern about it and was constantly throwing it away. I couldn't stop him from spending it foolishly or being an easy touch, but I could make it difficult. The scheme I devised was actually an idea my father gave me. It was Pop's plan to get Larry to agree to turn over to me a certain amount of money each week, which I dutifully put in a safe-deposit box in his name. What made the scheme work was that Larry had no idea where the safe-deposit box was located.

Later our friends Edna Ferber and Peggy Pulitzer recommended a wonderful man named Willy Kron to handle all of Larry's finances. Willy was far more than just a financial wizard who advised his client where to invest his money. He loved Larry and spent a great deal of time with him trying to keep him out of trouble. Larry was grateful enough to Willy to put him in his will.

There was a time when I thought psychiatry might help. Once, following a three-day drinking binge, Larry agreed to go to Doctors Hospital to get dried out. While he was there, I went to see Dr. Richard Hoffman, a well-known psychiatrist, and told him about Larry's problems. I knew that Larry would never voluntarily submit to psychoanalysis, but the doctor told me not to worry: he'd simply pass himself off as a hospital staff member and drop in to see him from time to time. He was sure that the deception would work and promised to keep me advised. That night I received a telephone call from Larry. All he had to say was, "Your witch doctor was in to see me," and that was the end of that.

I have made much of Larry's "disappearances" in this book. The logical question is, "Where did he go?" and my honest answer is, "I don't know." After our working day was over, I would go home to my family. I was never with Larry on any of his binges, though I did know that he liked hanging around Ralph's Bar on Forty-fifth Street in the heart of the theatre district. I also know that he frequently went to the Luxor Baths to get steamed out. Other than that—what he did, where he went, and with whom —I have no idea. What mattered to me, as far as our work was concerned, was that he was never available in the morning, and that when he did show up sometime in the afternoon he would be fresh from the barber, with his face heavily powdered and his eyes deeply pouched. Occasionally he might mumble something about having overslept, or having had a rough night, but most of the time he never gave any excuse. After our many years together I knew better than to press him for details.

One of the odd aspects of our partnership was that we never had a fight. Disagreements, of course, but only about work and never about anything serious. Basically he was such a sweet guy that it was impossible to be angry with him. I could be angry with what he was doing to himself and what this was doing to our relationship, but I never reached the point of issuing ultimatums or expressing my displeasure in a direct manner.

Perhaps at an early stage a confrontation might have done some good. Perhaps not. I was always so anxious to get on with my work and so impressed with the quality of work Larry produced that I was genuinely fearful of upsetting what was, to judge by the finished product, a closely coordinated, harmonious team.

One of the questions I'm most frequently asked is about our working method. This cannot be answered simply, because there were many methods. Larry seldom gave me a completed lyric; at best it would be no more than a verse or opening chorus. Occasionally he would give me a title which would suggest a melody. Most of the time I would play a completed melody for him and we'd sit around tossing titles and lyric ideas at each other. Once we agreed on the general theme, Larry would write the words and we'd have a finished song. For example, one afternoon I said to him, "Why don't we start off with a title that doesn't suggest a typical lyric, that has absolutely nothing to do with a romantic expression?"

"For instance?"

"Oh . . . 'I've Got Five Dollars.' "

As the years went on, Larry's concentration span became shorter and shorter. He could never work alone, so I knew that if he didn't show, it meant that no work was being done. During all our sessions he was good-natured and usually willing to compromise. For my part, I not only had to supply the musical themes to get him started, I also had to supply him with periodic drinks. He was a phenomenally fast worker and luckily I was too, because he could be controlled for just so many hours. Then, with little warning, he'd grab his hat and coat and be gone.

Much as I loved Larry and much as I took pride in what we had accomplished together, in the summer of 1941 I realized that the situation was becoming critical. I was thirty-nine years old, in good health and supremely grateful to be able to do the kind of work I loved, but I was linked professionally to a man forty-six years old who was compulsively bent on self-destruction and who no longer cared about his work. I *had* to think about the unthinkable: I had to think about a life without Larry Hart.

At first I felt guilty about it. Everybody thought of Rodgers and Hart as an indivisible team. People never thought of one without the other; in fact, it was almost one word: Rodgersandhart. Those who didn't know us personally neither knew nor cared if we had first names or that we were two totally dissimilar human beings. Never before had there been a writing team with such a long partnership in the history of the Broadway theatre, nor one more closely associated in the public mind.

I was even more concerned about what a break would do to Larry. He always looked on me as something of a big brother. Though he had a mind of his own when it came to the kind of songs and shows we should do, in almost every other professional area he was totally dependent on me. Pounding out songs for potential backers, auditioning singers, discussing terms, even tracking down producers who owed us money—these were always my jobs. The thought of leaving Larry was the most painful aspect of the entire situation. For the first time since the days when I was struggling unsuccessfully to get a start in the theatre, I was plagued by insomnia. I just couldn't see any way to avoid hurting someone. Still, I knew that I had to start planning for the day when Larry would no longer be able to work.

Once I began thinking of this inevitability, I was faced with the problem of finding someone to replace Larry. Who could equal his talent and also be the kind of partner with whom I could work closely and successfully? Many gifted lyric writers came to mind, but I always returned to one man: Oscar Hammerstein.

There were many reasons why I should not have thought of Oscar. He had always been part of a romantic, florid kind of theatre, more operetta than musical comedy, which was quite different from Larry's and mine. He had written his best lyrics with men of traditional, classical European backgrounds or training, such as Rudolf Friml, Sigmund Romberg and Jerome Kern. Also, I had to face the fact that he had not had a solid Broadway success in almost ten years.

But the main point was that I had absolute faith in Oscar's talent. I had seen show after show in which his lyrics were of high quality but whose productions were so stale, flat and obviously unprofitable that nothing could have helped them. I was convinced that any man who could write *Show Boat, Sweet Adeline* and the lyric to Jerome Kern's "All the Things You Are" was far from being through, that his talent was being misused rather than used up. Oscar's kind of theatre was rapidly becoming passé and mine was all too often in a rut. If we both were flexible and dedicated enough, perhaps something fresh and worthwhile could emerge from our combined efforts.

There were other considerations. Oscar was an old friend. I had known him ever since I was a kid and had even written a few songs with him. Though we did not see each other regularly, I always felt that I could turn to him if I had a problem, and I think he felt the same way about me. I was also aware that his background was not dissimilar from mine, and that, apart from the theatre we shared many similar views. Nor was it lost on me that Oscar was considered something of an anomaly on Broadway: a genuine pipe-and-slippers man who abhorred night life, had a closely knit family and was devoted to a warm, charming, attractive wife whose name also happened to be Dorothy. Thus, almost from the start the possibilities narrowed to one.

During the period that I was most despondent about Larry's condition, George Abbott asked me to read the script of a musical comedy he was planning to produce. It turned out to be another collegiate story, with some funny lines and clever situations, but this time George was not interested in a Rodgers and Hart score. He was, understandably, anxious to try his luck with a new team, though he wanted me to join him as co-producer and general overseer of the musical department. I agreed, but only on one condition: fearing that people might interpret this activity as a rift between Larry and me, I insisted that my name not be used in publicity or listed in the program credits. Because we had the libretto before we had a composer and lyricist, George and I held a number of auditions before giving the assignment for the show, which we eventually called *Best Foot Forward,* to two gifted newcomers, Hugh Martin and Ralph Blane.

I was in Philadelphia with the show during its pre-Broadway tryout in September 1941 when I unburdened myself to Abbott about my fears concerning Larry. George was even more pessimistic than I was. Almost instinctively, I picked up a telephone and called Oscar Hammerstein at his farm in Doylestown, Pennsylvania. The place was only about an hour's drive from Philadelphia, and I invited myself over for lunch the next day.

Seeing Oscar again in the surroundings of his rustic, solid farmhouse gave me a feeling of assurance that the situation could not be as bleak as I feared. Dependable, realistic, sensitive Oscar Hammerstein was the right man, possibly the only man, who not only would be understanding about my problem but would make constructive suggestions.

Over lunch I told him what was happening between Larry and me, and of my concern for the future of our partnership. Oscar listened without saying a word. He thought for a minute or two after I finished, and then said, "I think you ought to keep working with Larry just so long as he is able to keep working with you. It would kill him if you walked away while he was still able to function. But if the time ever comes when he cannot function, call me. I'll be there."

It was exactly what I had hoped to hear. Then he said something that revealed even more the kind of selfless person he was. "I'll even go a step further," he told me. "If you and Larry are in the middle of a job and he can't finish it, I'll finish it for him, and nobody but the two of us ever need know."

I left Oscar that day with enough of the weight removed from my shoulders to make me feel a bit more optimistic than I had for months.

My personal problems were real enough, but at this particular time, worrying about a songwriting partnership was quickly put into perspective by even a cursory glance at the daily headlines. A state of unlimited national emergency had existed in the United States since the previous May, and almost everything that happened in the world seemed to be moving us inexorably into a global conflict. At last others were beginning to realize what the Rodgers family had already learned in a very personal way: that the fate of the United States was inescapably linked to the fate of Great Britain.

Because of our emotional involvement, Dorothy and I were active in organizations that aided the Allies. Just three weeks prior to the Pearl Harbor attack, we were in Canada—along with Larry, Jane Froman and André Kostelanetz—to do what we could to help the Canadian War Savings drive. Since the United States was not yet on a wartime footing, it was a shock to visit a country that was. During the day we talked, sang and performed at at least half a dozen army camps near Toronto, and at night we took part in a radio broadcast. We had been on the go ever since seven o'clock in the morning and by midnight, when we caught the train back to New York, we were all exhausted but also exhilarated. As we walked through the station to our train, Jane Froman, who was so tired that I had to support her, suddenly burst out laughing. "You know, Dick," she said, "if we were getting paid to do this, we'd all raise hell!"

I remember the Canadian trip for another reason: Larry. On the night train going up he had spent almost all the time drinking himself into a stupor. After we arrived at the hotel in Toronto the next morning for breakfast, with many local dignitaries there to greet us, he got as far as the corridor outside the dining room when he got violently sick all over the floor. Dorothy and I shared a two-bedroom suite with Larry, and when we came back upstairs she went directly into his room, and for the first and only time in all the years that she knew him, let him know that she was aware of his drinking. All she said was, "Give me the bottles," and Larry, probably because he was so shocked by the order, meekly handed them over. As she was leaving the room he pleaded, "When can I have a drink?" "Tonight after the radio show" was Dorothy's no-nonsense answer.

Larry comported himself fairly well during the day and made the tour of the camps and the city hall reception without any mishaps, but by the time we reached the radio station he was in bad shape. The Rodgers and Hart contribution to the program was to read a war savings appeal. Larry read his lines all right, but I noticed that his right hand, which was holding the pages of his script, was shaking uncontrollably. After our turn was over, we went backstage and there was Dorothy, true to her word, waiting for him with a tumbler of whiskey. He drank it down in one gulp.

Once war finally came to the United States, my first thought was to apply for a commission. I took the Air Force physical examination and to my surprised satisfaction passed it. The only trouble was that because of a sudden crackdown on civilian commissions, I was never able to get one. This was a bitter disappointment, particularly because so many people close to me were either enlisting or otherwise engaged in work directly related to the war. Even my father, then seventy-two, had come out of retirement to volunteer his services examining draftees. Eventually I came to accept the fact that the best thing I could do to help the war effort was to continue doing exactly what I had always been doing: writing songs and shows that could make some small contribution to the morale of our armed forces and of the people supporting them.

At about this time a literary agent named Audrey Wood asked me to read the script of a play written by one of her clients. It was *The Warrior's Husband,* by Julian Thompson, which had been successfully presented on Broadway some ten years before with Katharine Hepburn in the leading role. The play dealt in a light-hearted fashion with the conflict between the Amazons and the Greeks and had some amusing things to say about the male-female relationship in a society in which the women dominated the men.

I thought the story could be turned into an amusing book for a musical, and Larry, who had been going through an extended depression, perked up noticeably when I told him about it. In fact, we decided to write the adaptation ourselves. I also decided that having gained some experience in the management field with *Best Foot Forward,* I would produce the new musical. But aware that I still had much to learn in this area, I formed a partnership with the more experienced Dwight Deere Wiman.

Now that I was both co-creator and co-sponsor, I had two problems. One was that I could never find Larry; the other was that I could never find Wiman. I was used to Larry's disappearing act, but Wiman's absences were a surprise. He was a very social, "clubby" man who always managed to find more time for his outside activities than for what should have been his primary concern.

In one instance this proved to be especially embarrassing. Like all Broadway shows, ours needed outside financial backing, and though it was really Wiman's job to find the "angels," I did manage to come up with one myself. This was Howard Cullman, a wealthy cigar manufacturer and patron of the arts who had expressed interest in investing in the show. Howard and I made an appointment to see Wiman in his office, but he kept us waiting for well over an hour—a breach of etiquette which, for a producer, is roughly akin to self-immolation. Fortunately for all of us, Howard had enough faith in the show, if not in Wiman, to put money in it.

Another person who helped finance the musical, which was eventually called *By Jupiter,* was Richard Kollmar, the young actor who had played the juvenile lead in *Too Many Girls.* He came into the office one day and said simply, "I hear you need thirty-five thousand dollars. If I can find it for you, will you give me credit as associate producer?" We agreed, Kollmar came up with the money, and that's how he got his start as a producer. I never did find out where he got that $35,000.

I had hoped that Larry's enthusiasm for the show would, however temporarily, keep him relatively sober, but he was less dependable than during any previous production. Weeks would go by before I'd hear from him. One day his doctor and I went over to his apartment, where we found him lying on his bed in a semistupor. We bundled him into a taxi and rushed him over to Doctors Hospital for the drying-out treatment. Now that I had him where I could keep an eye on him, I also took advantage of his confinement by putting him to work. In those days, Doctors Hospital had guest rooms that could be rented by the day by patients' relatives and friends, so I simply rented a hospital room as my office and had Steinway send up a piano. It was only after we had completed the score that Larry's doctor permitted him to be discharged. But once we got to Boston for the tryout, Larry was up to his old tricks and disappeared for three days.

Right from the start we'd had no other actor in mind than Ray Bolger for the lead of *By Jupiter.* He had scored a tremendous success in *On Your*

*Toes* and we were sure that his new part, that of the effeminate husband of the Amazon chieftain, played by Benay Venuta, would give even greater scope to his remarkable talent.

The production also marked the first time that I was associated professionally with John Green, then known as Johnny, who was our musical director. Johnny and I had been friends ever since he was a Harvard undergraduate; he was probably the only conductor on Broadway whose credits included leading a popular dance band, writing durable song hits (including "Body and Soul" and "Out of Nowhere"), and—years later—conducting symphony orchestras. (It was partly because of my admiration for Johnny's songs for *Beat the Band,* a 1942 George Abbott musical, that I joined George as co-producer. As in the case of *Best Foot Forward,* I took no official billing.)

Among the songs Larry and I had written for *By Jupiter,* we had thought the most popular would be the torch ballad "Nobody's Heart." The show-stopper, however, turned out to be a minor song called "Life with Father," thanks to a dance Bolger did with the sixty-year-old Bertha Belmore. Another song, "Wait Till You See Her," in which the hero describes his beloved, was well received, but after we opened in New York we decided to cut it for no other reason than that the show was running late. We didn't put it back until toward the end of the run, but despite this lack of exposure it was picked up by singers and orchestras and today is the best-known piece in the score.

*By Jupiter* had the longest run of any Rodgers and Hart show presented on Broadway except for the revival of *Pal Joey,* and it could have run even longer than its 427 performances if Ray Bolger had not decided to quit the cast to entertain American troops in the Far East. Since it was clear that the customers wouldn't come without him in the lead, we ruled out finding a replacement and closed up shop.

During the run, however, we did have to replace the feminine lead, Constance Moore, who had to leave because of a film commitment. We auditioned a number of girls to succeed her, but none seemed exactly right. Eventually, we found what we were looking for in a vivacious, snub-nosed singer named Nanette Fabray, but before she was picked, our endless auditions were responsible for my favorite story involving that tenacious breed known as the talent agent. One day I was walking through Shubert Alley when I was stopped by an agent whom I knew slightly.

"Understand you're auditioning for a new girl to take over Connie Moore's part," he said.

"That's right. Any suggestions?"

"Sure have. Leila Ernst would be great in the part. Remember how good she was in *Too Many Girls* and *Pal Joey*?"

"Leila's certainly a talented girl," I said, "but she's too tall for the part."

"Oh, I don't know," said the agent. "Have you seen her lately?"

At Rockmeadow in the summer of 1951

Rockmeadow

Picking up the Tony Awards for *The King and I* with Oscar, Gertrude Lawrence and Yul Brynner in 1952. Other winners that year included Helen Hayes, Phil Silvers and Judy Garland.

With Robert Russell Bennett and Pete Dulomon going over the score of *Victory at Sea* (1952)

At the piano under Doris Lee's painting of *Oklahoma!* (1953)

At the television salute to Rodgers and Hammerstein, which was carried by four channels on March 28, 1954

Rehearsing the New York Philharmonic for a concert of my music in 1954

SAM FALK

Cutting the cake at our 25th Wedding Anniversary Party on March 5, 1955

SAM FALK

Marilyn Monroe with an admirer on the same evening

At the recording session of the album I conducted with the New York Philharmonic in December. 1955

Rehearsing Julie Andrews for the television musical *Cinderella* (1957)

With Richard Kiley, Samuel Taylor, conductor Peter Matz, Diahann Carroll, Don Chastain, Bernice Massi and Mitchell Gregg at a rehearsal of *No Strings* (1962)

During the liturgical concert at Manhattanville in preparation for *The Sound of Music* (1959)

Mary

Linda

At our house in Fairfield, Connecticut (1967)

With Mayor John V. Lindsay at Mt. Morris Park on June 27, 1970

## 16

# ST. JAMES THEATRE

SELECT THEATRES CORPORATION

EMERGENCY NOTICE: In the event of an alert, remain in your seats. A competent staff has been trained for this emergency. Keep calm. You will receive information and instructions from the stage.
F. H. La GUARDIA, Mayor

FIRE NOTICE: The exit indicated by a red light and sign nearest to the seat you occupy is the shortest route to the street. In the event of fire please do not run—WALK TO THAT EXIT.
Patrick Walsh, Fire Commissioner and Chief of Department

It is urged for the comfort and safety of all, that theatre patrons refrain from lighting matches in this theatre.

THE · PLAYBILL · A · WEEKLY · PUBLICATION · OF · PLAYBILL · INCORPORATED

Matinees Thursday and Saturday

Beginning Wednesday, March 31, 1943

### THE THEATRE GUILD

presents

# OKLAHOMA!

A Musical Play

Based on the play "Green Grow the Lilacs" by Lynn Riggs

Music by RICHARD RODGERS
Book and Lyrics by OSCAR HAMMERSTEIN 2d
Production directed by ROUBEN MAMOULIAN
Dances by AGNES de MILLE

Costumes by
MILES WHITE

Settings by
LEMUEL AYERS

with
JOSEPH BULOFF
CELESTE HOLM

JOAN ROBERTS
RALPH RIGGS

BETTY GARDE
LEE DIXON

ALFRED DRAKE
HOWARD da SILVA
GEORGE CHURCH
MARC PLATT

KATHARINE SERGAVA

Orchestra directed by Jacob Schwartzdorf
Orchestrations by Russell Bennett
Production under the supervision of
Theresa Helburn and Lawrence Langner

Three of my Connecticut neighbors were Terry Helburn and Lawrence and Armina Langner. Ever since Larry and I wrote the scores for the Theatre Guild's first two *Garrick Gaieties,* and particularly since our return from Hollywood, Terry and Lawrence had often brought up the subject of our writing another show for the Guild. We never got down to specifics until shortly after *By Jupiter* opened, when Terry asked me to read the script of a play that the Guild had produced eleven years before. It was *Green Grow the Lilacs,* by Lynn Riggs, and I only had to read it once to realize that it had the makings of an enchanting musical. Set in the Southwest shortly after the turn of the century, with a cast of farmers and ranchers, it was a distinct departure from anything I had ever done before. I promptly told Terry and Lawrence that I wanted very much to write the score.

Of course, the Theatre Guild was assuming that they would have a musical with a score by Rodgers and Hart, since neither Terry nor Lawrence had any idea of Larry's condition. Though I knew that Oscar Hammerstein was waiting in the wings, I wanted to make one last effort to continue with Larry. I told him of my desire to do the show, sent him a script and made an appointment to meet him at the offices of Chappell and Company, our music publisher.

I was in the company's board room when a haggard and pale Larry walked in. He had obviously not had a good night's sleep in weeks, and I realized that I could no longer avoid talking about what was on my mind —that, if necessary, I'd have to be brutal to make him understand what he was doing not only to himself but to our partnership. I began by telling him I wanted to get started on the new show right away but that he was obviously in no condition to work. Larry admitted this and said that he needed a rest and was planning to leave soon for a vacation in Mexico. He was sure it would straighten him out and he'd return feeling much better.

This was nonsense; he knew it and I knew it.

"Larry," I said, "the only reason you're going to Mexico is to drink. When you come back you'll be in worse shape than ever."

Larry looked as if I had stabbed him. This was the first time in all the years we'd been together that I had ever spoken to him this way.

"We've got to work something out for the good of both of us," I continued. "I want you to have yourself admitted to a sanitarium, and I'll have myself admitted along with you. We'll be there together and we'll work together. The only way you're ever going to lick this thing is to get off the street."

Larry, who had been avoiding my eyes, looked at the floor and said, "I know, Dick. I'm sorry. But I want to go to Mexico. I have to."

I felt the blood rushing to my head. "This show means a lot to me," I told him. "If you walk out on me now, I'm going to do it with someone else."

"Anyone in mind?"

"Yes, Oscar Hammerstein."

Even the realization that I wasn't bluffing, that I actually had someone else waiting to take over, couldn't shake him. Still looking at the floor, all that Larry said was, "Well, you couldn't pick a better man." Then, for the first time, he looked me in the eyes. "You know, Dick," he said, "I've really never understood why you've put up with me all these years. It's been crazy. The best thing for you to do is forget about me."

There wasn't much more either one of us could say. Larry could no more fight his compulsive drinking than I could have thrown aside my family and career. He got up to leave and when he reached the door he turned around and said, "There's just one more thing. I really don't think *Green Grow the Lilacs* can be turned into a good musical. I think you're making a mistake."

With that he was gone, and so was our partnership.

I walked out of the board room to tell Max Dreyfus, who was waiting in his office, what had happened. But I never got there; I simply broke down and cried.

Larry did go to Mexico. When he returned a month later he had to be carried off the train on a stretcher.

As he had assured me, Oscar was ready to go to work. He read the script and saw the musical possibilities immediately. Because he was a librettist as well as a lyricist, he also saved us the problem of finding someone else to write the adaptation. And so Rodgers and Hart became Rodgers and Hammerstein.

It is only natural to feel some apprehension in forming a new partnership, especially after having worked exclusively with one man for so long a time, but because of the circumstances that brought Oscar and me together and because of the kind of man he was, I never had to go through a period of adjustment.

Our first meeting on the project that eventually became known as *Oklahoma!* took place at my home in Connecticut. We sat under the huge oak tree and tossed ideas around. What kind of songs were we going to write? Where would they go? Who would sing them? What special texture and mood should the show have?

We had many such sessions until we became thoroughly familiar not only with every aspect of the play but with each other's outlook and approach as well. Fortunately, we were in agreement on all major issues, so that when we finally did begin putting words and notes on paper—which didn't occur until we'd gone through weeks of discussions—we each were able to move ahead at a steady pace.

The first problem was, appropriately, how to open the show. We didn't want to begin with anything obvious, such as a barn dance with everyone a-whoopin' and a-hollerin'. After much thought and talk we simply went back to the way Lynn Riggs had opened his play, with a woman seated alone on the stage churning butter. For the lyric to the first song, Oscar developed his theme from the description that Riggs had written as an introduction to the scene: "It is a radiant summer morning several years ago, the kind of morning which, enveloping the shape of earth—men, cattle in a meadow, blades of the young corn, streams—makes them seem to exist now for the first time, their images giving off a visible golden emanation that is partly true and partly a trick of imagination focusing to keep alive a loveliness that may pass away . . ."

This was all Oscar's poetic imagination needed to produce his lines about cattle standing like statues, the corn as high as an elephant's eye, and the bright golden haze on the meadow. When I read them for the first time I could see those cattle and that corn and bright golden haze vividly. How prophetic were Oscar's words "I've got a beautiful feelin' / Ev'rything's goin' my way."

By opening the show with the woman alone onstage and the cowboy beginning his song offstage, we did more than set a mood; we were, in effect, warning the audience, "Watch out! This is a different kind of musical." Everything in the production was made to conform to the simple open-air spirit of the story; this was essential, and certainly a rarity in the musical theatre.

Oscar and I made few changes in the basic plot and the characters. We added the part of Will Parker, Ado Annie's boyfriend, and we made her a more physically attractive girl. For the ending, we tied the strands together a bit more neatly than in the play by having Curly being found innocent of murdering Jud Fry, rather than being given his freedom for one night to spend with his bride.

Most of the musical numbers presented no great problems. One, which every songwriter must face over and over again, is how to say "I love you" in a way that makes the song different from any other romantic ballad ever written. In "People Will Say We're in Love," Oscar hit on the notion of having the young lovers warn each other against showing any signs of affection so that people won't realize they're in love. (Larry and I had already written a different song of this kind in "This Can't Be Love," and later Oscar and I would try another variation on the theme with "If I Loved You.")

This song also demonstrates another familiar problem, especially for lyric writers. There are, after all, only so many rhymes for the word "love," and when Oscar decided to call the duet "People Will Say We're in Love," he was determined to avoid using any of the more obvious ones. After spending days thinking about this one rhyme, he called me up exultantly to announce that he'd solved the problem. His solution: the girl ends the refrain by admonishing the boy:

> Don't start collecting things,
> Give me my rose and my glove;
> Sweetheart, they're suspecting things—
> People will say we're in love.

Earlier in the story we needed a song in which Curly, who is stuck on Laurey, tries to tempt her into going to a box social with him by describing an imaginary "Surrey with the Fringe on Top." Oscar's lyric suggested both a clip-clop rhythm and a melody in which the straight, flat country road could be musically conveyed through a repetition of the straight, flat sound of the D note, followed by a sharp upward flick as fowl scurry to avoid being hit by the moving wheels.

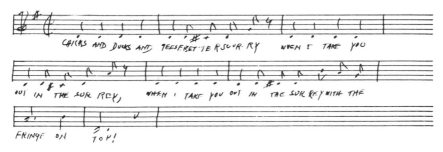

Oscar was so moved by this song that just listening to it made him cry. He once explained that he never cried at sadness in the theatre, only at naïve happiness, and the idea of two boneheaded young people looking forward to nothing more than a ride in a surrey struck an emotional chord that affected him deeply.

Though the words could be poetic and the music tender and romantic, Oscar and I were both careful in writing the score and lyrics to make the songs sound natural when sung by cowboys, ranchers and farm girls living in Indian Territory at the turn of the century. Though I had no prior experience creating melodies indigenous to this period and locale, I felt it important that the songs be my kind of music, though they could be embellished with a certain amount of regional flavoring. I remember that shortly before beginning the score Oscar sent me an impressively thick book of songs of the American Southwest which he thought might be of help. I opened the book, played through the music of one song, closed the book and never looked at it again. If my melodies were going to be authentic, they'd have to be authentic in my own terms.

This is the way I have always worked, no matter what the setting of the story. It was true of my "Chinese" music for *Chee-Chee,* of my "French" music for *Love Me Tonight,* and later of my "Siamese" music for *The King and I.* Had I attempted to duplicate the real thing, it would never have sounded genuine, for the obvious reason that I am neither Chinese, French, Siamese, nor from the Southwest. All a composer—any composer —can do is to make an audience believe it is hearing an authentic sound without losing his own musical identity.

In my judgment, the musical theatre has never had two greater lyric writers than Larry Hart and Oscar Hammerstein, yet they were as different in personality, appearance and technique as any two men could be. Working with Oscar was a brand-new experience. For twenty-five years, the only way I could get Larry to do anything was virtually to lock him in a room and stay with him until the job was finished. Oscar's working habits were entirely the opposite. I remember that when I first started talking to him about our method of collaborating, he seemed surprised at my question.

"I'll write the words and you'll write the music" was all he said.

"In that order?" I asked.

"If that's all right with you. I prefer it that way. You won't hear from me until I have a finished lyric."

And for 90 percent of the time, that's the way we worked together. Larry needed the stimulus of the music to get him started; Oscar needed nothing more than an agreement about what was required. Once Larry heard the music, he was a rapid, almost spontaneous worker, devoting little more time than it took to jot down the words. Oscar was slower and more painstaking, a characteristic partly dictated by his method of collaborating. I found no problem whatever in working this way. It gave Oscar the freedom he needed, and it helped me a good deal to have a completed lyric in front of me. It also offered me the opportunity to break away—even more than I had in the recent past—from the generally accepted "AABA" thirty-two-bar song construction. Lastly, I did not have to be with Oscar every time he got the urge to write a lyric. Since the actual creation of a melody has always come quickly to me, I was spared the endless hours I'd formerly had to spend playing nurse.

Oscar usually created his lyrics with "dummy" melodies going through his head—which he frankly admitted were stolen from fragments of other people's tunes. Often the melodies I wrote for his lyrics did not subscribe in time signature or scansion to his concept. For instance, he might have conceived of a melody in 3/4 time, but when I'd finished, it would appear with a 4/4 time signature. For some reason the change always pleased him. Though Oscar was not a musician, he did possess a superb sense of form. He knew everything about the architecture of a song—its foundation, structure, embellishments and because we always had thorough discussions on the exact kind of music that was needed, this method of collaboration helped us enormously in creating songs that not only were right for the characters who sang them but also possessed a union of words and music that made them sound natural.

The most important member of the production staff of any musical is the director. In Hollywood, Larry and I had worked with Rouben Mamoulian on *Love Me Tonight,* and Oscar and Jerry Kern had worked with him on *High, Wide and Handsome.* Moreover, both Oscar and I realized what a magnificent job he had done on the Theatre Guild's production of the Gershwin opera, *Porgy and Bess.* A musical like ours, we reasoned, required someone who was both creative and not too steeped in the conventions of traditional Broadway musical comedy. Mamoulian seemed ideal.

But not, strangely enough, to Terry and Lawrence. Why? Because he was Russian, and they didn't think he could handle a story about the American Southwest. Oscar and I were dumfounded; my God, if he could direct a story about Negroes living in a Southern ghetto, why couldn't he do an equally good job with cowboys living in Indian Territory? Well, that was different, they said. No, it wasn't, we said. Eventually we got Mamoulian.

Because our story required dances more in the style of ballet than musical comedy, we were on the lookout for someone with a background in classical choreography. Terry had already seen *Rodeo,* sponsored by the Ballet Russe de Monte Carlo, and she raved about the work of a young choreographer named Agnes de Mille. Once Oscar and I saw it, we too felt that she would be just right to handle the dances.

These were the major people in the production end: Terry Helburn and Lawrence Langner, Rouben Mamoulian, Agnes de Mille, Oscar Hammerstein and me. With one exception, none of us had had any Broadway successes recently, and some of us had never had one. Terry and Lawrence freely admitted that the new production was the Theatre Guild's last chance to reverse its dwindling fortunes. Mamoulian had staged only one previous musical on Broadway, and that had been over seven years before. Agnes de Mille's Broadway experience was limited to one show, which had been a flop. Oscar had done nothing memorable since *Music in the Air* ten years before. I was the lone exception in this rather unpromising lineup, and this, according to those supposedly in the know, was the most convincing reason of all why our new venture had no chance of success. Because of my string of hits with Larry Hart, everyone was certain that I could not possibly do well with any other partner.

From the start, Oscar and I were determined that a musical such as ours required actors and singers who had to be right for their parts, regardless of whether or not they were box-office names. Terry Helburn, however, perhaps because of the financial plight of the Guild, felt that the only way to stage a musical was to spend little on scenery and costumes and to concentrate on established stars who could lure both backers and customers. She came up with the likes of Shirley Temple for our heroine and Groucho Marx for the peddler, but Oscar and I held fast, and after some discussion we were able to assemble exactly the kind of cast we wanted.

Auditions began in the fall of 1942. One of the first to try out was Celeste Holm, who had her eye on the part of Ado Annie. Knowing that she had a trained voice, I was surprised that she would want such a hoydenish role. I told her that I wanted to hear her sing as if she had never taken a lesson in her life and was simply a gawky farm girl. That's exactly what she did, even to throwing in a sample of uninhibited hog-calling, and she got the part.

I had seen Joan Roberts before, in a recently produced operetta Oscar had written called *Sunny River*, and she easily won out over Shirley Temple. Alfred Drake, our hero, came right out of my past, since he had been the robust youth who introduced the title song in *Babes in Arms*. Betty Garde, our Aunt Eller, was a well-established character actress, and Joseph Buloff, the peddler, had spent most of his years in the Yiddish theatre.

For the dancing role of Will Parker we cast the boyish-looking Lee Dixon, who had appeared in *Higher and Higher* and had begun his career in Warner Bros. musicals. When we signed him he told us that he had a drinking problem but that he was confident he could control it. He did for a while, but after the show opened he began drinking heavily again and tried to cover up his whiskey breath by eating garlic. The odor made things pretty unpleasant for the other members of the cast, especially for Celeste Holm, with whom he played most of his scenes. After a year and a half he left the show of his own volition.

Initially, both Rouben Mamoulian and Agnes de Mille were determined to maintain their authority within their respective domains. One of their battles was over three girls whom Agnes brought in—Bambi Linn, Joan McCracken and Diana Adams—who were all brilliant dancers and strikingly attractive. For some reason Rouben strongly objected to their being in the show. Agnes got her way, but Rouben retaliated by preempting the stage of our rehearsal theatre for the book rehearsals and forcing Agnes to use whatever other space she could find.

One day Jerome Whyte, whom we had brought over from the George Abbott office to be our chief stage manager, came over to me and said, "Sneak down into the lounge and take a look at what Agnes is doing." There was Agnes, leading her dancers through some of the most dazzling routines I'd ever seen anywhere. If something could look that great in the men's room, I had no doubt it would be breath-taking onstage.

At the beginning, Rouben Mamoulian did not have the security of command that I had remembered from our experience in filming *Love Me Tonight*. His clashes with Agnes were unquestionably a result of this insecurity, and it was further apparent when he flew into a rage upon discovering that Oscar and I had been shown the costume and set designs before he'd seen them. Gradually, though, he settled down, and his brilliance in weaving together the component parts of the musical soon became obvious to us all.

Raising the money to put on this musical was one of our biggest hurdles. Apart from the spotty track record of the people involved, there was the production itself. Who ever heard of a successful "cowboy" musical, as one prospective backer called it? Who wants to see chorus girls in long dresses? What kind of musical keeps the dancers offstage until almost halfway through the first act? Could anyone give a damn about a story whose burning issue was who takes whom to a box social? "C'mon, Dick," my friends kept saying, "go back to Larry. Give us another *Boys from Syracuse* or *By Jupiter* and you'll get all the money you need for the show."

In order to help raise whatever backing we could, Oscar and I—usually with Alfred Drake and Joan Roberts—had to tour the "penthouse circuit," playing our songs and reading from the script. One such evening was held at the palatial home of a woman named Natalie Spencer, a friend of Terry Helburn's. Her apartment was not only large enough to have a ballroom in it, it actually *had* a ballroom in it. There must have been seventy people there to see us audition our material. We even rented a second piano so that Margot Hopkins and I could play four-handed accompaniment. It was an elegant evening of song, story, bright chatter and many complimentary words—but we didn't get a penny from anyone there.

What money we did get came in relatively small figures—a thousand here, five thousand there. One day Terry Helburn got the bright notion of going to Metro-Goldwyn-Mayer with the idea of their putting up the amount still needed. Since M-G-M owned the rights to *Green Grow the Lilacs,* Terry offered them 50 percent of the profits for a $75,000 investment, plus the movie rights for another $75,000. If the show succeeded, they'd get back their initial $75,000 and then some, so the movie rights really wouldn't cost them anything, and if the show failed, it would cost them no more than $75,000, since they wouldn't have to buy the movie rights. Despite the attractiveness of the proposal, the studio turned her down.

Then Terry said to them, "Look, since you're not giving us the money, you're making it impossible for us to get backing from any other studio because you still own the rights to *Green Grow the Lilacs.* Why don't you let us have an option to buy back the rights once the show opens?" This the company agreed to do, but with the proviso that we'd have to exercise the option within thirty days after the New York opening. We did it within thirty hours.

Through our friend Max Gordon, the Broadway producer, we then approached Harry Cohn, the powerful head of Columbia Pictures, with an offer similar to the one Terry had made to M-G-M. When we auditioned the songs for him at Steinway Hall, he was so enthusiastic that he told us that not only would he get Columbia to put up the money but Oscar and I must write the screenplay. Now we were really in business; everyone knew that Harry Cohn always got Columbia to do what he wanted.

This time, however, Columbia balked. The board of directors simply refused to go along with Cohn. To show his good faith, however, Harry put up $15,000 of his own money, which was of enormous help in convincing other investors, and Max Gordon made a sizable investment of his own.

Until the beginning of rehearsals in February 1943, we used the working title of *Green Grow the Lilacs.* We had no intention of keeping it, but we were stumped in coming up with something better. More out of desperation than anything else, we settled on *Away We Go!* The idea of calling the musical *Oklahoma* was mentioned, but we were reluctant to name it after a state. If the show turned out to be a success, fine, but if it was less than a smash, it would seem presumptuous and therefore self-defeating.

*Away We Go!* opened in New Haven on March 11. There was no advance sale and little publicity, but the reception on opening night was phenomenal. New Haven is not New York, we kept telling ourselves, but we were so encouraged that we tossed caution aside and changed the name to *Oklahoma!* Who should get credit for the title I really can't recall; nor do I remember whose idea it was to add the exclamation mark. It was, however, too late to use the new title in Boston, our next pre-Broadway stop, so we were still stuck with *Away We Go!*

There were few changes in the production between New Haven and Boston. We took out one of the songs, "Boys and Girls Like You and Me," a second-act love duet for the hero and heroine, because it tended to slow down the action. We also changed the song "Oklahoma," the final number in the show, from a solo for Alfred Drake to a rousing chorale for the entire company.

Boston turned out to be even more receptive than New Haven. We were all still concerned, however; nothing is "in" until it reaches New York. Many a show has been ruined by complacency because of favorable reactions on the road, and many others have been ruined by too much tinkering because a critic or a stagehand thinks it needs work. Yet with this particular production I was always confident that everything was going to work out. If anything, Dorothy was even more optimistic. I remember a run-through early in March while we were still in rehearsal. There were no costumes or scenery and the only accompaniment was a piano. Some people in the audience, including Dorothy, left immediately after the performance while I spent the next few hours at a production meeting. When I got home, on the pillow of my bed was a message which read: "Darling, This is the best musical show I have ever seen. Love."

Though things were going beautifully in Boston, the Broadway savants who'd gone to New Haven were apparently unwilling or unable to believe what they saw and heard around them, and they quickly spread the word that the show wouldn't make it. There was a celebrated remark, "No legs, no jokes, no chance," quoted in Walter Winchell's column. Somehow people got the mistaken idea that he'd made it up, but he had used it merely to show how wrong the Broadway crowd had been about *Oklahoma!'s* chances. The man generally believed to have originated the line was producer Michael Todd. Everyone knew that he had left in the middle of the show in New Haven. Later he apologized to me, explaining that a friend of his was in jail in New York and he had to rush back to bail him out.

But I didn't let anything get me down. In Boston we were playing at the Colonial Theatre, just across the street from the Common. At night after each performance, Terry, Lawrence, Oscar and I used to walk back to the Ritz-Carlton, where we were all staying. Whenever one of the others would express doubts about our prospects, I'd point out—song by song and scene by scene—that it simply couldn't miss. Never before had I had the assignment of keeping up the morale of the troops, but that's exactly what I found myself doing during this period.

Our opening in New York took place on March 31, 1943, at the St. James Theatre. Just as I knew it would, the audience responded to everything. Not only could I see it and hear it, I could feel it. From the time Alfred Drake began the opening bars of "Oh, What a Beautiful Mornin' " to the last exultant chorus of "Oklahoma," everything really was going our way.

After the final curtain we all went over to Sardi's to await the *New York Times* review. As we jostled our way into the restaurant, I suddenly saw a little man break through the crowd. It was Larry. Grinning from ear to ear, he threw his arms around me. "Dick," he said, "I've never had a better evening in my life! This show will still be around twenty years from now!" And I knew he meant it.

We'd been at Sardi's a little over an hour when the phone call came from our press agent, who read us the *Times* review. Lewis Nichols, who had succeeded Brooks Atkinson as the paper's drama critic for the duration of the war, gave us our first rave. "Wonderful is the nearest adjective," he wrote, "for this excursion combines a fresh and infectious gaiety, a charm of manner, beautiful acting, singing and dancing, and a score which does not do any harm either, since it is one of Rodgers' best."

Now even the last lingering doubts were removed. We whooped it up a little more at Sardi's, and then left for the party Jules Glaenzer was throwing for the entire cast. As I walked into his apartment Jules asked me if I wanted a drink. "No, thanks, Jules," I said. "I'm not going to touch a drop. I want to remember every second of this night!" I didn't have anything stronger than ginger ale the whole evening.

Our opening night had not been sold out completely, but the rave notices in the press guaranteed that the line at the box office would start queuing up early. Oscar and I went to the theatre the next day around noon, and it was bedlam. Everyone was pushing and shoving to get to the box office. There was even a policeman trying to keep order.

Since Oscar and I had made an appointment for lunch, I asked him, "Shall we sneak off to someplace quiet where we can talk, or shall we go to Sardi's and show off?"

"Hell, let's go to Sardi's and show off," said Oscar, and we did. From the moment we walked in until we left, everyone kept crowding around us, congratulating us, hugging us, kissing us, telling us they were on their way to buy tickets—or asking us to get them some—all the while assuring us that they'd known right from the start that the show would be a hit.

I have long held a theory about musicals. When a show works perfectly, it's because all the individual parts complement each other and fit together. No single element overshadows any other. In a great musical, the orchestrations sound the way the costumes look. That's what made *Oklahoma!* work. All the components dovetailed. There was nothing extraneous or foreign, nothing that pushed itself into the spotlight yelling "Look at me!" It was a work created by many that gave the impression of having been created by one.

In addition, *Oklahoma!* had two external factors working for it. In the spring of 1943 the Broadway musical stage was not enjoying the best of health. *By Jupiter* was still running, as was *Something for the Boys,* starring Ethel Merman. So much for conventional musical comedy. In addition, there was Olsen and Johnson's raucous revue, *Sons o' Fun;* a glorified burlesque show called *Star and Garter;* a vaudeville show called *Show Time;* a new version of *Die Fledermaus* called *Rosalinda;* and an ice show called *Stars on Ice.* That was the competition. Even if *Oklahoma!* had been created less skillfully, it would have stood out in this company.

Then there was the fact that we were in the midst of a devastating war. People could come to see *Oklahoma!* and derive not only pleasure but a measure of optimism. It dealt with pioneers in the Southwest, it showed their spirit and the kinds of problems they had to overcome in carving out a new state, and it gave citizens an appreciation of the hardy stock from which they'd sprung. People said to themselves, in effect, "If this is what our country looked and sounded like at the turn of the century, perhaps once the war is over we can again return to this kind of buoyant, optimistic life."

It was also extremely gratifying to have written music for this production that people so obviously enjoyed singing. This was brought home in a very personal way just two mornings after the show's Broadway opening. My family was in the country and I had to spend the night at a hotel just off Park Avenue. I was awakened in the morning by the sun streaming through my window and the sound of children singing something familiar. I looked down into the courtyard and there was a group of kids singing "Oh, What a Beautiful Mornin'." The show had just opened and they knew the song already! What a lovely feeling it was to realize that I was reaching not only the theatregoing adults but their children as well.

*Oklahoma!* was more than just another Broadway success. It was an event, something that transcended theatre, music, dance or anything confined to a specific production in a specific place. I was forty at the time, with a number of hit shows behind me, but nothing had ever remotely compared to this. It was a rebirth, both in my associations and in my career.

What kept going around in my head was the title of a once best-selling book called *Life Begins at Forty.*

Everyone, it seemed, just had to see *Oklahoma!,* and people outdid themselves in making up stories about how hard it was to get tickets. I do know one story whose truth I'll vouch for. Oscar had a farmer working for him in Doylestown whose son was about to get married. The farmer wanted to give the couple a pair of tickets as a wedding gift, the idea being that they would see the show following the wedding ceremony. Of course Oscar promised to get the tickets, and asked when the wedding would take place. "The day you can get the tickets," the farmer replied.

Right from the start, there was considerable competition for the rights to record the songs from the show. None of the offers appealed to Oscar or me until Jack Kapp, the president of Decca Records, came to us with a revolutionary idea. He wanted to use our cast, our conductor and our orchestra to reproduce on records the same musical program that people heard in the theatre. It was the most exciting recording concept we'd ever heard of, and naturally we consented. From *Oklahoma!* on, the original-cast album has become a major by-product of Broadway musicals, but this was the first time it had been done.

Another first for me was that the Guild sent out a road company while the New York company was still performing. The tour began in New Haven in October 1943 and ended ten and a half years later in Philadelphia. In all, it played over 150 cities in the United States and Canada, with many return engagements. The London company, which began its stay in April 1947, was also assembled by the Theatre Guild, with our stage manager, Jerry Whyte, as the on-the-scene producer.

In 1944 the Pulitzer Committee awarded a special drama prize to *Oklahoma!* The reason for this unusual citation was that word had spread that I was to be the recipient of the prize in music, an honor that I did not feel I could accept without sharing it with Oscar. Therefore the special award to *Oklahoma!* was given as something of a compromise.

It wasn't until November 1946 that the road company of *Oklahoma!* gave its first performance in Oklahoma. Governor Robert Kerr decided to turn the event into a statewide celebration, and invited Terry Helburn, the Lawrence Langners, Agnes de Mille, Lynn Riggs, Rouben Mamoulian, the Oscar Hammersteins and Dorothy and me to participate. A private railroad car transported us to Oklahoma City, where we were met by the governor, who put us all in a surrey with a fringe on top for the ride to the hotel. That morning there was to be a mammoth parade, with no fewer than forty-seven marching bands and thousands of Indians on horseback. Just as we were leaving the hotel to watch this spectacle, however, the weather suddenly changed into a sleet storm. They canceled the parade not, we were advised, because the kids who had been let off from school might catch pneumonia, but because the horses might slip and break their legs.

The performance of the show went on that night as scheduled and was followed by a formal ball in our honor. We were also made honorary Kiowa Indians, and each of us was presented with a chief's headdress. As if that wasn't enough, a few years later they made "Oklahoma" the official state song. Our show was apparently a great morale booster for citizens of the state who had long been stigmatized by the words "dust bowl" and "Okies," and they did everything they could to show their appreciation.

On December 4, 1947, we passed the 2,000th-performance mark on Broadway, a milestone then unheard of for a musical. Since I've always enjoyed conducting my own music, I took over the baton that evening for the second act. After it was over, members of the company complained that I took the tempos too fast—and they were right.

Perhaps of all the pleasures associated with *Oklahoma!* the one that gave me the greatest satisfaction was an arrangement we made to give forty-four special matinées for the armed forces. No one paid to get in and no one was paid to work, and everyone connected with the show always looked forward to these performances.

*Oklahoma!* did, of course, have an effect on the musicals that came after it. Everyone suddenly became "integration"-conscious, as if the idea of welding together song, story and dance had never been thought of before. There were also a number of costume musicals, and no self-respecting production dared open without at least one "serious" ballet.

But in a broader sense I feel that the chief influence of *Oklahoma!* was simply to serve notice that when writers came up with something different, and if it had merit, there would be a large and receptive audience waiting for it. Librettists, lyricists and composers now had a new incentive to explore a multitude of themes and techniques within the framework of the commercial musical theatre. From *Oklahoma!* on, with only rare exceptions, the memorable productions have been those daring to break free of the conventional mold. Freedom is the sunniest climate for creativity, and *Oklahoma!* certainly contributed to that climate.

The world outside was still torn by devastating warfare, but my little world within the theatre in 1943 brought me nothing but happiness. Still, there was someone tugging at my conscience: Larry Hart. Following *Oklahoma!* I very much wanted to continue the partnership with Oscar Hammerstein, but it was impossible to make a clean break with Larry. I even fantasized that the shock of *Oklahoma!*'s success might provoke him to getting back to work and possibly keep him from destroying himself. Ours was a one-way partnership in the sense that while I could work with another lyricist, it was inconceivable for Larry to work with another composer.

Oscar understood my apprehension about Larry; in fact, at about this time he became preoccupied with a separate project of his own. For some years he had been obsessed with the idea of turning Bizet's opera *Carmen* into an updated Broadway musical with an all-black cast. He called it *Carmen Jones,* and following the reception of *Oklahoma!,* he had little difficulty in securing Billy Rose as producer.

Since the rest of the year found Oscar involved with Bizet, it left me free to try to work again with Larry. But what could we do? Because of the endless problems I'd had with him in our most recent shows, I was afraid of attempting a new one that would be too much for him to handle.

One day I discussed the matter with Herb Fields, and together we hit on a solution of sorts: a revival of *A Connecticut Yankee,* with Larry's dear friend Vivienne Segal in the role of Morgan LeFay. But it wouldn't be just a word-for-word, note-for-note revival of the sixteen-year-old show. It would have new dialogue and half a dozen new songs augmenting the more familiar numbers from the original. In this way, we thought, Larry would not be overburdened; it would be familiar territory for him, he'd be working with people he liked, and most important, it might prove therapeutic for him. At least that was the idea.

Larry behaved beautifully during the months we spent preparing the show. He would come up to stay at our place in Connecticut and we'd work regularly at reasonable hours. I don't think he took a drink the entire time. There was no question that he was making a genuine effort to rehabilitate himself and to prove that the team of Rodgers and Hart was still a going concern. As a result he turned out some of the most charming and witty lyrics he had ever written, including "To Keep My Love Alive," a riotous account of the way Queen Morgan LeFay got rid of all her husbands.

But once rehearsals were over and there was nothing further for Larry to do, he simply caved in. All those months of self-denial had taken a lot out of him and he could no longer resist his thirst. He had proved that he could still work, but in so doing, he had stretched his nerves to the breaking point. The night *A Connecticut Yankee* opened in Philadelphia, Larry went on a drinking binge from which he never recovered. He'd always had the habit of leaving his coat and hat in bars, and since it rained or snowed almost every day that week, this only accelerated his physical deterioration.

On the show's opening night in New York, I was so worried about Larry that I instructed two men from our company to stand near him as he weaved back and forth in the rear of the theatre. My concern was not only for his health but for what he might do to cause a disruption of the performance onstage. As it turned out, this concern was well founded. Suddenly, in the middle of the first act, he began talking incoherently to the actors, at which point the men standing near him simply picked him up and took him home.

Two days later Willy Kron, Larry's friend and financial adviser, came up to me in the back of the theatre and said, "Larry has pneumonia. Probably more like double pneumonia. He's a very sick man."

"Willy," I said, "Larry isn't just sick. He's dying."

This time, I knew, he would never recover. But we did what we could. We got him to Doctors Hospital, but all his strength had been sapped and his resistance was gone. On the night of November 22, 1943, Dorothy, Larry's doctor and I had dinner at the hospital restaurant. None of us could eat or say very much, for we all knew that the end was not far off. When we returned upstairs, a dozen of his friends were in the corridor, none saying a word. Larry was in a coma.

Since we were at war at the time, there were air alerts and practice blackouts. Suddenly the wailing of sirens broke the hospital stillness, and the entire building, except for shaded emergency lights, went dark. One of these lights was in Larry's room because he was getting oxygen. All of us stood there in the darkness outside his room, our eyes on the door. Presently the doctor came out of the room, and as he told us that Larry was dead, we heard the all-clear siren and the lights throughout the hospital immediately came on again.

We may scoff, of course, but everyone has a natural inclination to believe in signs and portents and to attribute ordinary occurrences to psychic phenomena. To those of us in the hospital that night, the lights going on again at that moment was some sort of cosmic assurance that the darkness which had always surrounded Larry had suddenly disappeared— that in death he could at last enjoy the warmth and brightness that had eluded him all his life.

## 17

One evening during the run of *Oklahoma!* I got a telephone call from Sam Goldwyn, who was at the show and was calling during intermission. He asked me to meet him at the theatre after the performance and go out for a drink. An hour later I took a taxi to the St. James just as the people were streaming out of the theatre. Sam was walking up the aisle, and when he saw me he danced over and planted a kiss on my cheek.

"This is such a wonderful show!" he bubbled. "I just had to see you to give you some advice. You know what you should do next?"

"What?"

"Shoot yourself!"

This was Sam's blunt but funny way of telling me that I'd never create another show as good as *Oklahoma!* What to do after a hit is always a problem, though the magnitude of *Oklahoma!*'s success made the problem greater than at any time in the past. Still, there was never any thought of quitting. I knew it wouldn't be easy, but *Oklahoma!* was finished. If I had become absorbed in trying to duplicate what I had just done, nothing would have been accomplished; I would have been immobilized. The only solution was to move ahead, doing my damnedest to be as good as I possibly could be, without dwelling on any of the head-turning events that had happened in the past.

The revival of *A Connecticut Yankee* was only a stopgap production which gave me a chance to catch my breath and to help postpone a dear friend's drinking himself to death. My main objective following *Oklahoma!* was to establish a strong working relationship with Oscar. But it wasn't simply a matter of deciding what show to write next. Right from the start, our partnership embraced a number of varied but related projects.

The first was publishing. Even before rehearsals of *Oklahoma!* had begun, we wanted to show our faith in the production in a very concrete way: we decided to publish the score. We went up to Bronxville, where Max Dreyfus lived, to discuss the matter with him, since he had been Oscar's publisher as well as mine during most of our careers. Max was highly receptive to the idea, and we arranged to form a company in partnership with his own company, Chappell. Thus, Williamson Music came into existence with *Oklahoma!*—which wasn't a bad way to begin. As to the name of our firm, since Oscar and I were both sons of men named William, it seemed a fitting way to pay our respects to our fathers.

Oscar and I never had any kind of agreement to continue together after we had finished *Oklahoma!*, but I felt strongly that it would be wrong—once *Carmen Jones* and *A Connecticut Yankee* were out of the way—for us to split up even temporarily. One morning I heard that Oscar's lawyer, who by then was also my lawyer, was trying to line up a new musical for Oscar to write with Jerry Kern, another one of his clients. This so upset me that I went to see the lawyer and told him how I felt.

That afternoon I had lunch with Oscar at Dinty Moore's, and he brought up the matter. I told him of my conviction that it would be a serious mistake, except in an emergency, for either of us to do anything professional without the other. Oscar was in complete agreement.

"Then we can consider this a permanent partnership?" I said.

"As permanent as any partnership can be."

And it was, for the seventeen remaining years of Oscar's life.

At first, since *Oklahoma!* was still playing to packed houses, we didn't want to step on our own heels by writing a new musical. However, we were anxious to keep active in the theatre and also to establish our names as a team. This led to our becoming producers. Dorothy had read a novel by Kathryn Forbes called *Mama's Bank Account,* and she thought it could be successfully adapted as a play. Oscar and I thought so too, and we quickly obtained the dramatic rights. To write the adaptation we chose John Van Druten, who'd had a tremendous success the previous year with a three-character comedy called *The Voice of the Turtle.* In John's skilled hands, *Mama's Bank Account* was transformed into *I Remember Mama,* which, with Mady Christians giving a memorable performance, became one of the Broadway successes of 1944.

Now that Oscar and I were in the business end of the theatre, we were expected to act like businessmen. The first step was to open our own offices, which we did at 1270 Sixth Avenue. Morris Jacobs, a feisty, highly skilled theatre pro, joined us as general manager, and remained with the firm until his retirement in 1971.

*I Remember Mama* made it two in a row for Rodgers and Hammerstein. Though I can't say it gave us the heady excitement of writing a musical, producing a play had its own gratifications, particularly because our first effort was a success.

It was inevitable that eventually we would receive an offer from a film studio. 20th Century-Fox, which was planning a musical remake of its ten-year-old hit *State Fair,* was interested in having Oscar and me write the score. We went to a special screening of the movie at the studio's Fifty-sixth Street office, and were immediately won over. We made sure, though, that our contract included one provision. Because of our multiple activities in

New York, we had no intention of spending an extended length of time in Hollywood, and we insisted that we be allowed to write the songs in the East. Though they found the request a bit unusual, the studio people agreed; the story, which was set in Iowa, would be filmed in California, while the music and lyrics would be written in Fairfield, Connecticut, and Doylestown, Pennsylvania.

It turned out to be a satisfactory arrangement all around. The only disagreement we had with the company was over the proper tempo for the song "It Might as Well Be Spring." I had written the music at a bright, medium tempo, and the studio's musical director wanted it done as a slow ballad. We argued the matter until the studio promised to reshoot the number if it did not go over well at a preview performance. After the preview they telephoned us to say that the song had been enthusiastically received and that it would be a serious mistake to change it. There was no point in pushing the matter any further, so we reluctantly agreed. Later, when we saw the picture, we had to admit that they were right and we were wrong.

The song itself deserves some additional comment, both on its lyric and on its music. Initially Oscar had planned to write about a girl with spring fever, but then he discovered that state fairs are held only in the fall. This gave him a far more original idea: the self-portrait of a girl who shows all the symptoms of spring fever even though it isn't spring. As for the melody, it is a good example of the way a tune can amplify the meaning of its lyric. The first lines are: "I'm as restless as a willow in a wind storm, / I'm as jumpy as a puppet on a string." Taking its cue directly from these words, the music itself is appropriately restless and jumpy. Moreover, since the song is sung by a young girl who can't quite understand why she feels the way she does, I deliberately ended the phrase on the uncertain sound of the F natural (on the word "string") rather than on the more positive F sharp:

One unusual aspect of our work for *State Fair* was that after we had completed the score, we were told that Darryl F. Zanuck, then the head of 20th Century-Fox, wanted to see us in Hollywood before shooting was to begin. Since the company had been extremely cooperative in letting us do the job the way we wanted, it would have been ungracious to refuse— particularly as we were to be guests of the studio for a week and they were even thoughtful enough to invite our wives. Obviously there must be important things that Zanuck wanted to discuss with us that required a face-to-face meeting.

So the Hammersteins and the Rodgerses got on the cross-country train and spent a week in Hollywood. The accommodations were elegant, we met friends, attended some parties and saw a few screen tests of actors who were being considered for roles in the film. It wasn't until the day before we were to return home that Oscar and I were at last summoned by Zanuck. We were ushered into his pale-green office and there he was, riding crop across his lap, sitting behind a huge desk chewing on a huge cigar. And what did we talk about? Actually, I can't recall that Oscar or I said much. For twenty minutes Zanuck held center stage as he reminisced about his recent wartime experiences in North Africa. Then, when our allotted time was over, he rose, we rose, and we were ushered out of the office. We never saw him again.

Why was Zanuck so anxious to have us travel three thousand miles to see him after we had completed our work? Largely, I think, it was a matter of pride and muscle. He had paid us a lot of money and had acceded to our working conditions, but he wanted the satisfaction of being able to make us do as he wished. It was one more example of the kind of ego-satisfying extravagance that eventually helped contribute to the downfall of the Hollywood studio system.

Publishing songs, producing plays and writing songs for moving pictures were profitable and challenging enterprises, but Oscar and I never thought of ourselves as anything but writers for the Broadway musical theatre. After spreading our wings in diverse fields, we were anxious to get back to our first order of business.

Again what interested us was an idea that originated with Terry Helburn and Lawrence Langner. In 1921 the Theatre Guild had produced a play called *Liliom* by the Hungarian playwright Ferenc Molnár. Simply put, Terry and Lawrence felt that Oscar and I could do for *Liliom* what we had already done for *Green Grow the Lilacs.*

But this time we said no. A musical *Liliom* seemed totally impossible. It was a fantasy, which always presents problems; it was set in Budapest, and neither Oscar nor I had any feeling for the locale; it had a bitter, pessimistic ending that was unsuitable for a musical; and it was a recognized theatre classic which was continually being revived without any help from a songwriting team. Besides, what about Molnár himself? It was common knowledge that he'd already turned down offers from both Puccini and Gershwin to adapt his work for the musical stage.

But Terry and Lawrence were persistent. It didn't have to be set in Budapest, they pointed out; it could be anywhere we wanted. Terry suggested changing it to New Orleans, but that didn't seem right either. Eventually, I threw in the idea of relocating the story in New England, which somehow won unanimous agreement. We could always alter the ending, of course. In the play, the dead father returns to earth and slaps his daughter, which she feels as if it were a kiss. Certainly we could strengthen the importance of the man's return in helping to give the girl a more optimistic view of life. We couldn't do much about the fact that *Liliom* was an internationally celebrated play, but we were impressed to learn that Molnár, after having seen a performance of *Oklahoma!,* had voiced his approval of Oscar and me as possible adapters.

But there was still a major problem: what kind of music to write and where should it go? How do you sing *Liliom*? Oscar and I kept reading and rereading the play, searching for clues. Suddenly we got the notion for a soliloquy in which, at the end of the first act, the leading character would reveal his varied emotions about impending fatherhood. That broke the ice. Once we could visualize the man singing, we felt that all the other problems would fall into place. And somehow they did.

Though the bittersweet fantasy of *Carousel,* the name we gave our musical, was far different from the sunny pleasures of *Oklahoma!,* we assembled the same basic team to put it together. We reasoned—rightly, as it turned out—that with *Oklahoma!* behind them, both director Rouben Mamoulian and choreographer Agnes de Mille would feel secure enough to work smoothly together this time. We also decided that we would again have a cast consisting largely of unknown actors. Armina Marshall, Lawrence Langner's wife, had heard a singer named John Raitt in California and sent him East to audition for *Oklahoma!* He was a big, brawny fellow with a magnificent baritone who would be perfect either for Curly in *Oklahoma!* or Billy Bigelow (the name we gave Liliom) in *Carousel*—so we agreed to cast him as both. Since we weren't yet ready to begin rehearsals for *Carousel,* we put him in the Chicago company of *Oklahoma!* just to keep him busy. Jan Clayton, equally unknown, was cast as the heroine.

Preparations for *Carousel* were in welcome contrast to those we'd had to undergo for *Oklahoma!* We had no money or reputation worries. I won't say that *Carousel* was easier to put together than *Oklahoma!,* but it certainly was easier for Oscar and me to work with the people putting it together. And I think they found it easier to work with us.

Again, as in *Oklahoma!*, Oscar went directly to the text of the original play for his ideas. For example, the main love duet, "If I Loved You," evolved from the following dialogue in *Liliom:*

> LILIOM: But you wouldn't dare to marry any one like me, would you?
>
> JULIE: I know that . . . that . . . if I loved any one . . . it wouldn't make any difference to me what he . . . even if I died for it.
>
> LILIOM: But you wouldn't marry a rough guy like me—that is . . . eh . . . if you loved me—
>
> JULIE: Yes, I would . . . if I loved you, Mr. Liliom.

The dialogue is like this throughout the scene—awkward, hesitant, slightly disconnected—as the two leading characters try to express their feelings. Oscar caught the mood in a lyric that eloquently expressed the emotions of these two young people, even having the girl admit:

> If I loved you,
> Time and again I would try to say
> All I'd want you to know.
> If I loved you,
> Words wouldn't come in an easy way—
> 'Round in circles I'd go!

For the overture to *Carousel* I decided not to have an overture. I had become weary—I still am, in fact—of the sound that comes out of an orchestra pit during an overture. All that is ever heard is the brass because the orchestra never has a sufficient number of strings, and the audience must make a concerted effort to pick up any melody that is not blasted. Instead I tried to avoid this problem by making the audience pay attention, which I did simply by opening on a pantomime scene, with the orchestra playing a single piece, the "Carousel Waltz," rather than the usual medley. In this way we also gave the audience an emotional feeling for the characters in the story and helped to establish the mood for the entire play.

As for the "Soliloquy," which had played such an important part in our doing the show in the first place, it turned out to be an unusually lengthy number which took Oscar two weeks to write. Of course we had discussed the kind of music for the song ever since we'd begun the project, so that once I had Oscar's words before me, it did not take long to create the music.

Which brings up a point I'd like to emphasize. Whenever I get an idea for a song, even before jotting down the notes, I can hear it in the orchestra, I can smell it in the scenery, I can see the kind of actor who will sing it, and I am aware of an audience listening to it. When we began discussing the "Soliloquy" well before either of us did any writing, I asked Oscar, "How would this be for the music?" At the piano I gave him an idea—not the actual melody, but the general tone, color and emotion I thought would be appropriate. I know this helped him when he wrote the words, and it certainly helped me when I wrote the music.

"You'll Never Walk Alone," which was used in the play to give hope and strength both to the heroine, Julie, and to her daughter, has become something of a universally accepted hymn. Fred Waring once told me a remarkable story about it. His mother had died in a small town in Pennsylvania, and he went home for the funeral. It was a thoroughly miserable day, with leaden clouds hanging ominously over the entire sky. Among the musical pieces chosen for the service, which was held in the local church, was "You'll Never Walk Alone." The choir sang, the organist played and the melody ascended step by step until it reached the climax, the syllable "nev-" in the final line, "You'll never walk alone." Just as the singers hit that climactic note, the sun broke through the clouds, streamed through the stained-glass windows and cast a beam directly on the coffin. The entire congregation was so overcome that everyone, as if on cue, let out a spontaneous, audible gasp.

On the day of the first run-through of the play, I was sitting next to Oscar midway in the orchestra. For some reason I happened to turn around. There, in the back of the theatre, his coat draped around his shoulders and a monocle stuck in his right eye, sat Ferenc Molnár. We had never met before, no one had given any indication that he'd be there, and I was terrified.

"Don't look now," I whispered to Oscar, "but Molnár is sitting in the last row." We both began to sweat. Nothing looked or sounded right that afternoon. Whatever we saw was through Molnár's haughty gaze; whatever we heard was through his disapproving ears. I began making mental lists of excuses and explanations. One thing I was certain he would hate was our new ending. In order to give the story some measure of hope, we'd changed the scene to a high-school graduation in which Louise, the unhappy, frightened daughter of the leading characters, is encouraged by her dead father to heed the words of the song "You'll Never Walk Alone." Just before the ending, the girl sitting next to Louise shyly puts her arm around her, they smile, and we know that Louise will no longer be afraid. This so completely changed the spirit of the original that we awaited a humiliating dressing-down from the playwright.

When the run-through ended, I nudged Oscar. "Well, we might as well face it. Let's meet Molnár." We walked to the back of the theatre and Lawrence Langner introduced us.

Molnár opened his mouth and the monocle popped out of his eye. "What you have done," he said, "is so beautiful. And you know what I like best? The ending!"

It was better than a rave notice in the *Times.*

Thereafter Molnár came to almost every rehearsal. Only once did he express an opinion. That was after Mamoulian had directed a big scene and had jumped down from the stage to look at it from the viewpoint of the audience. As he headed back for the stage, a voice called out, "Mr. Mamoulian, please." There was dead silence as Mamoulian walked over to where the playwright was sitting. "Mr. Mamoulian," Molnár said, his face wreathed in a smile, "when you direct a large scene with a lot of people, you make it look as though there were twice as many people. You handle crowds better than any director I've ever known." Rouben beamed. "And, Mr. Mamoulian," Molnár continued, "when you have a love scene, you bring out such tenderness, such feeling. I've never known anybody who did it so well." By now Rouben was positively glowing. "But, Mr. Mamoulian" —and here Molnár's voice suddenly turned to ice and Rouben's jaw dropped—"but, Mr. Mamoulian, there is one thing I do not like. You smoke too much."

Our New Haven opening in March 1945 went well except for the scene in which we depicted a "Mr. and Mrs. God" as a New England minister and his wife. Oscar rewrote the scene and substituted the Starkeeper. The other major change was to add a reprise of "If I Loved You" in the second act because we felt it needed more music.

When one is preoccupied with a new show the work becomes so all-consuming that it tends to block out all personal considerations. I've always tried to guard against this, particularly in my relationship with my wife, because I know that Dorothy has contributed vitally to whatever success I have achieved, even though she has always had her own activities and interests. Among her accomplishments, she not only started the business called Repairs, Inc., which I mentioned earlier, she also invented a toilet cleaner aptly known as a Jonny-Mop and devised a basic dress-pattern fabric which she sold to McCall's.

Still, despite an extremely heavy schedule, Dorothy was never reconciled to the necessity of my leaving without her whenever I had to go out of town with a new production. At the time I was in Boston with *Carousel,* she wrote me a letter which, though full of warm praise and encouragement, voiced the normal reactions of a wife who felt she was being a bit shut out. This was my answer:

THE RITZ-CARLTON
Boston 17, Massachusetts

April 3, 1945

Darling,

Now I can write you because last night we had a SHOW! I'm a very cautious kid, as you know, but there are certain bits of evidence that cannot be refuted. Best of all, I know how I feel, and I feel that there are many moments of extreme beauty here and that the public will want to see and hear them.

Which brings me to your letter. It would be disingenuous to say that I disagree with your feelings that my work is improving. There are many reasons for this, and we've discussed most of them. But I think it's awfully important to both of us to recognize the part you play in my work. If the things a man writes are an expression of his personality (and they can't be anything else), then what greater influence can his personality and his writings have than a woman with whom he has lived for fifteen years? It's terribly important for you to understand and remember that. It's *your* name on the program or in the newspaper, and its meaning goes far deeper than a bow to custom. When an audience applauds something I've done, you are certainly entitled to a gracious nod of the head and I think you ought to do it. I recognize and understand the demands of your own ego. You wouldn't be worth much without it, but the next time you feel shut out of things try to realize that you never can be, any more than Mary and Linda can ever stop being the children of both of us.

To this testimony of devotion I set my hand and seal this 3d day of April, 1945.

In other words, I'm crazy about you.

Dick

The Boston tryout was clouded by the death of President Roosevelt. No one who lived through the Roosevelt years can ever forget the day it happened, or the strangely personal loss that was felt throughout the country.

I was in the Colonial Theatre holding understudy auditions when our musical director, Joseph Littau, crawled through the rows of seats and whispered the news in my ear. He didn't want to interrupt the auditions, but when word got around, everyone was so upset that we canceled them. We were undecided about giving a performance that evening, but after checking on what other shows were doing, we decided to go ahead. I remember telephoning Dorothy as soon as I could get out of the theatre. We could hardly speak; all we did was cry over the phone.

Immediately following the Boston tryout I had a strange accident that put me on my back for several weeks. I was returning to my home in Fairfield via train and got off at the Bridgeport station, where Dorothy and Mary were waiting for me. Because of the war, there weren't any porters, and I had to lug my two heavy bags to my car. I suffered no ill effects that night, but the next morning when I got up I coughed. With that I felt a pain in my back that was so excruciating that I simply collapsed on the floor. I had wrenched one of my lumbar vertebrae. The doctor told me I had to stay in bed, but I wanted to be at the final dress rehearsal in New York. Dorothy drove me from Fairfield to the Volney Hotel, which was then our city residence. I was in bed for several days, and on the night of the dress rehearsal I was taken by ambulance to the Majestic Theatre. There I was laid out, on a stretcher in the middle of the center aisle, from which position I conducted the rehearsal as best I could.

The following night, the opening, I again was taken to the theatre via ambulance. The Majestic has curtains that descend from the upper boxes, and I was placed, still on my stretcher, behind the ones on the left-hand side. From this biased position I could see only part of the stage, but since I was drugged with morphine, I could not have appreciated what was happening even if I'd had the best seat in the house. In fact, so fortified was I against pain that I was also unaware of the laughter and applause, and was convinced that the show was a dismal failure. It was only afterward, when people came over to me—making me feel like an Egyptian mummy on display—that I realized that *Carousel* had been enthusiastically received.

Molnár was there, too, of course, as proud and as happy as if he had written the adaptation himself, and I introduced him to Morty. "He may be your brother," Molnár said to Morty, patting my hand, "but he is my son."

One of the most frequent questions I am asked is: "What is your favorite of all your musicals?" My answer is *Carousel.* Oscar never wrote more meaningful or more moving lyrics, and to me, my score is more satisfying than any I've ever written. But it's not just the songs; it's the whole play. Beautifully written, tender without being mawkish, it affects me deeply every time I see it performed.

## 18

I cannot speak with authority about any other field, but I've always felt that a theatrical production is a success or failure the moment someone says, in effect, "Let's do a show about . . ." Given the fact that the people involved are at least competent in writing, casting and producing, this is where everything starts and ends. If the "about" is a bad idea, no matter what is done with it, the show is almost certain to fail. If it's a good idea, there have to be almost catastrophic mistakes to keep it from being a success.

One morning Dorothy Fields and her brother Herb came to see Oscar and me in our office and asked, "What do you think of Ethel Merman in a show about Annie Oakley?" Without hesitation we answered, "Go home and write it and we'll produce it." It was a one-sentence suggestion and a one-sentence acceptance. With Dorothy and Herb writing it, with Merman playing the colorful sharpshooter, there was no way the show could fail.

The idea of our writing the score was never brought up because neither Oscar nor I thought we were the right ones for it. We had been going in a certain direction with *Oklahoma!* and *Carousel,* and this did not seem to be along the same path. Besides, since Dorothy Fields was a highly skilled lyricist, she naturally expected to collaborate on the score. Choosing a composer was easy; Oscar's friendship with Jerome Kern and my near idolatry of him dictated the selection.

Kern's most recent Broadway musical had been *Very Warm for May,* which he wrote with Oscar in 1939. Although he was reasonably active in Hollywood, where he was now living, he had made it clear that he was anxious to return to Broadway if the right project could be found. We mailed him a script and I sent him a wire: IT WOULD BE ONE OF THE GREATEST HONORS IN MY LIFE IF YOU WOULD CONSENT TO WRITE THE MUSIC FOR THIS SHOW. Soon afterward we received an enthusiastic response.

Jerry arrived in New York early in November 1945, and had been in the city for three days when he suddenly collapsed on a sidewalk, suffering from a cerebral hemorrhage. An ambulance was quickly summoned. Going through his wallet, the attendant found an ASCAP membership card and called the society to say that he was taking Kern to the Welfare Island Hospital. Someone at ASCAP had the presence of mind to get in touch with Oscar, who was then with me at a meeting of the Dramatists Guild at the St. Regis Hotel. When we were notified of what had happened, we got a cab and rushed over to the hospital.

Jerry had been put in a regular charity ward, and I was frankly apprehensive of entering it, not knowing the conditions that would exist in such a place. To my surprise, it was spotlessly clean, and the fifty or so other patients—mostly derelicts and alcoholics—were all very quiet. We soon found out that the doctor in charge had already told them who Jerry was and had requested that they behave themselves. He was getting exceptionally good care, but his wife, Eva, did not want him in a public institution and insisted that he be taken to Doctors Hospital. But there was really nothing to be done for him, and within a few days he was dead.

I never knew Jerry Kern well. He wasn't really an easy person to know, partly because his wife was so overprotective. A year or so before his death I was going to the Coast, and Max Dreyfus, who had been his publisher long before he became mine, asked me to see Jerry because he had recently suffered two strokes and Max was concerned about him. In Hollywood, Eva kept putting me off, which of course only made me fear the worst. Finally, when we did meet, I was delighted to find him in good health. His mind was alert, he moved without difficulty, and we chatted beside his swimming pool for most of the afternoon.

Kern's death affected me deeply, primarily because of what his music had meant to me ever since I'd been a teen-ager scurrying up to the balcony to sit absorbed in the wonders of his earliest shows. No matter what I myself accomplished, I always felt I was continuing to build the same kind of musical theatre that Kern had helped to create. To me, the greatest gratification allowed anyone is to be able to gather a large group of people under one roof, and through words and music, impel them to feel something deeply and strongly within themselves. This was Kern's mission and he accomplished it superbly.

Once the shock of Jerry's death had faded, Oscar and I were faced with the problem of finding a composer to replace him on the Annie Oakley musical. Having already chosen Kern, we felt it was extremely important to get another composer of equal stature, and this could only mean Irving Berlin.

"We're aiming awfully high to try to get Berlin," I said to Oscar.

"What can we lose?" he answered. "The worst that can happen is that he'll refuse."

One hurdle would be Dorothy Fields's reaction, since she had already been signed to write the lyrics and Berlin wrote both words and music. Dorothy, however, was enthusiastic about bringing in Berlin, though like the rest of us, she was afraid that he would feel miffed at being our second choice.

Apparently this never played any part in Berlin's thinking. When he came to see us, we outlined exactly the kind of show it was going to be and what we wanted him to do, but our enthusiasm barely made a dent. Irving was simply not interested in writing the score for a book show. His latest had been about six years earlier, and many changes had taken place in the theatre since then. As a result of *Oklahoma!*, everyone was upholding the importance of "integration" in creating musicals, and he feared that sticking closely to the story line would inhibit him. We argued that just the opposite would be true: a good libretto could offer tremendous help in stimulating ideas for songs and in showing exactly where they would be the most effective. Still, Berlin remained unconvinced. Finally I said, "Irving, there's only one way to find out. Here's the script. Take it home, write a couple of numbers and then see how you feel about it."

That was on a Friday. On Monday morning Berlin came bounding into the office with a big grin on his face and handed over three songs. They were "You Can't Get a Man with a Gun," "There's No Business Like Show Business" and "Doin' What Comes Natur'lly." They were all brilliant, and there was no further need to convince him that he could write the songs for *Annie Get Your Gun*. In fact, he was so grateful to Dorothy and Herb for the help their script had given him that he insisted that they receive part of his percentage of the show. Generosity such as this is an exceedingly rare commodity.

Although he was justifiably proud of all the numbers he wrote for the score, Berlin was extremely sensitive about their reception. In the early days of preparation, we had a series of evenings in which his pianist played the score for all the staff connected with the production. Everyone adored the songs, of course, but at one performance I noticed that one of them had not been played. When I asked Berlin what had happened to it, he said, "I dropped it because the last time it was being played I didn't like the expression on your face. I didn't think you were happy about it and I decided not to use it."

"My God, Irving," I said, "don't ever pay any attention to the expression on my face. I love that song. I looked sour only because I was concentrating on where it should go."

That's how "There's No Business Like Show Business" almost got cut out of *Annie Get Your Gun*.

My relationship with Berlin during the preparation of the show couldn't have been better, perhaps because everything worked without a hitch almost from the very start. Everything, that is, except for the orchestrations. We were in New Haven for the tryout, and with opening night just a few days away, we spent one morning listening to the first orchestra rehearsal. I was not satisfied with what I'd heard, and I was sure Irving wasn't either.

During the lunch break, the two of us walked across the street to Kaysey's restaurant. Berlin didn't say a word until we sat down. "Well, Mr. Rodgers," he began—and I knew that when he called me "Mr. Rodgers," he was deeply troubled, "I'm very unhappy about the orchestrations." I confessed that I was, too, and after lunch I telephoned Max Dreyfus. "Max," I said, "I need Russell Bennett immediately." Russell was out of town with another show, but the next morning, promptly at ten, he was at the Shubert Theatre in New Haven. He reorchestrated the entire score, did his customary superlative job, and soon Irving was again calling me by my first name.

I had never worked with Ethel Merman before *Annie Get Your Gun.* There was no question that she was "the star," but this was an innate part of her personality and had nothing to do with anything she said or did. Throughout her entire association with the show she was totally dependable and disciplined. I suppose I've accomplished as much as I ever dreamed of in the theatre, but the one thing I've missed was hearing Ethel Merman belt out one of my songs clear up to the second balcony.

The only major problem we had with *Annie Get Your Gun* had nothing to do with the show or the people involved. The day before the scheduled Broadway opening at the Imperial Theatre, I was standing on the stage watching the crew hang the scenery when suddenly I heard a frighteningly loud cracking sound above me. One of the stagehands, with the knowledge stagehands always seem to have about such matters, ran over to me and shoved me into the wings. The steel girder holding up the top of the stage had buckled. Fearing the entire roof might cave in, we quickly cleared everyone out of the theatre, but luckily the buckled girder was the extent of the damage. Still, we couldn't risk opening the show until the building was safe.

Oscar and I rushed over to the Shubert office and told Lee Shubert, who owned the theatre, that he had to give us an interim out-of-town booking. At first he blamed the scenery rather than his theatre, but eventually he agreed to let us play the Shubert Theatre in Philadelphia while the necessary repairs were being made. There was the small matter of another show then playing at the Shubert, but Lee managed to have it transferred to Boston, and a week later we moved in. Though we had taken out only a tiny ad in the Philadelphia papers, we were sold out for our entire two-week run even before the opening. No one had to beat drums to make people flock to see Merman sing songs by Berlin in a show written by Dorothy and Herb Fields.

It was the same in New York. When the Imperial had been repaired, *Annie* scored what the press, in near unison, liked to call a bull's-eye. But how could it have been otherwise? It was a bull's-eye from the moment

Dorothy and Herb walked into our office with the idea of Ethel playing Annie.

With *Annie Get Your Gun* out of the way, Oscar and I turned our attention to producing a more modest attraction that Helen Hayes brought us. It was called *Happy Birthday,* and had been written for Helen by her dear friend Anita Loos. After its opening some of the daily reviewers loftily held that the First Lady of the Theatre was wasting her time in such an obvious trifle, but we thought it worth doing if only to give Helen a change of pace and to demonstrate her considerable talents as a comedienne. In any case, Rodgers and Hammerstein had another hit. Would it never end?

It didn't end with our next production, either: *John Loves Mary,* by Norman Krasna. It was only a fair play, but it certainly was entertaining and the public kept it going for almost five hundred performances.

On October 10, 1947, the Theatre Guild presented *Allegro,* the third Rodgers and Hammerstein musical, at the Majestic Theatre in New York. On that same day, *Oklahoma!, Annie Get Your Gun, Happy Birthday* and *John Loves Mary* were all playing on Broadway, the touring *Oklahoma!* was in Boston, the touring *Carousel* was in Chicago, and the touring *Annie Get Your Gun* was in Dallas. In London, both *Oklahoma!* and *Annie Get Your Gun* were sellouts, and within ten days Oscar and I would send out a road company of *Show Boat.*

Even now, it is hard to write calmly about this extraordinary period in my life. There was just no letup. No sooner had we stopped one project than we began another. Most of the time we worked on a number of shows simultaneously. Every day required an unending stream of decisions. Who would succeed Ethel Merman during her vacation? Which moving-picture company offer should we consider for *John Loves Mary*? What record company should we choose for the original-cast album of our next show? Could I afford the time to see the young interviewer from the Los Angeles *Times*?

Because Oscar and I were primarily writers, not businessmen, it was vital that we surround ourselves with competent people who could handle the variety of problems that were constantly arising. In addition to our general manager, Morris Jacobs, we now had Jerome Whyte supervising our shows in London, and we hired John Fearnley as casting director. Our lawyer, Howard Reinheimer, handled many of the details of our productions, and from time to time we hired others for specific jobs when they were needed.

In this way Oscar and I were more or less able to devote most of our attention during 1947 to writing *Allegro*. In fact, we were so determined to be free of the production headaches involved that we took the show to our old friends Terry Helburn and Lawrence Langner, who were eager to have the Theatre Guild sponsor it.

*Allegro* was the first musical Oscar and I wrote that was not based on a previous theatre production. From a practical point of view, adaptations are helpful, since they enable the writer to work from a source that already has a shape and form. But an original concept gives you a feeling of special pride, and you don't have to worry about a playwright approving or disapproving what you've done to his creation. It's all yours, and if you can pull it off, the mere fact that it's difficult to do makes the success all the more rewarding.

Still, the terms "adaptation" and "original" are tricky. In a way, everything is an adaptation. We get ideas from people we know or items we read about or events that happen to us. But whatever its origin, a musical must stand on its own. It isn't necessary to be familiar with the literary source of an adaptation; why should anyone care how faithfully a work has been changed into another form? All that really counts is the finished product itself, and its effect upon an audience.

*Allegro* was Oscar's idea. Originally, he had wanted to write an ambitious work about the life of a man from the cradle to the grave, and thought of making him a doctor because of his close friendship with his own doctor. Perhaps because my own father and brother were also doctors, I was immediately drawn to the idea. I also liked the questions the play raised: How does a doctor maintain his integrity when tempted by an easy practice of wealthy hypochondriacs? How can he avoid compromising his principles when he is caught up in the politics of a large hospital?

In discussing the way the story would take shape, we decided that we would have to limit the action from the hero's birth to his mid-thirties. We also realized that such an episodic story would need something like a Greek chorus to bridge the scenes, comment on the action, and talk and sing directly to the actors and the audience. Further, to avoid specific sets, we proposed suggesting various locales through lighting and different stage levels.

To achieve a smooth interflow of narrative, songs and dances, we were convinced that a single guiding hand should be in charge of every element of the production. This led us to Agnes de Mille. She is supreme as a choreographer, but to our dismay we found that she was unprepared to take on the additional chores of directing the dialogue and staging the musical numbers. Hence, we ended up with a divided command: Oscar directed the book, I staged the songs, and Agnes did what she did best. It was not a satisfactory solution by any means.

The New Haven opening of *Allegro* was unforgettable—and unpredictable. Lisa Kirk, the brightest performer in the show, had a number called "The Gentleman Is a Dope," in which, while putting down the man, she reveals how much she loves him. Lisa is a tall, hourglass-shaped girl who puts everything she has into a number, and that night she became so involved that she stepped right into the orchestra pit. The two cellists who caught her simply hoisted her back onto the stage, and she didn't stop singing through the entire accident! I don't think anyone ever got a bigger hand after a song.

There was another, even more frightening incident that night. During the second act, someone sitting on the right side of the orchestra suddenly got up and yelled, "I smell smoke!" At this the audience started to move toward the exit doors. Suddenly, from the other side of the house came the sound of an even more authoritative voice booming: *"Sit down!"* It was Joshua Logan, and when he commanded, everyone obeyed. Not sure where the smoke was coming from, I dashed out into the stage-door alley and discovered that someone in the building across the street was burning trash and that a draft was pulling the odor into the theatre. Because it was such a muggy September night, all the exit doors had been left open. By running around and closing them we let the people know that there wasn't a fire in the theatre.

In addition to the major problems of *Allegro,* an unusual one affected my department. For the scene at the college prom, which was set in the mid-twenties, everyone connected with the show thought it would be a clever stroke to have the band play "Mountain Greenery"—everyone, that is, except me. I hated the idea of dredging up something from the past for its obvious applause-catching effect, and felt that if something authentic was needed it should be by Gershwin or Berlin. Somehow, though, I was talked into it. What particularly rankled was that after our New York opening, Richard Watts, the drama critic of the *Post,* who was otherwise one of the production's greatest boosters, wrote that I'd had to fall back on "Mountain Greenery" to come up with anything tuneful in the score. What is tuneful or not tuneful is, of course, subjective, and Dick knew nothing of my objection to using the song. Still, it hurt to read such a misinterpretation.

The show got a genuinely mixed bag of reviews, ranging from the loving (Brooks Atkinson's "A musical play of superior quality") to the loathing (Louis Kronenberger's "An out-and-out failure"), with the loving very much in the majority. *Allegro* ran for nine months on Broadway and toured for another seven. Nothing to be ashamed of, certainly, but after *Oklahoma!* and *Carousel* it was a disappointing reception.

Trying to assess the musical **now,** I suppose that it probably was too preachy, as many people claimed. Audiences usually don't enjoy shows that moralize, and this one went a bit overboard in that direction. One reaction that did bother me was that some people seemed to feel that two men who had succeeded in the city were claiming that city life was no good. This was a misconception, but since it was a prevalent one I must conclude that the fault was ours for not stating our point of view more clearly. We never condemned big-city life; what we were against was the corrupting effect of big institutions. At the end of the story, the hero does leave the big city for the small town in which he grew up, but this was only so that he could work in a clinic and devote himself exclusively to healing the sick. It could have been a clinic in Harlem or in Des Moines; the locale had nothing to do with the point we were trying to make.

Of all the musicals I ever worked on that didn't quite succeed, *Allegro* is the one I think most worthy of a second chance. Some of the observations we made, particularly about what ambition does to a man's integrity, are in no danger of ever becoming dated. From time to time, various ideas for revising *Allegro* have been proposed, and though so far none has seemed feasible, I still keep hoping.

## 19

# Majestic Theatre

Magee Corp.

FIRE NOTICE: The exit indicated by a red light and sign nearest to the seat you occupy is the shortest route to the street. In the event of fire please do not run—WALK TO THAT EXIT.
Frank J. Quayle, FIRE COMMISSIONER

Thoughtless persons annoy patrons and distract actors and endanger the safety of others by lighting matches during the performance. Lighting of matches in theatres during the performances or at intermissions violates a city ordinance and renders the offender liable to ARREST.

THE · PLAYBILL · A · WEEKLY · PUBLICATION · OF · PLAYBILL · INCORPORATED

Week beginning Monday, December 26, 1949

Matinees Wednesday and Saturday

RICHARD RODGERS and OSCAR HAMMERSTEIN 2nd
In association with LELAND HAYWARD and JOSHUA LOGAN
present

## MARY MARTIN     EZIO PINZA

In The Critics Award Musical Play

## SOUTH PACIFIC

Music by RICHARD RODGERS
Lyrics by OSCAR HAMMERSTEIN 2nd
Book by OSCAR HAMMERSTEIN 2nd and JOSHUA LOGAN
Adapted from JAMES A. MICHENER'S Pulitzer Prize Winning
"TALES OF THE SOUTH PACIFIC"

Book and Musical Numbers Staged by JOSHUA LOGAN
Scenery and Lighting by JO MIELZINER

with

JUANITA HALL

WILLIAM TABBERT

MYRON McCORMICK

MARTIN WOLFSON

HARVEY STEPHENS

BETTA ST. JOHN

Archie SAVAGE     Fred SADOFF

Don FELLOWS

Henry SLATE

Orchestrations by ROBERT RUSSELL BENNETT

Costumes by MOTLEY

Musical Director SALVATORE DELL'ISOLA

E/ven if I'd been a four-year honor student at Columbia rather than a two-year extension dropout, I doubt that I'd ever have been a rah-rah alumnus rushing up to root for the football team on gray autumn afternoons. But I have always had a special affection for the college because it offered me the chance to write two Varsity Shows which helped set the course of my future career.

In 1948 I embarked on a project that I felt would benefit both Columbia and the cultural life of New York. For some time I'd had an idea for an art center, and the logical place for it seemed to be at Columbia. I strongly believed that the largest university in the largest city in the country should have one building set aside exclusively for the arts, a place where a boy from Mobile or a girl from Bombay could come to study painting, architecture, music, theatre or the dance. New York is the hub of the world's cultural activity; it has more concerts, plays, art exhibits—more of everything—than anywhere else. We can see all these forms of artistic expression around us; yet we still lack one central educational institution where they can be taught. Art does not exist in a vacuum, and its various forms should not be learned as departmentalized entities. An architect should be familiar with music, just as a sculptor should know the difference between a tour jeté and an arabesque. If they were taught within one building, every form of art would be enriched by feeding all the others.

I discussed this project with friends on the Columbia faculty and was gratified by the response. The board of trustees also reacted favorably, and I had the backing of the then president of the university, Dwight D. Eisenhower. Given his military background, Eisenhower's genuine enthusiasm for the plan surprised me, but even more important, he immediately got down to specifics and threw himself wholeheartedly into our efforts to secure financial backing. I am convinced that if Eisenhower had not resigned his position to become commander in chief of the NATO forces, Columbia would have an arts center today.

During the period that I was working on this project, I saw the General quite often. He was a thoroughly likable man without any pretense, and I was delighted by his desire to help. But one thing I found odd was his occasional naïveté, particularly in areas with which he should have been thoroughly familiar. I remember visiting him one morning after he had been to the theatre the previous night to see *Mister Roberts*. When I asked him if he had enjoyed it, he said he hated it. Why? "Our boys don't talk like that." I couldn't argue with him about the accuracy of the language "our boys" used, since he'd been to war and I hadn't, but I couldn't help wondering what war he'd been to if such relatively mild expletives annoyed him so much.

Later, when Ike ran for President, I supported him initially but became increasingly disillusioned when he failed to take a stand against the contemptible behavior of Senator Joseph McCarthy. Weakness was not what I had expected of him, and it certainly wasn't a trait I admired in a President. Therefore, midway through the campaign, I switched my support to Adlai Stevenson. Why this change of heart by a Broadway composer was deemed so important I'll never know, but the story was carried as front-page news clear across the country. Since Ike had been such a loyal supporter of my arts-center project, I was certain that this would signal the end of our friendship.

But Eisenhower was not a small man. After being in office for two years, he invited Oscar and me to the White House for dinner. It was one of those stag dinners he enjoyed giving for twenty or thirty men, mostly industrial tycoons, and to my surprise I was seated next to him. It was a delightful dinner, Ike couldn't have been more charming, and it was obvious that he harbored no grudge. After dinner we all went into the Red Room. By then McCarthy had been censured by Congress and was no longer a threat, but for some reason his name came up in the course of conversation. Eisenhower, who was sitting some distance away, leaned forward and said, "You see, Dick, sometimes if you don't talk about things, they go away."

It was incredible to me that anyone, especially someone of Eisenhower's intelligence, could feel that by disregarding a man like McCarthy, he would simply disappear. This silent treatment didn't destroy McCarthy; it was the very vocal objections by members of Congress who had the courage to censor him that ensured his downfall. To me, Ike's attitude was on the same order as saying, "If you don't call the fire department, the fire will go out."

My efforts to establish an arts center at Columbia occupied my time for a number of years. After Eisenhower resigned as president of the university late in 1950, his place was taken by Grayson Kirk, who was sympathetic but never seemed fired with enthusiasm. The main problem, of course, was raising the necessary funds, and Kirk was nothing if not blunt. One night at a dinner party I discussed this matter with him.

"I guess a project to benefit the arts is the toughest thing to get people to support."

"No," he said, "it's next to the toughest. The toughest is dentistry."

Obviously, people in the food-packaging business or steel can be found to make contributions to studies that have some relationship to their own industries. Chemistry, medicine, business administration and engineering are where the money goes. Dentistry is too unromantic, I suppose, and art too romantic, so my dream got nowhere.

During 1948 I was also concerned about a more personal matter. Pop was still at the Hotel Croydon, but his health was now steadily deteriorating. He had been an invalid for about a year, suffering from a lingering but mercifully painless form of cancer, and died in November at the age of seventy-seven. His passing was not the tragic shock that my mother's had been. He had lived a full life, devoted to his family and his profession, and he died peacefully.

Ten years earlier Garson Kanin had told me that for a movie he had written he had used my father as something of a model for the leading character, a hard-working, unsung doctor. The picture was called *A Man to Remember.*

Though we had no new shows opening during 1948, there were many duties to occupy my time professionally, particularly holding auditions for the many cast changes that were needed for our long-running Broadway and touring companies. Naturally, however, I was always on the lookout for something new. One day I was going through a little black notebook I always carry and found a notation: "Fo' Dolla'." Did I owe someone money, or did someone owe me? And why the devil had I suddenly started writing in dialect? Very puzzling, but I soon put it out of my mind. Some days later I received a telephone call from Josh Logan wanting to know if I'd ever bothered to take his suggestion and read "Fo' Dolla'." Then I remembered; meeting Josh at a party a few weeks earlier, we'd chatted about what we were working on, and I had to confess that I still hadn't found an idea for a musical that excited me. Thereupon Josh told me about a story he'd read called "Fo' Dolla'," which was in James Michener's collection of short stories, *Tales of the South Pacific.* He thought it had the makings of a great musical libretto and urged me to read the book. He wanted to direct it and had already lined up Leland Hayward as co-producer, but if Oscar and I were interested in writing it, he thought that we could all sponsor it together.

At the time of Josh's call I was in bed again with my back ailment, so with little else to do I read not just the one story but the entire collection. I could see immediately what Josh had in mind, and after Oscar read it, he could too. I told Josh we were interested, but suggested that we secure the dramatic rights not only to "Fo' Dolla' " but for the entire book. In this way we would have the opportunity, should the need arise, of using characters and situations from other stories.

It turned out to be a wise move. A couple of months later Oscar and I were in Los Angeles for the opening of *Annie Get Your Gun,* in which

Mary Martin was appearing, and sitting beside the pool at the Bel Air Hotel one afternoon, we began discussing the show. The story of "Fo' Dolla' " dealt with a South Seas native named Bloody Mary whose sixteen-year-old daughter, Liat, has a brief but intense affair with an American naval officer named Joe Cable. The more we talked about the plot, the more it dawned on us that onstage it would look like just another variation of *Madama Butterfly*. Though we liked the story, we became convinced that it was not substantial or original enough to make a full evening's entertainment.

Since we now had the rights to the entire book, we began discussing some of the other Michener stories that could either be substituted for "Fo' Dolla' " or run parallel to it. The most likely one was called "Our Heroine" and dealt with a romance between a middle-aged French planter named Emile de Becque and a young American nurse from Little Rock named Nellie Forbush. This, we decided, had to be the main story. The contrast between the two characters and the strong appeal of their attraction to each other virtually dictated that it would be a more dramatic and unusual plot. But the surprising thing was that we didn't have to abandon our original story. The stories of Nellie and Emile and Liat and Joe could complement each other and make for a fuller evening. Later we even managed to interweave them more closely by having Emile accompany Joe on a mission behind Japanese lines.

All this was against the accepted rules of musical-play construction. If the main love story is serious, the secondary romance is usually employed to provide comic relief—such as Ado Annie and Will Parker in *Oklahoma!* or Carrie Pipperidge and Mr. Snow in *Carousel*. But in *South Pacific* we had two serious themes, with the second becoming a tragedy when young Cable is killed during the mission. Breaking the rules didn't bother us, but we did think the show needed comic leavening, so we went to still a third story for an affable wheeler-dealer named Luther Billis and added him to the cast.

By a remarkable coincidence, late in the same day that Oscar and I had replotted the script, I received a telephone call from Edwin Lester, the West Coast producer. "Dick, I've gotten myself in a jam," he said. "As you probably know, Ezio Pinza has given up opera and wants to appear in a musical. I have him under contract, but there's a penalty clause in it. The trouble is, I haven't been able to come up with a damn thing that's right for him, and if I don't find something in a hurry, I'm going to have to pay him twenty-five thousand dollars. Do you and Oscar have anything cooking that might be suitable?"

"Yes," I said, as the whole picture suddenly began to take shape before my eyes. "I think I do. I think I do."

I hung up and ran back to Oscar, who saw exactly what I saw: handsome, virile, mature Ezio Pinza, the acclaimed Metropolitan Opera basso, as Emile de Becque. After our return to New York, Oscar, Ezio and I had our first meeting at lunch in the Oak Room at the Plaza. Though we had neither script nor songs, within two hours we'd managed to accomplish two things. We had our male lead and we had saved Edwin Lester $25,000.

With so formidable an attraction we were now confronted with finding the right girl to play opposite him. We needed someone young, pretty and lively, who could sing well but not necessarily with an operatic range, and who could project the quality of believable innocence. Oh, yes, and it wouldn't hurt if she had a slight Southern accent. At the time there seemed to be just one actress who could fill that bill, and we had just seen her on the West Coast as Annie Oakley. I put in a call to Mary Martin and told her what we had in mind. She was apprehensive, however. She'd played opposite musical-comedy juveniles and leading men but, my gosh, this was Don Giovanni himself! How could we possibly expect her to sing on the same stage with Ezio Pinza? Because there was some logic in what she said, I assured her that we'd write the score without a single duet for her. Mary promised to think it over, and when she came East in July we arranged to have her listen to the five songs we'd written. She and her husband, Richard Halliday, drove to Fairfield, where they heard the songs, and promised to call us in the morning to give their decision. That evening at dinner the telephone rang. It was Mary. She said that she couldn't wait until the morning for fear that we might change our minds and give the part to someone else overnight.

As soon as Oscar and I had finished congratulating ourselves on getting the two leads we wanted, we sat down with our general manager, Morrie Jacobs, to to take a look at the budget. What we saw convinced us that we had just cast ourselves out of a show. Adding what we would be expected to pay Mary, based on her salary for *Annie Get Your Gun*, to what we were already committed to pay Pinza, there was no way that *South Pacific* could be anything but an economic disaster, no matter how long it ran. So we called a meeting, explained the situation, and asked our two stars a simple question: "How much does it mean to both of you to work together?" After only a minimum amount of consultation, both Ezio and Mary did something unheard of in the theatre: they agreed to cut their salaries and percentages in half. Thereafter *South Pacific* never had any financial problems.

Mary and Ezio worked extremely well together, and their rapport showed in their performances. Mary was a thorough professional, strong-willed and tough-minded when necessary, but always deeply concerned that whatever she did be in the best interest of the production as a whole.

Pinza, too, was a joy. The only problem was that his English wasn't always distinct, a situation that precipitated the only major fight that Oscar and I had with Josh Logan and Leland Hayward. We were in the midst of rehearsals when Josh stormed over one night insisting that Pinza simply could not be understood and that we'd have to replace him. Leland backed Josh, but Oscar and I managed to prevail upon them to give Pinza a little more time. We knew that he was working diligently to overcome the problem, and we had confidence that he would. He had to; establishing himself as a Broadway star was vitally important to Pinza at this stage of his career. His ego simply would not let him fail, and it didn't.

One decision we made early in the preparation of *South Pacific* was that we would not have the kind of choreography to which audiences had been accustomed in previous Rodgers and Hammerstein musicals. We had two strong, dramatic stories, and we didn't need extended dance routines to flesh them out in any way. With his tremendous gift for staging, Josh managed individuals and groups so well that there wasn't a static moment. He brought a feeling of movement to the entire production which brilliantly disguised the fact that its dancing was minimal and basically formless.

As I had promised Mary, she had no duets with Pinza. Her songs were colloquial, direct, sunny and youthful, whereas his were sophisticated, romantic, even philosophical. Both had pieces that said "I love you," but there is a world of difference between a Nellie Forbush who scampers about, flinging her arms in the air and radiantly declaring, "I'm in love with a wonderful guy," and an Emile de Becque who fervently reveals his emotion by describing that "enchanted evening" when a man first looks at a woman and for some inexplicable reason decides to make her his own.

Some years before *South Pacific* went into production, I was idly playing the piano at home when a tune suddenly came to me. Since this was unusual, I played it for Dorothy and my two daughters. I promptly forgot about it, but they didn't, and one day when Oscar was at the house the girls asked me to play the melody because they thought it might fit a certain scene. Sure enough, Oscar agreed that it had exactly the qualities of romantic innocence for the song Cable sings to Liat. He took the music home, wrote the lyric and called it "Younger than Springtime."

Another song for Joe Cable, "Carefully Taught," has been denigrated in some quarters because it is considered propagandistic. The fact is that the song was never written as a "message" song, though it has, I know, provided ministers of many faiths with a topic for a sermon. It was included in *South Pacific* for the simple reason that Oscar and I felt it was needed in a particular spot for a Princeton-educated young WASP who, despite his background and upbringing, had fallen in love with a Polynesian girl. It was perfectly in keeping with the character and situation that, once having lost his heart, he would express his feelings about the superficiality of racial barriers. End of sermon.

Probably the most often repeated story about my method of composing has to do with the writing of "Bali Ha'i." Unfortunately, it is another example of the wrong emphasis being placed on my so-called speed. It is true that Oscar spent the better part of a week sweating over a lyric to the song, and that one day when we were lunching at Josh Logan's apartment he handed me a typewritten sheet with the words on it. I spent a minute or so studying the words, turned the paper over and scribbled some notes, then went into the next room, where there was a piano, and played the song. The whole thing couldn't have taken more than five minutes.

But it is also true that for months Oscar and I had been talking about a song for Bloody Mary which would evoke the exotic, mystical powers of a South Seas island. I knew that the melody would have to possess an Oriental, languorous quality, that it would have to be suitable for a contralto voice, and even that the title was going to be "Bali Ha'i." Therefore, as soon as I read the words I could hear the music to go with them. If you know your trade, the actual writing should never take long.

One lyric Oscar never liked was "This Nearly Was Mine." The reason was the word "paradise." Oscar hated such cliché words as "paradise" and "divine," which have been used over and over again by hacks because they are so easy and "poetic." But though he tried hard, he was unable to come up with anything better for the lines that required three-note endings. Admittedly, the word did convey exactly the way the character felt; he *was* close to paradise, whether Oscar liked it or not.

Basically, I had the same feeling about *South Pacific* that I had had about *Oklahoma!* and *Annie Get Your Gun*. It was failure-proof. The story was honest and appealing, the songs were closely interwoven but still had individuality, the staging was masterly, and it certainly didn't hurt to have the leading roles played by two such luminaries. Even before rehearsals began, and notwithstanding Pinza's cut-with-a-knife accent, I was dead sure there was nothing wrong with the show that couldn't be fixed.

We took *South Pacific* to our two favorite tryout cities, New Haven —where we cut two songs—and Boston. After making some other changes and tightening scenes here and there, it was tied with a ribbon and ready for Broadway.

The opening night at the Majestic Theatre, on April 7, 1949, was every bit as exciting as that of *Oklahoma!* Though in the past others had given parties for the shows I'd been associated with, I'd always been afraid of throwing one myself. What if you're clobbered by the critics? Is there anything more dispiriting than dozens of people frantically trying to reassure one another that reviewers don't know what the public likes and that the show is bound to run forever? But this time I thought we could risk it, and Oscar and I booked the St. Regis Roof. Then, to show how really cocky we were, even before Mr. Atkinson's comments appeared in print, we ordered a couple of hundred copies of the *Times* to give to the guests. Fortunately our gamble paid off (Brooks called *South Pacific* "as lively, warm, fresh and beautiful as we had all hoped it would be"), and the merrymaking went on until dawn. Again I was happy to remain cold sober in order to enjoy every minute of that night.

Once launched, *South Pacific* immediately joined that rare company of such musicals as *Oklahoma!*, *My Fair Lady* and *Fiddler on the Roof* which are not only successful stage productions but major social, theatrical, historical, cultural and musical events. We even made it into something of a philanthropic occasion by setting aside preferred locations at every performance for people who made sizable contributions to the Damon Runyon Cancer Fund.

All that marred the show's run was the frequency of Mr. Pinza's absences. He loved basking in the adulation bestowed on him as a middle-aged matinée idol, but he never could be counted on to show up for performances. He couldn't wait for his year-long contract to expire, and the minute it was up, he was on a plane for Hollywood—where he made two of the deadliest bombs ever released.

*South Pacific* surpassed *Oklahoma!* in one respect. It was awarded an honest-to-God Pulitzer Prize for drama, not a consolation "special award" that had gone to the other musical. This was tremendously gratifying, and I felt especially honored because it was the first time that the committee had included a composer in the drama prize. For some absurd reason, George Gershwin had not been included in the citation when the prize went to *Of Thee I Sing*, even though every other writer of the show was. It was also gratifying that the Michener book on which we had based our musical had previously won the Pulitzer Prize for literature.

*South Pacific* ran for almost five years on Broadway and for a while was second only to *Oklahoma!* as the longest-running musical. The closing night was especially emotional. Myron McCormick, who'd played Luther Billis ever since the show opened, stepped to the footlights after all the bows had been taken, and with tears in his eyes announced that the curtain would never be lowered on *South Pacific*. Everyone was then invited to sing "Auld Lang Syne," after which they were supposed to file out of the theatre. But with the curtain still up, the audience apparently thought there was going to be some kind of onstage party and no one wanted to leave. After remaining in their seats for half an hour, they reluctantly departed.

Mary Martin was with the show for over two years, then left to star in the London production, which despite some critical carping ran for two years at Drury Lane. At first, however, I didn't think it would run for two weeks. Josh Logan had gone over to rehearse the company but I didn't get to London until a few days before the opening. Expecting to see a reasonable facsimile of our New York production, I was shocked at what I saw at the dress rehearsal. Apparently tiring of his original concept, Josh had so deliberately altered and rearranged the show that it no longer held together. I couldn't understand what he was trying to do, and during the intermission I made my feelings known. Josh, however, remained unconvinced.

At the conclusion of the rehearsal, Mary sent word that she wanted to see Josh, Oscar and me in her dressing room. We found her crying hysterically. Between sobs, she told us that if the show wasn't put back the way it was originally, she wasn't going to open in it. We all tried to calm her, and Josh agreed to her demand. But Mary was still uncontrollable. She was sitting facing her dressing-room mirror and I happened to be standing in a spot where I was the only one who could see her reflection. It was barely perceptible, but as our eyes met in the mirror, Mary winked.

## 20

The most distinctive characteristic of the theatre is simply that it's alive. A play can't be put into a can like a movie or a television program to be taken out and shown without change. Theatre exists only when there are real people on both sides of the footlights, with audiences and actors providing mutual stimulation. No two performances or audiences are ever exactly alike; it is this unpredictability that makes the stage a unique art form.

In the theatre we use the term "frozen" to denote that a show requires no further changes before the Broadway opening. But nothing that is alive can ever be truly frozen. Even after the opening, even after the show seems on its way to a lengthy run, we must always be on our guard against complacency. One of the toughest jobs is the day-to-day task of keeping the production fresh. Rehearsals are constantly held to make sure that the people who buy tickets will always get the best performance possible. Actors take sick, go on vacation or leave to accept other jobs, and replacements must be found. Last-minute crises—anything from a torn curtain to a broken toe—must be faced and overcome. Consequently, now that Oscar and I had added *South Pacific* to our other shows, as well as acquiring the rights to *Oklahoma!, Carousel* and *Allegro* from the Theatre Guild, there was no end to the problems requiring our constant attention. Much as I felt stimulated by my work, my multiple professional activities might have put a severe emotional and physical strain on me had Dorothy not made sure that I enjoyed a home life that was so well attuned to my particular personality and needs.

In 1945, having grown increasingly uncomfortable in the cramped quarters of the Volney Hotel, Dorothy and I decided to move. Our friends the Andrew Goodmans had an apartment at 70 East Seventy-first Street, but because the building was about to become a cooperative, they had made plans to move to the country. Their place was a spacious duplex with fifteen rooms, though no view, and Dorothy and I promptly fell in love with it. Since co-ops were relatively new at the time and were considered by some to be a risky investment, my lawyer was dead set against the move. He reasoned that if one owner in the building went broke, the others would have to share the responsibility of the empty apartment. I secured a list of the other owners and discovered, not surprisingly, that if anybody were to go broke, I was likely to be the first one. Probably the greatest advocate of our buying the place was my father, usually an extremely cautious man, and he helped us make up our minds. Though we feared the cost would be prohibitive, we were happy to find out that when rented apartments went cooperative in those days, the asking price was quite low. My offer was quickly accepted and we moved in that June. Twenty-six years later, when we finally sold the apartment, we realized a handsome profit. Pop would have been proud.

To describe the apartment briefly, on the main floor we had a good-sized library which led into a huge living room where my two pianos fit quite cozily. Across a large foyer was the dining room and an extra room, which we combined into one L-shaped dining room with space enough for a sofa and a coffee table. Up a short circular staircase were the bedrooms. I cannot go into details about the decorating job Dorothy did, but I do know she managed to combine style with comfort, two qualities that are not always compatible.

The social highlight of our years on Seventy-first Street was the annual Christmas Eve party. Initially these get-togethers were intended primarily for non–New Yorkers who, for one reason or another, were unable to return home for the holiday; gradually, however, they grew until in later years we found ourselves with seventy or eighty guests. There were always small gifts for everyone—Dorothy took special pains in wrapping each one individually—and omelet-master Rudolf Stanish was always on hand to whip up his specialties. But eventually these affairs became too much of a chore for Dorothy and we gave them up just before we gave up the apartment.

Between 1945 and 1949 we divided our time between our city apartment and our country house on Black Rock Turnpike. Soon after *South Pacific* opened, however, we sold the house and moved to Rockmeadow, a Colonial house with gray shingles and imposing white chimneys situated on about forty acres in Southport, Connecticut. All our summers were spent at Rockmeadow, as well as most weekends, except during the extreme cold. Dorothy and I did a good deal of informal entertaining there, and especially enjoyed competing with friends who were fellow addicts of that curiously frustrating game known as croquet.

One particular occasion will always stand out in my memory. In June 1950, a few days before my birthday, Oscar and his Dorothy were spending the weekend with us. On Sunday morning we heard over the radio that two criminals had escaped from a nearby work farm, and at lunch we noticed two strange men walking around outside our dining-room window. My wife, however, assured me that they were only friends of our caretaker.

After lunch we were sitting in front of the house when we heard the sound of police sirens coming closer and closer. Because Rockmeadow was situated in such a way that it was impossible for us to see the curved driveway, I became increasingly apprehensive. When at last a police car loomed up in front of the house, I was certain that the two strange men I had seen were the two fugitives and that soon we'd be caught in the crossfire of a shoot-out. But then I noticed something else: following the police car was a caravan of a dozen automobiles, and out of the first one jumped Mary Martin! Then more familiar faces kept appearing as people tumbled out of the other cars. They were all members of the cast and crew of *South Pacific*, who proceeded to serenade me with "Happy Birthday." My surprise was so total that it amounted to a small shock. I actually felt my knees trembling as Mary rushed up and threw her arms around me.

How Dorothy had managed the whole thing with such secrecy I'll never know. She'd arranged for our guests to go swimming in the pool, and had even marked out a baseball field for the boys. That night, also as a result of Dorothy's prearrangement, we all square-danced at a neighbor's barn to the music of a small orchestra.

Somehow Dorothy had even provided us with a full moon, and when we returned home, the kids all went swimming again. I'll never forget the sight of the lovely Betta St. John, who played Liat in the show, diving from a stone wall into the water with the moonlight shining on her. At about midnight when they all departed, they left behind one emotionally drained but terribly happy birthday boy.

In a way, *South Pacific* presented Oscar and me with a problem similar to the one we'd had to face after *Oklahoma!* opened. With the show obviously set to run for years, we saw no point in competing with ourselves by following it up with another musical of our own. Therefore we did as before: we turned to producing other people's plays, though this time we found ourselves working on two projects almost simultaneously.

The first was *The Happy Time*, which Samuel Taylor, an old friend, had adapted from a novel by Robert Fontaine. Many years before, when Sam was a fledgling playwright, the Dramatists Guild had sent him over as an "observer" to study the production of *The Boys from Syracuse* straight through from casting to opening night. This was intended to give him practical knowledge in the theatre which presumably would help him in his writing. We had never lost touch, and now when he came to us with his warm and amusing story of a French Canadian family, Oscar and I produced it and everything turned out fine.

The other production, however, didn't turn out fine at all. This was an adaptation of a Graham Greene novel, *The Heart of the Matter*, which the author had written with a fellow Englishman named Basil Dean. We opened in Boston in February 1950, just one month after unveiling *The Happy Time* on Broadway. Unfortunately, it turned out to be one of those plays that are better on paper than on the stage. We were all realistic enough to see that it had no chance on Broadway, so we closed it within a week. It is the only production I've ever been associated with that failed to open in New York.

Later the same year we tried again with another serious play, *Burning Bright*, by John Steinbeck. Like Sam Taylor, John was an old friend; we had met through his wife, Elaine Anderson, who had been an assistant stage manager of *Oklahoma!* Oscar and I had always hoped that someday we might be associated with John on either a play or a musical, and when we read *Burning Bright* we were impressed and put it into immediate production. Perhaps our admiration for the author blinded us to the play's shortcomings; in any case, we found that while we thought highly of *Burning Bright*, most others did not, and it ended its Broadway run after only two weeks.

The play also ended Rodgers and Hammerstein's career as producers of works by other writers. This was not because we'd had two failures in a row; rather, it was because we'd had five previous hits with little to show for them. There are really only two basic reasons why people produce plays: the satisfaction of presenting something of quality, and to make money. We had the satisfaction, but since our own musicals were doing so well, we discovered that once we'd finished paying our taxes as writers, there was nothing left of our profits as producers. There is just so much time and energy that anyone can devote to the theatre, and we had enough to do concentrating on the shows we wrote ourselves. Hence, thereafter we served as producers only for our own musicals—and the only reason we did even this was simply that we had assembled a highly capable staff and it was easier for us to make decisions with people we knew well than to put our fate in the hands of others.

Despite our curtailment of the purely managerial end of Rodgers and Hammerstein, we had outgrown our offices. With the number of productions we now controlled, and with the ever-increasing requests we were getting from summer theatres and amateur groups to present our musicals and plays, it was necessary to move to an office large enough for a "library," where we could store all the scripts and musical parts. In addition, we also wanted a spot where, if necessary, we could hold auditions in the privacy of our own office without the bother of hiring a hall every time we wanted to hear someone sing. Consequently, in mid-1950, we moved to 488 Madison Avenue, occupying part of the ninth floor, and remained there for fourteen years.

In addition to general manager Morrie Jacobs and casting director John Fearnley, a third major member of our staff joined us at about this time. Jerry Whyte, who had been the chief stage manager for the Theatre

Guild and who had supervised our productions in London, was now with us on a permanent basis, alternating his time between serving as production supervisor in New York and heading our producing firm, Williamson Music Ltd., in London. Jerry was probably the most able man in his field, and he was a close friend and adviser until his death in 1974.

All of the first four stage musicals Oscar and I wrote together began with a story idea, which then suggested certain performers suitable for various parts. *The King and I* completely reversed the process. For the first time in our career, a project was submitted by someone who wanted to play the leading role.

Early in 1950 we received a call from Fanny Holtzmann, Gertrude Lawrence's lawyer, asking if we would be interested in writing and producing a musical adaptation of *Anna and the King of Siam*. It had been both a popular novel and a successful moving picture, and Gertrude was convinced that it would make an appealing and colorful vehicle for her.

At first our feelings were decidedly mixed. As mentioned above, we had never before written a musical specifically with one actor or actress in mind, and we were concerned that such an arrangement might not give us the freedom to write what we wanted the way we wanted. What also bothered us was that while we both admired Gertrude tremendously, we felt that her vocal range was minimal and that she had never been able to overcome an unfortunate tendency to sing flat.

On the other hand, here was an opportunity to write for one of the theatre's genuine stars. Gertrude had a distinctive quality all her own, a sort of worldly fragility, and she had won deserved acclaim in modern, sophisticated comedies and musicals. From what we knew about *Anna and the King of Siam*, the role would mark an obvious departure for her, and this alone made the project highly tempting. But before we came to a definite decision, we arranged to see a private screening of the film at the 20th Century-Fox office.

That did it. It was obvious that the story of an English governess who travels to Siam to become a teacher to the children of a semibarbaric monarch had the makings of a beautiful musical play. There was the contrast between Eastern and Western cultures; there was the intangibility of the attraction between teacher and king; there was the tragic subplot of the doomed love between the king's Burmese wife and the Burmese emissary; there was the warmth of the relationship between Anna and her royal pupils; there was the theme of democratic teachings triumphing over autocratic rule; and lastly, there were the added features of Oriental pomp and atmosphere. Here was a project that Oscar and I could really believe in, and we notified Fanny that we were ready to go to work.

With the "I" in *The King and I* already cast, we began thinking about "The King." Since Rex Harrison had given such a splendid performance in the movie version, we got in touch with him. Though he had never before sung in a stage musical, Rex was interested and was sure he could handle whatever singing was required. We had one meeting, but unfortunately were never able to come to terms.

The more we worked on the story, the more we wanted the one actor we felt could play the king with the power and authority the part needed. Our *Oklahoma!* hero, Alfred Drake, who had just left the cast of *Kiss Me, Kate,* was unquestionably the biggest male star in the musical theatre at the time, but we were confident that he would be interested. Oddly enough, we found him hard to pin down. After considerable effort on our part, including transatlantic telephone calls when we were in London for the opening of *Carousel,* he finally agreed to meet us for lunch at the Oak Room.

Oscar and I arrived at the restaurant first and were ushered to a table for four in a corner. Presently Alfred came bursting in with an armful of scripts, which he proceeded to dump on the unused chair. Suitably impressed that he was obviously much in demand, we enumerated the reasons why he should give preference to appearing in our musical. Alfred listened intently and then uttered the words we'd been waiting for months to hear: "I'd love to do it." Unfortunately, this was followed by a "but," and after the "but" came two provisions: 1) he could not remain in the show longer than six months because he had a commitment in London; 2) following the London commitment, he wanted us to buy a particular play from Gilbert Miller and produce it with him in the leading role. This seemed a bit much, so I said, "Alfred, let's forget the whole thing. You've obviously got too much on your mind right now. We'll get together on something else in the future."

Alfred said he understood, and we parted amicably in front of the Plaza. Thoroughly discouraged, Oscar and I hopped into a cab and went directly to the Majestic Theatre, where John Fearnley was holding auditions for the part of the king. The first candidate who walked out from the wings was a bald, muscular fellow with a bony, Oriental face. He was dressed casually and carried a guitar. His name, we were told, was Yul Brynner, which meant nothing to us. He scowled in our direction, sat down on the stage and crossed his legs, tailor-fashion, then plunked one whacking chord on his guitar and began to howl in a strange language that no one could understand. He looked savage, he sounded savage, and there was no denying that he projected a feeling of controlled ferocity. When he read for us, we again were impressed by his authority and conviction. Oscar and I looked at each other and nodded. It was no more than half an hour after we had left Drake, and now, out of nowhere, we had our king. (Incidentally, I never found out what happened to Alfred's London commitment or the play Gilbert Miller controlled, but eventually Alfred did play the king for two and a half months in 1952, when he temporarily took over the part while Yul was on vacation. He gave a superb performance, as Oscar and I had known he would.)

Yul Brynner turned out to be particularly helpful with a talent he possessed that we knew nothing about when we signed him: his ability as a director. Our director for *The King and I* was John Van Druten, who did a capable job except that he lacked the kind of strength needed to direct Gertrude Lawrence. Fortunately, Yul had that strength, and when he spoke, Gertrude listened. We might have been in serious trouble had it not been for Yul.

I had known Gertie for many years, ever since 1924, in fact, when she and Beatrice Lillie made such a notable Broadway debut in *Charlot's Revue*. We had been at many parties together, and I always found her to be light-hearted and self-assured, and to embody everything that means theatrical glamour. Once she started working on *The King and I,* however, all her insecurities came to the surface.

The trouble began early in 1951 when we invited Gertrude to our office to hear the score on the day before rehearsals were scheduled to begin. Because we wanted the numbers to sound as good as possible, I had asked Doretta Morrow, who was playing Tuptim, the king's Burmese wife, to do the singing. Doretta was a dark-haired, ravishingly attractive girl with a rich, lyrical, highly trained voice, and she performed beautifully. Gertrude seemed to approve of what she had heard and I was under the impression that we all parted the best of friends.

The first day of rehearsals is always important. Everyone there is conscious that it is the beginning of a production that may turn out to be not only successful but even historic. Now, at last, after months of preparation, one gets the first taste of what the songs and scenes will sound and look like when the actors perform them onstage. Usually there is a certain amount of excessive gaiety as old friends meet and newcomers try to feel at ease, but there is a deeper feeling of genuine camaraderie, born out of unspoken knowledge that each person has a contribution to make that will affect the final results.

As Gertrude strode into the crowded rehearsal hall, Oscar and I jumped up to welcome her. She greeted Oscar warmly, waved to others she knew, and cut me dead. There could be no misunderstanding; it was obvious to everyone. What had I done? Why, on the very first day of rehearsals, would the star deliberately snub the composer and co-producer? That afternoon, though Gertrude and I were scheduled to go over the songs together, she was still giving me the silent treatment, and I made some excuse about having to be somewhere else.

As soon as I could, I talked the matter over with Oscar and we both came to the conclusion that Gertrude's unhappiness must have something to do with the audition of the songs the day before. Apparently she felt so insecure about her vocal limitations that she had deeply resented hearing her numbers first sung by someone so vocally well equipped as Doretta Morrow, and since I had been the one who had asked Doretta to do it, Gertrude simply took the whole thing out on me.

We hoped that she would soon get over this antagonism, but she didn't. As the days progressed, and despite my efforts to achieve some kind of détente, there were no signs of any thaw. It was unthinkable to replace Gertrude, so I did the only thing possible: I hired an excellent vocal coach named Joe Moon to work with her on the songs. Happily, the two got along well, and Joe's efforts showed. Still, he couldn't cure her of singing flat. Even after the show had opened on Broadway and was attracting huge crowds, audiences were noticeably uncomfortable during her singing and showed it with muffled but audible sounds.

Though I had known all along that her singing would be a problem, I also knew something else about Gertrude Lawrence: she had a radiance that could light up an entire stage. Even during rehearsals it was obvious that she would be magnificent in the role of Anna. I also felt that her intrinsic style and feeling for music would compensate for her faulty pitch, and most of the time it did. Taking no chances, though, I was careful to write songs for her that were of relatively limited range—"I Whistle a Happy Tune," "Hello, Young Lovers" or "Shall We Dance?"—while saving the more demanding arias and duets—"We Kiss in a Shadow" or "Something Wonderful"—for those singers whose voices could handle them.

In composing the score, I followed my usual custom of writing the best music I could for the characters and situations without slavishly trying to imitate the music of the locale in which the story was set. Not only would I have been incapable of creating anything authentically Siamese, but even if I could, I wouldn't have done it. Western audiences are not attuned to the sounds of tinkling bells, high nasal strings and percussive gongs, and would not find this kind of music attractive. If a composer is to reach his audience emotionally—and surely that's what theatre music is all about— he must reach the people through sounds they can relate to. I have always compared my approach to this particular score to the way an American painter like Grant Wood might put his impressions of Bangkok on canvas. It would look like Siam, but like Siam as seen through the eyes of an American artist. Any other approach would be false and self-defeating.

Even though our view of Siam couldn't be completely authentic, Oscar and I were determined to depict the Orientals in the story as characters, not caricatures, which has all too often been the case in the musical theatre. Our aim was to portray the king and his court with humanity and believability, while avoiding the disease Oscar used to call "research poison."

*The King and I* was the only production in which I've ever been associated with a slim, intense, supremely gifted young choreographer named Jerome Robbins. It was Jerry who devised the amusing staging of "Getting to Know You," as well as the delightfully varied entrances for the princes and princesses during the "March of the Siamese Children." But the main ballet, the one we were counting on to be the highlight of the second act, gave him great trouble during the initial stages. One morning I walked into the Broadway Theatre, where we were holding rehearsals, before anyone else had arrived—at least I thought I did. As I entered the darkened theatre I could see Jerry sitting on the steps leading from the orchestra floor to the stage, staring into space. When I asked him what was wrong he confessed that he was stumped by the second-act ballet. It was to be a climactic scene in which, like Claudius in *Hamlet,* the king would observe a pantomimed story revealing his misdeeds.

Trying to be helpful, I mentioned to Jerry that he had already created one of the funniest ballets ever staged on Broadway, the Keystone Kops chase in *High Button Shoes,* and suggested that he might consider approaching the ballet for *The King and I* from a comic rather than tragic viewpoint. Jerry said he'd think about it. What resulted, of course, was his brilliant creation of "The Small House of Uncle Thomas." While the purpose of the ballet was serious, the juxtaposition of Oriental movements within the melodramatic Harriet Beecher Stowe saga—complete with King Simon of Legree chasing Eliza over the ice—made the work both funny and touching.

We made our customary New Haven stop and listened carefully to the advice of all our friends. The most drastic suggestion came from Leland Hayward, who said we ought to close the show. Luckily, we didn't listen. The main rewriting was done in Boston. We all agreed that there was something heavy about the show—we had purposely avoided any overtly comic character—and it was Gertrude who suggested that we could perk up the first act by giving her a song to sing with the children. She was absolutely right. For the music, I went back to a melody I had originally planned for Joe Cable to sing to Liat in *South Pacific,* but had discarded in favor of "Younger than Springtime." For the words, Oscar wrote a charming lyric about Anna's pleasure in getting to know the Siamese people, which he appropriately called "Getting to Know You." It not only gave the act a much-needed lift, it also voiced a philosophical theme for the entire story. Another piece written out of town was "I Have Dreamed," sung by the two young lovers.

*The King and I* opened in New York at the St. James Theatre (our first time back since *Oklahoma!*) on March 29, 1951. As usual, Dorothy and I sat in the last row of the orchestra, and I had the dread feeling I occasionally get that suddenly the whole production was falling apart before my eyes. I was delighted to be proved wrong; the headlines in the next day's papers told the story without even making it necessary to read the notices: "They Do It Again" . . . "Another Triumph for the Masters" . . . "Another Great Hit for Dick and Oscar" . . . "Another Enchanted Evening." Curiously, the score received mostly offhanded comments, implying that it was little more than a satisfactory accompaniment to the play. I don't know why it took the songs so long to catch on, but thanks in part to the excellent film version, they eventually won widespread popularity.

Gertrude appeared in the show for well over a year before going on an extended vacation during the summer of 1952. According to her husband, Richard Aldrich, she was in good health the entire time she was away. She returned to *The King and I* in mid-August (Celeste Holm had been her replacement) looking fit and well rested, and was in such high spirits that she even treated me as if there had never been the slightest rift between us. After she had been back only a few days, however, she began complaining of severe pains, and her doctor recommended that she check into a hospital for tests. At first her ailment was diagnosed as hepatitis which, though serious and painful, was no cause for undue alarm. Soon, however, it became clear that she was actually suffering from a rare form of cancer which was not accompanied by a lingering period of physical deterioration. She died relatively peacefully within a week after being admitted to the hospital.

As I wrote at the beginning of this chapter, the theatre exists only because it is alive, and because it is alive it must perpetually adjust to all sorts of emergencies. The tragic death of a star casts a pall over everything, but if you believe in the theatre you know that, like life itself, it must continue. There is no alternative but to find a replacement and go on. In the case of *The King and I,* it was Gertrude's friend and understudy, Constance Carpenter. Later the part was played by Annamary Dickey and

Patricia Morison in New York, Valerie Hobson in London, Deborah Kerr in the movie, and by many others throughout the world. Each brought something special to the role, and each was certainly more vocally secure than Gertrude Lawrence. Just the same, whenever I think of Anna I think of Gertie.

## 21

"If you were approached to do some work for the United States Navy, we'd like your assurance that you wouldn't refuse to consider it."

"Well, of course I wouldn't refuse to consider an offer from the United States Navy."

This peculiar exchange took place during a telephone conversation I had early in the fall of 1951 with Sylvester "Pat" Weaver, then vice-president in charge of television at NBC. His curiously negative question, it turned out, was simply a matter of protocol. The Navy had approached NBC with the idea of presenting a television documentary series about its exploits during World War II, but before a definite offer could be made I had to give my assurance in advance that I would at least consider composing the score. One simply does not say no to the United States Navy—not out of hand, anyway.

An appointment was set up in my office for the producer-writer of the series, a tall, affable young man named Henry Salomon who, for reasons of his own, was nicknamed Pete, to fill me in. It was to be a series, called *Victory at Sea,* made up of twenty-six half-hour programs winnowed from over a million feet of film from the files of some ten different countries, Axis as well as Allied. Each segment would deal with a phase of our Navy's activities, the only addition being a voice-over commentary and musical score.

It was tempting. Apart from *Love Me Tonight,* I'd never before written any background music, nor had I ever written anything for television. In addition to the appeal of working in a new field in a new medium, I would meet a new array of heroes and heroines. Any composer would have been intrigued by the challenge of creating music to accompany the movements of ships, planes and submarines.

But I held back; to be frank, I was concerned about my ability to do the job. All my previous work had been in the theatre or films. In many ways, this would be a far more demanding job than anything I had ever done. It required an almost continuous stream of music, unaided by song titles or lyrics. I asked for two weeks to make up my mind.

During those two weeks, desire finally overcame doubt; of course I could do it. Despite my inexperience in the field, I couldn't let this opportunity slip through my fingers. No matter what was required, it would still be music, would still deal with emotions, would still be used to enhance dramatic situations. If I could reach people in a theatre audience, I was confident that I could also reach them in their homes, and if the U.S. Navy and NBC thought that I was the man for the job, who was I to disagree?

When I told Salomon that I'd undertake the assignment, I made one stipulation. Since the United States government was involved, I did not think *Victory at Sea* should be a moneymaking project, at least not until the initial series had appeared. After the twenty-six programs were shown for the first time, the network could make whatever syndication arrangements it wished, and I would be only too happy to share in the proceeds. NBC agreed, and I soon found myself back in the world of Guadalcanal, the Aleutians, Anzio and Leyte Gulf.

The months of working on *Victory at Sea* were one of the most satisfying periods of my life. Pete Salomon, who died only a few years after the documentary was shown, was a tremendous help, and together we evolved an agreeable *modus operandi*. I had neither the time, patience nor aptitude to sit in a cutting room hour after hour going over thousands of feet of film with a stopwatch in my hand in order to compose themes that fit an inflexible time limit. We agreed that Pete and the film editor, Isaac Kleinerman, would first do the rough cutting and editing, and then let me see sections of the episodes. They also supplied me with written breakdowns— or logs—of all the action. In this way, with the visual image in my mind and the logs in my hand, I was free to compose the music on my own time in whatever surroundings I chose.

I took those logs everywhere with me. Whenever I had some spare moments, I'd take them out and read, say, "Airplane carrier. Planes landing on deck," which would trigger the mental image I needed to write the music I thought appropriate to accompany the scene. During this period Dorothy and I took a vacation in Florida, and every afternoon I'd consult my logs and scribble away for an hour. It was fragmented work, not like sitting down and composing a symphony, or even a score for a show. Often there was little continuity from one sequence to another. Many of the segments were extremely short, some lasting no more than a minute and a half.

As a result, what I composed were actually musical themes. For the difficult technical task of timing, cutting and orchestrating, I turned to my old friend Russell Bennett, who has no equal in this kind of work. He fully deserves the credit, which I give him without undue modesty, for making my music sound better than it was.

*Victory at Sea* was successfully launched late in the fall of 1952. Since it attracted huge audiences right from the start, NBC was immediately inundated with offers of commercial sponsorship. True to our agreement, however, they waited until the twenty-six weeks were over before entering into any syndication arrangements. Apart from the public's continued approval, which kept the series running for years, I also had the gratification of being honored with the Navy's Distinguished Public Service Medal.

In addition, the *Victory at Sea* score has become a best seller in RCA's classical-records division.

Soon after this program began, I was invited to conduct the St. Louis Symphony, with Marguerite Piazza, Thomas Hayward, Claramae Turner and Robert Weede singing a program of my songs. The concert was scheduled for the afternoon of Washington's Birthday at the Keil Auditorium in St. Louis. Since the hall seats nearly fifteen thousand people, I told the sponsors that I couldn't imagine anything near that size crowd willing to sit still at a concert during a holiday afternoon. They told me to stick to conducting; they'd worry about filling the hall. It turned out to be a sellout, which was especially gratifying since it was the first time I'd ever conducted a full symphony orchestra.

The fact that *Victory at Sea* can sell in the millions as a classical-record album and that a program of theatre songs performed by a symphony orchestra is able to fill an enormous auditorium is a healthy indication of the universal appeal of music of all kinds. Unfortunately, too many people still believe that there are only two kinds of women and two kinds of music —one too popular to be good, the other too good to be popular. Why should we assume that goodness and popularity can't coexist?

In school I can even remember being taught that there were two kinds of "good" music, program and absolute—in other words, descriptive and abstract. There was always a snide connotation that descriptive music lacked the purity of the abstract composition and was thus of a lower order. This undoubtedly grew out of the fact that the great symphonies are allegedly abstract. I say "allegedly" because I believe that while it may be possible to create an unspecific work, the listener supplies his own description. He will hear surf pounding on rocks, relive the parting from a loved one, or even feel impending doom creep down his spine. Painters often see color combinations while listening to music, and I'll bet that the Schumann Piano Concerto makes a first-class cook water at the mouth. The horn solo in the second movement of Tchaikovsky's Fifth has always evoked my mother because it has a contralto voice, as she had, and because it even sounds the way she looked.

Musical labels have always bothered me, in part because the terms in common usage are imprecise and confusing. Is every "classical" work a classic? Aren't there any unpopular "popular" songs? Are we to assume that all forms of music other than "serious" must be "frivolous"? Is there no heavy "light" music—or light "heavy" music? All too often such words merely serve to build barriers around each form, attracting one group of people while putting off others. What we enjoy should have nothing to do with the descriptive labels currently in fashion. The most important function of any composition, whether song or symphony, is that it has the power to affect its listener's emotions. I cannot simply admire a piece of music; I must also feel it. In fact, when I feel it strongly enough the hairs on my arms actually stand straight out.

People have an emotional need for melody, just as they need food or personal contact. By this I don't mean to denigrate the contributions of atonal, so-called "modern" music. Nothing should be brushed off because it is not immediately understood. What may be far-out to one listener may very well be near-in to another. When I was a kid and first heard a Strauss tone poem I found it exciting but I didn't really understand it. Now it's too easy. I can't say that I fully appreciate rock music, but there's no denying that it fills an emotional need for a large part of the population.

Personally, I'd like to see musical labels disappear entirely. Whether it's Bach or Bacharach, the important thing is not the label or the name of the composer, but the music itself. Symphonies abound with dance tunes. The popular music of Italy is grand opera. Within the last ten years or so the theatre music of Gershwin, Bernstein, Kurt Weill, Fritz Loewe and others has become a fixture in the repertories of symphony orchestras. Whenever barriers crumble, the result can only be the broadening and strengthening of music's appeal.

In a small way, I did a little barrier-breaking myself. In my "symphonic" score for *Victory at Sea* was a theme for an episode called "Beneath the Southern Cross" that I wrote as a languid tango to accompany the activities of our Navy in South American waters. The motif attracted a considerable amount of interest as soon as it was heard, and I felt sure that I could find a place for it in a Broadway score. The opportunity presented itself in the very next Rodgers and Hammerstein show, *Me and Juliet,* and Oscar supplied the words and title, "No Other Love."

*Me and Juliet* grew out of our fascination with the theatre. It was our second production not adapted from a specific literary source, and while it fared a bit better on Broadway than *Allegro,* it was not a wholly satisfactory work. One of our aims was to avoid all the clichés usually found in backstage stories. Though the plot focused on various people associated with a stage musical, we established the fact at the beginning that the show within a show was a success. The backer didn't pull out, the star didn't quit and the chorus girl didn't take over. We simply used the production as a framework for a love story, though of course we did take advantage of the theme to reveal some aspects of the world of the theatre. For the actual setting, we decided to restrict the action to the theatre building itself, thereby giving the production a unity that we felt would contribute to its dramatic impact. For example, the number "Keep It Gay" began with an electrician on a light bridge singing along with the actor supposedly on the stage below during a performance of our play within a play. Then blackout, and the audience saw the same number being danced by the onstage chorus. Then another blackout, and the dancers were in practice clothes continuing the routine on a bare stage during a rehearsal.

This musical gave us the chance to put into song some of the things we felt about the theatre. One piece, "The Big Black Giant," dealt with that indispensable and unpredictable element, the audience. Another number, "Intermission Talk," opened the second act with the familiar sight of theatregoers having a smoke in the lobby between the acts. Here we first picked up the chatter—no one can remember how the songs go—which then leads into one group singing, "The theatre is dying,/ The theatre is dying,/ The theatre is practically dead . . ." Though another group cites currently successful shows, these "Happy Mourners" continue their gloomy predictions of the theatre's demise. Eventually the more satisfied patrons become dominant and end by proclaiming, "The theatre is living!"

It's nice to end on a positive note, but the truth is that the theatre has always been a Fabulous Invalid. Somehow, though, it always pulls through. I don't deny the multitude of problems that currently exist, but many of them have nothing to do with the theatre itself. It cannot accept responsibility for the disreputable elements invading the Times Square area or the fact that you can't get a taxi. Nor can it be held accountable for the high cost of living. It's easy to say that tickets cost too much. Of course they do, but so does everything else. In 1943 the top price for an orchestra seat for *Oklahoma!* was $4.80. Today the highest weekend price for a musical is $15. That's an increase of a little more than three times in over thirty years, which is about the same as that of a loaf of bread or a quart of milk. A New York subway ride costs seven times as much as in 1943. And these are necessities, not luxuries.

But if we can't be optimistic about the state of the Broadway theatre today, we can't deny that it not only survives but even thrives on occasion. When a worthwhile production comes along, nothing can keep the audience away. There is no force quite like that magnetic strength which the theatre has to draw people out of their homes to spend an evening with others watching real actors on a real stage.

Because Jo Mielziner's brilliant scenery for *Me and Juliet* was complicated, we opened the pre-Broadway break-in tour at the more commodious Hanna Theatre in Cleveland rather than the usual Shubert in New Haven. The next stop was Boston.

When a show is in good shape you don't have to wait for the newspapers to tell you; you can feel it in the air. In the same sensory way, you also know when a show is not in good shape. Whatever flickering optimism any one of us may have had about *Me and Juliet* was quickly doused when we heard people raving about the sets, without a word being said about the rest of the show. We opened on Broadway late in May 1953 and received the expected unenthusiastic notices, but thanks largely to a healthy advance sale still managed to run for ten months. As it turned out, early in the fall Oscar and I had four productions running in New York at the same time: *Me and Juliet* at the Majestic, *The King and I* at the St. James, *South Pacific* at the Broadway, and in a Jean Dalrymple revival, *Oklahoma!* at the City Center.

Shortly after the opening of *Me and Juliet,* Oscar and I became involved in our first venture as film producers. Just as soon as *Oklahoma!* had begun its record-breaking run, we were receiving offers from major studios for the screen rights. At one point Paramount, figuring to make their money solely out of the distribution rights, offered us 100 percent of the profits if we chose them. But this was early in the show's run and we thought it wiser to wait until the stage production ended before coming to terms with Hollywood. What sold us on the outfit that eventually did produce the picture was a film process called Todd-AO.

The "Todd" of Todd-AO stood for a pugnacious, imaginative showman named Michael Todd. Mike had been involved with Cinerama, the wide-screen three-camera screen process, and was anxious to perfect a wraparound projection that used a single camera and a single projector. He made a deal with the American Optical Company—the "AO" in the name —which agreed to undertake the research. Eventually the firm came up with an entirely new wide-angle camera, complete with new lenses, new 65-mm. film, and a magnetic sound track equipped for full stereophonic sound.

It was Arthur Hornblow, the Hollywood producer responsible for getting Larry Hart and me to write the score for *Mississippi,* who first told Oscar and me about Todd's new process. Arthur was associated with Mike's production company and he was anxious that the first Todd-AO movie be *Oklahoma!* He assured us that we would have complete artistic control over the picture, and that we would become part of the company then being organized to release films in Todd-AO.

Along with Sam Goldwyn, Arthur was one of the few men in Hollywood in whom I had total confidence, and in August, Dorothy and I traveled to Buffalo to see a demonstration of the new process at the Regent Theatre. We both came away tremendously impressed. The audience felt that it was part of the action, and the depth, clarity and sound were all remarkably lifelike. Best of all, Todd-AO didn't have those irritating jumpy seams that divided Cinerama into three panels. The filming of *Oklahoma!* would have been an important event in any case, but making it the debut of this exciting new process made the offer even more appealing.

To finance the process and the production, a company called Magna Theatre Corp. was set up, with George Skouras, head of United Artists Theatre Circuit, as president, and Arthur Hornblow as vice-president. At a preliminary meeting Todd and Skouras got into a furious name-calling brawl. Oscar and I were there with our lawyer, Howard Reinheimer, and after we left I said that I didn't want to have anything further to do with these people. Oscar's opposition was, if anything, even stronger.

To my amazement, without consulting me Oscar and Reinheimer went back to the Magna people a day or two later and told them we'd be delighted to become associated with them in the *Oklahoma!* production. Reinheimer must have thought the deal was so good that he was able to convince Oscar. Had I made an issue of this, I'm sure it would have caused a serious rift between Oscar and me, and this was one thing I wanted to avoid. Furthermore, I had to admit that my opposition was based solely on the behavior of Todd and Skouras at one meeting and had nothing to do with the business arrangement. So I said nothing and went along. Actually, though I approached the enterprise with a good deal of trepidation, the contract was highly satisfactory, both artistically and financially, and all things considered, the movie itself turned out to be creditable.

Except for location scenes (filmed near Nogales, Arizona, because the terrain was closer to turn-of-the-century Oklahoma than 1954 Oklahoma), most of the film was shot on the M-G-M lot in Culver City. Oscar and I flew to California in the summer and were met at the airport by assorted production and publicity wheels, who went to great lengths to describe the cottage on the M-G-M grounds that they had refurbished for our use. As we drove toward it my mind raced back twenty years. This was the very house that had been Irving Thalberg's office, where I had gone to say good-bye the day Larry Hart and I left Hollywood. Then Thalberg hadn't had the slightest idea who I was; now, with many a flourish, I was being royally welcomed to the very same place.

Though Oscar and I were the "executive producers," the actual producing chores were handled by Arthur Hornblow. The director we chose was Fred Zinnemann, who had recently won high praise for his work on

*High Noon* but who had never before directed a musical. As musical-theatre insurance, we signed Agnes de Mille to restage her dances. Oddly enough, she turned out to be the most temperamental person associated with the project. On one occasion she had the door locked on a sound stage during a dance rehearsal and made Arthur and me—both her employers—wait outside until she deigned to let us in.

Visually, parts of the film were impressive, with some stunning shots of elephant-eye-high corn, the surrey ride, and the cloud-filled Arizona sky. But the wide-screen process was not always ideal for the more intimate scenes, and I don't think the casting was totally satisfactory. At any rate, from then on—except for *South Pacific*—Oscar and I left moving pictures to moving-picture people and stayed clear of any involvement with subsequent film versions of our musicals.

We were both anxious to get back to New York to start work on a project we had been interested in for about two years. As I have mentioned earlier, Elaine and John Steinbeck had long been our good friends. John had once tried to adapt his *Cannery Row* stories into a musical, but it didn't work out and instead he wrote a novel called *Sweet Thursday,* using some of the characters in the stories. The producing team of Cy Feuer and Ernest Martin wanted to turn this into a musical, but it never got off the ground. It was then that John approached Oscar and me.

We read the book and were enchanted by the raffish characters and the colorful California locale. As soon as we returned East, we began plans for what eventually became known as *Pipe Dream.*

Sometime during the summer of 1955, I started feeling a pain in my left jaw which I assumed was caused by a tooth. My dentist examined me and told me not to worry, but asked me to return for periodic checkups. It didn't get any better, and one day in mid-September he took one look and told me that I was in trouble. Five minutes later I was in my doctor's office, and that evening my doctor and my brother made an appointment with Dr. Hayes Martin, a specialist in head and neck surgery, for the next morning. After the examination Dr. Martin asked me to sit with Dorothy in the reception room while he talked to Morty in his office. The wait was interminable, and I knew something serious was going on. Finally we were ushered into the office where Morty and Dr. Martin's colleague, Dr. Amoroso, were also waiting. Dr. Martin looked at me calmly and said, "It isn't too early but it still isn't too late." This was his way of telling me I had cancer. While the realization was disturbing, I somehow found the mournful expressions on the faces around me—particularly Dorothy's and Morty's—even more upsetting than the news itself.

It was a Friday. Dr. Martin made arrangements with Memorial Hospital to admit me the following Tuesday, with the operation scheduled for Wednesday. The rest of the morning was spent with an X-ray specialist whose office was a block away.

By coincidence, *Pipe Dream* was to begin its rehearsals on the Tuesday that I was to enter the hospital. Over the weekend I wrote a new song and finished three piano manuscripts. Because I was anxious to see the *Pipe Dream* cast in action and because I thought it was important that they see me, I managed to get permission to spend Tuesday morning at the rehearsal. At noon I took Dorothy to lunch at Dinty Moore's, and then she drove me to the hospital.

That afternoon there was a steady stream of medical and surgical technicians popping in and out of my room. It was all good-natured, without any gloom or tension, which helped overcome any feelings of fear. All I needed was one pill to give me a good night's sleep.

In the morning there were a couple of hypodermic injections, and shortly after noon I was wheeled upstairs. There was one more shot, this time Sodium Pentothal. What a miracle it is! I never felt the sensation of falling asleep or even blacking out. The next thing I knew I was conscious again in the recovery room, minus one malignant growth, a part of one jaw, and numerous lymph nodes. What actually woke me was the unexpected sound of applause, which came from the patient in the next bed being shown the headline in the *Daily News:* "MARCIANO KAYOS ARCHIE MOORE."

Sometime later they wheeled me back to my own room. I had no real pain, only enormous pressure from the bandages, and the first thing I did was walk unaided to the bathroom. Thereafter I received nothing stronger than an aspirin derivative, and at night only a mild sleeping pill. Oddly, I discovered that it was more comfortable to sleep in a chair than in a bed.

I can't say that the surgical and medical procedures of my hospital experience were enjoyable, but there was nothing horrible about them either. What sticks in my mind was the infinite patience of Dr. Martin and Dr. Amoroso, and the pervasive atmosphere of optimism in an institution where terror is thought to be the common emotion. I'm also aware that my recovery was greatly helped by Dorothy, who managed to remain cool and unhysterical at all times, no matter what she may have been going through inside. She also had the marvelous faculty of being exactly in the right place whenever I needed her.

On the eighth day after the operation, Dorothy took me for a ride in the park. I felt miserable. On the ninth day she took me to a movie. I was bored. On the tenth day, still making my home in the hospital, I went to a rehearsal of *Pipe Dream.* I loved every minute of it.

I left Memorial Hospital on the twelfth day after the operation, and went right back to work. I found it tremendously stimulating. Going to rehearsals, surrounded by healthy young people was the greatest possible boost for my morale.

For the first month or so I had handicaps but no visible scars. I couldn't eat properly or speak well, because my tongue hadn't yet learned how to behave. For a while, too, my left arm was quite stiff and I was afraid I'd never be able to play the piano again. But I insisted on going to New Haven and Boston for the *Pipe Dream* tryouts. My wife was my only nurse, and I can't imagine a professional one being more understanding or efficient. Since then, I have had no physical trouble that could be related in any way to the operation. My left jaw is slightly out of line, but it's far from being a major deformity.

If I learned anything from this particular episode, it was simply that the more honest we are about our ailments, the better off most of us will be. Though we recognize that our attitude is illogical, many of us are reluctant to admit that we've had cancer, even after a complete cure. People seem to feel that there is some sort of stigma attached to it, almost as if it were a social disease. The point is that if there are signs of trouble, a person should go for early help—not in fear but in hope.

Had this episode been made into a movie in the heyday of Hollywood musicals, the scenario would have ended with the composer recovering from his operation just in time to attend the opening-night performance of his latest work. With tears in his eyes he acknowledges the thunderous ovation signaling his crowning achievement. Well, if there were any tears in my eyes, it was because *Pipe Dream* was universally accepted as the weakest musical Oscar and I had ever done together.

Just before the Broadway opening we had written a piece for the *New York Times* in which we admitted: "It is not likely that *Pipe Dream* will prove to be exactly what is expected of us. We only know that the rule of thumb of 'expectability' is just about impossible for us to follow."

And that was the problem: we had simply gone too far away from what was expected. People were unwilling to accept the show on its own terms. It had to be compared with our other works and that indefinable thing called the Rodgers and Hammerstein image. Had we been a couple of unknowns, I'm convinced that *Pipe Dream* would have been better received. Which is not to say that it was an unflawed gem; far from it. We were well aware that it was something of a mood piece with little real conflict, and that we weren't as well acquainted as we might have been with bums, drifters and happy houses of prostitution. Also, we made mistakes in casting, and signing opera star Helen Traubel as a warm-hearted madam was certainly one of them. It wasn't Helen's fault; we chose her after Dorothy and I had heard her in a Las Vegas night club, and that was terribly misleading. We did, however, have two fine musical-theatre talents, Bill Johnson and Judy Tyler, in the romantic leads. By tragic coincidence, both died within a year after *Pipe Dream* closed.

## 22

I n 1956, Lerner and Loewe's *My Fair Lady* glided, waltzed and skipped into town to win immediate acceptance as a classic of the musical theatre. Not only was it a rich and endearing work, it also served to establish Julie Andrews as Broadway's most radiant new star. There wasn't a composer or lyricist who didn't start dreaming of songs for her to sing or roles for her to play.

Luckily, Oscar and I didn't have to do any dreaming at all. One day in late summer I received a telephone call from Charles Tucker, Julie Andrews' agent. Hesitantly, he wanted to know if Oscar and I might be interested in writing a television adaptation of *Cinderella* for his client. At the time, thanks largely to Mary Martin's success in *Peter Pan,* children's stories were much in demand for television, but what sold us immediately was the chance to work with Julie. Casting her as Cinderella was like casting Ethel Merman as Annie Oakley. It was right right from the start.

The CBS production took shape quickly, with Dick Lewine, a distant cousin of mine and close friend, as producer, and Ralph Nelson as director. In writing the story and songs, Oscar and I felt that it was important to keep everything as traditional as possible, without any "modernizing" or reaching for psychological significance. One of the major changes, though, was making the two stepsisters less frightening and more comic. We also decided to make our Fairy Godmother an attractive young woman—played by Edie Adams—rather than the customary old crone.

Most good collaborations between a lyricist and a composer depend on give and take, a willingness to accept suggestions and make concessions in the interest of the project as a whole. This was one of the most rewarding aspects of working with Oscar. He was never afraid to voice his ideas if they differed from mine, nor did he ever make me afraid to voice mine if they differed from his. Since we respected each other's views, even in our own particular bailiwicks, we were always grateful for the other's help.

In November 1956, during the early stages of our work on *Cinderella,* Oscar and his Dorothy spent a few weeks in Australia—Dorothy was born in Tasmania—at the Olympic Games. Because we were separated during this period by over ten thousand miles, we had to thrash out whatever problems we had by mail. To document our method of collaborating, I have extracted sections from four letters dealing with the writing of the song "Do I Love You Because You're Beautiful?"

From Oscar:

> I've been brooding about a line in "Do I Love You Because You're Beautiful?" I don't like "Am I *making believe,* etc.?" "Making believe" (outside of the fact that I cashed in on that phrase some years ago) seems an unimportant expression in this connection. How about this?
>
> > Am I telling my heart I see in you
> > A girl too lovely to be really true?
>
> Let me know what you think.
>
> The last time we went over this number, I suggested that you stay up on the higher notes, going into the phrase: "Are you the sweet invention, etc.?" First, you said you had wanted to finish in minor, then you said you could do what I was asking for and still finish in minor.
>
> Now I have a new idea. Would it not be more exciting and psychologically sounder to finish the refrain in major, even though you have started in minor? It is my conception that although the last line is a question, the lover really believes she is "as beautiful as she seems." So after starting with doubt (minor key) the major finish would imply: "Oh, hell, I love you and I really think in my heart of hearts that you *are* as beautiful as you seem." This is based, of course, on the assumption that it is not musically ungrammatical to start with minor and finish with major.

From me:

> I have no particular qualms about using the line "Am I making believe, etc.?" It occurs to me that this is simply a part of the language and it is not connected with you any more than it is with dozens of other authors. I am not devoted to the line "A girl too lovely to be really true," for the simple reason that it sounds like a split infinitive.
>
> Apparently you don't remember that you gave me a pretty good briefing on the subject of going into a climax on the phrase, "Are you the sweet invention, etc.?" At the time I agreed that you were absolutely right and I changed the tune to subscribe to your suggestion. It still reaches higher for its climax and ends in major rather than minor. There is absolutely nothing ungrammatical about ending in major when you start in minor. It is quite conventional and extraordinarily effective. I think you will find that you have the lift at the finish that you expected.

From Oscar:

> My reason for wanting to change "make believe" was not chiefly because of my earlier use of the phrase. In my letter to you I mentioned that only parenthetically. I think it is a "little" phrase and I think "telling my heart" has more emotional importance. You, apparently, don't because you don't even mention it. Let us wait until we get together, which will be in two weeks. I don't share your split-infinitive phobia, but I tried very hard to dodge "really" and couldn't get out of it. I even considered asking you to eliminate the two notes and substitute a long one, thus: "a girl too lovely to be true," but feared it was less interesting musically.

From me:

> As I said in my last communication, once you and I sit down in a room and discuss these matters of syllables and notes there isn't the remotest possibility of disagreement. I know we can conform to what the other would like to do quite easily. In any event, it will be good to have you back and to sit down and talk things over.

When Oscar returned, we discussed this problem—and we compromised. Oscar agreed that "Am I telling my heart" was not appreciably stronger than "Am I making believe." And I agreed to accept "too lovely to be really true" because, no matter how it sounded, it wasn't really a split infinitive.

All this may strike some readers as more of a case of splitting hairs than infinitives, but the fact is that songwriting is made up of small things. It is concerned not only with emotional expression but with emotional compression. An inexact note or an imprecise word can ruin the desired effect simply because a song must convey a particular feeling within a relatively constricted form.

In mid-March, two weeks before the scheduled *Cinderella* telecast, we mounted a full-scale production—not just a dress rehearsal—which we recorded via kinescope. Though it lacked an audience, it was our equivalent to a New Haven tryout. We studied the production carefully and did whatever rewriting or restaging was necessary, A week later we ran a second kinescope—the Boston tryout—which helped us with last-minute polishing.

Other than mechanical differences, putting together a television musical is really not much different from working on a Broadway or Hollywood musical. We still had to create a show intended to produce an emotional reaction in the audience, to create musical sequences that conformed to the action and the mood of the piece. The main difference about writing for television is that the very size of the screen dictates a more intimate approach, while the rigid time limitations prescribe stories that can be told as succinctly as possible.

Though a few of its songs have become popular, our score for *Cinderella* is another example of what theatre music is really all about. No matter what the medium, a score is more than a collection of individual songs. It is, or should be, a cohesive entity whose words and music are believable expressions of the characters singing them. When the lonely, bullied heroine sings "In My Own Little Corner," it's not merely a song, it's a revelation of the girl herself. When she finishes, we know something more about her than we had before—her sense of humor, her naïve optimism, her imagination and her relationship to the rest of her family. It's fair to say that this song is familiar to a vast number of people, but it has never made anyone's hit parade and never will; it is simply part of a score, and it is the score *in toto* that either succeeds or fails. Like a symphony, concerto or opera, some portions have greater appeal than others, but it is the work as a whole that makes the overall impression.

Because there was no video tape in 1957, *Cinderella* was given one performance only, on March 31. By coincidence, this was also the fourteenth anniversary of the Broadway opening of *Oklahoma!*, a fact that invites a startling comparison of the number of people who saw both productions. *Oklahoma!*, our longest-running Broadway show, took over five years in New York to play to more than four million people, and ten years on the road to play to almost eight million. According to CBS, the single performance of *Cinderella* was seen by 107 million viewers.

Seven years after the live show was broadcast, CBS decided to film *Cinderella* with a new script and a new cast. The Rodgers and Hammerstein score remained the same, except that I added the song "Loneliness of Evening," which had been cut from *South Pacific*. Because it is on video tape, this production has been shown annually since 1964.

Early in the spring of 1957, soon after my work for *Cinderella* was completed, I first became aware of a new and mystifying illness: depression. I began sleeping late, ducking appointments and withdrawing into long periods of silence. I lost all interest in my work and barely spoke either to Dorothy or to my children. I simply didn't give a damn about doing anything or seeing anyone. One of the most disturbing manifestations was that I began to drink. This never grew to the point of my becoming an alcoholic, but it was a symptom of my emotional condition.

As these periods of depression became longer and more intense, those around me became increasingly worried, and so did I. What was especially upsetting was that I had no idea of its cause. It had nothing to do with my work. I'd had flops before *Pipe Dream,* and successes before *Cinderella,* and I didn't suffer from a loss of confidence. I am not a doctor, so I cannot speak from scientific knowledge, but I've always felt that the one thing that might have triggered the situation was my returning to work so soon after the cancer operation. It was great for my morale at the time, but one's nervous system is unpredictable and unfathomable, and there's no telling when or how it will react to an experience such as having part of one's jaw removed. Whatever, it is the only reason I can come up with for an extremely baffling and frightening period of my life.

During this time I was never so far gone that I was unaware of what was happening to me. I knew something drastic had to be done. One weekend Dorothy and I asked both my doctor and a psychiatrist to come up to visit us at our house in Connecticut. After discussing my condition we all agreed, calmly and rationally, that the best thing for me would be to spend some time at the Payne Whitney Clinic. So in the summer of 1957 I voluntarily separated myself from my family, from my work, from life itself.

Once I was in the clinic, untroubled by problems and pressures, I felt fine. My spirits soon picked up, and before long I was so well adjusted that I became something of a doctor's helper. Dorothy visited me, as did Oscar and a few close friends, but most of the time I read, played cards or chatted with the other patients, some of whom were confined for the same reason. The time passed quickly.

After a self-imposed exile of twelve weeks, I returned to my family and my work as if nothing had happened. Fortunately, it has never happened again. Fortunately, too, I soon plunged into a rewarding new project.

As the reader knows, I had always been close to Lew Fields and his family, both socially and professionally. Lew had given me my start in the theatre, Herb was the librettist for most of the Rodgers and Hart shows in the twenties, and Herb and Dorothy had written *Annie Get Your Gun.* But there was still one writing member of the family, Lew's eldest son, Joseph, with whom I had never worked. Our chance came in 1958.

Joe had read a book called *The Flower Drum Song,* by a Chinese-American novelist named C. Y. Lee, which dealt with the conflicts between the older and younger generations of Chinese Americans living in San Francisco. Joe saw the dramatic possibilities, secured the rights and approached Oscar and me about collaborating on a musical version. We were charmed by the story and before long we were under way.

While all of the characters in the play were of Chinese ancestry, it was impossible to find Chinese actors to fill every part; in fact, most of our leads were played by non-Chinese. Josh Logan had told me about a Japanese girl named Miyoshi Umeki who had a slight but adequate voice, and she turned out to be just right for the shy heroine. In the brassier role of a night-club stripper was a Japanese-American song belter named Pat Suzuki. For other main roles we cast Juanita Hall, who was black; Ed Kenney, who was Hawaiian; and Larry Blyden, who was Houston, Texas. Keye Luke, formerly Charlie Chan's number-one son, was the only actor of Chinese background who had a major part.

This ethnically mixed cast certainly didn't lessen the total effect; what was important was that the actors gave the illusion of being Chinese. This demonstrates one of the wonderful things about theatre audiences. People want to believe what they see on a stage, and they will gladly go along with whatever is done to achieve the desired effect. Ask them to accept Ezio Pinza as a Frenchman, Yul Brynner as Siamese or a heterogeneous group of actors as Chinese, and they are prepared to meet you nine tenths of the way even before the curtain goes up.

In selecting a director, we did the unexpected and went to Gene Kelly. I had known Gene ever since he was our Pal Joey, and had helped him get the job of choreographer for Best Foot Forward. Though his directing experience was limited to the screen—including Joe Fields' last picture—we were confident he could do a beautiful job. He did.

Rather than book Flower Drum Song into the Shubert in New Haven, we decided to go straight to Boston, where the show remained a full month. Part of the time was needed to rehearse Larry Blyden, who took over one of the leading parts. Musically, our major problem was with a song, "My Best Love." At first it was sung by Keye Luke, but that didn't work. Then we gave it to Juanita Hall, and that didn't work either. Then Oscar and I decided to scrap the number completely and write something new for another character in the same scene. That was the role played by Larry Blyden, who initially had an exchange with Miyoshi Umeki, his intended "picture bride" from China, in which he tried to talk her out of marrying him. Oscar simply put the dialogue into a lyric, "Don't Marry Me," and I set it to music on a piano I'd discovered in the Shubert Theatre's ladies' lounge.

One other song is particularly interesting because of the poetic form Oscar used. This was "I Am Going to Like It Here," which Miyoshi sang soon after her arrival in San Francisco. To achieve an appropriately naïve, singsong flavor, Oscar went back to an ancient Malaysian form called the "pantoum," in which the second and fourth lines of each four-line stanza become the first and third lines in the following stanza. It was meticulously worked out, though it's unlikely that many people were conscious of the technique—which is just as it should be.

Oscar was a perfectionist not only about his own work but about every aspect of a production. He was also the most self-controlled person I've ever known. During the Boston tryout of *Flower Drum Song* one of the actors, despite repeated warnings, continued to sing a line incorrectly for seven straight performances. Oscar may have been seething inwardly, but the strongest reproach he could muster was, "I'm not very good-natured about this any more."

The musical opened in New York on December 1, 1958, and ran for a year and a half on Broadway. Later it toured for another year and a half and also had a successful London run. The entire experience of working on *Flower Drum Song* was rewarding in many ways, not the least of which was that it convinced me that I had overcome all traces of my depression. My only thought was to keep on doing what I was doing, and I saw nothing in the future that could stop me.

## 23

$M$ost people have a strong desire for continuity. One way we continue ourselves is through our work; what we create or accomplish is our method of reaching out and becoming part of others. But the most basic way we manifest our desire for continuity is by having children. This is biological continuation, but it can also be a form of creative continuation when one's children become involved in the same field that we are.

Both our daughters, Mary and Linda, have many traits and characteristics that are to be found in Dorothy and me, but from a purely selfish point of view, it is especially gratifying to me that not only do they have a strong love of music, they also have been gifted with the ability to perform and compose. (Geneticists may note, however, that all but one of Mary's five children have shown little interest in the musical arts but, like their grandmother, have demonstrated notable aptitude for the visual arts.)

Naturally, Mary and Linda grew up surrounded by music, and I did what I could to encourage their interest. I remember that we used to make a game of ear-training. For example, I'd strike a minor sixth and the girls would try to compete in identifying it first. In the early forties, when I began taking piano lessons again, the fact that I was always rushing to the piano to practice made it all the more desirable for Mary and Linda. If the old man could bang away at the keyboard for hours, maybe it wasn't so boring after all.

Though I have tried to help my daughters' ambitions, my attitude has always been that encouragement should remain within the confines of our home. While it is vital that young people interested in the theatre get as much practical experience as possible, I think it would have been wrong to have employed either of my daughters to work on any of my shows. Whatever talents they possessed had to be recognized on their own, without any close identification with me. I don't deny that the name Rodgers may have opened some doors, but both Mary and Linda were smart enough to realize that to keep those doors open, their work would have to possess both quality and individuality. Nobody hires a composer on the basis of having a relative in the business.

Linda was the first to exhibit musical talent. Since she is four years younger, this turned Mary away from music for a while. Dorothy and I then became convinced that Mary's talents lay more in words, but she surprised us all by majoring in music at college.

Though for a time Mary diligently pursued a career as a composer, she has recently emerged as a successful writer of fiction with two well-received books, *Freaky Friday* and *A Billion for Boris*. In addition, she and her mother write a column, "Of Two Minds," for *McCall's* magazine, which answers written-in questions about problems facing wives and mothers today. The column is an offshoot of the book they wrote together, *A Word to the Wives*. On her own, Dorothy has brought further literary distinction to the family by writing *My Favorite Things* (her feelings about various people, places and objects) and *The House in My Head* (her experiences in the building and decorating of our country house).

For their first stage score our daughters collaborated, with Linda as composer and Mary as lyricist. It was a charming mini-musical for kids called *Three to Make Music,* which Mary Martin performed in concert and on television.

Mary first won recognition as a composer with her score for *Once Upon a Mattress*. Mixed with my pride in her accomplishment was my concern that she should receive all the credit that was her due. Because it is always a temptation for outsiders to assume that I must have had a hand in the writing, I studiously avoided giving suggestions about the music or the show. I was, in fact, so sensitive about it that once when a photographer asked me to pose at the piano with Mary listening, I insisted that the positions be reversed: Mary was photographed at the piano while I was doing the listening.

Six months after the opening of Mary's first musical, Rodgers and Hammerstein's last musical, *The Sound of Music,* opened on Broadway.

The production's genesis, so far as Oscar and I were concerned, went back to the beginning of the previous year. Mary Martin, her husband Richard Halliday and producer Leland Hayward had just seen a German-language film, *The Trapp Family Singers,* and were all agog over its stage potential. But initially they envisioned it as essentially a dramatic play, featuring authentic Trapp family songs with one new number by Rodgers and Hammerstein.

Oscar and I saw the picture and agreed that it had the makings of an impressive stage production, but we disagreed with their concept. If they wanted to do a play using the actual music the Trapps sang, fine, but why invite a clash of styles by simply adding one new song? Why not a fresh score? When I suggested this to Leland and Mary they said they'd love to have a new score—but only if Oscar and I wrote it. We had to explain that we would be tied up with *Flower Drum Song* for a year, but they came back with the two most flattering words possible: "We'll wait."

Rodgers and Hammerstein joined Hayward and Halliday as co-sponsors, though the actual staff was recruited from the Hayward office. Because Howard Lindsay and Russel Crouse had already been signed to supply the libretto before Oscar and I became involved, *The Sound of Music* was one of the few productions for which Oscar's writing was confined to lyrics.

In creating their story, Howard and Russel tried to steer clear of making it one more old-fashioned dirndl-and-lederhosen Austrian operetta, and to keep the plot believable and convincing. Admittedly, it was a sentimental musical, but the truth is that almost everything in it was based on fact. No incidents were dragged in to tug at heart strings. This, more or less, is what had happened:

A young postulant named Maria Rainer went to work as governess for the children of an autocratic army captain named Baron Georg von Trapp. Postulant and baron fell in love, the girl left her order, the two were married, organized a family singing group and eventually were forced by the Nazis to flee Austria.

Had such a story come out in any way other than sentimental it would have been false. To be sure, too much of anything is harmful. No one is comfortable with an excess of hearts and flowers, but there is no valid reason for hiding honest emotion. This has always been a major element in the theatre, and it's my conviction that anyone who can't, on occasion, be sentimental about children, home or nature is sadly maladjusted.

My concentration on *The Sound of Music* during its preparation was tempered by my concern for Oscar. He was not a well man. During the writing he began to complain of discomfort, and in September, just before rehearsals began, he was operated on for an ulcer. Though they hid the truth from Oscar, the doctors told his family—and Dorothy and me—that he had cancer, and that there was only a slim chance of his pulling through.

It was devastating news. Still, we always clung to the chance that somehow he would be able to lick the disease just as I had. The seriousness of his condition was simply too awful to grasp. This couldn't be allowed to happen. Oscar would get over it; there was still time; somewhere, we were confident, there had to be a cure. Unfortunately, we were all afflicted with what Larry Hart had once called "the self-deception that believes the lie."

Oscar was too sick to go to New Haven for the first tryout stop, but he did get to Boston to write the lyric for a melody that Von Trapp sang as an expression of his love for his homeland. "Edelweiss" was the last song Oscar and I ever wrote together.

For this one, as well as for all the other songs in the score, it was essential that we maintain not only the genuineness of the characters but also of their background. "The Sound of Music," the first real song in the play, was an arm-flinging tribute to nature and music. "Do-Re-Mi" offered an elementary music lession that Maria employed to ingratiate herself with the Von Trapp children. "My Favorite Things," a catalogue of simple pleasures, had a folkish quality, while "The Lonely Goatherd" and the instrumental "Laendler" evoked the atmosphere of the Austrian Alps. "Climb Ev'ry Mountain" was needed to give strength to Maria when she left the abbey, and at the end to the whole family when they were about to cross the Alps.

One musical problem confronting me was the opening piece. Rather than begin with the customary overture, we decided to open immediately on a scene in Nonnberg Abbey, in which the nuns are heard chanting a Catholic prayer, "Dixit Dominus." Since I had been so strongly against a score that combined old music with new, I could hardly fall back on using a traditional melody for the mass. Writing "Western" songs for *Oklahoma!* or "Oriental" songs for *The King and I* had never fazed me, but the idea of composing a Catholic prayer made me apprehensive. Given my lack of familiarity with liturgical music, as well as the fact that I was of a different faith, I had to make sure that what I wrote would sound as authentic as possible.

So for the first time in my life I did a little research—and it turned out to be one of the most rewarding music lessons I've ever had. Through friends I got in touch with Mother Morgan, the head of the music department at Manhattanville College in Purchase, New York. She was not only willing to help; she even invited Dorothy and me to a specially arranged concert at which the nuns and seminarians sang and performed many different kinds of religious music, from Gregorian chants to a modern work by Gabriel Fauré. An unexpectedly amusing moment came when Mother Morgan, waving her arms like a cheerleader at a football game, was vigorously conducting a particularly dramatic passage. As the music built to its peak, above the singing could be clearly heard Mother Morgan's booming command: "Pray it!"

Working with Mary Martin again made me appreciate even more what an extraordinary trouper she is. During rehearsals and during the run of the show on Broadway she was constantly in training, both vocally and physically. Nothing we ever suggested was considered too demanding. Even after it seemed impossible to do anything more with the part, Mary was still working to improve her interpretation. In all the years I've known her, I have never seen her give a performance that was anything less than the best that was in her.

Nor have I ever known Mary to be anything less than kind to everyone. She does, however, have one unusual trait. Possibly because of her family background, she cannot utter even the mildest form of profanity. Strangely, though, her strait-laced innocence has led her to use euphemisms that sound even more scatological than the words she carefully avoids. Instead of saying "Oh, damn!"—or worse—Mary always substitutes "Oh, plop!" The strongest expression I have ever heard her use about anyone—and he has to be a true monster to earn it—is "He's a son-of-a-bear!"

*The Sound of Music* opened in New York almost exactly a year after *Flower Drum Song*. The line-up of talent ensured a healthy advance sale at the box office, but the notices were decidedly mixed, with most carping aimed at the book, which, predictably, was labeled too sentimental. Still, the production remained on Broadway for over three and a half years and had a London run of almost twice as long. Its longevity in the West End was all the more remarkable because of blistering first-night reviews—again chiefly because of the play's alleged sentimentality. Fortunately, the English have a habit of making up their own minds.

As we'd all feared, Oscar was getting progressively worse. During the following winter I continued to make believe—at least in front of him—that everything was fine. We held auditions for cast replacements, discussed possible future properties and even flew over to London at the end of March for the West End premiere of *Flower Drum Song*. Early in the summer I also tried to keep from thinking about the inevitable by becoming involved in the writing of the background score for a television series, *Winston Churchill—The Valiant Years*.

But Oscar could not be kept from the truth indefinitely. One morning he went to his doctor and insisted on knowing exactly how serious his condition was. That afternoon we met for lunch, and Oscar told me what his doctor had said. He had three alternatives: he could have another operation, which would leave him in great discomfort but would still not cure him completely; he could go down to Washington, where they had a highly sophisticated X-ray machine, but this treatment would also prove both painful and temporary; or he could do nothing. He revealed this quietly, in a calm, matter-of-fact voice, as if he were discussing a series of rhyming alternatives. He also told me that he had already chosen the third alternative: he would do nothing. "I'm just going down to Doylestown," he said, "and stay on the farm until I die."

Then he talked of the future. He had no financial problems, so his family would be well taken care of. As for me, he said he thought I should try to find a younger man to work with; it would prove stimulating for me, and he was sure that my experience would be of great help to someone just beginning. We discussed many things that day, two somber, middle-aged men sitting in a crowded restaurant talking unemotionally of the imminent death of one and the need for the other to keep going. Toward the end of lunch, a man seated a few tables away came over to us with his menu in his hand. He introduced himself, told us he was from the Midwest, and asked for our autographs. After we had scribbled our names, the man said, "I hope you won't mind my saying this, but one thing bothers me. You're both extremely successful men, at the top of your profession, and I'm sure you don't have a worry in the world. I was just wondering what could possibly make you both look so sad."

Oscar did as he said he would. He went back to his farm to spend his last remaining days with his family in the countryside that he loved. He died on August 23, 1960.

Larry Hart's death had affected me deeply, but Larry was a man whose death could have been predicted at any time during the twenty-five years we knew each other. When he did succumb he was only forty-eight with a career that was all but over. Oscar's death was the greater blow simply because almost to the day he died everything about him was an affirmation of life. He was then in his sixty-sixth year, but he was infused with a faith and an optimism that only grew stronger as he grew older.

In many ways Oscar was a study in contrasts. He was a passionately loving man, yet he never gave any overt indication of that love except through his lyrics. He was a meticulously hard worker, yet he'd roam around his farm for hours, even days, before putting words to paper. In business dealings he was practical and hard-headed, yet he was always willing to lend his support to idealistic causes. He was quiet-spoken and gentle, yet I saw him rise to heights of fury at the injustices around him, especially those dealing with the rights of minorities. He was a genuinely sophisticated, worldly man, yet he will probably be best remembered for his unequaled ability to express the simplest, most frequently overlooked pleasures of life.

For all his days Oscar sang with a clear voice about everything that was good and decent and enjoyable. It's still a clear voice, but now we must do his singing for him.

## 24

$O_f$ all the theatrical art forms, none is more of a collaborative effort than the musical play. While most of the essential components—the libretto, direction, dancing, set designs, lighting, and the others—can be and usually are handled by a single person in each area, the one department that generally requires the services of two people is the score. A composer can provide only half the finished product; without a lyricist he simply cannot function.

Composer-lyricist partnerships seldom last long. A writer must be able to work with someone new whenever the occasion arises. At the time of Oscar's death I had spent over forty years in the theatre, and in all that time I'd had only two partners. I don't think such fidelity has ever been equaled. When I turned to Oscar because of Larry's problems, there were never any adjustment difficulties, chiefly because our outlook on life and work was so similar. With Oscar gone it was simply too much to expect that I could adjust to anyone else without a lengthy interval between.

Still, there was never any question of my determination to continue. Primarily this was a matter of creative drive. After the shock and grief of the loss of a dear friend and partner it's easy to consider chucking everything and spending the rest of your life puttering around a garden or traveling around the world. Had I succumbed to that feeling I'd be dead —not physically, perhaps, but mentally and emotionally dead. For me, work is simply a matter of survival. I was only fifty-eight at the time of Oscars' death, and while my career had been long and fulfilling, I could not imagine spending the rest of my days reliving past glories and withdrawing from the vital, exciting world that I loved.

Under the circumstances, there was only one logical path: I had to try to write my own lyrics. The roster of men who are adept at writing both words and music is not long, but it does include some of the elite members of my profession. Frank Loesser, Cole Porter, Irving Berlin, Noël Coward and Harold Rome all have excelled in both fields. While I had no illusions about matching their lyric-writing skills, I knew that something must have rubbed off on me after all those years with Larry and Oscar. In fact, I had already had some limited experience; because of Larry's numerous disappearances, I'd frequently been forced to supply additional lyrics of my own during out-of-town tryouts. After Larry's death, I was also called on to update some of his lines for revivals of our shows.

Luckily, I had the chance to test my ability as a lyricist even before I was faced with writing a new score. At this time 20th Century-Fox was planning a remake of *State Fair*. Perhaps suffering from the misapprehension that anything bigger is necessarily better, they planned to change the locale from Iowa to Texas, and they also wanted some additional songs. I told them that I intended to write my own lyrics, but that if I didn't like them, they'd never see them. I also assured the studio that if they didn't like what I'd written, they didn't have to use it. Within a few weeks I sent them three songs which apparently won their approval because they then asked me for two more. While they weren't exactly world-beaters—and neither was the picture—they did give me enough confidence to plan on writing the lyrics for my next show, whatever it would be.

One evening in April 1961 I switched on the television set to watch Jack Paar's program, which I often used as something of a talent audition. That night his guest was the stunning Diahann Carroll, a singer whom I'd greatly admired ever since seeing her in Harold Arlen's musical, *House of Flowers*. I had even tested her for the lead in *Flower Drum Song*, but we never were able to make her appear Oriental. On Paar's program she sang an old Johnny Mercer number, "Goody-Goody," with such distinctiveness that it sounded like a brand-new song written expressly for her. But there was more to Diahann than vocal ability. Wearing a black chiffon cocktail dress with her hair in a stylish bouffant, she looked as if she had just stepped off the cover of a fashion magazine. Her singing and her appearance immediately gave me the idea of starring her in a musical in which she would play a chic, sophisticated woman of the world. She would not represent a cause or be a symbol of her race, but a believable human being, very much a part of a stratum of society that the theatre thus far had never considered for a black actress. Such casting, I felt, would be more effective than anything strident or preachy in breaking down racial stereotypes that had persisted far too long on Broadway.

This concept became so fixed in my mind that the very next day I called Diahann on the phone, and that afternoon we met for a drink. I told her my general idea—and at the time it was nothing if not general—and she responded to it immediately. Simply having a black actress in the starring role would, we both felt, give the play an extra dimension that made it unnecessary for anything in the dialogue or action to call attention to the fact. Rather than shrinking from the issue of race, such an approach would demonstrate our respect for the audience's ability to accept our theme free from rhetoric or sermons.

Now that I had a star and a general concept, as well as a fledgling lyricist, my job was to find a librettist to devise a suitable story. In thinking of various writers, I kept coming back to Sam Taylor. He had never before written a musical-comedy book, but I had known him for many years and admired his work. After Oscar and I had produced his first play, *The Happy Time,* Sam went on to write such equally charming comedies as *Sabrina Fair* and *The Pleasure of His Company.* Another factor was simply that I felt comfortable with Sam. He was a thoughtful, accommodating, highly skilled craftsman, with just the right outlook the project needed. We talked the matter over, he liked the idea, and I had a book-writer.

Early in the summer Dorothy and I went up to Sam's place in East Blue Hill, Maine, where we discussed various aspects of the story which by now we had decided to call *No Strings.* It was then that the basic form emerged: Diahann would play an American model living in Paris who meets and falls in love with another American, a former Pulitzer Prize-winning novelist who is now just another expatriate bum sponging off wealthy tourists. The girl helps restore his self-confidence and his desire to resume writing, but the distractions of the affluent life around him are too much. He can only work if he returns home to Maine—Sam's only autobiographical touch—but when he asks the girl to go with him they both realize that it could never work out, and they part. Even at the end, when the reason for the breakup is clearly because of anticipated racial prejudice, we were careful to avoid mentioning the issue directly.

With the outline and the basic characters decided on, I began work on the score. I soon discovered the major benefit of writing one's own lyrics: I was always there when I wanted me. Of course I missed Oscar's help, but I also was stimulated by being able to do the entire job myself. I loved the independence it gave me. If I wanted to, I could work until four in the morning—or I could get up at four and start working. I've always had a compulsion to finish something once I've started it, and at last I had the opportunity of polishing off a complete song at one sitting.

As any songwriter will tell you, writing lyrics is more demanding than writing music. Music is created with broad strokes on a large canvas, whereas lyrics are tiny mosaics that must be painstakingly cut and fitted into a frame. I found that I never really had any method of self-collaboration. Sometimes the title of a song and the first few bars would occur to me simultaneously and I'd finish them together. At other times I'd jot down a few lines of a lyric which would suggest a melody. Occasionally this would be reversed and I'd think of the musical phrase first. Never, however, did I write a complete lyric and then set it to music.

As I became more deeply involved in the production, I discovered that the theme lent itself to a technical innovation that had never before been attempted in the theatre. In any musical production, there is a built-in chasm, the orchestra pit, that separates the audience from the performers, and it has long been accepted as a convention that singers sing on the stage and musicians play in the pit. Since our story was of such an intimate nature, I began to think about putting the musicians on the stage, both in the wings and in full view of the audience. Instrumental soloists and small groups of musicians could then be involved visually with the play and players, thereby providing physical as well as musical cohesion.

Most of this aspect of the show was worked out with our director, Joe Layton, a tall, lean, intense fellow who heretofore had been known primarily as a choreographer. I had first become familiar with his work in my daughter Mary's show, *Once Upon a Mattress*, and later the same year Oscar and I hired him to stage the musical numbers in *The Sound of Music*. Since then he had done other impressive choreography and musical staging on Broadway. As *No Strings* began to evolve, it seemed to require the kind of fluidity of movement that could only come when the choreographer and the director were the same man, and I was convinced that Joe had the ability to handle the overall production.

Because it was important that audiences accept our concept right from the start, we did away with the overture and had the curtain rise on a darkened stage with Diahann Carroll, strikingly gowned in white, picked out by a spotlight. But she isn't alone. As she sings "The Sweetest Sounds," a musician plays a flute obbligato. The song is then sung by the male lead (played by Richard Kiley) with a clarinetist near him playing the accompaniment. Even though as an augury of their future romance they sing together, the girl and boy are unaware of each other's existence, and the instrumentalists, though in full view, are meant to be musical abstractions rather than characters in the story.

This was further developed in other scenes. During the song "Love Makes the World Go," we used a trombonist in an even more direct manner for comic effect. For the last scene in the first act, which takes place in the heroine's apartment, an invisible drummer first beats out a tense rhythm while the lovers express their feelings in "Nobody Told Me." Then, as they disappear into the bedroom offstage, a panel rises and the spotlighted drummer brings the act to a close with a blazing interpretation of their passion.

It should be stressed that while these innovations worked within the context of this play, they were not introduced to impress people with our cleverness. It was simply that given the kind of story we had, it seemed imperative that the entire musical and dramatic effect come from a single source—the stage—without the distractions of the structural chasm yawning in front of it.

Since we were trying so many innovations, we decided on a few more. To help maintain the flow of the narrative, which covers a number of French locales, we decided to have mobile sets moved by the dancers in full view of the audience. In one scene, at Honfleur, the beach was represented by a sand-colored slab. Because there were only two characters on the stage, at the end the girl changed the setting simply by tilting up one end of the slab—and the couple was now on a terrace overlooking the water.

Two major songs were sung during the beach scene. One was "Look No Further," a plaintive love song written in traditional "AABA" form. Here the only rhymes used in each "A" section fell on the two successive words in the fourth and fifth bars. Then, to start the next line, I repeated the second rhymed word, though with a slightly different meaning:

> 1.
> Don't move an inch away, stay.
> Stay with one who loves you.
>
> 2.
> This is the journey's end, friend.
> Friend has turned to lover.
>
> 3.
> Making it all complete, sweet.
> Sweet it is to hold you.

While there was no direct reference to race in either lyrics or libretto, the song "Maine," also sung in the Honfleur scene, was intended to make audiences aware of the disparity in background of the two leading characters. Even here, though, the mood was light and the attitude nostalgic. At first the boy sings:

> Let the snow come down
> Before the sun comes up.
> Maine is the main thing.
> Let the lake and hills
> Become a frozen cup.
> Twenty below in Maine . . .

Then, to the same melody, the girl sings:

> When the sun goes down
> The kids are up and out,
> East of the Hudson.
> There's a sidewalk symphony
> Of song and shout
> Up north of Central Park . . .

While the play's title fitted the situation of the story, during the preparation of the show we also decided to make it refer to the fact that aside from a harp, our orchestra would consist entirely of brass, percussion and woodwinds.

*No Strings* had an unusually lengthy break-in period—two months—during which we played Detroit, Toronto, Cleveland, and New Haven. We took our time primarily because so much of what we were doing technically had never been tried before. Musicians had to feel comfortable onstage, and dancers had to become familiar with stage markings in order to move the scenery with grace and precision.

We opened at the 54th Street Theatre (later the George Abbott) in New York in March 1962. In general, the reviewers applauded the physical production, raved about Diahann, were complimentary about the music and lyrics, and had reservations about the book. Though no smash, *No Strings* had a successful run of seventeen months.

But most important to me was the assurance it gave me that I could pick up the pieces of my career and start all over again with new people and new techniques. Well-meaning friends complimented me for my daring in attempting so many innovations, but this was only because they didn't know what I knew. Playing it safe is really playing it dangerous. Taking a chance is always far less risky, and it's a lot more fun.

## 25

Although I scarcely considered myself Broadway's latest lyric-writing genius, I felt generally satisfied with the job I had turned in on *No Strings*. There was no question in my mind that if necessary, I could always do it again. But once I'd proved this to myself, I was anxious to team up with a new partner.

Why? Simply because having worked with the two men who were the best in the field, I wanted the benefit of working again with a lyricist of comparable stature. There is nothing more stimulating to the creative process than the interchange of ideas with someone who is both a gifted writer and one with whom you can also establish a close personal rapport.

Almost inevitably, this led me to Alan Jay Lerner. He had written brilliant lyrics and librettos for a notable succession of musicals—*Brigadoon, My Fair Lady, Camelot*—to music by Frederick Loewe. Because of failing health, Fritz had decided to retire, and I was told that Alan was looking for a new collaborator. Anyone's list of Broadway's outstanding lyricists at that time would have to place Alan's name at the top, but even more important to me was the kind of theatre he had come to represent. It had taste and style, and it "said something." From what I knew about Alan, his general philosophy and attitude toward the musical theatre seemed closest to mine of any lyricist then active on Broadway. Further, since I was more than fifteen years older, working with him would even follow Oscar's advice to collaborate with a younger writer.

Early in 1961, at about the same time I began thinking of *No Strings*, Alan and I had a few preliminary meetings. One of his ideas, which I didn't like, was a musical about Coco Chanel; another, which I did, was to be an original story about extrasensory perception. Soon after *No Strings* opened, we agreed to work together on the ESP musical, which we called *I Picked a Daisy*.

It didn't take too long, however, for me to realize that Alan's working habits were far different from mine. I knew that he was then occupied with the screen version of *My Fair Lady*, but I couldn't understand why, once having made an appointment, he would often fail to show up or even offer an explanation—or if he did arrive, why the material that was supposed to be completed was only half finished. On one occasion, the Friday before the Labor Day weekend in 1962, Alan told me that he was planning to remain in New York and work during the three days because no one would be around to disturb him. The next morning, just before driving to the country, I telephoned him. The maid answered the phone: "Mr. Lerner 'e is not 'ere. 'E is in Capri."

It wasn't all Alan's fault. Perhaps he felt uncomfortable working with someone he found too rigid, and so had to show his independence. In any case, by the summer of 1963, when it was clear that nothing would come of it, we agreed to terminate our partnership. Soon afterward Alan found another composer, Burton Lane, with whom he apparently felt more compatible, and eventually the ESP musical—now called *On a Clear Day You Can See Forever*—was presented on Broadway. Though it caused no box-office crush, it did benefit from a score that I have always felt was one of the finest either man has ever turned out.

Devoting so many unproductive months to this enterprise was extremely frustrating, particularly at this stage of my career. Fortunately, at about this time I was given something else to think about: a new theatre.

William Schuman, the president of Juilliard, had recently resigned to accept the highly prestigious presidency of the newly completed Lincoln Center. I had known Bill for some time, primarily because of our mutual interest in Juilliard, and one day he asked me to lunch. He was satisfied, he told me, with the progress of all the component elements at the Center except for one, the New York State Theater. The New York Opera Company and the New York Ballet Company filled the theatre during most of the year, but he was worried about the summer months. What he had in mind was the creation of an autonomous producing organization, to be called the Music Theater of Lincoln Center, which would offer a series of musical revivals, and he wanted me to be in charge.

Bill touched a highly sensitive nerve. Ever since my abortive effort to get Columbia University to establish a center for the arts, I have tried to encourage such projects. Everyone knew that Lincoln Center was going to be the country's major performing arts center, and now I was being offered the opportunity to become part of it. There would be no salary—nor did I want any—but I was assured complete artistic control of a separate division which would be on an equal footing with those of concert music, opera, ballet and drama. How could I possibly refuse?

The initial plan was to offer two productions during the summer, each running a little over a month, which would then go out on tour. These would not be hand-me-down revivals, but would be mounted as carefully as if they were being shown on Broadway for the first time. There was one problem: the theatre was so huge that we had to limit our choices to musicals that required sizable casts.

Our first two productions, shown in 1964, were *The King and I* and *The Merry Widow*. Aided by the attraction of the glittering new playhouse, both shows did extremely well. We maintained the policy of two shows per season for three years, until rising costs forced us to cut down to one. Despite the size of the theatre and the expenses involved, we somehow managed to turn a profit during the first five years. Perhaps because it had been revived too often, the only production to lose money was *Oklahoma!*, the attraction for our sixth and final season.

One of the most exciting revivals was that of *Annie Get Your Gun* in 1966. After twenty years Ethel Merman was back in her original role, with possibly even more energy than before. Irving Berlin helped make the production truly memorable by writing two new songs, though one had to be dropped during the Toronto tryout. The song that remained, "An Old-Fashioned Wedding," was the kind of contrapuntal number that Irving writes with such skill that it always stops the show.

The second production that summer was *Show Boat,* which turned out to be an unusually expensive undertaking. The greatest acclaim was won by Constance Towers, a tall willowy blonde who auditioned for Magnolia but ended up playing Julie, the mulatto, in a black wig. Connie has a magnificent voice and more nerve than almost any actress I know. After singing "Bill" seated on top of an upright piano, she never failed to receive enthusiastic and prolonged applause. She also never failed to milk it by walking into the wings and then strolling back to the piano, picking up the pocketbook that she had presumably forgotten, and then strolling off again.

By 1969 the operation of the State Theater had been taken over by the New York City Center people, and they seemed agreeable that I continue the Music Theater seasons. For some reason, however, they began pressing me in the fall for my plans for the following summer. Obviously it was impossible for me to come up with anything definite so far in advance.

Sometime in January a representative of the City Center came to my office.

"When do you have to have my decision?" I asked him.

"Well, we'd like to have it pretty soon."

"You've got it now. I'm not going to do anything."

Despite his surprise, my impression was that this was really what the man wanted to hear. It was becoming obvious that the City Center management wanted to run things alone, which was perfectly all right with me. Quitting certainly caused no financial hardship; simply on a time basis, a minimum of a third of my year—as well as that of my office staff—was involved with the Lincoln Center operation. Unfortunately, the result of the City Center takeover was that for the first time the State Theater had what Bill Schuman had feared—a dark house during the summer.

Besides launching the Music Theater of Lincoln Center in 1964, I also helped launch a more modest theatrical undertaking, one which in a way meant even more to me: the Amphitheater in Mt. Morris Park. The park had changed, of course, since the days when I played there as a kid, and so had the neighborhood, but I still felt close to it and I wanted to do something both for the city and this particular area. Somehow the idea of contributing money for the construction of an outdoor theatre seemed appropriate; happily, the city thought so too.

The two architects, John Stonehill and Oliver Lundquist, came up with an interesting concept. The backstage, which ordinarily would be for dressing rooms, was also designed to include rooms for different functions, such as art classes and places where the elderly might go to play chess or cards. The productions themselves would be given without charge, with the community itself deciding on the different kinds of entertainment to be presented. Dorothy and I were there the day the Amphitheater was dedicated, and were joined by Mayor John Lindsay and Jerome Weidman, an old friend, and his wife.

Following the brief ceremony, the Weidmans and the Rodgerses walked over to the house at 3 West 120th Street, where I had lived as a boy.

As we approached the brownstone building I could see a sign where once "WILLIAM RODGERS, M.D." had been. Now it read "COME INTO MY HOUSE, MY CHILD." We climbed the steps and walked in to discover that the house was a drug rehabilitation center for kids up to fourteen years old. Not a thing seemed familiar. I remembered the spacious reception room for my father's patients and Pop's imposing office, with its huge Mussolini desk; now it all looked cramped and tiny. As happens so often, everything had shrunk in scale.

Though my association with Alan Jay Lerner had proved fruitless, it did nothing to lessen my resolve to keep on looking for the right partner and the right property. I had spent an unusually long unproductive period and I was eager to get going again. Given a good idea and some talented people who were willing to work, I was sure we would come up with something.

The next something was *Do I Hear a Waltz?*, based on Arthur Laurents' play *The Time of the Cuckoo,* in which Shirley Booth had appeared on Broadway. Later a movie was made of it called *Summertime,* with Katharine Hepburn. I'd always liked the story, and when Arthur and Stephen Sondheim came to me with the idea of making it into a musical, I told them I was their man.

Steve, who was almost half my age, had already demonstrated his considerable gifts as Leonard Bernstein's lyricist for *West Side Story* and as Jule Styne's for *Gypsy.* He displayed further ability by creating the music as well as the words for *A Funny Thing Happened on the Way to the Forum.* Three hits in three times at bat is a pretty good average in any league.

What also gave our partnership a certain blessing was that Steve happened to be something of a protégé of Oscar Hammerstein, who had taken him under his wing and taught him a good deal. Steve was opinionated but terribly self-critical and totally dedicated to his craft, and I thought it would be especially challenging to work with someone so thoroughly trained in music as he was.

At first we worked closely and well. There was no particular *modus operandi.* Sometimes a quatrain would start me thinking of a melody; sometimes it would be a completed lyric. Occasionally I thought of a melodic theme first and Steve would then write the words. If I changed his lyric pattern, we'd discuss it, and Steve would either rewrite or we'd agree to discard the number entirely. I was working again and I was happy again.

From the start Arthur, Steve and I decided that we would purposely avoid the clichés that we could easily fall into with a story about an American tourist in Venice. We weren't going to resort to tarantellas or a comic ballet featuring gondoliers; in fact, there would be no formal choreography at all, or any booming choral numbers. Instead, under our director, John Dexter, the aim was for stylized movement which would convey the quality we wanted. The story was touching and intimate, and this was exactly the way we planned to keep it. Every element was going to have so much integrity that we were all practically shining each other's halos.

Unfortunately, when we put our touching, intimate story on the stage, we found that instead of a musical we had a sad little comedy with songs. It simply didn't work. During the tryout in New Haven, we held a conference and decided to call in a choreographer, Herb Ross, to put some life into the show. This was especially needed in the first-act scene on the Piazza San Marco, where the heroine sits alone surrounded by tourists and Venetians. Originally she had a song called "Two by Two," which was accompanied by strollers acting out the lyric by walking around two by two. There was no real development or commentary. Then Steve and I wrote a new song, the self-mocking "Here We Are Again," and Ross devised dance steps for the amorous couples that emphasized and contrasted with the girl's loneliness.

This helped, but not enough. Changes of this sort are always tricky. When you start rebuilding a show you must always be careful that the number you may feel is delaying the action does not actually support the dramatic structure of the entire play. If you replace a song, you may find yourself with a problem in another scene fifteen minutes later. It's like pulling out one seemingly inconsequential brick from a wall, only to find the entire wall collapsing. And no one ever really knows why.

There was one fundamental problem with the story that I never realized until too late. It wasn't only that Elizabeth Allen, the actress playing the heroine, was younger and less spinsterish than either Miss Booth or Miss Hepburn; it was simply that in a crucial scene in the second act the girl gets drunk and tells a young wife that her husband has had a dalliance with the owner of their *pensione*. I felt that this made the heroine unsympathetic and that audiences would not accept it, no matter what the provocation might have been, but despite my objection, Sondheim and Laurents were adamant about retaining the scene.

The more we worked on the show, the more estranged I became from both writers. Any suggestions I made were promptly rejected, as if by prearrangement. I can't say that all this tension was to blame for the production being less than the acclaimed triumph we had hoped for, but it certainly didn't help. *Do I Hear a Waltz?* was not a satisfying experience.

Given the impermanence of life, it is only natural that people cling to the security of certain objects and places that seem impervious to time. Perhaps this is especially strong in me because of the intangibility of my work and the entertainment world of which I am a part. Ever since 1949, our place in Southport, Connecticut, had been more of a home to Dorothy and me than our city apartment. Rockmeadow was our refuge and retreat, where we enjoyed entertaining friends and where, just in walking through the grounds, I often thought of melodic themes or ideas for musical development. By mid-1965, however, it was no longer a haven of durability and dependability; it had simply become too difficult for Dorothy to maintain. The house itself, with three floors and numerous guest rooms, required constant cleaning, polishing and waxing. Outside, there were seemingly endless lawns to mow, hedges to trim and earth to reseed. It was a place that required year-round, sleep-in help, and we were unable to get it.

To Dorothy, the solution was to move not merely to a new house, but to a newly built house. Only in this way, she felt, could we live in a country place that would accommodate our particular needs. This meant a place that would require a minimal amount of care, with everything as functional as possible, while still possessing the features that enhanced the style of life we enjoyed.

When Dorothy first revealed her need for a change, I strongly resisted it. I could understand and sympathize with her many problems, but I didn't see why a less drastic solution wouldn't work as well. Couldn't we cut down on entertaining? Couldn't we live in just one wing? Couldn't we try to import help from Europe? And, most important, how could we possibly build a new house that would be ready for us to move in the following summer?

As patiently as she could, Dorothy shot down all of my arguments. Her strongest point was that it was wrong for us to make our lives conform to a house, no matter how much we loved it. Eventually—and grudgingly—I consented. Because we had definite ideas of what we wanted, Dorothy felt that the wisest course was to engage an architect without too many fixed ideas of his own. This led us to John Stonehill, who had been one of the designers of the Mt. Morris Park Amphitheater. A cousin of Dorothy's and a frequent guest at Rockmeadow, he had never designed a private home before. With his approval, Dorothy and I selected an area in Fairfield County of about ten acres of farmland, which we bought from our friends Margot and Roy Larsen.

We spent our last days at Rockmeadow on Labor Day weekend in 1965. Leaving the place was a painful experience for me. I felt comfortable there and hated the idea of change. With her miraculous ability to picture things to come, Dorothy had the joy of looking forward to a new house, new surroundings and a new life. I found the prospect intimidating, and it took months before I was able to appreciate what she had done.

The foundation for the new house was laid in the fall. With Dorothy and John supervising every step of the way, the contractor, true to his word, had the place ready for us to move in the following July. What they had accomplished was truly remarkable. Though functional and far from palatial, the house had a feeling of spaciousness and warmth that made it seem a part of the surrounding landscape. Everything fit comfortably on one level, without stairs to climb or wasted areas. There was one large central room, with plenty of space for both the piano and the dining area. I also appreciated the fact that I could go from my bedroom directly to the swimming pool without having to walk through the rest of the house. As Dorothy has said, our only regret is that we didn't build the place ten years earlier.

After the experiences with my most recent collaborators, it had become increasingly clear that I would probably never again have the kind of long-term working relationships I had enjoyed with Larry and Oscar. Each partnership would have to be for a specific project. If a lyricist came to me with an idea I liked, I'd work with him; if I thought someone the right person for a project I was interested in, I'd get in touch with him—and if I thought I could do the lyrics myself, that would be all right too. Most important, despite my recent setbacks I was determined to keep working.

In 1967 I was approached to write the score for a television adaptation of Bernard Shaw's *Androcles and the Lion,* with a book by Peter Stone. Since I could choose my own lyricist, I simply went back to my *No Strings* collaborator—me—and we got along just fine. The show itself didn't come off well, I'm afraid, but it did give me the chance to be professionally associated with Noël Coward, who played Julius Caesar as a wickedly charming Noël Coward.

Though I find satisfaction working in any medium, nothing can match the exhilaration of the Broadway theatre, and I was anxious to return to it. During this period I heard many ideas and read many scripts, some actually scheduled for production, but for some reason—perhaps because I had become overcautious—none of them ever got off the ground.

Eventually, early in 1969, one finally looked promising.

Martin Charnin, a young lyricist who had written songs with my daughter Mary, came to me with the idea for *Two by Two*. (Neither the title nor the title song had anything to do with the discarded number from *Do I Hear a Waltz?*) I liked Marty and admired his work, but what really excited me was the concept—a musical version of Clifford Odets' *The Flowering Peach*. The story dealt with Noah and the flood, and though written in 1954, covered such contemporary themes as the generation gap and ecology. There was even a parallel between the flood and the atom bomb. We got in touch with Peter Stone, who had just had a tremendous hit with *1776*, and he agreed to join us as librettist. In June we announced our plans to the press. Since Dorothy and Mary were off on a trip to the Soviet Union that summer, I looked forward to an extended period of concentrated work.

One Friday morning in July I was getting ready for a weekend in Fairfield, where my production manager, Jerry Whyte, and his wife, Jeannette, would be my guests. I bent over to tie my shoelaces, and when I straightened up I had trouble catching my breath. A bit concerned, I telephoned my doctor, Frode Jensen, and his nurse told me to come right over.

After doing a cardiograph and giving me a thorough examination, Frode said, "You're not going to Fairfield, you're going to Lenox Hill Hospital. I want you where I can keep an eye on you. Your blood pressure is going crazy and I can't find your pulse."

I did as I was told. At the hospital I spent a reasonably comfortable day on Saturday, but on Sunday morning, as I was leaving the bathroom, I collapsed. The next thing I was aware of was a soothing voice saying, "Breathe normally," and I opened my eyes to see a roomful of doctors and nurses and an oxygen tank near the bed. Only then did I know I'd had a heart attack.

Later that day I was transferred to the coronary-care unit. When my daughter Linda was allowed to see me, the first thing she said was, "You're going to be sore as hell, but we're sending for your wife." I confess that it didn't make me sore at all.

But what nobody realized was how difficult it would be to make contact with Dorothy and Mary, who were then in Leningrad. In fact, it was only with the help of Mayor Lindsay that Linda and her husband, Danny Melnick, were able to put the call through. Dorothy and Mary immediately canceled their trip to Finland, scheduled for the following day, and through Danny's efforts, managed to get a reservation on the once-a-week flight to Paris, which fortunately left Leningrad on Monday. They spent that night in Paris, and on Tuesday were on the Air France flight to New York.

Later Dorothy told me that she had expected to see a desperately ill patient; instead, she found me reasonably strong and in excellent spirits—unquestionably due to the fact that she was there. If I learned anything from my experience, it was that the best place to be at the time of a cardiac arrest is in a hospital. Had I been in my apartment, on the street or in Fairfield, it is doubtful that I'd be writing about it today.

Possibly, too, this is the reason I never felt fear at any time. I had total confidence in my doctors and the hospital staff. I knew that they would do everything necessary and that all I had to do was put myself in their hands. My attitude was not merely one of hope or expectation; just as in the case of my cancerous jaw, I was sure I'd pull through.

This illness served to bring me in contact again with a remarkably dedicated young woman. Several years before, during the building of our new house, Dorothy had broken her knee and was operated on at the Hospital for Special Surgery. One of her nurses was a bright-eyed little Irish girl named Eileen Gurhy. After Dorothy was well enough to leave the hospital, we took Eileen with us to Fairfield, where she saw Dorothy through the transition from wheelchair to crutches to cane. Because of a problem in getting nurses following my heart attack, one of the first things Dorothy did after her return to New York was to telephone Eileen. Eileen's roommate said that she was home in Ireland but that she would call her and tell her what had happened. Soon afterward, Eileen telephoned Dorothy from Cork, and on Thursday morning at 8 A.M. she was in my hospital room ready for duty.

With the kind of care I received from Dorothy and Eileen, my recovery was rapid enough for me to return to *Two by Two* without much delay. One of our first steps was to sign Danny Kaye for the role of Noah. The notion of Danny in the part was especially intriguing. Though he hadn't been in a Broadway show since the early 1940s and was primarily identified as a zany comic, Danny was anxious to try something meatier than the parts he'd been given in the movies. Our script called for a bravura performance, requiring the actor to appear both as a doddering old man of six hundred and a bounding youth of ninety, and we were confident that it would benefit from his special brand of showmanship.

*Two by Two* has left a sour taste in my mouth not because of the mixed reception (it ran almost a year and showed a small profit), but because of Danny's behavior after the show had opened in New York. Early in February 1971 he tore a ligament in his left leg during a performance and had to be hospitalized. Apparently unable to submit to the discipline of the theatre, when he returned to the show he decided to adapt the entire production to his infirmity. He appeared with his leg in a cast and either rode around the stage in a wheelchair—in which he sometimes would try to run down the other actors—or hobbled around the stage on a crutch—which he used to goose the girls. In addition, he began improvising his own lines and singing in the wrong tempos. He even made a curtain speech after the performances in which he said, "I'm glad you're here, but I'm glad the authors aren't." Apparently there was a certain curiosity value to all this, because people actually went to see *Two by Two* because of Danny's one-by-one vaudeville act. Others, of course, were appalled and expressed their irritation in letters to the *Times*.

What was especially disturbing was that there was nothing I or anyone else could do about all of this; Danny simply could not take criticism. The minute someone faulted him, he'd just sulk and slow down, and figuring that slowing down was worse than cutting up, we reluctantly said nothing.

# Coda

$A$t the time I am writing these words—April 1975—I find that I am probably more active than at any other period during the past ten years. Even though I shall soon be seventy-three, this would hardly be worth mentioning except for the fact that nine months ago I underwent a laryngectomy. The operation was successful, I feel perfectly well and, thanks to therapy, I have mastered what is known as esophageal speech. So my days are happily devoted to assisting with the production of a Rodgers and Hart revue slated for Broadway, attending auditions for a revival of *Oklahoma!* at the Jones Beach Theatre—and working on the score for a new musical. Of course it is impossible to foresee what will happen to the musical by opening night, but what's important to me is that I have a new show, and there's no feeling like it in the world. Nothing else matches the exhilaration of helping to conceive, plan and create something that has no purpose other than to give people pleasure.

Yet there is more to it than that. Naturally, I'd like the show to be a hit, but it has to be creatively new, not just chronologically new. I don't want more of the same; I want everything I do to make some contribution, no matter how small, to push out the theatre's walls a bit further. The past is helpful; it can guide us in giving shape and direction to our work. But no production ever succeeds by looking over its shoulder. I know the form can be expanded because every day people are doing it, whether through a new approach in stagecraft, a new theme or a new sound in music.

I am often asked where I think the musical theatre is heading. It's one question I always try to dodge because I don't think it's heading anywhere until it's already been there. One night a show opens and suddenly there's a whole new concept. But it isn't the result of a trend; it's because one, two, three or more people sat down and sweated over an idea that somehow clicked and broke loose. It can be about anything and take off in any direction, and when it works, there's your present and your future.

There is a traditional trick that theatre people have played as long as I can remember. A veteran member of a company will order a gullible newcomer to find the key to the curtain. Naturally, the joke is that there is no such thing. I have been in the theatre over fifty years, and I don't think anyone would consider me naïve, but all my life I've been searching for that key. And I'm still looking . . .

# Index

# Other titles of interest